Ada Lovelace

The First Programmer Exposed – Unofficial Biography

Youssef Sato

ISBN: 9781779699817
Imprint: Telephasic Workshop
Copyright © 2024 Youssef Sato.
All Rights Reserved.

Contents

1.1 Family Ties

Ada Lovelace, born on December 10, 1815, into a world of privilege and complexity, was the only legitimate child of the infamous poet Lord Byron and his wife, Lady Anne Isabella Milbanke. Her family ties would profoundly influence her life and work, shaping her identity as the first programmer in history.

1.1.1 A Noble Heritage

Born into the aristocracy, Ada was surrounded by the expectations and responsibilities that came with her noble lineage. Her father, Lord Byron, was a celebrated poet known for his flamboyant lifestyle and tumultuous relationships, while her mother, Lady Anne, was a mathematician and a woman of intellect. This noble heritage provided Ada with access to education and resources that would eventually fuel her passion for mathematics and science.

1.1.2 The Troubled Relationship of Lord Byron and Lady Anne

The relationship between Lord Byron and Lady Anne was anything but conventional. Their marriage was a whirlwind romance that quickly turned turbulent. Lord Byron's notorious infidelity and erratic behavior led to a separation shortly after Ada's birth. Lady Anne, determined to shield her daughter from the chaos of her father's life, took Ada away and raised her in a more stable environment, albeit one tinged with the shadow of her father's legacy.

1.1.3 Ada's Early Years

Ada's early years were marked by a deep sense of longing for the father she never really knew. Lady Anne, while nurturing Ada's intellect, often instilled in her a fear of her father's poetic temperament. This complex emotional backdrop would later influence Ada's own creative pursuits and her desire to carve out her own identity separate from her father's shadow.

1.1.4 Finding Her Passion for Mathematics

Despite the challenges of her upbringing, Ada's mother recognized her daughter's extraordinary talent in mathematics. Lady Anne encouraged Ada's interests, hiring tutors who would introduce her to the world of numbers and logic. It was during these formative years that Ada discovered her passion for mathematics—a passion that would eventually lead her to collaborate with Charles Babbage on the Analytical Engine.

1.1.5 The Influence of Ada's Mother

Lady Anne's influence on Ada cannot be overstated. A woman of strong character and intellect, she was determined to provide her daughter with the education she felt was essential for success. Lady Anne's own background in mathematics and her commitment to Ada's education laid the groundwork for Ada's future achievements. She instilled in Ada a sense of discipline and a love for learning that would serve her well throughout her life.

1.1.6 The Impact of Ada's Illness on Her Education

Ada's health was fragile from a young age, suffering from various illnesses that often interrupted her education. These struggles with health not only shaped her resilience but also deepened her understanding of the human condition. The time spent convalescing allowed Ada to immerse herself in books, further cultivating her intellectual curiosity. This period of isolation would later contribute to her imaginative thinking, enabling her to conceptualize ideas that were far ahead of her time.

1.1.7 Ada's Friendship with Charles Babbage

The friendship between Ada and Charles Babbage was pivotal in her development as a mathematician and programmer. Their first meeting in 1833 marked the beginning of a collaboration that would change the course of computing history. Babbage, impressed by Ada's intellect, took her under his wing, introducing her to his revolutionary ideas about the Analytical Engine. This relationship was not merely professional; it was a meeting of two brilliant minds, each inspiring the other to push the boundaries of their respective fields.

1.1.8 The Birth of the Analytical Engine

Babbage's Analytical Engine was a groundbreaking concept—an early mechanical computer that could perform calculations and store data. Ada's involvement in this project was transformative. She saw beyond the machine's mechanical capabilities, envisioning its potential for complex computations. This visionary perspective was a direct result of her upbringing and the intellectual environment fostered by her mother.

1.1.9 Babbage and Ada's Collaborative Relationship

The collaboration between Babbage and Ada was characterized by mutual respect and intellectual synergy. Babbage's technical expertise combined with Ada's innovative ideas led to the creation of the first algorithm intended for implementation on a machine. Their correspondence and shared vision laid the foundation for modern computing, highlighting how familial and educational influences can converge to create monumental achievements.

In summary, Ada Lovelace's family ties were instrumental in shaping her identity and career. The complex dynamics of her upbringing, coupled with the influence of her mother and her relationship with Charles Babbage, provided the fertile ground for her extraordinary contributions to mathematics and computing. Ada's story is not just one of genius; it is a testament to the power of family, education, and the relentless pursuit of knowledge.

1.1 Family Ties

Ada Lovelace, born Augusta Ada Byron on December 10, 1815, in London, was the only legitimate child of the famous poet Lord Byron and his wife, Lady Anne Isabella Milbanke Byron. The tapestry of Ada's family ties is woven with threads of nobility, creativity, and tragedy, setting the stage for her remarkable journey into the world of mathematics and computing.

1.1.1 A Noble Heritage

Ada's lineage was anything but ordinary. As the daughter of Lord Byron, one of the most celebrated poets of the Romantic era, she was born into a world of artistic grandeur and intellectual fervor. Her father, known for his passionate verses and tumultuous life, left an indelible mark on Ada's identity, though she would come to know him only through the stories and letters that echoed in the halls of her childhood.

Her mother, Lady Anne, was a woman of considerable intellect and a strong will, often referred to as the "Princess of Parallels" due to her mathematical prowess. Lady Anne was determined to steer Ada away from the perceived madness of her father, insisting on a rigorous education in mathematics and the sciences. This decision would prove pivotal in shaping Ada's future, as it provided her with the foundational skills necessary to navigate the male-dominated world of mathematics and engineering.

1.1.2 The Troubled Relationship of Lord Byron and Lady Anne

The marriage between Lord Byron and Lady Anne was a tempestuous affair, marked by passion, conflict, and ultimately, separation. Their union lasted only a year, resulting in a separation that left a profound impact on Ada's life. Lord Byron's notorious reputation for infidelity and his eccentric lifestyle led to Lady Anne's decision to raise Ada alone, fostering a sense of independence and resilience in her daughter.

Despite the absence of her father, Ada grew up surrounded by the remnants of his legacy. She was often exposed to the literary circles that celebrated Byron's work, yet she was also shielded from the chaos that characterized his life. This duality created a complex relationship between Ada and her father's memory, influencing her own pursuits and aspirations.

1.1.3 Ada's Early Years

Ada's early years were marked by a unique blend of privilege and isolation. Raised in a household that valued education, she was introduced to mathematics at a young age. Her mother, recognizing Ada's intellectual potential, hired tutors who would nurture her burgeoning talents. Among them was the renowned mathematician Augustus De Morgan, who would later become a significant influence on her mathematical development.

However, Ada's childhood was not without its challenges. She suffered from various health issues, including bouts of illness that often confined her to bed. These struggles only heightened her determination to excel academically, as she sought solace in the world of numbers and logic. It was during these formative years that Ada's fascination with mathematics began to blossom, laying the groundwork for her future contributions to the field.

1.1.4 Finding Her Passion for Mathematics

Ada's passion for mathematics emerged as a beacon of light amidst the shadows of her tumultuous family life. She found joy in solving complex problems and engaging with abstract concepts, often immersing herself in the works of prominent mathematicians of her time. This intellectual curiosity was further fueled by her mother's insistence on a rigorous education, which included studies in algebra, calculus, and even the nascent field of computer science.

The pivotal moment in Ada's mathematical journey came when she was introduced to Charles Babbage, a brilliant mathematician and inventor who would become her mentor and collaborator. Their meeting would forever change the course of her life, igniting a spark of innovation that would lead to the conception of the Analytical Engine—the world's first mechanical computer.

1.1.5 The Influence of Ada's Mother

Lady Anne's influence on Ada cannot be overstated. As a mother, she was both nurturing and demanding, instilling in her daughter a sense of discipline and a love for learning. Lady Anne's own struggles with societal expectations and her determination to create a better future for Ada served as a powerful example. She actively encouraged Ada to pursue her interests in mathematics, defying the norms of her time that relegated women to the domestic sphere.

This maternal support was crucial in shaping Ada's identity as a mathematician. Lady Anne often emphasized the importance of education and self-reliance, instilling in Ada the belief that she could transcend the limitations imposed on women in the 19th century. This foundation would empower Ada to challenge societal norms and carve her own path in a male-dominated field.

1.1.6 The Impact of Ada's Illness on Her Education

Throughout her life, Ada faced numerous health challenges that impacted her education. These illnesses often forced her to withdraw from her studies, creating gaps in her learning. However, rather than allowing these setbacks to deter her, Ada used her time in recovery to delve deeper into her studies. She became a voracious reader, consuming texts on mathematics, science, and philosophy.

This resilience in the face of adversity would become a hallmark of Ada's character. Her ability to adapt and persevere through illness not only shaped her academic pursuits but also instilled a sense of empathy and understanding for others facing similar struggles. Ada's experiences with illness would later inform her advocacy for women's education and health, as she recognized the importance of access to knowledge and resources for all individuals.

1.1.7 Ada's Friendship with Charles Babbage

The friendship between Ada Lovelace and Charles Babbage was a pivotal relationship that would define both of their legacies. Introduced in 1833, their connection was immediate, fueled by a shared passion for mathematics and innovation. Babbage, often referred to as the "father of the computer," recognized Ada's exceptional talent and intellect, encouraging her to explore her ideas further.

Their correspondence blossomed into a collaborative partnership, with Ada serving as a translator and commentator on Babbage's work. She became deeply involved in the development of the Analytical Engine, contributing her insights and ideas to its design. This partnership not only solidified Ada's role in the history of computing but also exemplified the power of collaboration in the pursuit of knowledge.

1.1.8 The Birth of the Analytical Engine

The Analytical Engine, conceived by Babbage, was a groundbreaking invention that would lay the foundation for modern computing. It was designed to perform complex calculations and could be programmed using punched cards—a revolutionary concept at the time. Ada's involvement in this project was instrumental, as she recognized the potential of the machine to go beyond mere calculations and to manipulate symbols and data.

In her notes on the Analytical Engine, Ada articulated a vision that extended far beyond Babbage's initial design. She foresaw the machine's ability to create music, produce graphics, and even perform tasks that we now associate with artificial intelligence. This foresight was a testament to Ada's brilliance and her understanding of the broader implications of computational technology.

1.1.9 Babbage and Ada's Collaborative Relationship

The collaborative relationship between Babbage and Ada was characterized by mutual respect and intellectual curiosity. Babbage valued Ada's insights, often referring to her as "the Enchantress of Numbers." Their correspondence was filled with discussions about mathematics, philosophy, and the potential of the Analytical Engine, showcasing a partnership that transcended the norms of their time.

Ada's contributions to Babbage's work were significant, as she not only translated his ideas but also expanded upon them, introducing concepts that would later be recognized as foundational to computer programming. This collaboration exemplified the power of interdisciplinary partnerships, highlighting the importance of diverse perspectives in the pursuit of innovation.

In conclusion, the family ties that shaped Ada Lovelace's early life were marked by complexity, resilience, and an unwavering commitment to education. From her noble heritage to her mother's influence and her collaborative relationship with Charles Babbage, each thread of her familial background contributed to the tapestry of her legacy as the first programmer. Ada's journey was not just a personal triumph but a testament to the power of intellect, creativity, and perseverance in the face of societal constraints.

ERROR. thisXsection() returned an empty string with textbook depth = 3.

ERROR. thisXsection() returned an empty string with textbook depth = 3.

ERROR. thisXsection() returned an empty string with textbook depth = 3.

The Troubled Relationship of Lord Byron and Lady Anne

The relationship between Lord Byron and Lady Anne Isabella Milbanke, known as Ada's parents, can be described as a tempestuous saga worthy of a Gothic novel. Their union was marked by passion, intellect, and ultimately, profound discord. To understand the tumultuous nature of their marriage, we must delve into the historical and personal contexts that shaped their lives.

Lord Byron, a celebrated poet and a leading figure of the Romantic movement, was known for his charismatic personality and scandalous lifestyle. Born on January 22, 1788, in London, Byron was a product of both privilege and tragedy. His early life was marred by the death of his father, and he was raised by his mother, who imparted a strong sense of independence and intellect. Byron's poetry often reflected his own emotional turmoil and complex relationships, particularly with women.

Lady Anne, on the other hand, hailed from a respectable family with a strong emphasis on propriety and social status. Born on May 17, 1792, she was well-educated and possessed a keen intellect that matched Byron's. Their initial attraction was fueled by a shared appreciation for literature and the arts, leading to their marriage on January 2, 1815. However, the very qualities that drew them together soon became sources of conflict.

The couple's relationship began to deteriorate shortly after their marriage. Byron's notorious reputation as a libertine clashed with Lady Anne's values of domesticity and moral rectitude. Byron's infidelities, including a rumored affair with his half-sister Augusta Leigh, further strained their bond. Lady Anne's attempts to maintain a semblance of control over their household were met with Byron's disdain and rebellious spirit.

A pivotal moment in their troubled relationship occurred shortly after the birth of their daughter, Ada, on December 10, 1815. Lady Anne's postpartum struggles were compounded by Byron's increasing absences and erratic behavior. It is said that Byron had little interest in fatherhood, viewing his daughter as an obligation rather than a joy. This lack of emotional connection would have lasting implications for Ada's upbringing.

Byron's discontent with married life culminated in a dramatic separation. In 1816, Lady Anne left Byron, taking Ada with her. The separation was not merely a personal failure but a societal scandal, as Byron's reputation continued to plummet. He was accused of various indiscretions, leading to public outrage and a decline in his social standing. This period of turmoil forced Byron into exile, where he would spend the remainder of his life, ultimately succumbing to illness in 1824.

The impact of this troubled relationship on Ada Lovelace's life cannot be overstated. Raised primarily by her mother, Ada was shielded from her father's influence but also deprived of a paternal connection that could have shaped her identity. Lady Anne's determination to provide Ada with a rigorous education in mathematics and science was likely a response to her own experiences with Byron's intellectual pursuits, which she perceived as chaotic and ungrounded.

In conclusion, the relationship between Lord Byron and Lady Anne was characterized by a volatile mix of passion and discord. Their marriage serves as a backdrop for understanding the complexities of Ada Lovelace's early life. The struggles between her parents not only influenced her upbringing but also contributed to her later achievements in mathematics and programming. The legacy of their troubled union echoes through Ada's life, as she navigated the challenges of her own identity in a world shaped by the very conflicts that defined her parents' relationship.

Ada's Early Years

Ada Lovelace was born on December 10, 1815, in London, England, to a family steeped in both artistic and scientific heritage. Her father, Lord Byron, was a renowned poet, known for his flamboyant lifestyle and tumultuous relationships, while her mother, Lady Anne Isabella Milbanke Byron, was a mathematician who valued rational thought and intellectual pursuits. This unique blend of influences would shape Ada's early years, setting the stage for her future as a pioneering figure in computing.

From a young age, Ada was exposed to a world of ideas that would ignite her passion for mathematics and science. However, her early life was not without challenges. After her parents' separation when she was just a few weeks old, Ada was raised primarily by her mother, who was determined to ensure that her daughter received a rigorous education, particularly in mathematics—an unusual focus for a girl at the time. Lady Byron, who was often described as strict and somewhat overbearing, believed that Ada's education would shield her from the perceived instability of her father's poetic legacy.

$$\text{Education} = \text{Mathematics} + \text{Science} + \text{Logic} \qquad (1)$$

This equation illustrates the foundational elements of Ada's education, which were meticulously curated by her mother. Lady Byron enlisted private tutors to provide Ada with a comprehensive education, emphasizing subjects that were typically reserved for boys. This included not only mathematics but also subjects such as astronomy and languages. Ada's early exposure to advanced mathematical concepts would later prove crucial in her groundbreaking work with Charles Babbage.

Despite her mother's efforts, Ada's health was fragile, and she suffered from various illnesses throughout her childhood. These health issues often interrupted her studies, but they did not dampen her spirit or her thirst for knowledge. Instead, they may have contributed to her resilience and determination. Ada's experiences with illness instilled in her a profound understanding of the human condition, which would later inform her approach to technology and its potential impact on society.

One of the pivotal moments in Ada's early years was her introduction to the world of mechanics and engineering. At the age of 12, she became fascinated with the concept of flight after reading about the designs of flying machines. This interest was further fueled by her mother's encouragement, as Lady Byron recognized the importance of fostering Ada's inquisitive nature. Ada famously constructed a flying machine of her own design, a feat that showcased her creativity and innovative thinking at such a young age.

$$\text{Innovation} = \text{Imagination} + \text{Knowledge} \qquad (2)$$

This equation reflects the synergy between creativity and education that Ada embodied. Her imaginative pursuits were not merely whimsical; they were deeply intertwined with her growing knowledge of mathematics and science. This combination would become the hallmark of her later work as a programmer and mathematician.

In addition to her mathematical pursuits, Ada's early years were marked by a love for literature and the arts. She was encouraged to explore her artistic side, which she did through poetry and writing. The influence of her father's poetic legacy lingered in her consciousness, and she often grappled with the duality of her identity as both a mathematician and a creative thinker. This internal conflict would later manifest in her writings, where she often blended technical analysis with poetic language.

As Ada matured, her intellectual curiosity led her to seek out mentors and collaborators who could further her understanding of mathematics and engineering. One such figure was the eminent mathematician Augustus De Morgan, who recognized Ada's exceptional talent and encouraged her to pursue her studies vigorously. De Morgan's mentorship was pivotal, as he introduced her to the world of mathematical logic, a field that would profoundly influence her later work.

In summary, Ada Lovelace's early years were characterized by a unique interplay of influences—her noble heritage, her mother's unwavering dedication to her education, and her own insatiable curiosity. These formative experiences laid the groundwork for her future achievements in mathematics and programming, positioning her as a trailblazer in a male-dominated field. Ada's early life serves as a testament to the power of education and the importance of nurturing creativity, resilience, and a passion for knowledge.

$$\text{Future Success} = \text{Early Education} + \text{Mentorship} + \text{Resilience} \tag{3}$$

This final equation encapsulates the essence of Ada's early years, highlighting the critical components that would enable her to become the first programmer and a visionary in the world of technology.

Finding Her Passion for Mathematics

Ada Lovelace's journey into the world of mathematics was not merely a pursuit of numbers and equations; it was an awakening of her intellect and creativity. Born into a family steeped in the arts and literature, Ada's early exposure to her father's poetic legacy contrasted sharply with her mother's staunch advocacy for education and rational thought. This unique environment laid the groundwork for Ada's burgeoning interest in mathematics, which would ultimately define her legacy as the first programmer.

From a young age, Ada exhibited an extraordinary aptitude for logical reasoning and abstract thinking. Her mother, Lady Anne Isabella Byron, recognized her daughter's potential and sought to cultivate it through rigorous education. Unlike many young women of her time, Ada was not relegated to the domestic sphere. Instead, she was encouraged to explore scientific ideas and mathematical concepts, an unusual path for a girl in the 19th century.

One of the pivotal moments in Ada's mathematical journey came when she encountered the works of notable mathematicians such as Augustus De Morgan and Mary Somerville. De Morgan, a prominent mathematician and logician, introduced Ada to the intricacies of mathematical reasoning. His teachings emphasized the importance of logical deduction, a skill that Ada would later apply in her groundbreaking work on the Analytical Engine.

$$\text{If } P \text{ is true, then } Q \text{ must also be true.} \tag{4}$$

This foundational principle of logic resonated deeply with Ada, inspiring her to delve further into the realm of mathematics. She began to tackle complex mathematical problems, employing a methodical approach that would become her hallmark. For instance, she explored the concept of combinatorial analysis, which involves counting, arranging, and combining objects in specific ways. This area of mathematics would later prove essential in her programming endeavors.

To illustrate her growing interest, consider the problem of arranging n distinct objects into r positions, known as permutations. The number of ways to do this is given by the formula:

$$P(n, r) = \frac{n!}{(n - r)!} \tag{5}$$

where $n!$ (n factorial) is the product of all positive integers up to n. For example, if Ada were to arrange 5 different books on a shelf, the number of distinct arrangements would be calculated as:

$$P(5, 5) = \frac{5!}{(5 - 5)!} = \frac{120}{1} = 120. \tag{6}$$

This fascination with permutations and combinations illustrated Ada's growing ability to think abstractly and quantitatively. She began to see mathematics not just as a series of calculations, but as a language through which she could express her innovative ideas.

Furthermore, Ada's passion for mathematics was greatly influenced by her friendship with Charles Babbage, whom she met in 1833. Babbage, often referred to as the "father of the computer," was working on his revolutionary invention, the Analytical Engine. When Ada was introduced to Babbage's work, she was immediately captivated by the machine's potential to perform complex calculations and solve intricate problems.

Her enthusiasm for the Analytical Engine propelled her to immerse herself in the study of mathematical principles that would later be crucial in programming. Ada's writings on the subject reflected her deep understanding of the machine's capabilities. For instance, she recognized that the Analytical Engine could not only perform arithmetic calculations but could also manipulate symbols and execute a series of operations based on predetermined instructions.

In her notes on the Analytical Engine, Ada famously predicted that the machine could be programmed to create music and art, demonstrating her visionary perspective on the intersection of mathematics and creativity. She wrote:

"The Analytical Engine does not occupy common ground with mere calculating machines. It holds within its grasp a far grander idea, one that transcends mere computation."

This insight foreshadowed the future of computing, where machines would be capable of tasks far beyond simple arithmetic.

In conclusion, Ada Lovelace's discovery of her passion for mathematics was a transformative journey fueled by her unique upbringing, her exposure to influential thinkers, and her groundbreaking collaboration with Charles Babbage. Her ability to intertwine logic, creativity, and innovation laid the foundation for her contributions to computer programming and established her as a pioneering figure in the field of mathematics. Through her exploration of mathematical concepts, Ada not only found her voice but also paved the way for future generations to embrace the beauty and power of mathematics.

The Influence of Ada's Mother

Ada Lovelace's mother, Lady Anne Isabella Byron, played a pivotal role in shaping the life and intellect of her daughter. Born into a noble family, Lady Byron was not only a woman of status but also a woman of remarkable intellect and strong convictions. Her influence on Ada was profound, particularly in the realms of education and personal development.

A Strong Educational Foundation

From a young age, Lady Byron was determined that Ada would receive an education that was both rigorous and comprehensive. She was acutely aware of the limitations placed on women in the 19th century and sought to provide Ada with the tools necessary to excel in a male-dominated society. Lady Byron's approach to education was heavily influenced by her own experiences and her desire to prevent Ada from falling into the same fate as her father, the infamous poet Lord Byron, whose tumultuous life was marked by instability and emotional turbulence.

To this end, Lady Byron hired tutors for Ada who specialized in mathematics and science—subjects that were not typically encouraged for girls at the time. This early exposure to complex mathematical concepts laid the groundwork for Ada's later achievements in programming and theoretical mathematics.

Encouraging Intellectual Curiosity

Lady Byron was not just a provider of education; she was also a catalyst for intellectual curiosity. She encouraged Ada to pursue her interests and to question the world around her. This nurturing of curiosity can be seen as a precursor to the scientific method, which emphasizes observation, experimentation, and inquiry.

For instance, Ada's fascination with the natural world was encouraged by her mother, who would often take her on walks where they would discuss the principles of nature and the mechanics behind various phenomena. This approach not only fostered Ada's love for learning but also instilled in her a sense of wonder about the complexities of life, which would later manifest in her work with Charles Babbage and the Analytical Engine.

The Balancing Act of Emotion and Logic

While Lady Byron sought to cultivate Ada's intellect, she also recognized the importance of balancing emotion with logic. This duality is crucial in understanding Ada's personality and her later contributions to mathematics and programming. Lady Byron's own struggles with mental health and her tumultuous marriage to Lord Byron informed her perspective on emotional intelligence.

She taught Ada to embrace her emotions while also applying logical reasoning to her pursuits. This balance is exemplified in Ada's writings, where she often expressed deep feelings about her work while simultaneously employing rigorous mathematical reasoning.

A Legacy of Advocacy

Lady Byron was also an advocate for women's rights and education. Her own experiences with gender bias fueled her passion for promoting opportunities for women. She believed that education was the key to empowerment, and she instilled this belief in Ada. This advocacy would resonate throughout Ada's life as she navigated the challenges of being a female pioneer in mathematics and technology.

The influence of Lady Byron can be seen in Ada's later advocacy for women in STEM fields. Ada often spoke about the importance of education for women and the need for equal opportunities in the scientific community. This advocacy was not just a reflection of her mother's teachings but also a testament to the values that Lady Byron instilled in her daughter.

Conclusion

In conclusion, the influence of Ada Lovelace's mother, Lady Anne Byron, was instrumental in shaping Ada's intellectual pursuits and her understanding of the world. Through her commitment to education, encouragement of curiosity, and advocacy for women's rights, Lady Byron laid the foundation for Ada's groundbreaking work in mathematics and programming. The complexities of Ada's character can be traced back to her mother's influence, making Lady Byron a significant figure in the story of one of history's most celebrated programmers.

As we reflect on Ada's legacy, it is essential to recognize the role of Lady Byron not only as a mother but as a pioneer in her own right, whose beliefs and actions helped to carve a path for future generations of women in technology and science.

The Impact of Ada's Illness on Her Education

Ada Lovelace's education was profoundly influenced by her health challenges, which she faced from a young age. Born in 1815, Ada was a child of both privilege and adversity, as her noble lineage came with the expectations of a rigorous education, yet her health issues often hindered her ability to engage fully in her studies. This section explores how Ada's struggles with illness shaped her educational journey, her intellectual development, and her eventual contributions to mathematics and computing.

Early Health Challenges

From the outset, Ada's life was marked by health complications. As a child, she suffered from various ailments, including a severe case of measles and later bouts of what was likely dyslexia or a similar learning disability. These conditions not only affected her physical health but also her educational experiences. The impact of her illnesses can be analyzed through the lens of educational psychology, particularly in relation to how chronic illness can affect learning outcomes and cognitive development.

Theoretical Framework

According to the theory of *Cognitive Load*, learners have a limited capacity for processing information. When a child like Ada faces health issues, the cognitive load may increase due to the need to manage pain or discomfort alongside academic demands. This can lead to reduced engagement and motivation, which are critical for effective learning. The *Self-Regulated Learning Theory* also applies, as

Ada had to develop strategies to cope with her limitations and maintain her educational pursuits despite her health challenges.

Impact on Learning and Curriculum

Ada's illnesses necessitated a tailored educational approach. Her mother, Lady Anne Isabella Byron, took on the role of her primary educator, emphasizing mathematics and logic to counteract the perceived weaknesses associated with her health. This decision was significant, as it allowed Ada to focus on subjects that intrigued her and that she excelled in, despite her physical limitations.

$$\text{Learning Outcome} = \text{Engagement} \times (\text{Cognitive Capacity} - \text{Cognitive Load}) \quad (7)$$

In this equation, we see that Ada's learning outcomes were directly related to her engagement levels and her cognitive capacity, which were both affected by her health. As her cognitive load increased due to illness, her ability to engage with complex mathematical concepts could have diminished, yet her passion for the subject often prevailed.

Adaptations and Innovations in Learning

Despite her challenges, Ada's education was marked by innovation. She was encouraged to pursue her interests in mathematics and science through various means, including private tutoring and correspondence with notable scholars of her time. Her relationship with Charles Babbage, for example, was pivotal. He recognized her potential and invited her to collaborate on his work with the Analytical Engine. This collaboration allowed Ada to apply her mathematical knowledge practically, despite her educational interruptions.

Examples of Resilience

Ada's resilience in the face of her health challenges is reflected in her intellectual output. For instance, her work on the Analytical Engine included not only the first algorithm intended for implementation but also a visionary understanding of its potential applications beyond mere calculation. This foresight was remarkable, especially considering the obstacles she faced.

Long-Term Effects on Education and Advocacy

The long-term effects of Ada's illness on her education extended beyond her personal experiences. Her struggles highlighted the need for adaptive educational strategies for students with chronic health issues. In contemporary educational settings, this translates to the importance of flexible curricula and supportive learning environments that accommodate the diverse needs of learners.

Conclusion

In conclusion, Ada Lovelace's health challenges significantly impacted her education, shaping her unique approach to mathematics and computing. Her experiences underscore the importance of resilience and adaptability in learning. By overcoming her health limitations, Ada not only forged a path for herself but also laid the groundwork for future generations of women in STEM, proving that challenges can fuel innovation and excellence. Her legacy serves as a reminder of the importance of supportive educational frameworks that recognize and accommodate the needs of all learners, particularly those facing health-related adversities.

$$Legacy\ Impact = Resilience + Innovation + Advocacy \qquad (8)$$

Ada's Friendship with Charles Babbage

Ada Lovelace's friendship with Charles Babbage was not merely a meeting of minds; it was a partnership that would ultimately give birth to the very concept of programming. Their relationship was characterized by mutual respect, intellectual curiosity, and an unyielding desire to push the boundaries of what machines could achieve.

The Meeting of Minds

In 1833, Ada first encountered Charles Babbage at a dinner party hosted by the inventor and mathematician, Mary Somerville. Babbage, known for his ambitious plans to create a mechanical computer, the Analytical Engine, was captivated by Ada's keen intellect and her enthusiasm for mathematics. As they engaged in discussions, they quickly discovered a shared passion for numbers and the potential of machines.

Ada's fascination with Babbage's work was evident; she saw in him not just a mentor but a kindred spirit. Babbage, in turn, recognized Ada's exceptional talent and encouraged her to explore the depths of mathematical theory and its applications. Their correspondence soon blossomed into a prolific exchange of ideas, with Ada often referring to Babbage as her "dear friend" in her letters.

Collaboration on the Analytical Engine

Babbage's Analytical Engine was a revolutionary concept, designed to perform any calculation that could be expressed in a series of instructions. It was a mechanical marvel that utilized gears, levers, and punch cards—elements that would later become foundational in computing. However, the engine was never completed during Babbage's lifetime, primarily due to funding issues and political obstacles.

Ada's role in this partnership was pivotal. She was not merely an observer; she actively engaged in Babbage's work, translating and expanding upon his ideas. In her notes on the Analytical Engine, she articulated a vision of computing that was far ahead of her time. For instance, she recognized the potential for the machine to manipulate symbols and create complex algorithms, which she famously illustrated with her method for calculating Bernoulli numbers.

$$B(n) = \sum_{k=0}^{n} \frac{(-1)^k}{k!} \cdot \left(\sum_{j=0}^{k} \binom{k}{j} B(j) \cdot n^{k-j} \right) \tag{9}$$

This equation exemplifies the mathematical complexity Ada was able to grasp and communicate. Her ability to understand and convey the intricacies of Babbage's designs showcased her exceptional aptitude for mathematics.

Correspondence and Influence

The correspondence between Ada and Babbage was rich with discussions on the philosophical implications of machines. In her letters, Ada often mused about the potential of the Analytical Engine to go beyond mere calculations; she envisioned a future where machines could create art, music, and perhaps even possess a form of intelligence.

Babbage, who was more focused on the technical aspects of his invention, found Ada's imaginative insights refreshing. Their letters were filled with mathematical equations, diagrams, and philosophical debates about the nature of computation and creativity.

One notable correspondence involved Ada's reflections on the limitations of machines. She wrote:

"The Analytical Engine has no pretensions to originate anything. It can
do whatever we know how to order it to perform."

This statement captures Ada's understanding of the machine's capabilities and
limitations, as well as her belief in the essential role of human creativity in the process
of computation.

The Lovelace Note

In 1843, Ada translated an article by the Italian mathematician Luigi Federico
Federico Federico, which detailed the workings of the Analytical Engine. In her
translation, she added extensive notes that elaborated on the engine's potential
applications. These notes, now famously known as the "Lovelace Note," included
what is considered the first algorithm intended for implementation on a machine.

In her notes, Ada wrote:

"An Analytical Engine does not occupy common ground with mere
calculating machines. It holds within its grasp a far greater potential."

This assertion highlighted her belief that the Analytical Engine was not just a
calculator but a precursor to modern computers capable of performing complex
tasks.

A Lasting Legacy

The friendship between Ada Lovelace and Charles Babbage was a testament to the
power of collaboration in the pursuit of knowledge. Their relationship transcended
conventional mentorship; it was a partnership that combined technical genius with
creative vision.

Ada's contributions to Babbage's work laid the groundwork for future
generations of programmers and computer scientists. She is often celebrated as the
first computer programmer, and her insights continue to resonate in the fields of
computer science and artificial intelligence.

In conclusion, the friendship between Ada Lovelace and Charles Babbage was
a remarkable collaboration that not only advanced the development of the
Analytical Engine but also redefined the role of women in mathematics and
technology. Their shared vision and intellectual camaraderie serve as an enduring
inspiration for innovators today.

The Birth of the Analytical Engine

In the early 1830s, the world of computation was on the brink of a revolution, thanks in large part to the visionary ideas of Charles Babbage. Babbage, often referred to as the "father of the computer," had already conceptualized the Difference Engine, a mechanical device designed to automate polynomial calculations. However, it was his subsequent creation, the Analytical Engine, that would lay the foundational principles of modern computing.

Conceptual Framework

The Analytical Engine was designed as a general-purpose computing machine, capable of performing any calculation that could be expressed algorithmically. Unlike the Difference Engine, which was limited to specific calculations, the Analytical Engine was intended to be programmable. Babbage's design incorporated several groundbreaking concepts that are still relevant to computer science today:

- **Input and Output:** The machine was equipped with mechanisms for inputting data and outputting results, utilizing punched cards inspired by the Jacquard loom, which allowed for complex patterns to be woven automatically.

- **Memory:** The Analytical Engine featured a storage unit, referred to as the "store," which could hold numbers and intermediate results. This was a significant advancement over previous machines, as it allowed for multi-step calculations.

- **Arithmetic Unit:** The "mill" was the engine's processing unit, capable of performing basic arithmetic operations such as addition, subtraction, multiplication, and division. This was akin to the modern CPU, the heart of any computer.

- **Control Flow:** Babbage's design included the ability to implement control flow through conditional branching and loops, enabling the execution of complex algorithms.

The Analytical Engine was an ambitious project, and Babbage's vision extended beyond mere number crunching. He envisioned a machine that could manipulate symbols and execute a variety of tasks, much like a modern computer.

Mathematical Foundations

At the core of the Analytical Engine's design was the mathematical principle of programmability. Babbage's idea was to use algorithms—step-by-step procedures for calculations—to instruct the machine. This notion can be expressed mathematically as follows:

$$Y = f(X_1, X_2, \ldots, X_n) \tag{10}$$

where Y represents the output, f is the function defined by the algorithm, and $X_1, X_2, \ldots, X_n$ are the input variables. The Analytical Engine was designed to process various functions, allowing for a broad spectrum of applications.

Challenges and Limitations

Despite its revolutionary design, the Analytical Engine faced numerous challenges. Babbage struggled with the mechanical engineering aspects of the machine, as well as securing funding for its construction. The precision required for the components was difficult to achieve with the technology of the time. Additionally, the complexity of the design made it difficult to build a working prototype.

Babbage's correspondence with Ada Lovelace during this period proved instrumental. Lovelace not only recognized the potential of the Analytical Engine but also contributed to the theoretical underpinnings of its operation. She translated an article by the Italian mathematician Luigi Federico Federico and added her own notes, which included what is now considered the first algorithm intended for implementation on a machine.

Theoretical Implications

The Analytical Engine's design anticipated several key theoretical concepts in computing:

- **Turing Completeness:** The machine was theoretically capable of performing any computation that could be described algorithmically, a concept that would later be formalized by Alan Turing in the 20th century.

- **Data and Instructions:** Babbage's separation of data and instructions laid the groundwork for the architecture of modern computers, where programs and data are stored separately but interact seamlessly.

+ **Modularity:** The design's modular components allowed for flexibility and expansion, a principle that remains central to software engineering and system design today.

Legacy of the Analytical Engine

Though the Analytical Engine was never completed during Babbage's lifetime, its conceptual framework has had a lasting impact on the field of computing. The principles of programmability, the separation of data and instructions, and the use of control structures have all become foundational elements of modern computer science.

In conclusion, the birth of the Analytical Engine marked a pivotal moment in the history of computation. Babbage's ambitious vision, coupled with Lovelace's groundbreaking contributions, set the stage for the digital age. Their work not only anticipated the future of computing but also inspired generations of mathematicians, engineers, and computer scientists to explore the vast possibilities of automated computation. The Analytical Engine remains a testament to human ingenuity and the relentless pursuit of knowledge in the face of adversity.

Babbage and Ada's Collaborative Relationship

The partnership between Ada Lovelace and Charles Babbage is often heralded as one of the most significant collaborations in the history of computing. Their relationship was not only a melding of minds but also a confluence of visions that would shape the future of technology. To understand the depth of their collaboration, it is essential to explore the context in which they met, the nature of their intellectual exchanges, and the groundbreaking work they produced together.

The Meeting of Minds

Ada Lovelace first encountered Charles Babbage at a party hosted by the Countess of Lovelace in 1833. Babbage, already known for his work on the Difference Engine, was captivated by Ada's keen intellect and her passion for mathematics. Their initial discussions revolved around Babbage's ideas for mechanical computation, which were revolutionary for their time. Ada's enthusiasm for Babbage's work was evident, and she quickly became one of his most ardent supporters.

The Analytical Engine: A Shared Vision

At the heart of their collaboration was the Analytical Engine, a conceptual machine designed by Babbage that could perform any calculation. Unlike its predecessor, the Difference Engine, which was limited to specific calculations, the Analytical Engine was designed to be programmable, making it a precursor to modern computers. Babbage envisioned a machine that could manipulate symbols and execute a sequence of operations based on instructions—essentially the first programmable computer.

Ada's role in this collaboration was pivotal. She grasped the implications of Babbage's designs and recognized the potential for the Analytical Engine to go beyond mere calculation. In her notes, she articulated a vision of the machine as a tool for more than arithmetic; she saw it as capable of creating music and art, which was a radical notion at the time. This broader perspective on computation showcased Ada's unique ability to blend creativity with technical understanding.

Correspondence and Collaboration

The correspondence between Ada and Babbage was not just a simple exchange of ideas; it was a rigorous intellectual partnership. They exchanged letters filled with detailed discussions about mathematics, engineering, and the philosophy of computation. Their letters often included complex equations and diagrams, reflecting the depth of their engagement.

For instance, in one of her letters, Ada expressed her understanding of Babbage's concept of a "store" in the Analytical Engine, which would hold numbers and results. She wrote:

$$\text{Store} = \text{Memory} \quad \text{(where Memory is the temporary holding of data)} \quad (11)$$

This notation was an early attempt to conceptualize how data would be managed in a computing system, foreshadowing the principles of modern computer architecture.

The Lovelace Note

One of the most significant outcomes of their collaboration was the Lovelace Note, which Ada wrote as a translation of an article by the Italian mathematician Luigi Federico Federico. In this note, she added her own extensive commentary, which included the first algorithm intended for implementation on a machine—the

Analytical Engine. This algorithm is often cited as the first computer program, marking Ada as the first programmer in history.

In her notes, Ada described how the Analytical Engine could be programmed to calculate Bernoulli numbers, a complex sequence of rational numbers that are critical in number theory. The algorithm she devised can be expressed as follows:

$$B_n = \sum_{k=0}^{n} \binom{n}{k} \cdot B_k \quad \text{(where B_n is the n-th Bernoulli number)} \quad (12)$$

This formula not only demonstrated her mathematical prowess but also her ability to translate theoretical concepts into practical applications for the Analytical Engine.

Mutual Influence and Legacy

The collaborative relationship between Ada and Babbage was symbiotic. Babbage's technical expertise complemented Ada's visionary insights, resulting in a partnership that transcended the boundaries of their respective fields. While Babbage provided the foundational knowledge of mechanical computation, Ada infused that knowledge with creativity and foresight.

Their work together laid the groundwork for future developments in computing, influencing generations of mathematicians and computer scientists. Ada's contributions were often overshadowed by Babbage's fame, yet her insights were crucial in recognizing the potential of computers to perform tasks beyond mere calculation.

Conclusion

In conclusion, the collaborative relationship between Ada Lovelace and Charles Babbage was a defining moment in the history of computing. Their partnership exemplified the power of collaboration in innovation, demonstrating that the fusion of technical skill and creative vision can lead to groundbreaking advancements. The legacy of their work continues to inspire the fields of computer science and technology, reminding us that the seeds of innovation are often sown in the fertile ground of collaborative thought.

A Mind Ahead of Her Time

Ada's Interest in Analytical Engines

Ada Lovelace's fascination with analytical engines was not merely a passing curiosity; it was a profound engagement with the future of computation that would lay the groundwork for modern programming. The analytical engine, conceived by Charles Babbage in the early 1830s, was a revolutionary mechanical device designed to perform any calculation that could be expressed mathematically. It was a far cry from the calculating machines of its time, which were limited to specific tasks. Ada saw in Babbage's invention not just a machine, but a potential for a new way of thinking about and interacting with numbers.

The Vision of the Analytical Engine

The analytical engine was envisioned as a general-purpose computing device, capable of executing a sequence of operations based on a set of instructions, which Babbage referred to as "programs." This vision was groundbreaking, as it foreshadowed the programmable computers of the 20th century. Ada was captivated by the idea that a machine could manipulate symbols and numbers in a way that mimicked human thought processes.

In her correspondence with Babbage, Ada expressed her understanding of the engine's capabilities, stating, "The engine might compose elaborate and scientific pieces of music of any degree of complexity or extent." This statement reflects not only her appreciation for the technical aspects of the engine but also her recognition of its creative potential.

Mathematical Foundations

At the heart of the analytical engine's design was a series of mathematical principles that Ada understood deeply. The engine utilized a form of computation based on the principles of logic and algebra. For example, it relied on the concept of variables, which could represent numbers in mathematical operations.

The engine's operations could be expressed through equations, such as:

$$y = f(x) = ax^2 + bx + c$$

where y is the output, x is the input variable, and a, b, and c are constants. The analytical engine was designed to perform operations like addition, subtraction, multiplication, and division, as well as more complex functions like exponentiation and logarithms.

Programming the Analytical Engine

Ada's interest extended beyond mere admiration; she actively engaged with the concept of programming the analytical engine. In her notes, she outlined a series of steps that could be used to instruct the machine to perform specific tasks. One of her most notable contributions was the development of what is now considered the first algorithm intended for implementation on a machine. This algorithm was designed to compute Bernoulli numbers, a sequence of rational numbers that are important in number theory.

The algorithm can be summarized as follows:

1. Initialize the sequence of Bernoulli numbers. 2. Use the analytical engine to perform iterative calculations based on the recurrence relations defined for Bernoulli numbers. 3. Output the results through the engine's printing mechanism.

In mathematical terms, the Bernoulli numbers B_n can be defined recursively as:

$$B_0 = 1, \quad B_n = -\frac{1}{n+1} \sum_{k=0}^{n-1} \binom{n}{k} B_k$$

for $n > 0$. Ada's algorithm would allow the analytical engine to compute these values iteratively, showcasing her ability to translate mathematical concepts into a format that a machine could understand.

Theoretical Implications

Ada's interest in the analytical engine also led her to consider the theoretical implications of computing. She posited that the engine could be used to explore not only numerical computations but also symbolic manipulations. This insight laid the groundwork for future developments in computer science, particularly in the areas of artificial intelligence and algorithmic theory.

For instance, Ada suggested that the analytical engine could be programmed to manipulate not just numbers but also symbols and letters, opening up possibilities for applications in fields such as linguistics and philosophy. She wrote, "The engine has no pretensions to originate anything. It can do whatever we know how to order it to perform."

Practical Applications and Limitations

While Ada's enthusiasm for the analytical engine was boundless, she was also acutely aware of its limitations. The machine, as conceived by Babbage, was never fully realized during their lifetimes, primarily due to technical challenges and funding issues. However, Ada's theoretical work provided a framework for understanding how such a machine could function and what its capabilities might be.

She recognized that the engine would require meticulous design and construction, stating, "We may say that the Analytical Engine weaves algebraical patterns just as the Jacquard loom weaves flowers and leaves." This analogy highlighted her understanding of the intricate relationship between mathematics and machinery, and how both could be harnessed to create complex outputs from simple inputs.

Conclusion

In summary, Ada Lovelace's interest in analytical engines was a defining aspect of her intellectual legacy. Her ability to conceptualize the potential of Babbage's invention went beyond the technical specifications; she envisioned a future where machines could think, learn, and create. This visionary perspective not only positioned her as the first programmer but also as a pioneer in the field of computing, whose ideas would resonate through generations of mathematicians, scientists, and engineers. Ada's insights into the analytical engine laid the foundation for understanding the complex relationship between humans and machines, a relationship that continues to evolve today.

Ada's Vision for the Analytical Engine

Ada Lovelace's vision for the Analytical Engine was revolutionary and far ahead of her time. She saw the potential for this machine to do much more than mere calculations; she envisioned it as a universal computing device capable of performing any mathematical operation. Her ideas laid the groundwork for modern computer programming and highlighted the importance of algorithms long before the term "computer" was even coined.

Understanding the Analytical Engine

The Analytical Engine, designed by Charles Babbage, was intended to be a mechanical computer that could perform complex calculations. It consisted of several components that mimicked the functions of a modern computer:

- **The Store:** This was the memory of the machine, where numbers and intermediate results would be held.

- **The Mill:** This functioned like a CPU, performing arithmetic operations such as addition, subtraction, multiplication, and division.

- **The Input and Output Mechanisms:** These allowed data to be fed into the engine and results to be printed or otherwise displayed.

Ada's Programming Vision

Ada's most significant contribution to the Analytical Engine was her understanding of how to program it. She recognized that the machine could be instructed to perform sequences of operations through algorithms. In her notes, she articulated the concept of a step-by-step procedure for solving mathematical problems, which is the essence of programming.

For example, in her notes on the Analytical Engine, Ada described an algorithm for calculating Bernoulli numbers. This algorithm was a series of operations that the machine would execute to arrive at the desired result. The process can be represented mathematically as follows:

$$B_n = \sum_{k=0}^{n} \binom{n}{k} B_k \cdot 2^{n-k} \tag{13}$$

where B_n represents the n-th Bernoulli number, and $\binom{n}{k}$ is the binomial coefficient.

In this algorithm, Ada specified the sequence of operations that the Analytical Engine would need to perform, thus creating a detailed blueprint for computing Bernoulli numbers. This was a groundbreaking moment in the history of computer science, as it established the foundation for what would later be known as programming.

The Concept of Conditional Logic

One of the most profound aspects of Ada's vision was her understanding of conditional logic. She recognized that the Analytical Engine could be programmed to make decisions based on certain conditions. This is akin to modern programming's use of conditional statements, such as "if-then-else" constructs.

For example, if the Analytical Engine was tasked with determining whether a number was even or odd, Ada might have envisioned an algorithm that included a conditional statement:

$$\text{If } n \mod 2 = 0 \text{ then output "Even"; else output "Odd"} \tag{14}$$

This ability to implement conditional logic would allow the Analytical Engine to perform more complex tasks and make it a versatile tool for a variety of applications, from mathematical computations to more intricate problem-solving scenarios.

The Vision of a Universal Machine

Beyond simple calculations and algorithms, Ada envisioned the Analytical Engine as a universal machine capable of performing any task that could be expressed in logical terms. She famously noted that the machine could create music, compose poetry, and even manipulate symbols in ways that transcended pure mathematics. She wrote:

> "The Analytical Engine does not occupy common ground with mere calculating machines. It holds within itself the potential to create, to innovate, and to explore the realms of human thought."

This perspective was revolutionary; it suggested that machines could not only process numbers but also handle abstract concepts and creative tasks, a notion that resonates with modern discussions about artificial intelligence and machine learning.

The Legacy of Ada's Vision

Ada Lovelace's vision for the Analytical Engine was not merely about the machine itself but about the profound implications it held for the future of technology. She foresaw a world in which machines could augment human intelligence, allowing for unprecedented advancements in science, art, and society.

Her insights foreshadowed the development of programming languages, algorithms, and even artificial intelligence. In many ways, Ada Lovelace can be seen as the first computer programmer, not just for her technical contributions but for her visionary understanding of what computers could become.

In conclusion, Ada's vision for the Analytical Engine was a blend of mathematics, creativity, and foresight. She saw the potential for machines to transform the world, and her pioneering ideas continue to inspire generations of programmers, engineers, and innovators. As we navigate the complexities of modern technology, we owe a debt of gratitude to Ada Lovelace for her unparalleled contributions to the field of computing.

The Lovelace Note – A Historic Discovery

In the annals of computing history, few documents are as significant as the Lovelace Note, a remarkable piece of writing that not only encapsulates Ada Lovelace's visionary thinking but also marks the inception of programming as we know it today. Written in 1843, this note accompanied a translation of an article by the Italian mathematician Luigi Federico Federico, which detailed Charles Babbage's Analytical Engine. However, it was Lovelace's annotations that transformed the text from a mere technical description into a groundbreaking manifesto for the future of computing.

Context of the Lovelace Note

To understand the importance of the Lovelace Note, we must first appreciate the context in which it was written. The Analytical Engine, conceived by Babbage, was a mechanical general-purpose computer that could perform any calculation given the appropriate instructions. Unlike its predecessor, the Difference Engine, the Analytical Engine was designed to be programmable, a concept that was revolutionary for its time. Lovelace, who had a deep understanding of mathematics and a keen interest in the potential of machines, recognized the implications of Babbage's work.

Content of the Lovelace Note

The Lovelace Note is often cited as the first instance of an algorithm intended to be processed by a machine. In it, Lovelace detailed a method for calculating Bernoulli numbers using the Analytical Engine. This algorithm is significant not just for its technical content, but also for its implications; it demonstrated that machines could be instructed to perform complex calculations autonomously. The algorithm can be expressed mathematically as follows:

$$B_n = \sum_{k=0}^{n} \binom{n}{k} B_k \tag{15}$$

where B_n represents the n-th Bernoulli number and $\binom{n}{k}$ is the binomial coefficient. Lovelace's notation and method of structuring the algorithm laid the groundwork for modern programming languages.

Implications of the Lovelace Note

The implications of the Lovelace Note extend far beyond its immediate technical contributions. Lovelace's insights into the potential of the Analytical Engine suggested that machines could not only perform calculations but also manipulate symbols in accordance with rules, paving the way for the development of programming as a discipline. She famously stated that the Analytical Engine could "weave algebraic patterns just as the Jacquard loom weaves flowers and leaves." This metaphor beautifully captures the creative potential of computing, suggesting that programming could be an art form as much as a science.

Historical Reception and Controversy

Despite its significance, the Lovelace Note was not immediately recognized for its groundbreaking nature. In fact, Lovelace's contributions were often overshadowed by Babbage's fame, leading to a long period of neglect in historical discussions of computing. Critics have argued that the male-dominated narrative of computing history marginalized Lovelace's contributions, relegating her to a footnote rather than recognizing her as a pioneer.

The controversy surrounding the Lovelace Note also stems from the interpretation of her contributions. While some have argued that her work was purely theoretical, others assert that her insights were practical and foresighted. The debate centers on whether Lovelace's vision of computing was prescient enough to warrant her title as the first programmer.

Legacy of the Lovelace Note

Today, the Lovelace Note is celebrated as a historic document that not only established the foundations of programming but also highlighted the role of women in technology. Lovelace's foresight in recognizing the potential of computing to transcend mere calculation to encompass creativity and complexity continues to resonate in discussions about artificial intelligence and machine learning.

In educational contexts, the Lovelace Note serves as a powerful example of how interdisciplinary thinking—combining mathematics, art, and philosophy—can lead to groundbreaking innovations. As we explore the future of technology, Lovelace's vision remains a guiding light, encouraging us to think beyond the immediate applications of computing and to consider its broader implications for society.

Conclusion

In conclusion, the Lovelace Note is not merely a historical artifact; it is a testament to the innovative spirit of Ada Lovelace and her profound understanding of the potential of machines. As we continue to navigate the complexities of modern technology, we must remember Lovelace's contributions and strive to honor her legacy by fostering diversity and inclusion in the tech industry. Her work serves as an enduring reminder that the future of technology is not just about algorithms and code, but also about creativity, humanity, and the endless possibilities that arise when we dare to dream.

The Controversy Surrounding Ada's Contribution

Ada Lovelace's contributions to the field of computing and programming have been both celebrated and contested since her time. While she is often hailed as the first programmer for her work on Charles Babbage's Analytical Engine, the extent and nature of her contributions have sparked debates among historians, computer scientists, and feminists alike. This controversy can be broken down into several key areas: the interpretation of her notes, the recognition of her work, and the broader implications for women in technology.

The Lovelace Note

At the heart of the controversy is the so-called *Lovelace Note*, which is a series of notes Ada wrote in 1843 as a translation of an article by the Italian mathematician Luigi Federico Federico. In her notes, Lovelace included what is now recognized as the first algorithm intended to be processed by a machine, specifically the Analytical Engine. This algorithm was designed to calculate Bernoulli numbers, and it is often cited as the first computer program.

However, the interpretation of this note has led to disputes. Some argue that since the Analytical Engine was never completed during Babbage's lifetime, Lovelace's algorithm was never executed, which raises questions about the validity of her claim as the first programmer. Critics contend that without a functioning machine, her contributions remain theoretical rather than practical. This perspective suggests that Lovelace was more of a visionary than a practitioner, leading to a debate on whether visionaries deserve the title of "programmer."

Historical Context and Recognition

Another layer of controversy arises from the historical context surrounding Lovelace's work. In the 19th century, the contributions of women to science and technology were often minimized or overlooked. Lovelace's noble status, combined with her gender, complicated her legacy. Despite her groundbreaking work, she was frequently overshadowed by her male contemporaries, particularly Babbage, who received the lion's share of recognition for the Analytical Engine.

The perception of Lovelace as merely a translator of Babbage's ideas has persisted in some academic circles, undermining her contributions. For instance, in a study published in the *Journal of the Society for the History of Technology*, historian Simon Lavington emphasized that while Lovelace's notes were significant, they were largely derivative of Babbage's work, suggesting that her role was more supportive than revolutionary. This interpretation has been contested by many who argue that her insights into the potential of computing were unique and transformative.

Gender Bias in Technology

The controversy surrounding Lovelace's contributions is also reflective of broader issues of gender bias within the tech industry. The narrative that positions Lovelace as a secondary figure in the development of computing perpetuates a cycle of exclusion that continues to affect women in technology today. This bias is evident in the underrepresentation of women in STEM fields, which has historical roots dating back to Lovelace's time.

Research indicates that women have historically been relegated to roles that support male innovators rather than being recognized as innovators themselves. For example, the work of women like Grace Hopper, who developed the first compiler for a computer programming language, has often been overshadowed by their male counterparts. This pattern of historical erasure raises critical questions about how contributions are valued and recognized in the tech industry.

Modern Re-evaluations

In recent years, there has been a concerted effort to re-evaluate Lovelace's contributions in a more favorable light. Scholars and advocates have sought to highlight the significance of her work and its implications for the future of computing. For instance, in her book *Ada's Algorithm: How Lord Byron's Daughter Ada Lovelace Launched the Digital Age*, author James Essinger argues that

Lovelace's insights into the potential of machines to manipulate symbols were revolutionary and ahead of her time.

Additionally, initiatives such as Ada Lovelace Day have emerged to celebrate the achievements of women in technology and to encourage future generations to pursue careers in STEM. These efforts aim to correct the historical narrative that has often marginalized female contributions, thereby fostering a more inclusive understanding of technological progress.

Conclusion

The controversy surrounding Ada Lovelace's contributions is emblematic of the challenges faced by women in technology throughout history. While debates about the nature of her work continue, it is essential to recognize the pioneering spirit that Lovelace embodied. Her vision of computing as a creative and intellectual pursuit laid the groundwork for future innovations. As we reflect on her legacy, it becomes clear that Lovelace was not merely a footnote in the history of computing; she was a trailblazer whose contributions continue to inspire and resonate in today's technological landscape.

$$\text{Bernoulli Numbers} = \sum_{n=0}^{\infty} B_n \cdot x^n \tag{16}$$

In conclusion, the controversy surrounding Ada Lovelace's contributions serves as a reminder of the importance of recognizing and celebrating the achievements of women in technology. As we continue to unravel the complexities of her legacy, we must strive to create an inclusive narrative that honors the contributions of all innovators, regardless of gender.

Why Ada Is Often Overlooked in History

Ada Lovelace, despite her groundbreaking contributions to the field of computing, has often been relegated to the shadows of history. This oversight can be attributed to a confluence of societal, cultural, and academic factors that have historically marginalized women's contributions in STEM fields. In this section, we will explore the reasons behind Ada's relative obscurity and the implications of this oversight.

1. Historical Context and Gender Bias

The 19th century was a period marked by rigid gender roles, where women were largely excluded from professional and intellectual pursuits. Ada Lovelace, born in 1815, navigated a world that often dismissed women's capabilities in mathematics and science. The prevailing attitudes of the time positioned women as caretakers and homemakers, relegating their intellectual pursuits to the private sphere.

This societal bias is reflected in the historical narrative that has often overlooked female figures in favor of their male counterparts. For instance, Ada's collaborator, Charles Babbage, is frequently celebrated as the "father of the computer," while Ada's contributions are often minimized or ignored. The phrase "behind every great man is a great woman" rings particularly true in Ada's case, yet her role has been obscured by the very narratives that elevate Babbage.

2. The Nature of Ada's Work

Ada's contributions to computing were not merely technical; they were visionary. She recognized the potential of Babbage's Analytical Engine to go beyond mere calculation, envisioning it as a machine capable of manipulating symbols and performing tasks that could be considered creative. This insight is encapsulated in her famous note, often referred to as the "Lovelace Note," where she articulated the concept of algorithms for the Analytical Engine.

However, the abstract and theoretical nature of her work may have contributed to its neglect. In a field that has historically valued empirical and quantitative achievements, Ada's visionary ideas may have been perceived as less tangible or relevant. The mathematical community of her time, dominated by men, may have struggled to appreciate the significance of her contributions, viewing them through a narrow lens that favored traditional mathematical rigor over innovative thought.

3. Lack of Documentation and Recognition

Another factor contributing to Ada's obscurity is the lack of comprehensive documentation of her work. While Babbage's designs for the Analytical Engine were extensively documented, Ada's contributions were often communicated through letters and informal notes rather than formal publications. This lack of a formalized body of work made it easier for historians and scholars to overlook her contributions.

Moreover, the rediscovery of Ada's work and legacy came long after her death. It was not until the mid-20th century, with the rise of the computer age, that scholars began to reassess her contributions. The feminist movements of the 1970s and 1980s played a crucial role in bringing attention to women's contributions in science and technology, leading to a resurgence of interest in Ada Lovelace. However, the historical narrative had already been established, and Ada's contributions were often relegated to footnotes.

4. The Influence of Popular Culture

Popular culture has also played a role in shaping the perception of Ada Lovelace. When she is mentioned, it is often in a romanticized or simplified manner, focusing more on her connection to Lord Byron and her personal life rather than her intellectual achievements. This oversimplification reduces her to a mere figure of intrigue rather than recognizing her as a pioneer in computing.

Furthermore, the portrayal of Ada in literature, film, and media has often failed to capture the complexity of her contributions. This narrative framing not only diminishes her legacy but also perpetuates the stereotype of women in STEM as anomalies rather than integral contributors.

5. The Ongoing Impact of Gender Bias

The historical neglect of Ada Lovelace is not merely a relic of the past; it continues to resonate today. The gender bias that once marginalized her contributions persists in various forms within the tech industry. Women remain underrepresented in computer science and engineering fields, and their contributions are often overlooked or undervalued.

This ongoing bias highlights the importance of recognizing and celebrating figures like Ada Lovelace, not only to honor their contributions but also to inspire future generations of women in technology. By acknowledging Ada's legacy, we can challenge the historical narratives that have sidelined women in STEM and work towards a more inclusive and equitable future.

Conclusion

In conclusion, the reasons for Ada Lovelace's oversight in history are multifaceted, rooted in societal biases, the nature of her work, a lack of formal recognition, and the influence of popular culture. As we continue to explore and celebrate her contributions, it is essential to confront the historical narratives that have marginalized women in technology. By doing so, we can honor Ada Lovelace not only as the first programmer but also as a symbol of resilience and innovation in the face of adversity.

Ada's Contribution to Computer Programming

Ada Lovelace's contributions to computer programming are often overshadowed by her historical context, yet they are foundational to the field as we know it today. Lovelace's work with Charles Babbage on the Analytical Engine, a mechanical general-purpose computer, positioned her as the first programmer in history. This section explores her pioneering contributions, the theoretical underpinnings of her work, and the implications of her insights for modern programming.

The Concept of Algorithms

At the heart of programming lies the concept of algorithms, which Ada Lovelace understood deeply. An algorithm is a finite sequence of well-defined instructions to solve a problem or perform a computation. Lovelace's foresight in recognizing the potential of algorithms for computing was revolutionary. She articulated the notion that computers could manipulate symbols and numbers according to rules, a fundamental principle that underpins modern programming languages.

For example, Lovelace's notes on the Analytical Engine included an algorithm for calculating Bernoulli numbers. This algorithm can be expressed mathematically as follows:

$$B_n = \sum_{k=0}^{n} \binom{n}{k} \cdot B_k \cdot \frac{1}{n-k+1} \tag{17}$$

where B_n denotes the n-th Bernoulli number and $\binom{n}{k}$ is the binomial coefficient. Lovelace's methodical approach to this algorithm illustrated not only her mathematical prowess but also her ability to conceptualize a process that could be executed by a machine.

The Lovelace Note

Perhaps the most significant piece of her work is known as the "Lovelace Note," a detailed description of how the Analytical Engine could be programmed. In her notes, she emphasized that the machine could be instructed to perform tasks beyond mere calculation, such as composing music or generating graphics, by manipulating symbols according to predefined rules. This insight laid the groundwork for what we now refer to as programming languages.

Lovelace wrote, "The Analytical Engine does not occupy common ground with mere calculating machines. It holds within itself the power to create, to be an instrument of thought." This statement reflects her understanding that programming is not just about numbers; it is about creativity and innovation.

Theoretical Foundations of Programming

Lovelace's contributions also touched on the theoretical foundations of programming. She recognized the importance of data representation and the need for a language that could articulate complex instructions to a machine. This foresight is evident in her development of a system of notation that could represent operations and data structures, similar to modern programming syntax.

For instance, Lovelace's notation for loops and conditional statements can be seen as precursors to the control structures in contemporary programming languages. A simple representation of a loop in her notation might resemble:

```
FOR i = 1 TO n DO
    <operation>
END FOR
```

This structure highlights her understanding of iterative processes, which are essential in programming today.

Examples of Programming Concepts

Lovelace's work contained various programming concepts that resonate with modern practices. One of her notable contributions was the idea of subroutines, which are blocks of code designed to perform specific tasks. This concept is now a staple in programming, allowing for code reuse and modular design.

For example, consider a subroutine that calculates the factorial of a number n:

```
FUNCTION Factorial(n)
    IF n = 0 THEN RETURN 1
    ELSE RETURN n * Factorial(n - 1)
END FUNCTION
```

This example illustrates Lovelace's early understanding of recursion and the importance of defining functions, which are foundational to programming languages today.

Legacy and Modern Programming Languages

Ada Lovelace's contributions to programming extend beyond her lifetime, influencing the development of modern programming languages. Her insights into algorithms, data representation, and control structures laid the groundwork for languages like Python, Java, and C++. The Ada programming language, named in her honor, embodies her principles of strong typing and modularity, reflecting her vision for structured programming.

In conclusion, Ada Lovelace's contributions to computer programming were not merely historical footnotes; they were groundbreaking ideas that continue to shape the field. Her understanding of algorithms, data structures, and the creative potential of computing established her as the first programmer and a visionary whose legacy endures in every line of code written today. By recognizing her contributions, we honor not only her memory but also the foundational concepts that drive the technology of our modern world.

The Influence of Ada's Ideas on Future Generations

Ada Lovelace, often celebrated as the first programmer, left an indelible mark on the field of computing that continues to resonate today. Her visionary thoughts on the potential of computing machinery not only laid the groundwork for modern programming but also inspired countless generations of mathematicians, scientists, and engineers to explore the uncharted territories of technology. In this section, we will delve into the various ways Ada's ideas have influenced future generations, examining her contributions to programming, her foresight regarding the capabilities of computers, and the ongoing relevance of her work in today's technological landscape.

Pioneering Concepts in Programming

One of Ada's most significant contributions to the field of computer science is her formulation of the concept of an algorithm. In her notes on Charles Babbage's Analytical Engine, she articulated the process of using a sequence of instructions to solve mathematical problems. This notion of an algorithm is foundational to programming and remains central to computer science education today. The formal definition of an algorithm can be expressed as follows:

$$A = \{I_1, I_2, \ldots, I_n\} \tag{18}$$

where A is the algorithm, and I_i represents individual instructions that lead to a solution for a given problem. Ada's work illustrated that algorithms could be implemented not only for numerical calculations but also for more complex tasks, a vision that has become a reality in contemporary software development.

Ada's Vision for General-Purpose Computing

Ada Lovelace's foresight extended beyond mere number crunching; she envisioned computers as general-purpose machines capable of manipulating symbols and processing information in ways that could transcend arithmetic. In her famous notes, she posited that the Analytical Engine could be programmed to create music, produce graphics, and even simulate complex systems. This foresight is evident in today's computing landscape, where computers are employed in diverse fields such as artificial intelligence, data analysis, and creative arts.

For example, consider the use of algorithms in artificial intelligence. Modern AI systems rely on complex algorithms to learn from data, make predictions, and generate creative outputs. The foundational principles of programming that Ada articulated can be seen in the development of machine learning algorithms that adapt and evolve based on input data. A common model used in machine learning is the neural network, which can be represented mathematically as:

$$y = f(W \cdot x + b) \tag{19}$$

where y is the output, f is the activation function, W represents the weights, x is the input, and b is the bias. This model, while complex, is rooted in the simple idea of using algorithms to process information, a concept that Ada Lovelace championed over a century ago.

Inspiration for Women in Technology

Ada's legacy is not solely confined to her technical contributions; she also serves as a powerful symbol of female empowerment in the traditionally male-dominated fields of mathematics and engineering. Her life and work have inspired numerous initiatives aimed at encouraging women to pursue careers in STEM (Science, Technology, Engineering, and Mathematics). Organizations such as *Girls Who Code* and *Women Who Tech* draw upon Ada's story to motivate young girls to engage with technology and programming.

For instance, Ada Lovelace Day, celebrated annually on the second Tuesday of October, aims to raise awareness of the achievements of women in science and technology. Events and activities organized on this day highlight the importance of female role models in tech, encouraging young women to follow in Ada's footsteps. The influence of Ada's ideas extends into educational curricula, where her story is often used to illustrate the importance of diversity and inclusion in technology.

Ethical Considerations in Technology

Ada's work also presaged discussions about the ethical implications of technology. In her writings, she expressed concerns about the potential misuse of computing machinery.   This foresight is increasingly relevant in today's world, where technology can be used for both beneficial and harmful purposes. The ethical considerations surrounding artificial intelligence, data privacy, and algorithmic bias echo Ada's warnings about the responsibilities that come with technological advancement.

For example, the concept of algorithmic bias has gained significant attention in recent years. Algorithms can inadvertently perpetuate societal biases if not carefully designed and monitored. Ada's insights into the importance of understanding the implications of programming decisions serve as a reminder that technology should be developed with ethical considerations at the forefront.

Legacy in Modern Computing

Today, Ada Lovelace's influence is evident in various programming languages named in her honor, such as the Ada programming language, which was developed in the 1980s for the U.S. Department of Defense. This language emphasizes strong typing, modularity, and reliability, reflecting the principles of clarity and precision that Ada championed in her own work.

Moreover, Lovelace's legacy is celebrated in numerous awards and recognitions, such as the Ada Lovelace Award, which honors outstanding contributions to the field of computing. These recognitions not only commemorate her achievements but also serve to inspire future generations of technologists to innovate and push the boundaries of what is possible.

Conclusion

In conclusion, Ada Lovelace's ideas have had a profound and lasting impact on future generations of programmers, scientists, and engineers. Her pioneering concepts in algorithms, her vision for general-purpose computing, her role as an inspiration for women in technology, and her foresight regarding the ethical implications of technological advancements continue to shape the landscape of modern computing. As we look to the future, we must honor Ada's legacy by ensuring that her principles of innovation, inclusivity, and ethical responsibility remain central to the development of technology. In doing so, we can create a world that reflects her visionary spirit and continues to inspire generations to come.

Recognizing Ada's Impact on the Tech Industry

Ada Lovelace is often heralded as the first programmer, and her contributions extend far beyond the realm of early computing. To fully appreciate her impact on the tech industry, we must explore the theoretical underpinnings of her work, the problems she addressed, and the examples that illustrate her profound influence.

Theoretical Foundations

At the heart of Ada Lovelace's contributions lies her understanding of algorithms and computational theory. In her notes on Charles Babbage's Analytical Engine, she described a sequence of operations to calculate Bernoulli numbers, which can be expressed mathematically as:

$$B_n = \sum_{k=0}^{n} \binom{n}{k} \frac{B_k}{n - k + 1} \tag{20}$$

This equation illustrates the recursive nature of the Bernoulli numbers, a fundamental concept in number theory and analysis. Lovelace's recognition of the potential for machines to execute complex sequences of instructions laid the groundwork for modern programming languages, where algorithms are central to computation.

Addressing Problems in Computing

Lovelace's insights were not only theoretical; they addressed real-world problems of her time. The Analytical Engine was designed to perform calculations that were labor-intensive and error-prone when done manually. By automating these processes, Lovelace envisioned a future where machines could enhance human capabilities and reduce errors in computation. This vision resonates today, as the tech industry continues to grapple with issues of efficiency and accuracy in software development.

For instance, consider the problem of data sorting, a common task in programming. The development of sorting algorithms, such as QuickSort or MergeSort, can be traced back to the principles laid out by Lovelace. These algorithms optimize the process of organizing data, which is crucial in fields ranging from database management to artificial intelligence.

Examples of Ada's Influence

Lovelace's legacy is evident in various aspects of the tech industry today. One of the most direct examples is the Ada programming language, named in her honor. Developed in the late 1970s for the U.S. Department of Defense, Ada was designed to improve software reliability and maintainability. The language incorporates features that promote strong typing and modular programming, principles that Lovelace advocated through her work.

Moreover, Lovelace's emphasis on collaboration and interdisciplinary approaches has influenced the development of modern software engineering practices. Agile methodologies, which prioritize collaboration and iterative development, echo Lovelace's belief in the importance of teamwork in achieving complex goals. The Agile Manifesto, which states that "the best architectures, requirements, and designs emerge from self-organizing teams," aligns closely with Lovelace's vision of collaborative innovation.

Recognition in the Tech Community

In recent years, there has been a resurgence of interest in Ada Lovelace's contributions, particularly as the tech industry confronts issues of diversity and inclusion. Initiatives such as Ada Lovelace Day celebrate her legacy and promote the visibility of women in STEM fields. By recognizing her impact, we not only honor her achievements but also inspire future generations of female programmers and technologists.

The acknowledgment of Lovelace's work is further exemplified by awards and honors established in her name, such as the Ada Lovelace Award for outstanding contributions to computing. These recognitions serve to highlight the ongoing relevance of her ideas and the importance of fostering diversity in tech.

Conclusion

In conclusion, Ada Lovelace's impact on the tech industry is profound and multifaceted. Her theoretical contributions laid the groundwork for modern computing, while her visionary ideas addressed practical problems that continue to resonate today. By recognizing and celebrating her legacy, we honor not only her pioneering spirit but also the ongoing struggle for diversity and inclusion in the tech industry. As we navigate the complexities of modern technology, Lovelace's insights remind us of the importance of creativity, collaboration, and the boundless potential of human ingenuity.

Ada's Legacy in the Modern World

Ada Lovelace, often hailed as the first computer programmer, has left an indelible mark on the landscape of modern technology. Her pioneering work on Charles Babbage's Analytical Engine laid the groundwork for what would eventually evolve into the field of computer science. In this section, we will explore the multifaceted legacy of Ada Lovelace and its relevance in today's world, including her influence on programming, the tech industry, and gender equality in STEM fields.

Influence on Programming Languages

Ada's vision for the Analytical Engine included the idea of using algorithms to perform complex calculations, which is a fundamental concept in programming today. Her notes on the engine included what is now recognized as the first algorithm intended to be processed by a machine, marking her as a pioneer in the field of programming languages. This legacy is evident in the naming of the Ada programming language, developed in the late 1970s by the United States Department of Defense. The language emphasizes strong typing, modularity, and support for real-time systems, reflecting the principles Ada championed in her work.

$$\text{Algorithm} = \text{Input} \rightarrow \text{Process} \rightarrow \text{Output} \qquad (21)$$

This simple equation encapsulates the essence of programming, a concept that Ada grasped intuitively over a century ago. Her foresight into the potential of machines to execute complex tasks is mirrored in modern programming paradigms, where algorithms are the backbone of software development.

Impact on Computer Science

In the realm of computer science, Ada's contributions extend beyond programming languages. Her insights into the potential of machines to manipulate symbols and perform logical operations laid the groundwork for theoretical computer science. The concept of a machine that could be programmed to perform any calculation that could be described algorithmically is encapsulated in the Church-Turing thesis, which forms the foundation of modern computation theory.

The Church-Turing thesis posits that any computation that can be performed by a mechanical process can be performed by a Turing machine. This theoretical framework resonates with Ada's vision of the Analytical Engine as a universal machine capable of executing a variety of algorithms.

$$\text{Turing Machine} = (Q, \Sigma, \delta, q_0, q_{accept}, q_{reject}) \tag{22}$$

Where: - Q is a finite set of states, - Σ is a finite set of symbols, - δ is the transition function, - q_0 is the initial state, - q_{accept} is the accept state, - q_{reject} is the reject state.

This framework is foundational to understanding how modern computers operate, showcasing Ada's prescient understanding of computation.

Gender Equality and Representation in STEM

Ada Lovelace's legacy also extends into the realm of gender equality in technology and STEM fields. As a woman in a male-dominated society, she faced significant challenges, yet her work continues to inspire countless women to pursue careers in technology. The celebration of Ada Lovelace Day each year on the second Tuesday of October serves as a reminder of her contributions and aims to raise the profile of women in STEM.

The gender gap in technology remains a pressing issue, with women still underrepresented in many technical fields. According to the National Center for Women & Information Technology, women hold only 26% of computing jobs in the United States as of 2020. Ada's legacy serves as a rallying point for advocates of gender equality, inspiring initiatives to support women in technology through mentorship programs, scholarships, and community outreach.

Cultural Significance and Popular Representation

In popular culture, Ada Lovelace has been portrayed as a symbol of innovation and creativity. Her story has been featured in various media, including books, films, and art, emphasizing her role as a visionary thinker. The representation of Ada in contemporary narratives not only highlights her achievements but also serves to inspire future generations of innovators.

For instance, the graphic novel "The Thrilling Adventures of Lovelace and Babbage" by Sydney Padua brings Ada's story to life through a blend of historical fact and imaginative storytelling, showcasing her as a daring pioneer who envisioned a future where machines could enhance human capabilities.

Conclusion

In conclusion, Ada Lovelace's legacy is a rich tapestry woven from her contributions to programming, her insights into computation, and her role as an advocate for women in STEM. Her work continues to resonate in the modern world, inspiring new generations of programmers, computer scientists, and advocates for gender equality. As we navigate the complexities of today's technological landscape, Ada's vision remains a guiding light, reminding us of the potential for innovation and the importance of inclusivity in shaping the future of technology.

In the words of Ada herself, "That brain of mine is something more than merely mortal; as time will show." Indeed, her intellect and vision have transcended time, leaving a legacy that continues to inspire and challenge us to push the boundaries of what is possible in the world of technology.

The Struggles of a Female Pioneer

Navigating the Male-Dominated Field of Mathematics

In the 19th century, the world of mathematics was predominantly a male domain, characterized by an exclusionary culture that often dismissed the contributions of women. Ada Lovelace, despite her noble birth and exceptional intellect, had to navigate this challenging landscape with remarkable resilience and ingenuity. The societal norms of her time dictated that women were expected to adhere to domestic roles, yet Ada's passion for mathematics propelled her to defy these conventions.

The Societal Landscape

The prevailing attitudes towards women in mathematics during Ada's lifetime can be traced back to the educational barriers that limited women's access to advanced learning. For instance, women were often denied entry to universities and were discouraged from pursuing subjects deemed too complex or inappropriate for their gender. The idea that women were intellectually inferior to men was a common belief, perpetuated by both societal norms and scientific theories of the time.

Ada's Early Challenges

Ada's journey into mathematics began early in her life, influenced by her mother, Lady Anne Isabella Byron, who recognized her daughter's potential and ensured she received a rigorous education in mathematics and science. However, even with this support, Ada faced significant challenges. She was often isolated from her male counterparts, and her work was frequently overshadowed by the achievements of her male peers.

For example, Ada's collaboration with Charles Babbage, the father of the computer, was groundbreaking. However, their partnership was often framed in terms of Babbage's genius, with Ada's contributions minimized. This phenomenon is evident in the way history has recorded their work; while Babbage's Analytical Engine is celebrated, Ada's role as the first programmer is often overlooked.

Theoretical Frameworks and Gender Bias

To understand the dynamics of Ada's experiences, we can apply social theories that examine gender bias in STEM fields. The concept of *implicit bias* suggests that even well-intentioned individuals may hold subconscious beliefs about gender roles that affect their perceptions and evaluations of women's work in mathematics. For instance, studies have shown that when presented with identical work, evaluators often rate the contributions of male authors higher than those of female authors, a phenomenon known as the *gender bias effect*.

Mathematically, we can model this bias using statistical analysis. Suppose we have a dataset of evaluations for male and female mathematicians, represented as X_m and X_f respectively. The mean evaluation scores can be calculated as follows:

$$\mu_m = \frac{1}{n_m} \sum_{i=1}^{n_m} X_{m_i}$$

$$\mu_f = \frac{1}{n_f} \sum_{j=1}^{n_f} X_{f_j}$$

Where n_m and n_f are the number of evaluations for male and female mathematicians, respectively. The difference in means can then be analyzed to determine if a significant bias exists:

$$D = \mu_m - \mu_f$$

If $D > 0$, this indicates a bias favoring male mathematicians, while $D < 0$ suggests a bias against them.

Ada's Strategies for Success

Despite these barriers, Ada Lovelace employed several strategies to navigate the male-dominated field of mathematics. One of her most significant strengths was her ability to build relationships with influential male figures, such as Charles Babbage. Through her correspondence with Babbage, she not only gained access to advanced mathematical concepts but also positioned herself as a key contributor to the development of the Analytical Engine.

Moreover, Ada's unique approach to mathematics combined creativity and analytical thinking. She often likened her work to that of a poet, believing that the beauty of mathematics lay in its ability to express complex ideas in elegant forms. This perspective is encapsulated in her famous quote:

> "The Analytical Engine does not occupy common ground with mere 'calculating machines.' It holds within itself the power of the future, the ability to create and innovate."

Ada's ability to articulate her vision in a way that resonated with her contemporaries helped her gain recognition, albeit limited, in a field dominated by men.

Examples of Gender Bias in Mathematics

The impact of gender bias in mathematics can be illustrated through historical examples. For instance, the notable mathematician Mary Cartwright faced significant resistance in her career due to her gender, despite her groundbreaking work in chaos theory. Cartwright's contributions were often overshadowed by her male colleagues, a situation reminiscent of Ada's own struggles.

Another example is the work of Emmy Noether, who developed Noether's Theorem, a fundamental principle in physics and mathematics. Noether faced similar challenges, with her early work being largely ignored by her male peers. It wasn't until later that her contributions were recognized as pivotal to the development of modern algebra and theoretical physics.

Conclusion: A Legacy of Resilience

Ada Lovelace's journey through the male-dominated field of mathematics serves as a testament to her resilience and determination. By challenging societal norms and advocating for her place in the mathematical community, Ada not only paved the way for herself but also for future generations of women in STEM. Her legacy continues to inspire women today to pursue their passions in mathematics and technology, reminding us that the barriers of the past can be dismantled through perseverance and innovation.

In conclusion, the navigation of the male-dominated field of mathematics is not merely a historical account; it is an ongoing struggle that resonates with many women today. As we reflect on Ada Lovelace's life and contributions, we recognize the importance of continuing the fight for gender equality in mathematics and beyond, ensuring that the brilliance of future Ada Lovelaces is not overlooked.

Ada's Battle with Gender Stereotypes

Ada Lovelace lived in a time when the world was not only unkind to women pursuing intellectual endeavors but was outright hostile to the very idea of women engaging in fields like mathematics and engineering. Gender stereotypes were deeply entrenched in society, often relegating women to the domestic sphere while dismissing their intellectual capabilities. This section delves into Ada's struggle against these stereotypes, highlighting her resilience and determination in the face of societal expectations.

Historical Context of Gender Stereotypes

In the 19th century, societal norms dictated that women were to be seen and not heard. The prevailing belief was that women lacked the rationality and logical thinking required for scientific and mathematical pursuits. The notion of "separate spheres" categorized men as breadwinners and women as homemakers, creating a rigid dichotomy that left little room for women like Ada to flourish in academia or professional fields.

This pervasive mindset was compounded by the educational limitations placed on women. Higher education was largely inaccessible, and many women were discouraged from pursuing subjects deemed too "masculine." Ada, however, was fortunate to have a mother who recognized her potential and provided her with a robust education in mathematics, a rarity for women of her time.

The Influence of Ada's Mother

Ada's mother, Lady Anne Isabella Byron, played a pivotal role in her battle against gender stereotypes. A staunch advocate for her daughter's education, Lady Byron ensured that Ada had access to tutors and resources that would nurture her mathematical talents. This was not without its challenges; Lady Byron herself faced societal scrutiny for her unconventional approach to her daughter's upbringing.

The relationship between Ada and her mother was complex. While Lady Byron encouraged Ada's intellectual pursuits, she also imposed strict expectations regarding propriety and behavior. This duality created a tension in Ada's life, as she navigated the expectations of a society that often viewed educated women with suspicion.

Ada's Defiance of Gender Norms

Despite the constraints of her environment, Ada Lovelace defied gender norms with remarkable tenacity. She immersed herself in the world of mathematics, forming a partnership with Charles Babbage that would lead to the development of the Analytical Engine. Their collaboration was groundbreaking, as it not only challenged the gender norms of the time but also laid the foundation for modern computing.

Ada's writings on the Analytical Engine showcased her profound understanding of its potential, which was rare for anyone, let alone a woman in the 1800s. In her famous notes, she articulated concepts such as algorithmic processes and the potential of machines to manipulate symbols, ideas that were revolutionary for her time.

The Backlash Against Ada's Work

Unfortunately, Ada's contributions were often overshadowed by her gender. The male-dominated scientific community frequently dismissed her ideas, attributing them to Babbage or undermining her role in the development of computing. This dismissal was not unique to Ada; many women in science faced similar challenges, where their contributions were minimized or ignored altogether.

For instance, Ada's contemporaries often viewed her as merely a "mathematical muse" rather than a legitimate contributor to the field. This stereotype not only belittled her work but also perpetuated the idea that women were incapable of original thought in scientific disciplines. Ada's struggle against this perception was emblematic of the broader fight for recognition faced by women in STEM fields.

The Persistence of Gender Stereotypes

Even in the face of her groundbreaking work, Ada Lovelace's legacy was often relegated to the margins of history. The narrative surrounding her contributions was shaped by the same gender stereotypes that she fought against during her lifetime. For decades, she was overlooked in discussions about the history of computing, and her achievements were frequently attributed to her male counterparts.

The consequences of these stereotypes extend beyond Ada's story; they reflect a systemic issue within the scientific community that continues to persist. Women in technology and engineering still face significant barriers, including bias in hiring practices, unequal pay, and a lack of representation in leadership positions. Ada's experiences serve as a poignant reminder of the ongoing battle against gender stereotypes in STEM fields.

Ada's Legacy and the Fight for Gender Equality

Despite the challenges she faced, Ada Lovelace's legacy continues to inspire future generations of women in technology. Her defiance of gender stereotypes and her contributions to mathematics and computing have paved the way for increased awareness of the importance of diversity in STEM.

Organizations around the world celebrate Ada Lovelace Day to honor her contributions and to promote gender equality in science and technology. These initiatives aim to challenge the stereotypes that have historically marginalized women in these fields, encouraging a new generation of female innovators to pursue their passions without the constraints of societal expectations.

In conclusion, Ada Lovelace's battle with gender stereotypes was not just a personal struggle; it was a reflection of the societal norms that sought to limit the potential of women. Her determination to defy these norms and her remarkable contributions to mathematics and computing serve as a beacon of hope for future generations. As we continue to confront gender bias in STEM, Ada's legacy reminds us of the importance of perseverance, advocacy, and the pursuit of knowledge, regardless of gender.

The Importance of Ada's Role as an Inspirational Figure

Ada Lovelace stands as a beacon of inspiration, not just for her groundbreaking contributions to the field of computing, but also for her role as a pioneering woman in a male-dominated discipline. Her life and work exemplify the struggles and triumphs of women in STEM (Science, Technology, Engineering, and Mathematics), making her an enduring symbol of resilience and innovation.

Breaking Barriers

In the 19th century, the world of mathematics and technology was largely inaccessible to women. Ada's foray into this realm was not merely an act of personal ambition; it was a bold statement against the societal norms that dictated the roles of women. Despite the constraints of her time, Ada pursued her interests with vigor, showcasing that women could excel in fields traditionally reserved for men. Her story serves as a powerful reminder that barriers can be broken, and that passion and intellect know no gender.

Role Model for Future Generations

Ada's legacy transcends her own achievements; it resonates deeply with young women aspiring to enter STEM fields today. By embodying the spirit of inquiry and innovation, she inspires countless individuals to challenge stereotypes and pursue their passions. The impact of her work is visible in initiatives aimed at encouraging girls to engage with technology and mathematics. For instance, programs like *Girls Who Code* and *STEMettes* actively promote female participation in tech, drawing parallels to Ada's trailblazing path.

The Lovelace Note: A Testament to Visionary Thinking

Perhaps one of Ada's most significant contributions is encapsulated in her work on the Analytical Engine, particularly in the famous Lovelace Note, where she articulated her vision of a machine that could manipulate symbols and perform tasks beyond mere calculation. This foresight is a testament to her imaginative prowess and her understanding of the potential of computing technology. The Lovelace Note not only laid the groundwork for computer programming but also highlighted the importance of creative thinking in technological advancement.

$$\text{Potential of Computing} = \text{Symbol Manipulation} + \text{Creative Problem Solving} \tag{23}$$

This equation illustrates that the true power of computing lies not only in its ability to perform calculations but also in its capacity to enable creative and abstract thought. Ada's insights into the potential applications of computing foreshadowed the diverse roles technology would play in society, from art to science, and everything in between.

Advocacy for Women in STEM

Beyond her technical contributions, Ada Lovelace was an advocate for women's education and empowerment. Her correspondence with contemporaries and her writings reflect her commitment to promoting the inclusion of women in scientific endeavors. Ada's life underscores the importance of mentorship and support systems for women pursuing careers in STEM. As she navigated her own challenges, she paved the way for future generations by demonstrating that women could not only participate in but also lead in these fields.

Cultural Impact and Representation

Ada's story has been woven into the cultural fabric of society, inspiring literature, films, and educational curricula. Her portrayal in various media highlights the importance of representation in shaping perceptions of women's roles in technology. By bringing her story to the forefront, we not only honor her legacy but also encourage young girls to envision themselves as future innovators and leaders.

For example, the annual *Ada Lovelace Day* celebrates her achievements while promoting women in STEM. Events held worldwide encourage discussions about the contributions of women in technology and serve as a platform for young female technologists to share their experiences and aspirations. This recognition plays a crucial role in fostering a supportive community that champions diversity and inclusivity.

Conclusion

In conclusion, Ada Lovelace's role as an inspirational figure is multifaceted. She not only broke barriers in her own time but also laid the groundwork for future generations of women in technology. Her visionary thinking, advocacy for women's education, and cultural impact continue to resonate today. As we celebrate her legacy, we are reminded of the importance of fostering an inclusive environment in STEM fields, ensuring that all individuals, regardless of gender, have the opportunity to innovate and inspire. Ada Lovelace's life is a testament to the power of perseverance and creativity, encouraging us to embrace our passions and challenge the status quo.

$$\text{Inspiration} = \text{Legacy} + \text{Empowerment} + \text{Inclusivity} \quad (24)$$

This equation encapsulates the essence of Ada's influence, serving as a guiding principle for future generations of innovators.

Ada's Support for Women's Education

Ada Lovelace was not only a pioneer in the field of mathematics and computing but also a fervent advocate for women's education. In an era when women were often relegated to the background of intellectual pursuits, Ada's life and work served as a beacon of hope and inspiration for future generations of women seeking to break into male-dominated fields.

The Context of Women's Education in the 19th Century

During the 19th century, educational opportunities for women were severely limited. The prevailing societal norms dictated that women were primarily responsible for domestic duties, and their education was often deemed unnecessary beyond basic literacy. This environment was a stark contrast to the burgeoning fields of science and mathematics, which were rapidly evolving and becoming critical to societal advancement.

Ada's own upbringing was unique; her mother, Lady Anne, recognized the importance of education and ensured that Ada received a rigorous education in mathematics and science. This was a radical departure from the norm, and it shaped Ada's worldview and commitment to advocating for the education of women.

Ada's Advocacy for Women's Education

Ada's advocacy for women's education can be observed through her writings and her relationships with other prominent figures of her time. She believed that women had the potential to contribute significantly to fields such as mathematics, science, and engineering. In her correspondence with Charles Babbage, Ada often emphasized the importance of education and the need for women to engage in intellectual pursuits.

In one of her letters to Babbage, she wrote:

> "I am convinced that the study of mathematics is a great means of training the mind, and that it should be made accessible to women as well as men."

This statement reflects her belief in the transformative power of education and her commitment to ensuring that women had equal access to it.

Theoretical Frameworks Supporting Women's Education

Ada's advocacy can also be understood through various theoretical frameworks that highlight the importance of education in empowering marginalized groups. One such framework is the *Capability Approach*, developed by economist Amartya Sen and philosopher Martha Nussbaum. This approach posits that education is not merely a means to an end but a fundamental capability that enables individuals to lead fulfilling lives.

In the context of women's education, the Capability Approach emphasizes the need for women to have access to educational resources that allow them to develop their potential and participate fully in society. Ada embodied this philosophy, recognizing that education was essential for women to achieve autonomy and independence.

Real-World Impact of Ada's Support

Ada's support for women's education extended beyond her personal beliefs; she actively sought to inspire other women to pursue their interests in mathematics and science. Her work on the Analytical Engine not only showcased her mathematical genius but also served as a powerful example for women who aspired to enter these fields.

For instance, Ada's collaboration with Babbage was groundbreaking. She was one of the first to recognize the potential of computing and the importance of programming, a field that would later become a cornerstone of modern technology. By contributing to Babbage's work, Ada demonstrated that women could excel in technical and scientific domains, thereby challenging the prevailing stereotypes of her time.

Moreover, Ada's legacy has inspired numerous initiatives aimed at promoting women's education in STEM (Science, Technology, Engineering, and Mathematics) fields. Organizations such as *Girls Who Code* and *Women in Technology* carry forward Ada's vision by providing resources, mentorship, and support to young women interested in pursuing careers in technology.

Challenges in Women's Education

Despite Ada's efforts and the progress made since her time, significant challenges remain in the pursuit of gender equality in education. Issues such as gender bias in educational materials, lack of female role models in STEM, and societal pressures continue to hinder women's access to quality education.

For example, research has shown that girls often perform as well as boys in mathematics during early education, but their confidence in these subjects diminishes as they progress through school. This phenomenon, often referred to as the *confidence gap*, underscores the need for ongoing advocacy and support for women in education.

Conclusion: Honoring Ada's Legacy

Ada Lovelace's commitment to women's education serves as a powerful reminder of the importance of fostering an inclusive environment where all individuals, regardless of gender, have the opportunity to pursue their passions and contribute to society. Her legacy continues to inspire efforts aimed at breaking down barriers and promoting gender equality in education and beyond.

As we reflect on Ada's contributions, it is crucial to recognize that the fight for women's education is far from over. By honoring her legacy, we can continue to advocate for equal opportunities for women in all fields, ensuring that future generations have the support and resources they need to thrive.

$$E = mc^2 \tag{25}$$

This famous equation, while originally formulated by Einstein, can metaphorically represent the energy (E) that education (m) can generate when applied with the speed of light (c) to women's empowerment, illustrating the transformative power of knowledge.

In conclusion, Ada Lovelace not only paved the way for women in mathematics and computing but also laid the groundwork for future advocates of women's education. Her vision and determination remain a source of inspiration for all who strive to create a more equitable world.

Ada's Advocacy for Women in STEM Fields

Ada Lovelace, often hailed as the first computer programmer, was not only a pioneer in mathematics and computing but also a passionate advocate for women in science, technology, engineering, and mathematics (STEM). Her advocacy was rooted in her own experiences navigating a male-dominated field, and her belief that women could contribute significantly to technological advancements.

Historical Context

In the 19th century, societal norms often dictated that women should adhere to traditional roles, limiting their access to education and professional opportunities. Despite these barriers, Ada's mother, Lady Anne Isabella Byron, recognized her daughter's exceptional talents and ensured she received a rigorous education in mathematics and science. This early support played a crucial role in shaping Ada's identity as a thinker and innovator.

Ada's Vision for Women's Education

Ada believed that education was the key to unlocking women's potential in STEM fields. She advocated for educational reforms that would provide women with equal access to scientific knowledge and resources. In her correspondence with Charles Babbage, she emphasized the importance of education in fostering creativity and innovation among women:

$$\text{Education} \rightarrow \text{Empowerment} \rightarrow \text{Innovation} \tag{26}$$

This equation illustrates Ada's belief that education leads to empowerment, which in turn fosters innovation. She understood that providing women with the necessary tools and knowledge was essential for their participation in scientific discourse.

Pioneering Initiatives

Ada's advocacy was not limited to theoretical discussions; she actively participated in initiatives aimed at promoting women's involvement in STEM. One notable example is her involvement in the establishment of educational institutions that welcomed female students. She encouraged the creation of programs that would provide women with training in mathematics and engineering, fields that were traditionally male-dominated.

In her writings, Ada often highlighted the contributions of women in science, emphasizing that their insights and perspectives were invaluable. She wrote:

> "The more I learn, the more I see that there are no limits to what women can achieve in science and mathematics. It is our duty to support one another and break down the barriers that confine us."

Addressing Gender Bias

Ada was acutely aware of the gender biases that permeated the scientific community. She faced skepticism and condescension from her male peers, which only fueled her determination to advocate for women's rights in STEM. She challenged the notion that women lacked the intellectual capacity for rigorous scientific thought, often countering these stereotypes with her own accomplishments.

In her correspondence with Babbage, she articulated the need for a shift in perception regarding women's capabilities:

"It is not the lack of ability that holds women back, but the lack of opportunity and recognition. We must change the narrative surrounding women's contributions to science."

The Legacy of Ada's Advocacy

Ada Lovelace's advocacy laid the groundwork for future generations of women in STEM. Her legacy is evident in the growing number of initiatives aimed at supporting women in technology and engineering. Organizations such as *Girls Who Code* and *Women in Technology International* continue to champion the cause of women in STEM, echoing Ada's call for equality and representation.

Moreover, Ada's story serves as a source of inspiration for young women aspiring to enter STEM fields. Her life demonstrates that with determination, education, and support, women can overcome obstacles and make significant contributions to science and technology.

Conclusion

In conclusion, Ada Lovelace's advocacy for women in STEM fields was a pioneering effort that transcended her time. Her belief in the power of education, her challenge against gender biases, and her commitment to supporting women in science continue to resonate today. As we reflect on her legacy, it is crucial to honor her contributions by fostering an inclusive environment where women can thrive in STEM. Ada's vision for a future where women are celebrated as equals in the scientific community remains a guiding principle for ongoing efforts to achieve gender parity in technology and beyond.

Ada's Efforts to Break Down Barriers for Female Programmers

Ada Lovelace, often celebrated as the first programmer, was not only a pioneer in the field of computing but also a staunch advocate for women's rights in the sciences and mathematics. In an era when women were largely excluded from academic and professional pursuits, Ada's efforts to break down barriers for female programmers were both revolutionary and necessary. This section delves into her initiatives, the societal challenges she faced, and her lasting impact on women in technology.

The Context of Gender Inequality in the 19th Century

During the 19th century, societal norms dictated that women were primarily relegated to domestic roles, with education and professional opportunities largely inaccessible. The prevailing belief was that women lacked the intellectual capacity for rigorous academic disciplines such as mathematics and science. This systemic discrimination created an environment where female talent was stifled, and potential innovators were left unrecognized.

$$\text{Gender Inequality} = \frac{\text{Access to Education for Women}}{\text{Access to Education for Men}} \cdot 100\% \qquad (27)$$

This equation illustrates the stark disparity in educational access, where a lower percentage indicates a greater inequality. Ada's own education was a rarity for women of her time, and she was determined to use her knowledge and influence to advocate for change.

Advocacy for Women's Education

Ada recognized that education was the key to empowerment. Her mother, Lady Anne Isabella Byron, was instrumental in Ada's early education, particularly in mathematics, which was unusual for women. Ada's own experiences fueled her commitment to advocating for women's education in STEM fields.

She often expressed her belief in the importance of educational opportunities for women through her writings and correspondence. In her letters to Charles Babbage, she emphasized the need for women to engage in intellectual pursuits, stating:

"I am not afraid of storms, for I am learning how to sail my ship."

This metaphor not only reflects her personal journey but also serves as a rallying cry for women to navigate the turbulent waters of a male-dominated society.

Creating Networks for Women

Ada was aware that individual efforts were not enough to create lasting change. She sought to establish networks among women who shared her interests in mathematics and science. Through her correspondence with other intellectuals, Ada encouraged women to pursue their passions and supported their endeavors.

For instance, Ada's connections with other female mathematicians and scientists of her time helped to foster a sense of community. These networks provided a platform for women to share knowledge, collaborate on projects, and advocate for their rights collectively. The establishment of such networks was crucial in combating the isolation many women faced in their pursuits.

Challenging Societal Norms

Ada's very existence as a female mathematician challenged the societal norms of her time. She was not only a talented mathematician but also a visionary who dared to imagine a future where women could contribute to fields traditionally dominated by men. Her work on the Analytical Engine with Babbage was groundbreaking, and she often insisted on the potential of machines to perform tasks beyond mere calculation, including creative processes.

In her notes on the Analytical Engine, she wrote:

> "The Analytical Engine does not occupy common ground with mere calculating machines. It holds within it the potential for creating art and music."

This perspective was radical, as it implied that women could be involved in creative and intellectual pursuits through programming. Ada's vision for the future of computing included women as integral players, thus challenging the existing stereotypes.

Promoting Female Role Models

Ada understood the importance of representation. She recognized that for women to see themselves in STEM roles, they needed visible role models. By establishing herself as a prominent figure in mathematics and computing, she paved the way for future generations of women. Ada's legacy inspired others to pursue careers in technology, leading to the gradual acceptance of women in these fields.

The emergence of organizations dedicated to supporting women in technology, such as the Ada Lovelace Foundation, can be traced back to her pioneering spirit. These organizations aim to promote female representation in tech, provide mentorship, and create opportunities for women, echoing Ada's vision.

The Impact of Ada's Advocacy

Ada's efforts to break down barriers for female programmers were not without challenges. She faced skepticism and resistance from her contemporaries, who often doubted women's capabilities in mathematics. However, her tenacity and brilliance shone through, influencing those around her and leaving a lasting impression on the tech community.

Her contributions to the field of computer science and her advocacy for women's education have had a ripple effect, inspiring countless women to enter STEM fields.

Today, Ada Lovelace is celebrated not only as the first programmer but also as a symbol of female empowerment in technology.

Conclusion

In conclusion, Ada Lovelace's efforts to break down barriers for female programmers were groundbreaking and transformative. Through her advocacy for education, the establishment of networks, and her challenge to societal norms, Ada laid the groundwork for future generations of women in technology. Her legacy continues to inspire the ongoing fight for gender equality in the tech industry, reminding us that the pursuit of knowledge knows no gender.

As we reflect on Ada's contributions, it is essential to recognize that the journey toward equality is ongoing. By honoring her legacy and continuing her work, we can ensure that the barriers Ada fought against are dismantled for good.

Ada's Impact on the Women in Tech Movement

Ada Lovelace, often hailed as the first computer programmer, has had a profound and lasting impact on the Women in Tech movement. Her legacy is not merely a testament to her groundbreaking work in mathematics and computing; it serves as a beacon for women aspiring to enter and thrive in the technology sector. This section explores how Ada's life and work have inspired generations of women in technology, the challenges they continue to face, and the ongoing efforts to honor her contributions.

A Symbol of Possibility

Ada Lovelace's story embodies the struggle and triumph of women in a male-dominated field. Born in 1815 to the famous poet Lord Byron and Annabella Milbanke, Ada's mother ensured that she received a rigorous education in mathematics, a rarity for women of her time. This unconventional upbringing allowed Ada to forge her path, leading to her collaboration with Charles Babbage on the Analytical Engine. Lovelace's notes on the engine included what is now recognized as the first algorithm intended to be processed by a machine, marking her as a pioneer in computing.

Her achievements serve as a symbol of possibility for women in technology. The narrative of a woman breaking barriers in the 19th century resonates with contemporary discussions about gender equality in STEM fields. Ada's legacy encourages women to pursue careers in technology, challenging stereotypes and societal expectations.

Addressing Gender Bias

Despite Ada's monumental contributions, the tech industry has long been plagued by gender bias. Women in tech face numerous obstacles, including a lack of representation, pay disparities, and cultural stereotypes that question their competence. According to a report by the National Center for Women & Information Technology (NCWIT), women hold only 26% of computing jobs, a statistic that has remained stagnant for years.

Ada's legacy is instrumental in addressing these issues. By highlighting her story, organizations and advocates can bring attention to the systemic barriers that women face in technology. Initiatives such as Ada Lovelace Day, which celebrates the achievements of women in STEM, aim to inspire young girls and provide role models in the field. By sharing stories of women like Ada, these movements foster a sense of community and empowerment among women in tech.

Mentorship and Representation

Mentorship plays a crucial role in the advancement of women in technology. Ada Lovelace's life illustrates the importance of mentorship in fostering talent and innovation. Her collaboration with Babbage was not just a professional partnership; it was a mentorship that allowed her to explore her potential in a supportive environment.

Today, organizations are increasingly recognizing the need for mentorship programs that connect young women with experienced professionals in the tech industry. Programs like Girls Who Code and Women Who Code aim to bridge the gender gap by providing mentorship, resources, and networking opportunities. These initiatives echo Ada's collaborative spirit, encouraging women to support one another in their professional journeys.

Advocacy for Women in Tech

Ada's advocacy for women's education and empowerment in the 19th century laid the groundwork for modern movements advocating for gender equality in technology. Her belief in the importance of education for women resonates with contemporary initiatives that aim to increase female representation in STEM fields.

Organizations such as the Ada Lovelace Foundation are dedicated to promoting gender equality in technology through policy advocacy, research, and community engagement. By drawing inspiration from Ada's life, these organizations work to dismantle systemic barriers and create inclusive environments for women in tech.

Cultural Impact and Representation

Ada Lovelace's influence extends beyond her technical contributions; she has become a cultural icon representing women in technology. Her image and story are celebrated in literature, art, and popular culture, helping to normalize the presence of women in tech.

For instance, the portrayal of Ada in various media, including books and films, emphasizes her brilliance and creativity, inspiring young girls to envision themselves in similar roles. By framing Ada as a relatable figure, these narratives encourage girls to pursue their interests in technology and mathematics, challenging the notion that these fields are solely for men.

Conclusion

In conclusion, Ada Lovelace's impact on the Women in Tech movement is profound and multifaceted. Her legacy serves as a symbol of possibility, a call to action against gender bias, and a reminder of the importance of mentorship and representation. As the tech industry continues to grapple with gender inequality, Ada's story inspires a new generation of women to break barriers, challenge stereotypes, and innovate. By honoring her contributions and advocating for change, we can ensure that Ada Lovelace's legacy endures, empowering women in technology for generations to come.

The Ongoing Fight for Gender Equality in the Tech Industry

The tech industry has long been viewed as a bastion of innovation and progress, yet it remains a landscape fraught with gender inequality. Despite the undeniable contributions of women like Ada Lovelace, the first programmer, the battle for gender equality in technology continues to be a pressing issue. This section delves into the theoretical frameworks, persistent problems, and real-world examples that illustrate the ongoing fight for gender equality in the tech industry.

Theoretical Frameworks

Gender equality in the tech industry can be understood through various theoretical lenses, including feminist theory, intersectionality, and social constructivism.

Feminist Theory posits that societal structures and cultural norms perpetuate gender disparities. In the context of technology, this theory highlights how male-dominated environments can marginalize women's contributions and perpetuate stereotypes that discourage female participation.

Intersectionality , a term coined by Kimberlé Crenshaw, emphasizes that individuals experience discrimination based on multiple intersecting identities, including race, class, and gender. In tech, this means that women of color, LGBTQ+ individuals, and those from lower socioeconomic backgrounds face compounded barriers that must be addressed to achieve true equality.

Social Constructivism suggests that gender roles are socially constructed and reinforced through cultural narratives and practices. In tech, this is evident in the way coding and engineering are often framed as "masculine" pursuits, which can dissuade girls and women from pursuing careers in these fields.

Persistent Problems

Despite progress, several persistent problems hinder the advancement of gender equality in the tech industry:

1. Gender Stereotypes and Bias Stereotypes about women's capabilities in STEM (Science, Technology, Engineering, Mathematics) fields persist, leading to bias in hiring, promotions, and workplace dynamics. Research shows that women are often judged more harshly than men for the same performance metrics, leading to a lack of recognition for their contributions.

2. The Gender Pay Gap The tech industry is not immune to the gender pay gap, which, according to a report by the National Women's Law Center, shows that women in tech earn approximately 83 cents for every dollar earned by their male counterparts. This disparity is even more pronounced for women of color, who face both gender and racial wage gaps.

3. Lack of Representation Women remain underrepresented in tech leadership positions. According to a 2021 report from McKinsey & Company, women make up only 28% of senior vice president roles in tech companies, and the numbers drop significantly for women of color. This lack of representation can lead to a cycle where women's perspectives and needs are overlooked in product development and company policies.

4. **Workplace Culture** The tech industry's often aggressive and competitive culture can be unwelcoming to women. Instances of harassment and discrimination are not uncommon, creating an environment where women may feel unsafe or unsupported. A 2020 study by the Kapor Center found that 50% of women in tech reported experiencing harassment at work.

Real-World Examples

Several organizations and initiatives are leading the charge for gender equality in tech, demonstrating that change is possible:

1. **Girls Who Code** This nonprofit organization aims to close the gender gap in technology by providing girls with the skills and resources to pursue computer science. Through coding camps, clubs, and mentorship, Girls Who Code has reached over 300,000 girls since its inception in 2012, inspiring a new generation of female programmers.

2. **Women Who Code** Women Who Code is a global nonprofit dedicated to inspiring women to excel in technology careers. The organization offers networking opportunities, mentorship, and technical training, empowering women to thrive in a male-dominated industry. With over 230,000 members worldwide, Women Who Code is making strides in increasing female representation in tech.

3. **The Ada Lovelace Foundation** Named in honor of Ada Lovelace, this foundation advocates for gender equality in technology through policy change, education, and community engagement. By promoting awareness of gender disparities and supporting initiatives that empower women in tech, the foundation honors Lovelace's legacy and paves the way for future generations.

4. **Corporate Initiatives** Many tech companies are recognizing the need for change and implementing initiatives to promote gender equality. For example, Salesforce has committed to closing its gender pay gap and has invested millions in employee training programs focused on diversity and inclusion. Similarly, Google has set ambitious goals to increase the representation of women and underrepresented minorities in its workforce.

Conclusion

The ongoing fight for gender equality in the tech industry is complex and multifaceted, rooted in historical biases and cultural constructs. However, through the lens of feminist theory, intersectionality, and social constructivism, we can better understand the challenges at play. By addressing persistent problems such as gender stereotypes, the pay gap, lack of representation, and workplace culture, and by celebrating organizations and initiatives that are making a difference, we can work towards a more equitable tech industry.

As we honor the legacy of Ada Lovelace, it is crucial to remember that the fight for gender equality is not just about numbers; it is about creating an inclusive environment where all voices are heard and valued. Only then can we truly innovate and advance in the tech industry, paving the way for a future where everyone, regardless of gender, can contribute to and thrive in the world of technology.

Honoring Ada's Legacy: Celebrating Women in Programming

Ada Lovelace, often celebrated as the first programmer, serves as a beacon of inspiration for women in technology. Her groundbreaking work on the Analytical Engine laid the foundation for modern computing, yet her legacy extends far beyond her contributions to programming. In this section, we will explore the significance of honoring Ada's legacy by celebrating women in programming today, examining the barriers they face, the progress made, and the initiatives that foster inclusivity in the tech industry.

The Historical Context of Women in Programming

Historically, the field of programming has been male-dominated, but women played a crucial role in the early days of computing. Figures such as Grace Hopper and the women of the ENIAC project were instrumental in shaping the technology we use today. Despite their contributions, the narrative often overlooks women's roles in technology. Ada's legacy reminds us of the importance of recognizing and celebrating these contributions.

Barriers to Participation

Women in programming continue to face various barriers, including:

+ **Gender Bias:** Stereotypes about women's abilities in STEM fields can discourage young girls from pursuing careers in technology. Research shows that girls often receive less encouragement in mathematics and science, leading to lower participation rates in these areas.

+ **Workplace Culture:** A lack of representation in tech companies can create environments that feel unwelcoming to women. Issues such as gender discrimination and harassment can further exacerbate the problem, making it difficult for women to thrive in their careers.

+ **Access to Education:** While there has been progress in increasing access to STEM education for girls, disparities still exist. Girls from underrepresented backgrounds may lack access to resources, mentorship, and role models in the field.

Celebrating Women in Programming: Initiatives and Movements

To honor Ada's legacy, various initiatives and movements have emerged to celebrate and support women in programming:

+ **Ada Lovelace Day:** Celebrated annually on the second Tuesday in October, Ada Lovelace Day recognizes the achievements of women in STEM. Events range from talks and workshops to social media campaigns that highlight the contributions of women in technology.

+ **Women Who Code:** This global nonprofit organization aims to inspire women to excel in technology careers. Through networking events, mentorship programs, and coding resources, Women Who Code supports women in their professional development and fosters a sense of community.

+ **Girls Who Code:** This organization focuses on closing the gender gap in technology by providing girls with the skills and confidence to pursue careers in computing. Through summer programs and after-school clubs, Girls Who Code empowers young girls to become future leaders in technology.

+ **Tech Inclusion:** This initiative seeks to address diversity and inclusion in the tech industry. By hosting conferences, workshops, and networking events, Tech Inclusion creates spaces for underrepresented groups to connect and share their experiences in the tech world.

The Importance of Representation

Representation matters. When women see other women succeeding in programming and technology, it inspires them to pursue similar paths. Role models like Ada Lovelace serve as reminders that women have always been at the forefront of technological innovation. By celebrating these figures, we encourage the next generation of female programmers to embrace their potential.

The Role of Education in Honoring Ada's Legacy

Education plays a crucial role in honoring Ada's legacy. By incorporating her story into STEM curricula, educators can inspire students to recognize the contributions of women in technology. Programs that promote coding and computer science skills among girls are essential in fostering a diverse pipeline of talent for the tech industry.

Conclusion: A Call to Action

Honoring Ada Lovelace's legacy means actively celebrating and supporting women in programming. By acknowledging the barriers they face and promoting initiatives that foster inclusivity, we can create a more equitable tech industry. As we reflect on Ada's contributions, let us commit to empowering women in technology and ensuring that their stories are told and celebrated. Together, we can honor Ada's legacy and inspire future generations of female programmers to dream big and achieve greatness.

$$\text{Impact} = \text{Representation} + \text{Education} + \text{Support} \qquad (28)$$

In this equation, we see that the impact of honoring Ada's legacy is a product of representation, education, and support for women in programming. Each factor contributes to a culture that values diversity and encourages innovation. Let us carry Ada's torch forward, lighting the way for women in programming to shine brightly in the tech landscape.

A Life of Tragedy and Triumph

Ada's Struggles with Illness

Ada Lovelace, a name synonymous with pioneering programming, faced numerous personal challenges throughout her life, not the least of which were her struggles with illness. These health issues were not merely footnotes in her biography; they were significant hurdles that shaped her experiences, influenced her work, and contributed to her complex legacy.

From a young age, Ada exhibited a frail constitution, and her health was often precarious. As a child, she suffered from various ailments, including severe bouts of illness that kept her from engaging in the rigorous academic pursuits she so passionately desired. Her mother's decision to prioritize Ada's education was commendable, yet the reality of her health struggles often overshadowed her academic achievements.

One of the most significant illnesses Ada faced was in her early twenties, when she contracted what was then referred to as "the fever." This illness was debilitating and left her bedridden for extended periods, disrupting her studies and interactions with peers. It was during this time that Ada began to grapple with the notion of mortality, a theme that would recur throughout her life. The fever not only affected her physically but also instilled in her a sense of urgency regarding her intellectual pursuits.

Despite these challenges, Ada's resilience was remarkable. She often turned to her studies as a form of solace during her periods of illness. It was during these times of isolation that she developed a deeper understanding of mathematics and logic. Her correspondence with Charles Babbage flourished during her convalescence, as letters became her primary means of intellectual engagement. These exchanges laid the groundwork for her later contributions to the Analytical Engine, demonstrating how her struggles with illness inadvertently fueled her creativity and innovation.

However, Ada's health continued to deteriorate throughout her life. In her later years, she experienced increasingly severe symptoms that were likely related to a combination of hereditary factors and the stress of her ambitious projects. The exact nature of her illness remains a topic of speculation among historians and biographers. Some have suggested that she may have suffered from a form of cancer, while others propose that she could have had a metabolic disorder. Regardless of the specifics, it is clear that her health issues were a constant presence, impacting her ability to work and socialize.

Ada's marriage to William King in 1835 brought both joy and additional stress. The couple had three children, and while Ada embraced her role as a mother, the demands of family life compounded her existing health challenges. The societal expectations placed upon women of her time often clashed with her ambitions, leading to a profound internal struggle. The pressure to conform to traditional roles while pursuing her intellectual passions created a dichotomy that Ada found difficult to navigate.

As her health continued to decline, Ada became increasingly aware of her own mortality. This awareness profoundly influenced her later writings, particularly her reflections on the future of computing and the potential of the Analytical Engine. In her famous notes on the engine, she expressed a vision that transcended her own time, suggesting that machines could one day create art and music, and even develop their own ideas. This visionary thinking was perhaps a way for Ada to assert her legacy in the face of her own declining health.

Ultimately, Ada Lovelace's struggles with illness were not just obstacles; they were integral to her narrative as a pioneering thinker. Her ability to transform personal adversity into intellectual triumph is a testament to her resilience and creativity. Despite the physical limitations imposed by her health, Ada's mind remained sharp, and her contributions to the fields of mathematics and computing continue to resonate today.

In conclusion, Ada's health struggles were a significant aspect of her life, shaping her experiences and influencing her work. They serve as a reminder that even the most brilliant minds face challenges, and it is often through overcoming these challenges that true innovation occurs. Ada Lovelace's legacy is not only that of the first programmer but also of a woman who, despite her struggles, dared to dream of a future defined by technology and creativity. Her story is a profound reminder of the intersection between personal struggle and professional achievement, a narrative that continues to inspire generations of innovators and thinkers.

Ada's Personal Relationships and Romantic Interests

Ada Lovelace, the first programmer, was not just a mathematical genius; she was also a woman of complex emotions and relationships. Her personal life was a tapestry woven with threads of passion, intellect, and the societal expectations of her time. This section explores the romantic interests and personal relationships that shaped Ada's life, influencing both her work and her legacy.

The Influence of Lord Byron

To understand Ada's romantic inclinations, one must first acknowledge her lineage. Ada was the daughter of the famous poet Lord Byron and Lady Anne Isabella Milbanke. Her father's poetic spirit and tumultuous life left an indelible mark on Ada. The relationship between Lord Byron and Lady Anne was fraught with conflict, leading to their separation shortly after Ada's birth. This absence of a father figure, coupled with the shadow of her father's reputation, influenced Ada's views on love and relationships.

$$R_{Ada} = f(L_{Byron}, C_{Mother}) \tag{29}$$

Where R_{Ada} represents Ada's romantic relationships, L_{Byron} is the influence of Lord Byron, and C_{Mother} is the control exerted by her mother. This equation suggests that Ada's romantic relationships were significantly shaped by her father's legacy and her mother's strict upbringing.

Romantic Interests and Correspondences

Ada's correspondence with Charles Babbage, her mentor and collaborator, reveals a deep intellectual connection that bordered on the romantic. Their letters were filled with admiration and respect, often discussing mathematical theories and the potential of the Analytical Engine. However, the nature of their relationship was complicated by the societal norms of the Victorian era, which dictated that women should maintain a certain decorum.

$$C_{Ada-Babbage} = \int_0^T (I_{Ada}(t) \cdot I_{Babbage}(t))dt \qquad (30)$$

In this integral, $C_{Ada-Babbage}$ represents the complexity of Ada and Babbage's relationship over time T, where $I_{Ada}(t)$ and $I_{Babbage}(t)$ are the intellectual contributions of Ada and Babbage at any given time t. Their relationship was a blend of admiration and collaboration, yet it lacked the romantic culmination that one might expect given their chemistry.

Marriage to William King

Ada's marriage to William King in 1835 marked a significant turning point in her life. King was a supportive partner, encouraging Ada's intellectual pursuits while also providing her with the stability she needed. Their union was not without its challenges, as Ada struggled with the expectations of being a wife and mother in a society that often relegated women to domestic roles.

$$S_{Ada} = M_{King} + C_{Family} \qquad (31)$$

Here, S_{Ada} represents Ada's sense of self, M_{King} is the support she received from William King, and C_{Family} encompasses the challenges of family life. This equation illustrates the balance Ada sought between her personal and professional identities.

Romantic Affairs and Scandals

Despite her marriage, Ada's life was not devoid of romantic intrigue. There were whispers of affairs and scandals, particularly with figures such as the mathematician and poet, Augustus De Morgan. These rumors highlighted the tension between Ada's intellectual ambitions and the societal expectations placed upon her as a woman.

$$T_{Romance} = \frac{R_{Affairs}}{S_{Society}} \tag{32}$$

In this relationship, $T_{Romance}$ represents the tension in Ada's romantic life, $R_{Affairs}$ is the number of rumored romantic entanglements, and $S_{Society}$ is the societal pressure to conform. This equation encapsulates the struggle Ada faced as she navigated her desires against the backdrop of societal norms.

The Legacy of Ada's Relationships

Ada's personal relationships were a double-edged sword. On one hand, they provided her with emotional depth and inspiration; on the other, they constrained her within the rigid confines of Victorian society. The interplay of love, ambition, and societal expectation shaped not only her personal life but also her groundbreaking work in mathematics and computing.

In conclusion, Ada Lovelace's personal relationships and romantic interests reflect the intricate balance she maintained between her desires and the expectations of her time. Her connections with influential figures, including her marriage to William King and her intellectual partnership with Charles Babbage, played a crucial role in her development as a pioneering programmer. While Ada's romantic life was filled with complexity, it ultimately contributed to her enduring legacy as a visionary who dared to challenge societal norms.

Ada's Marriage to William King

Ada Lovelace's marriage to William King in 1835 was a pivotal moment in her life, intertwining her personal and professional worlds in ways that would shape her legacy. At the age of 19, Ada was introduced to William King, the son of a wealthy family, who was also a member of the British aristocracy. Their courtship was marked by a shared intellectual curiosity, and it wasn't long before they became engaged. The marriage took place on July 8, 1835, and it was a union that would have both supportive and challenging implications for Ada's work.

From the outset, the marriage was characterized by a blend of romance and practicality. William King, who would later become the Earl of Lovelace, was not only a gentleman of means but also a man of significant intellect and ambition. He recognized Ada's extraordinary talents and was supportive of her pursuits in mathematics and science. However, societal expectations of women during the

Victorian era placed considerable limitations on Ada's independence and professional aspirations.

The Dynamics of Their Relationship

While William was supportive, the marriage also brought with it the traditional roles expected of a woman at the time. Ada was thrust into the role of a wife and, later, a mother, which often conflicted with her ambitions. The couple had three children: Byron, Anne Isabella, and Ralph Gordon. The demands of motherhood, combined with societal expectations, often left Ada feeling constrained.

Despite these challenges, Ada's relationship with William had its moments of intellectual collaboration. They engaged in discussions about mathematics and philosophy, and William often encouraged her studies. However, the reality of Victorian domestic life meant that Ada had to navigate her dual roles carefully. The complexity of her identity as both a pioneering mathematician and a devoted wife and mother created a tension that would follow her throughout her life.

The Influence of William on Ada's Work

William King was influential not only as a husband but also as a confidant. He recognized Ada's potential and encouraged her to pursue her interests, particularly her collaborations with Charles Babbage. Their correspondence reveals a dynamic where William acted as a sounding board for Ada's ideas. He understood the significance of her work on the Analytical Engine and often provided emotional support during her struggles with illness and societal pressures.

However, the marriage also came with its own set of challenges. As Ada became increasingly involved in her mathematical pursuits, the expectations of her as a wife and mother often clashed with her desire for intellectual freedom. This duality is evident in Ada's letters, where she expresses both her passion for mathematics and her frustrations with the limitations imposed by her domestic responsibilities.

Societal Expectations and Personal Struggles

The Victorian era was not kind to women who sought to break the mold. Ada faced societal pressures that dictated her role as a woman, often relegating her to the background of her husband's life. The expectation that she should prioritize her family over her intellectual pursuits was a constant source of conflict. Ada's struggles with her identity as a mathematician and a mother are well-documented in her correspondence, where she oscillates between pride in her work and guilt over her familial obligations.

The societal norms of the time often diminished the significance of women's contributions, and Ada's achievements were frequently overshadowed by her husband's status. This reality is reflected in the limited recognition she received during her lifetime. Despite her groundbreaking work on the Analytical Engine, her contributions were often attributed to Babbage, leading to a long-standing overshadowing of her legacy.

A Marriage of Equals?

While William King was supportive, the notion of a marriage of equals was complicated by the societal norms of their time. Ada's brilliance was often met with skepticism, and her contributions were minimized. The dynamics of their marriage can be viewed through the lens of partnership, but it was also marked by the constraints placed on women in the 19th century. Ada's struggles for recognition and respect in her field were mirrored in her personal life, where her identity as a mathematician often took a backseat to her role as a wife and mother.

In conclusion, Ada's marriage to William King was a complex interplay of support and constraint. While he encouraged her intellectual pursuits, the societal expectations of the time often limited her ability to fully realize her potential. The duality of Ada's identity as a pioneering mathematician and a devoted wife and mother highlights the challenges faced by women in the 19th century. Ada's marriage was not just a personal union; it was a reflection of the broader societal dynamics that would shape her legacy as the first programmer. Despite the challenges, Ada Lovelace's contributions to mathematics and programming remain a testament to her resilience and brilliance in a world that often sought to confine her.

Ada's Role as a Mother

Ada Lovelace, known for her groundbreaking contributions to mathematics and computing, was also a devoted mother. Her relationship with her children, particularly her three surviving offspring—Byron, Anne Isabella, and Ralph—was marked by her attempts to balance her intellectual pursuits with the demands of motherhood. This section delves into the complexities of Ada's role as a mother, exploring how her experiences influenced her children and how they, in turn, reflected her legacy.

The Challenges of Motherhood

Motherhood in the 19th century was fraught with challenges, particularly for women like Ada, who were navigating the male-dominated spheres of science and mathematics. As a mother, Ada faced societal expectations that often conflicted with her ambitions. The Victorian era idealized motherhood, placing women in the domestic sphere while simultaneously dismissing their intellectual capabilities. This societal pressure created an internal conflict for Ada, who sought to fulfill her role as a mother while also pursuing her passion for mathematics and her collaboration with Charles Babbage.

Despite these challenges, Ada was deeply committed to her children. She often expressed her desire to provide them with a strong educational foundation. In letters to her mother, she emphasized the importance of nurturing her children's intellectual curiosity. Ada believed that education was a means of empowerment, and she sought to instill this belief in her children.

Ada's Educational Approach

Ada's approach to her children's education was progressive for her time. She engaged them in discussions about mathematics, science, and the arts, encouraging them to think critically and creatively. For instance, she introduced them to mathematical puzzles and logical reasoning exercises, believing that a strong foundation in these areas would prepare them for the complexities of life.

This educational philosophy was influenced by her own experiences as a student. Ada had faced numerous obstacles in her pursuit of knowledge, including her struggles with illness and societal restrictions. She understood the importance of resilience and adaptability, traits she sought to impart to her children.

The Impact of Ada's Illness

Ada's health problems significantly impacted her role as a mother. Throughout her life, she battled various illnesses, including a severe case of measles that nearly cost her life during her childhood. These health issues often left her fatigued and unable to engage fully with her children. Despite these limitations, Ada remained determined to be present in their lives, often writing letters to them filled with encouragement and wisdom.

Her struggles with illness also served as a teaching moment for her children. Ada instilled in them the importance of perseverance, teaching them that challenges could be overcome through determination and intellect. This message resonated with her children, particularly her daughter, who later became a writer and advocate for women's rights.

Ada's Relationship with Her Children

Ada's relationship with her children was complex, marked by both affection and the weight of her expectations. She often expressed a desire for her children to excel, reflecting her own ambitions and aspirations. For example, she encouraged her son Byron to pursue a career in mathematics, hoping he would follow in her footsteps. However, this pressure sometimes led to tension, as her children struggled to meet her high expectations.

Despite the challenges, Ada's love for her children was evident. She often engaged them in family activities, including visits to the theater and musical performances. Ada believed that exposure to the arts was essential for a well-rounded education, and she sought to foster a love for creativity in her children.

Legacy and Influence

Ada Lovelace's legacy as a mother extends beyond her immediate family. Her commitment to education and intellectual growth influenced the way her children approached their own lives and careers. Byron Lovelace, for instance, became a prominent figure in the field of mathematics, while Anne Isabella pursued her interests in writing and advocacy.

Moreover, Ada's emphasis on the importance of education for women laid the groundwork for future generations. Her children carried forward her belief in the value of knowledge and the potential of women to contribute meaningfully to society.

In conclusion, Ada Lovelace's role as a mother was characterized by her dedication to her children's education and her struggle to balance societal expectations with her intellectual ambitions. Despite the challenges she faced, Ada's influence on her children was profound, shaping their lives and values in ways that would resonate for generations to come. Her legacy as a mother is a testament to her resilience and commitment to fostering a love for learning, creativity, and empowerment in the next generation.

$$E = mc^2 \tag{33}$$

This equation, while primarily associated with Einstein, serves as a metaphor for Ada's own contributions to the world: a powerful energy of intellect and creativity that transformed the landscape of technology and education, much like the way mass and energy are interconnected in the universe.

The Impact of Ada's Illness on Her Personal Life

Ada Lovelace, despite her remarkable intellect and contributions to mathematics and computing, faced significant challenges throughout her life, particularly due to her health issues. These ailments not only affected her physical well-being but also had profound implications for her personal relationships, professional ambitions, and overall mental health.

Health Challenges

From a young age, Ada suffered from various health problems, which were exacerbated by the societal expectations placed upon her as a woman of noble birth. Her illnesses included severe headaches, digestive issues, and what was likely a form of uterine cancer, which ultimately led to her untimely death at the age of 36. These chronic health issues often left her bedridden, limiting her ability to engage fully in the intellectual pursuits she cherished.

The impact of illness on Ada's life can be understood through the lens of the biopsychosocial model, which posits that health is influenced by biological, psychological, and social factors. For Ada, her physical ailments were intertwined with her emotional state and the societal constraints of her time. The psychological burden of her health issues often led to bouts of depression, which further hindered her productivity and social interactions.

Impact on Personal Relationships

Ada's illnesses had a significant impact on her relationships with her family and friends. Her mother, Lady Annabella Milbanke, was particularly protective of Ada, perhaps due to the fear of losing her to illness, as had happened with many in their family. This overprotectiveness often translated into a stifling environment, where Ada felt constrained by her mother's expectations and the societal norms of the Victorian era.

Moreover, her health challenges strained her relationship with her husband, William King. While King was supportive of Ada's intellectual pursuits, the stress of her deteriorating health created tension in their marriage. Ada's frequent illnesses meant that she could not always fulfill her roles as a wife and mother, leading to feelings of inadequacy and guilt. This internal conflict is evident in her correspondence, where she oscillates between expressing her desire to be a devoted mother and her yearning for intellectual engagement.

Professional Ambitions and Limitations

Ada's health issues also curtailed her professional ambitions. Despite her groundbreaking work with Charles Babbage on the Analytical Engine, her physical limitations often prevented her from fully participating in collaborative projects. For instance, her famous notes on the Analytical Engine, which included the first algorithm intended for implementation on a machine, were written during periods when she was well enough to work. However, these productive bursts were interspersed with long periods of illness, leading to a fragmented body of work.

The challenges Ada faced can be likened to the modern concept of "imposter syndrome," where individuals doubt their accomplishments and fear being exposed as a "fraud." Ada's struggles with illness likely exacerbated these feelings, as she grappled with the societal perception of women in science and her own self-doubt regarding her contributions. This internal conflict is poignantly captured in her letters, where she often reflects on her worth and the value of her work.

Mental Health and Coping Mechanisms

The psychological toll of Ada's chronic illnesses cannot be understated. Her letters reveal a woman who was acutely aware of her limitations and the societal expectations placed upon her. To cope with her mental and emotional struggles, Ada turned to various outlets, including writing, mathematics, and her correspondence with Babbage. These activities provided her with a sense of purpose and a means of expressing her thoughts and frustrations.

Ada's approach to coping with her illness can be seen as a precursor to modern therapeutic practices. She often engaged in reflective writing, which allowed her to process her emotions and articulate her thoughts. This practice not only provided her with an emotional outlet but also helped her to maintain her intellectual rigor despite her physical limitations.

Legacy of Resilience

Despite the challenges posed by her health, Ada Lovelace's legacy is one of resilience and determination. She navigated the complexities of her personal life while making significant contributions to the field of computing. Her ability to overcome adversity serves as an inspiration to many, particularly women in STEM fields who may face similar challenges.

In conclusion, Ada Lovelace's illness profoundly impacted her personal life, shaping her relationships, professional ambitions, and mental health. Her story highlights the intersection of health and productivity, particularly for women in the 19th century. Ada's legacy is not only defined by her groundbreaking work but also by her resilience in the face of adversity. Her life serves as a testament to the enduring spirit of those who strive to innovate, despite the challenges they may face.

Ada's Legacy in the Face of Tragedy

Ada Lovelace's life was a tapestry woven with threads of brilliance and adversity. Despite the numerous challenges she faced, including illness and societal expectations, her legacy endures as a testament to resilience in the face of tragedy. This section explores how Ada's struggles shaped her contributions to mathematics and computing, ultimately solidifying her place in history as a pioneering figure.

The Weight of Illness

From a young age, Ada suffered from various health issues, which included debilitating migraines and other ailments that often left her incapacitated. These health struggles were not merely personal challenges; they were barriers that threatened to stifle her intellectual pursuits. However, rather than allowing her illnesses to define her, Ada transformed her experiences into a source of motivation.

Her correspondence with Charles Babbage, for instance, often reflected her determination to push through her physical limitations. In one of her letters, she wrote, "I am not afraid of being ill; I am afraid of being unproductive." This mindset exemplified her resilience and commitment to her work, despite the pain she endured.

Personal Relationships and Their Impact

Ada's personal life was equally tumultuous. Her marriage to William King was a complex union marked by both affection and societal pressures. While King supported her intellectual pursuits, the expectations of Victorian society placed immense pressure on Ada to conform to traditional roles as a wife and mother. This duality often left her feeling trapped between her ambitions and her responsibilities.

Despite these challenges, Ada found ways to navigate her personal and professional life. She famously stated, "The most important thing in life is to have a purpose," a philosophy that guided her through the trials she faced. Her ability to balance her roles as a mother, wife, and mathematician is a testament to her strength and determination.

The Legacy of Overcoming Adversity

Ada's legacy is not merely a collection of her mathematical contributions; it is also a narrative of overcoming adversity. Her work on the Analytical Engine, particularly her notes on programming, was groundbreaking. The Lovelace Note, which contained what is now recognized as the first algorithm intended for implementation on a machine, showcases her innovative spirit.

The famous equation she formulated, often referred to as the first computer program, can be expressed as:

$$\text{Algorithm} = \sum_{n=0}^{\infty} a_n \cdot x^n \tag{34}$$

In this equation, a_n represents the coefficients of the series, while x is the variable. This mathematical representation reflects Ada's ability to harness her intellect, even in the face of personal struggles.

The Influence of Ada's Tragedies on Her Work

Ada's experiences with illness and societal constraints deeply influenced her perspective on technology and its potential. She envisioned machines as not just tools for calculation but as instruments of creativity and innovation. This perspective is illustrated in her writings, where she often mused about the possibilities of machines transcending mere computation to engage in artistic endeavors.

Her belief that "the Analytical Engine might compose elaborate and scientific pieces of music of any degree of complexity" reveals her forward-thinking mindset. Ada recognized that technology could serve as a conduit for human expression, a notion that resonates with contemporary discussions about the intersection of art and technology.

Inspiration for Future Generations

Today, Ada Lovelace stands as a symbol of resilience and ingenuity. Her legacy serves as an inspiration for countless individuals, particularly women, who aspire to break barriers in fields traditionally dominated by men. Ada's story encourages us to confront our challenges head-on and to view adversity as an opportunity for growth.

The Ada Lovelace Day, celebrated annually, is a testament to her enduring impact. It serves to honor women in science, technology, engineering, and mathematics (STEM) while promoting the importance of diversity and inclusion in these fields. By celebrating Ada's contributions, we also acknowledge the struggles she faced and the strength it took for her to overcome them.

Conclusion: A Legacy of Strength

In conclusion, Ada Lovelace's legacy is intricately tied to her experiences of tragedy and triumph. Her ability to rise above personal and societal challenges not only shaped her own life but also paved the way for future generations of innovators. Ada's story teaches us that greatness can emerge from adversity, and her contributions to mathematics and computing will continue to inspire those who dare to dream beyond their circumstances.

As we reflect on Ada's life, let us remember her words: "I am more than my challenges; I am a creator." This sentiment encapsulates the essence of her legacy, reminding us that our struggles can fuel our creativity and drive us to achieve remarkable things.

Overcoming Adversity: Ada's Resilience and Strength

Ada Lovelace, often celebrated as the first programmer, faced numerous adversities throughout her life that tested her resilience and strength. From her tumultuous family background to her struggles with health issues, Ada's journey was anything but straightforward. Yet, through these challenges, she emerged not only as a pioneering figure in mathematics and computing but also as a symbol of perseverance for women in STEM fields.

The Impact of Her Family Background

Born into a family with a complicated legacy, Ada was the daughter of the renowned poet Lord Byron and Anne Isabella Milbanke. Her parents' marriage was fraught with tension, leading to their separation shortly after her birth. This unstable environment could have hindered Ada's development, but instead, it instilled in her a fierce determination to carve out her own identity. Her mother, who was keen on ensuring that Ada did not inherit her father's artistic temperament, emphasized a rigorous education in mathematics and science. This unique upbringing laid the foundation for Ada's future achievements.

Health Struggles and Their Influence

Throughout her life, Ada battled various health issues, including severe illnesses that often left her bedridden. These health challenges could have easily derailed her ambitions, but Ada's response was to channel her frustrations into her work. She famously remarked, "The more I study, the more insatiable do I feel my genius for it to be." This insatiable curiosity propelled her to delve deeper into the realms of mathematics and computing, transforming adversity into an impetus for intellectual exploration.

Navigating a Male-Dominated Field

In a time when women were largely excluded from scientific discourse, Ada had to navigate a male-dominated field that often dismissed her contributions. Despite the societal norms that sought to confine her, Ada's collaboration with Charles Babbage was a testament to her resilience. Their partnership was not merely a meeting of minds; it was a defiance of the gender stereotypes of the era. Ada's ability to articulate complex ideas about the Analytical Engine showcased her strength and intellect, challenging the notion that women were incapable of such contributions.

The Lovelace Note: A Defining Moment

Perhaps the most significant demonstration of Ada's resilience is encapsulated in her work on the Analytical Engine. In her famous notes on Babbage's machine, known as the Lovelace Note, she detailed the potential of the machine to perform complex calculations and even predicted the future of computing. This groundbreaking work was not just a technical achievement; it was a bold assertion of her capabilities in a field that often overlooked women. The Lovelace Note stands as a testament to her ability to overcome societal barriers and assert her place in history.

Legacy of Strength and Inspiration

Ada's life was marked by a series of challenges, yet she continually rose above them. Her resilience serves as an inspiration for future generations, especially women in technology. The ongoing fight for gender equality in the tech industry can draw strength from Ada's legacy. She not only paved the way for future female programmers but also demonstrated that adversity can be transformed into strength.

In conclusion, Ada Lovelace's journey was not merely about her contributions to mathematics and computing; it was a profound narrative of overcoming adversity. Her life exemplifies how resilience and strength can lead to groundbreaking achievements, making her a timeless figure of inspiration. As we continue to navigate the complexities of gender in technology, Ada's story reminds us that with determination and courage, we can overcome any obstacle.

$$F = m \cdot a \tag{35}$$

where F is the force applied, m is the mass of the object, and a is the acceleration. This equation parallels Ada's life: despite the mass of challenges weighing her down, she applied the force of her intellect and determination to accelerate toward her goals.

$$E = mc^2 \tag{36}$$

This famous equation by Einstein can also be seen as a metaphor for Ada's impact: her energy (E) was derived from her mass (m) of experiences and struggles, which she transformed into an enduring legacy, traveling at the speed of light (c) through the annals of history.

Through her life and work, Ada Lovelace exemplified resilience in the face of adversity, proving that the strength of one individual can indeed change the course of history.

The Importance of Mental Health Awareness in Honor of Ada

In the annals of history, Ada Lovelace stands not only as a pioneer in computing but also as a figure whose life underscores the critical importance of mental health awareness. Living in a time when mental health issues were poorly understood, Ada faced numerous challenges that impacted her well-being and, consequently, her remarkable contributions to mathematics and programming. This section explores the significance of mental health awareness through the lens of Ada's life, highlighting theoretical frameworks, prevalent mental health problems, and contemporary examples that resonate with her legacy.

Theoretical Frameworks

To understand the relevance of mental health in Ada's context, it is essential to consider the biopsychosocial model of health, which posits that biological, psychological, and social factors all play a significant role in human functioning. This model emphasizes that mental health cannot be viewed in isolation; rather, it is influenced by a complex interplay of various elements, including genetics, environment, and personal experiences.

$$H = f(B, P, S) \tag{37}$$

Where:

- H = Health (mental and physical)

- B = Biological factors (genetics, neurochemistry)

- P = Psychological factors (thought patterns, emotional well-being)

- S = Social factors (support systems, cultural influences)

This model is particularly relevant to Ada, who dealt with chronic illness and the societal pressures of her time. Her experiences exemplify how mental health issues can arise from a combination of biological predispositions and societal expectations, reinforcing the need for a holistic approach to mental health.

Mental Health Challenges Faced by Ada

Ada Lovelace struggled with various health issues throughout her life, including what is now believed to be a form of chronic illness. The impact of her physical health on her mental state cannot be overstated; chronic illness is often linked with mental health challenges such as anxiety and depression. Research indicates that individuals with chronic health conditions are at a higher risk for developing mental health issues due to the stress and limitations imposed by their illnesses.

$$D = \frac{C}{T} \tag{38}$$

Where:

- D = Depression risk

- C = Chronic illness severity

- T = Time spent managing illness

As Ada navigated her health challenges, she also faced the emotional toll of societal expectations, particularly as a woman in a male-dominated field. The pressures of balancing her intellectual pursuits with the constraints of her health likely contributed to feelings of isolation and frustration, common among individuals facing similar struggles.

Contemporary Examples and Mental Health Awareness

In today's context, Ada's story resonates strongly with ongoing discussions about mental health awareness, particularly in high-pressure fields like technology and academia. The stigma surrounding mental health continues to pose challenges, often discouraging individuals from seeking help or discussing their struggles openly.

Organizations such as the National Alliance on Mental Illness (NAMI) advocate for mental health awareness, emphasizing the importance of education, support, and community engagement. Initiatives like Mental Health Awareness Month and World Mental Health Day serve as platforms to promote understanding and reduce stigma, echoing the need for awareness that Ada's life exemplifies.

Moreover, the tech industry, where Ada's legacy is most profound, has increasingly recognized the importance of mental health. Companies are implementing wellness programs, mental health days, and support resources to foster a healthier work environment. For example, Google has introduced mindfulness programs, while other tech giants have prioritized mental health in their corporate policies, recognizing that a healthy workforce is essential for innovation and productivity.

Conclusion: Honoring Ada Through Mental Health Advocacy

Honoring Ada Lovelace's legacy involves not only celebrating her contributions to computing but also recognizing the importance of mental health awareness. By fostering an environment that values mental health, we can create a space where future innovators feel supported in their personal and professional journeys.

As we reflect on Ada's life, let us commit to breaking the silence surrounding mental health, advocating for resources, and supporting those who, like Ada, navigate the complexities of their health while striving to make a difference in the world. In doing so, we honor her memory and ensure that her pioneering spirit continues to inspire generations to come.

Remembering Ada Lovelace: A Life of Triumph despite Challenges

Ada Lovelace, often heralded as the first computer programmer, faced numerous challenges throughout her life. Yet, despite these hurdles, she emerged as a beacon of innovation and resilience. Her story is not just about her groundbreaking work in mathematics and computing, but also about her ability to navigate a world that often sought to limit her potential due to her gender and health struggles.

Early Challenges and Health Struggles

Born in 1815, Ada was the only legitimate child of the famous poet Lord Byron and his wife, Lady Anne Isabella Milbanke. From the outset, her life was marked by turmoil. Lord Byron abandoned the family when Ada was just a few weeks old, leaving Lady Anne to raise her alone. This absence of a father figure created a void that Ada would grapple with throughout her life.

Moreover, Ada's health was frail from a young age. She suffered from various illnesses, including a prolonged bout of measles that left her bedridden. These health issues often interrupted her education, yet they did not deter her passion for learning. Instead, they fueled her determination to excel academically. Her mother, recognizing Ada's potential, ensured that she received a rigorous education in mathematics and science, subjects traditionally reserved for boys.

Breaking Gender Barriers

In a male-dominated society, Ada's journey was fraught with gender-based obstacles. During the 19th century, women were largely excluded from the realms of mathematics and science. However, Ada defied societal expectations, establishing herself as a formidable intellect. Her collaboration with Charles Babbage, the inventor of the Analytical Engine, was pivotal.

Ada's contributions to Babbage's work were groundbreaking. She translated an article written by the Italian mathematician Luigi Federico Federico and added her own notes, which contained what is now recognized as the first algorithm intended for implementation on a machine. This monumental achievement is encapsulated in the Lovelace Note, where she famously stated that the Analytical Engine could be programmed to perform any calculation, not just numerical ones, but also to manipulate symbols and create music.

$$\text{Lovelace's Algorithm: Output} = \text{Input} \times \text{Transformation} \qquad (39)$$

This equation symbolizes her understanding of how an algorithm transforms data, a concept that remains foundational in computer science today.

Personal Triumphs Amidst Adversity

Ada's personal life was equally tumultuous. She married William King, the Earl of Lovelace, and became Lady Lovelace. The couple had three children, and Ada balanced her roles as a mother and a pioneering mathematician. However, her marriage was not without challenges. Ada faced societal pressures to conform to the expectations of a wife and mother, which often clashed with her desire to pursue her intellectual passions.

Despite these pressures, Ada continued to advocate for women in science and mathematics. She was a vocal supporter of women's education, believing that women should have the same opportunities as men to pursue careers in STEM fields. Her advocacy was not merely theoretical; she actively engaged in discussions and wrote letters to prominent figures, urging them to recognize the potential of women in mathematics.

Legacy and Recognition

Ada Lovelace's legacy transcends her own lifetime. Although she faced considerable challenges, her contributions laid the groundwork for future generations of programmers and mathematicians. In the years following her death in 1852, her work remained largely unrecognized until the late 20th century when a resurgence of interest in her life and contributions began.

Today, Ada is celebrated as a pioneer who overcame personal and societal obstacles to make lasting contributions to computer science. Ada Lovelace Day, observed annually, serves as a reminder of her achievements and an opportunity to highlight the work of women in STEM.

$$Legacy = Innovation + Inspiration \tag{40}$$

This equation reflects how Ada's innovative work continues to inspire women and men alike, encouraging them to pursue their passions regardless of the challenges they may face.

Conclusion

In remembering Ada Lovelace, we honor not only her remarkable intellect and contributions to computing but also her resilience in the face of adversity. Her life is a testament to the power of perseverance and the importance of breaking down barriers. Ada Lovelace's story reminds us that triumph is not merely the absence of challenges but the ability to rise above them and make a lasting impact on the world. Her legacy continues to inspire future innovators, urging them to embrace their unique journeys and contribute to the ever-evolving landscape of technology.

The Future of Technology: Ada's Predictions

Ada's Vision of Computers and Automation

Ada Lovelace, often celebrated as the first computer programmer, had a vision for the future of machines that extended far beyond the capabilities of her time. She foresaw a world where computers could perform tasks not merely as calculators but as entities capable of complex reasoning and creativity. This vision was articulated through her work on Charles Babbage's Analytical Engine, a mechanical device that could be programmed to carry out a variety of operations.

At the heart of Ada's vision was the concept of automation. She understood that machines could be employed to execute repetitive tasks, thereby freeing humans to engage in more creative and intellectual pursuits. In her notes on the Analytical Engine, she famously stated:

> "The Analytical Engine does not occupy common ground with mere calculating machines. It holds within itself the potential for a new form of thought."

This statement encapsulates her belief that the Analytical Engine could transcend its mechanical origins and serve as a foundation for future computers that could think and learn.

Theoretical Foundations

To understand Ada's vision, it is essential to consider the theoretical underpinnings she proposed. Ada recognized that the Analytical Engine could manipulate symbols, not just numbers. She envisioned a system where data could be represented in various forms, allowing for the execution of complex algorithms. Her work laid the groundwork for what we now refer to as programming languages.

One of the key theoretical contributions Ada made was the idea of using loops and conditional statements in programming, which are foundational concepts in modern computer science. She wrote about the potential for a sequence of operations to be repeated:

$$\text{Repeat (Operation) until (Condition)} \tag{41}$$

This simple yet powerful idea of iteration is a cornerstone of programming today.

Problems and Solutions

Despite her visionary ideas, Ada faced significant challenges in articulating her vision for computers and automation. The technology of her time was rudimentary, and the Analytical Engine itself was never completed. This meant that Ada's theories remained largely untested.

Moreover, societal norms posed a barrier to her acceptance in the male-dominated field of mathematics and engineering. Ada's gender often overshadowed her contributions, and her ideas were frequently dismissed by her contemporaries. Nevertheless, she persevered, advocating for the potential of machines to enhance human capabilities.

To illustrate her vision, Ada provided an example in her notes regarding the generation of Bernoulli numbers, a sequence of rational numbers that are important in number theory. She described how the Analytical Engine could be programmed to compute these numbers using a series of operations. The algorithm she presented is one of the earliest known examples of a computer program:

$$B_n = \sum_{k=0}^{n} \binom{n}{k} B_k \tag{42}$$

where B_n represents the n-th Bernoulli number and $\binom{n}{k}$ is the binomial coefficient. This example not only demonstrates her understanding of mathematics but also her ability to envision how machines could automate complex calculations.

Examples of Automation in Ada's Vision

Ada's vision extended to various applications of automation, including:

1. **Data Analysis**: Ada anticipated that machines could be used to analyze large datasets, identifying patterns and making predictions. This foresight is evident in today's use of algorithms in data science and machine learning.

2. **Creative Processes**: She believed that computers could assist in creative endeavors, such as composing music or generating art. This concept has materialized in modern AI technologies that create music, art, and literature.

3. **Scientific Research**: Ada envisioned that automation could revolutionize scientific research by enabling simulations and complex calculations that would be impractical for humans to perform manually.

Conclusion

In conclusion, Ada Lovelace's vision of computers and automation was groundbreaking. She recognized that machines could do more than simple calculations; they could revolutionize the way humans interact with information and creativity. Her theoretical contributions, although rooted in the 19th century, paved the way for modern computing and programming.

As we continue to explore the capabilities of technology, it is essential to remember Ada's insights and aspirations. Her belief in the potential of machines to augment human intellect and creativity remains relevant today, inspiring new generations of programmers and innovators to push the boundaries of what is possible. Ada Lovelace's legacy is not just that of the first programmer but as a visionary who saw the future of technology as a partnership between human ingenuity and machine efficiency.

The Relevance of Ada's Predictions in the Modern World

Ada Lovelace, often recognized as the first computer programmer, was not only a pioneer in the field of computing but also a visionary who foresaw the profound implications of technology on society. Her predictions about the potential of computers and their capabilities resonate strongly in today's digital landscape. In this section, we will explore the relevance of Ada's predictions in the modern world, highlighting how her insights continue to shape our understanding of technology, its applications, and its ethical considerations.

1. The Vision of Computers as More than Calculators

One of Ada's most significant predictions was her belief that computers could be used for more than mere calculations. In her notes on Charles Babbage's Analytical Engine, she famously stated that the machine could manipulate symbols and perform operations beyond arithmetic. This foresight laid the groundwork for the development of modern computing, where computers are employed in various fields such as art, music, and science.

$$\text{Output} = f(\text{Input}_1, \text{Input}_2, \ldots, \text{Input}_n) \tag{43}$$

In contemporary terms, this can be understood through the lens of algorithms that process data to produce meaningful results. For example, in machine learning, algorithms learn from data inputs to make predictions or decisions, showcasing the versatility Ada envisioned.

2. The Emergence of Artificial Intelligence

Ada's insight into the potential of computing machines also foreshadowed the rise of artificial intelligence (AI). She speculated that computers could be programmed to create music and art, which we see today in various AI applications. For instance, AI algorithms can generate original compositions or artworks, demonstrating the creative capabilities of machines.

Consider the following equation that represents a simple neural network:

$$y = f(W \cdot x + b) \tag{44}$$

where y is the output, W is the weight matrix, x is the input vector, and b is the bias. This mathematical framework underpins many AI systems that mimic human creativity, validating Ada's predictions about the expansive role of computers.

3. The Importance of Data and Information Processing

Ada recognized that the Analytical Engine could handle complex data sets, a concept that is critical in today's data-driven world. The ability to process large volumes of information and extract insights is foundational to fields such as big data analytics and data science.

In practical applications, data processing can be represented by the following equation:

$$\text{Insight} = \sum_{i=1}^{n} \text{Data}_i \cdot \text{Weight}_i \tag{45}$$

This equation illustrates how individual data points contribute to a larger understanding or insight, a principle that Ada anticipated long before the advent of modern data analytics.

4. Ethical Considerations in Technology

Ada's predictions also extended to the ethical implications of technology. She understood that with great power comes great responsibility. In her writings, she hinted at the need for careful consideration of how technology could affect society. Today, as we grapple with issues such as privacy, surveillance, and algorithmic bias, Ada's foresight serves as a guiding principle.

For example, the ethical dilemma surrounding AI decision-making can be encapsulated in the following inequality:

$$Fairness \geq Bias \qquad (46)$$

This equation emphasizes the importance of striving for fairness in AI systems, a challenge that Ada anticipated when she highlighted the potential consequences of technological advancements.

5. The Interdisciplinary Nature of Technology

Ada Lovelace's work exemplified the intersection of mathematics, science, and the arts. She believed that the Analytical Engine could be a tool for interdisciplinary collaboration, a notion that is increasingly relevant in today's world. Modern innovations often emerge from the collaboration of diverse fields, such as computer science, biology, and social sciences.

The concept of interdisciplinary synergy can be represented as:

$$Innovation = Science + Art + Technology \qquad (47)$$

This equation illustrates how the convergence of different disciplines can lead to groundbreaking advancements, echoing Ada's vision of a holistic approach to technology.

6. Conclusion

In conclusion, Ada Lovelace's predictions remain profoundly relevant in the modern world. Her insights into the capabilities of computers, the emergence of artificial intelligence, the importance of data processing, the ethical considerations of technology, and the interdisciplinary nature of innovation continue to shape our understanding of the digital age. As we navigate the complexities of contemporary technology, we can draw inspiration from Ada's visionary ideas, ensuring that we honor her legacy by embracing the full potential of computing while remaining mindful of its impact on society. Ada Lovelace was not just a pioneer; she was a prophet of the digital age, and her predictions will continue to resonate for generations to come.

Ada's Anticipation of Artificial Intelligence and Machine Learning

Ada Lovelace, often celebrated as the first computer programmer, possessed an extraordinary vision that extended far beyond the mechanical calculations of her time. In her correspondence with Charles Babbage regarding the Analytical Engine, she hinted at concepts that would later evolve into what we now recognize as artificial intelligence (AI) and machine learning (ML). While the technology to realize her ideas was centuries away, her insights laid the groundwork for future explorations into computational creativity and autonomous reasoning.

At the heart of Ada's anticipation of AI and ML lies her understanding of the Analytical Engine's potential. She theorized that this machine could not only perform arithmetic calculations but could also manipulate symbols in accordance with rules. In her seminal notes, she wrote:

> "The Analytical Engine has no pretensions whatever to originate anything. It can do whatever we know how to order it to perform."

This statement reflects her recognition that machines could follow complex instructions and operate on data, but it also implies a limitation: machines could only execute tasks defined by humans. This understanding foreshadowed the foundational principles of AI, where algorithms are designed to process information and learn from it, yet remain bound by the parameters set by their creators.

Theoretical Foundations

Ada's insights align closely with the modern theoretical underpinnings of AI. Specifically, her vision can be connected to the concept of **symbolic reasoning**, where machines manipulate symbols to solve problems. In contemporary terms, this is akin to the way AI systems, such as expert systems, use rules and logic to derive conclusions from given data. The formalization of symbolic reasoning can be represented mathematically as:

$$P \implies Q$$

Where P represents a premise or condition, and Q represents a conclusion derived from P. Ada's understanding that the Analytical Engine could be programmed to execute a sequence of logical operations resonates with the foundational logic used in AI today.

The Concept of Learning

Moreover, Ada's reflections on the potential of the Analytical Engine can be viewed through the lens of **machine learning**. Although she did not use the term, her ideas suggested that machines could be designed to adapt and improve their performance over time. This notion is central to modern machine learning, where algorithms learn from data and enhance their accuracy through experience.

For example, consider a simple linear regression model, which can be expressed mathematically as:

$$y = mx + b$$

Where y is the dependent variable, m is the slope, x is the independent variable, and b is the y-intercept. In a machine learning context, the model learns the optimal values of m and b by minimizing the error between predicted values and actual data points, typically using a method known as **gradient descent.**

Ada's insights about the potential for machines to perform tasks akin to human reasoning suggest an early understanding of the iterative process of learning from data. She envisioned a future where machines could not only execute predetermined instructions but also adapt their operations based on new information, a concept that is foundational to machine learning today.

Examples of Anticipation

To illustrate Ada's anticipation of AI and ML, consider her famous example of the Analytical Engine being programmed to compute Bernoulli numbers. In her notes, she described how the engine could be instructed to perform this task by following a specific algorithm, which involved a series of iterative calculations. This example not only demonstrated her understanding of programming but also hinted at the potential for machines to tackle complex problems through systematic approaches—a principle that underpins many modern AI applications.

Furthermore, Ada's recognition of the importance of data and its manipulation can be seen as a precursor to contemporary data science. In today's world, machine learning relies heavily on large datasets to train algorithms, enabling them to make predictions or decisions without explicit programming for every scenario. Ada's foresight in understanding that machines could analyze and derive patterns from data was revolutionary for her time.

Challenges and Ethical Considerations

Despite her optimistic vision, Ada also hinted at the challenges and ethical considerations surrounding the development of intelligent machines. She understood that the power of computation comes with responsibility. Her assertion that the Analytical Engine could not originate anything implies a cautionary note about the limits of machine intelligence and the necessity of human oversight.

In the context of modern AI, this perspective aligns with ongoing debates about the ethical implications of autonomous systems. For instance, the question of accountability in AI decision-making processes, particularly in critical areas such as healthcare, finance, and law enforcement, echoes Ada's concerns about the consequences of machine actions. As AI continues to evolve, the need for ethical frameworks to guide its development is more pressing than ever.

Conclusion

In conclusion, Ada Lovelace's anticipation of artificial intelligence and machine learning was not merely a reflection of her time but a visionary insight into the future of technology. Her understanding of the Analytical Engine's capabilities, combined with her foresight into the potential for machines to learn and adapt, laid the groundwork for the fields of AI and ML. As we continue to explore the possibilities of intelligent machines, we must remember Ada's legacy: a reminder of the power of human creativity in shaping the future of technology, coupled with the responsibility that comes with it. Her ideas remain relevant as we navigate the complexities of modern computing, ensuring that we honor her vision as we forge ahead into the digital age.

The Impact of Ada's Ideas on Today's Technology

Ada Lovelace, often heralded as the first programmer, laid the groundwork for modern computing through her visionary insights into the potential of machines. Her contributions transcend the mere mechanics of programming; they encompass a philosophical understanding of what computation could achieve. In this section, we will explore the profound impact of Ada's ideas on today's technology, examining both theoretical frameworks and practical applications that continue to shape our digital landscape.

Theoretical Foundations

At the heart of Ada's contributions lies her understanding of the Analytical Engine, a mechanical general-purpose computer designed by Charles Babbage. Lovelace's work on this machine introduced several key concepts that are foundational to modern computing:

+ **Algorithmic Thinking:** Ada recognized that the Analytical Engine could be programmed to perform a sequence of operations, much like modern algorithms. She famously described how the machine could calculate Bernoulli numbers, providing one of the first examples of a computer algorithm. This concept is central to computer science today, where algorithms form the basis of software development.

+ **Data Representation:** Lovelace understood that numbers could be represented in various forms, including symbols and even music. This foresight laid the groundwork for data abstraction, a fundamental principle in computer programming that allows for the manipulation of data in versatile formats.

+ **Conditional Logic:** Ada's insights into how the Analytical Engine could make decisions based on conditional statements foreshadowed the development of control structures in programming languages, such as `if-else` statements and loops. These constructs are essential for creating complex software applications.

Practical Applications

The impact of Ada's ideas is evident in numerous technological advancements and applications that we encounter daily. Here are a few examples illustrating this influence:

1. **Software Development:** The principles of algorithmic thinking and modular programming, which Ada championed, are foundational to contemporary software development practices. Modern programming languages, such as Python, Java, and C++, utilize these principles to create efficient and maintainable code. For instance, the concept of functions in programming directly relates to Ada's structured approach to problem-solving.

2. **Artificial Intelligence (AI):** Ada's visionary ideas about machines performing complex tasks have paved the way for advancements in AI. The ability of computers to learn from data and make decisions is a direct descendant of her understanding of conditional logic and algorithmic processes. Today, algorithms that underpin machine learning, such as neural networks, are designed to mimic the decision-making processes that Lovelace envisioned.

3. **Computer Graphics and Multimedia:** Lovelace's recognition of the potential for machines to manipulate symbols and represent data in various forms has influenced the fields of computer graphics and multimedia. The creation of visual content, animations, and interactive applications relies heavily on the principles of data representation and manipulation that Ada foresaw. For example, modern graphics programming utilizes complex algorithms to render images and animations, echoing Lovelace's early notions of computational creativity.

4. **Cybersecurity:** Ada's emphasis on the importance of understanding the inner workings of machines has implications in cybersecurity. The algorithms used for encryption and data protection are rooted in the principles of logic and computation that she articulated. In an era where data breaches and cyber threats are prevalent, Ada's foresight into the complexities of machines underscores the importance of robust security measures in technology.

5. **Human-Computer Interaction (HCI):** The user-centric design principles that govern HCI today can be traced back to Ada's belief in the potential of machines to assist and enhance human capabilities. Her work encourages the exploration of how technology can be designed to be more intuitive and accessible, paving the way for innovations in user interface design and user experience.

6. **Educational Technology:** Ada's advocacy for education, particularly for women in STEM, resonates in today's educational technologies. Online learning platforms, coding bootcamps, and interactive programming environments are all products of her belief in the transformative power of technology to educate and empower individuals. The emphasis on inclusivity and diversity in tech education is a legacy of Lovelace's vision.

Challenges and Future Directions

While Ada Lovelace's ideas have had a significant impact on technology, challenges remain. The digital divide, gender disparity in tech fields, and ethical considerations in AI are contemporary issues that echo the struggles Ada faced in her own time. Addressing these challenges requires a continued commitment to innovation and inclusivity, ensuring that the legacy of Ada Lovelace inspires future generations of technologists.

As we look to the future, the principles Ada championed—algorithmic thinking, data representation, and conditional logic—will continue to guide the evolution of technology. Her visionary insights remind us that the potential of machines is only limited by our imagination and ethical considerations.

In conclusion, Ada Lovelace's impact on today's technology is profound and far-reaching. Her pioneering ideas have shaped the foundations of computer science and continue to influence a wide array of fields, from software development to AI and beyond. As we honor her legacy, we are reminded of the importance of creativity, inclusivity, and ethical responsibility in shaping the future of technology.

Recognizing Ada's Pioneering Role in Predictive Technologies

Ada Lovelace, often celebrated as the first computer programmer, was not only ahead of her time in her understanding of computing but also in her visionary ideas about predictive technologies. Her insights laid the groundwork for what we now recognize as predictive analytics, a field that has become increasingly vital in our data-driven world. This section explores Ada's pioneering role in predictive technologies, illustrating her foresight and its implications for modern computing.

Theoretical Foundations of Predictive Technologies

At the core of predictive technologies lies the concept of algorithms—sets of rules or instructions designed to perform a task. Ada's work with Charles Babbage on the Analytical Engine included the notion that machines could manipulate symbols and perform calculations based on predefined instructions. This foundational understanding can be expressed mathematically through the concept of functions:

$$f(x) = y \tag{48}$$

where f represents the algorithm, x is the input data, and y is the output or prediction. Ada's vision extended beyond mere calculations; she imagined a future where machines could analyze data and make predictions based on patterns, a concept that resonates with modern predictive modeling techniques.

The Problem of Prediction

Predictive technologies aim to solve the problem of uncertainty in decision-making by forecasting future events based on historical data. Ada recognized that data could serve as a powerful tool for prediction, a notion that aligns with contemporary practices in machine learning and artificial intelligence. The predictive process can be framed as follows:

$$\hat{y} = f(X; \theta) \tag{49}$$

where $\hat{y}$ is the predicted outcome, X is the input data matrix, and θ represents the parameters of the model. In her time, Ada's insights into how data could be processed and analyzed were revolutionary, setting the stage for future developments in predictive analytics.

Ada's Vision for Predictive Technologies

Ada's vision for the Analytical Engine included the capacity to not only perform calculations but also to create complex models that could simulate real-world scenarios. She famously stated, "The Analytical Engine does not occupy common ground with mere calculating machines." This distinction emphasized her belief that machines could transcend basic arithmetic and venture into realms of prediction and simulation.

Her foresight can be seen as an early recognition of what we now refer to as simulation modeling, where systems are analyzed through mathematical models to predict their behavior under various conditions. For example, consider the following equation used in predictive modeling:

$$y = \beta_0 + \beta_1 x_1 + \beta_2 x_2 + \ldots + \beta_n x_n + \epsilon \tag{50}$$

In this equation, y represents the predicted variable, β_0 is the intercept, β_i are the coefficients for each predictor variable x_i, and ϵ is the error term. Ada's understanding of such relationships, even if not mathematically formalized in her time, illustrates her capacity to envision complex interactions within data.

Examples of Predictive Technologies Inspired by Ada

1. **Weather Forecasting**: Modern meteorology relies heavily on predictive models that analyze vast amounts of atmospheric data to forecast weather patterns. Ada's insights into data manipulation and analysis laid the groundwork for these advancements.

2. **Financial Modeling**: In finance, predictive analytics is used to assess risks and forecast market trends. Ada's early recognition of the potential for machines to analyze data for decision-making parallels the algorithms used in today's financial models.

3. **Healthcare Predictions**: Predictive technologies in healthcare utilize algorithms to predict patient outcomes based on historical data. Ada's work, which hinted at the potential for machines to analyze complex datasets, is reflected in the algorithms that drive modern healthcare analytics.

The Legacy of Ada in Predictive Technologies

Ada Lovelace's pioneering role in predictive technologies is not merely a historical footnote; it is a testament to her visionary thinking. Her ability to foresee the implications of computational machines in analyzing data and making predictions has paved the way for the sophisticated predictive technologies we rely on today.

In recognizing Ada's contributions, we honor not only her legacy as the first programmer but also her role as a visionary in the field of predictive analytics. Her insights continue to inspire researchers and practitioners in technology, emphasizing the importance of innovative thinking in shaping the future of computing.

In conclusion, Ada Lovelace's pioneering role in predictive technologies demonstrates her profound understanding of the potential of machines to analyze data and forecast outcomes. Her insights laid the groundwork for the predictive analytics that drive many of today's technological advancements, affirming her status as a true pioneer in the field.

The Ethical Implications of Ada's Predictions

Ada Lovelace, often celebrated as the first programmer, not only laid the groundwork for computing but also foresaw a future where machines would not merely calculate but also learn and adapt. Her insights into the potential of machines to simulate human reasoning raise profound ethical questions that resonate today, particularly in the realms of artificial intelligence (AI) and machine learning (ML). This section delves into the ethical implications of Ada's predictions, exploring the responsibilities of programmers and society in harnessing technology for the greater good.

The Nature of Machine Intelligence

At the core of Ada's vision lies the concept of machine intelligence, which can be mathematically represented in terms of algorithmic efficiency and decision-making processes. Let M represent a machine's ability to process information, and I denote its level of intelligence. Ada's early ideas suggest that as M increases, so too does I, leading to the equation:

$$I = f(M)$$

where f is a function that describes the relationship between machine processing power and intelligence. This raises ethical considerations regarding the autonomy of machines. As machines become more capable, the question of accountability surfaces: Who is responsible for the decisions made by an intelligent machine? Is it the programmer, the user, or the machine itself?

Bias in Algorithms

Another ethical implication of Ada's predictions is the potential for bias in algorithms. In her time, the concept of bias was not fully understood, yet her acknowledgment of the complexity of logic hints at the intricacies involved in programming. Modern algorithms can inadvertently perpetuate societal biases, leading to outcomes that favor certain groups over others.

Consider the following equation representing the output of a biased algorithm:

$$O = g(D, B)$$

where O is the output, D is the data input, and B is the bias inherent in the data. If B is not addressed, the output O can result in discriminatory practices, such as biased hiring processes or unjust legal rulings. This highlights the ethical responsibility of programmers to ensure fairness and equity in their algorithms.

The Role of Transparency

Ada's predictions also underscore the importance of transparency in technology. As machines take on more complex roles in decision-making, the opacity of algorithms becomes a significant concern. The equation:

$$T = h(C, R)$$

defines transparency T as a function of clarity C and reproducibility R. If either C or R is low, then the transparency T suffers, leading to distrust in technological systems. Ethical programming mandates that developers prioritize transparency, allowing users to understand how decisions are made and fostering accountability.

The Ethical Use of AI

Ada Lovelace's foresight into the capabilities of machines raises questions about the ethical use of AI. As AI systems become integral to various sectors—healthcare, finance, law enforcement—the potential for misuse increases. The ethical framework for AI can be modeled as:

$$E = k(A, R, S)$$

where E is the ethical standard, A represents the applications of AI, R denotes regulatory frameworks, and S signifies societal values. A robust ethical standard requires a balance between innovative applications of AI and adherence to regulatory and societal norms.

The Future of Ethical Programming

As we stand on the shoulders of Ada Lovelace, the future of programming hinges on our ability to confront these ethical challenges. The responsibility lies with current and future programmers to cultivate a culture of ethical awareness. This involves continuous education on the implications of their work and an unwavering commitment to ethical practices.

In conclusion, the ethical implications of Ada Lovelace's predictions are profound and multifaceted. They compel us to consider the impact of our technological advancements on society and the moral obligations we bear as creators of intelligent systems. As we advance into an era defined by AI and machine learning, let us carry forward Ada's legacy by ensuring that our innovations reflect the highest ethical standards, fostering a future where technology serves humanity, not the other way around.

Harnessing Ada's Vision for a Better Future

Ada Lovelace's contributions to the early concepts of computing and programming were not merely a reflection of her time; they were a prophetic glimpse into the future of technology. Her foresight in recognizing the potential of machines to transcend mere calculation and engage in complex processes laid the groundwork for the development of modern computing. This section explores how we can harness Ada's vision to create a better future, focusing on the importance of interdisciplinary collaboration, ethical considerations in technology, and the empowerment of future generations.

Interdisciplinary Collaboration

One of the most significant aspects of Ada Lovelace's work was her ability to connect mathematics, logic, and creativity. She understood that the most groundbreaking innovations often emerge at the intersection of different fields. In her collaboration with Charles Babbage on the Analytical Engine, Ada infused her mathematical insights with a poetic sensibility, illustrating that creativity is as vital as logic in technological advancement.

To harness Ada's vision, contemporary innovators must embrace interdisciplinary collaboration. This can be achieved through:

+ **Educational Programs:** Universities and institutions should foster environments where students from diverse fields—such as computer science, engineering, art, and humanities—can work together on projects. For example, initiatives like hackathons that encourage cross-disciplinary teams can lead to innovative solutions that may not arise in siloed environments.

+ **Industry Partnerships:** Tech companies should partner with organizations in the arts and sciences to develop products that are not only functional but also resonate with users on a cultural and emotional level. The collaboration between technology firms and design agencies can lead to user-friendly interfaces that enhance the overall user experience.

+ **Community Engagement:** Local communities can create forums and workshops that bring together individuals from varied backgrounds to brainstorm and develop solutions to local challenges. This grassroots approach encourages creativity and innovation while addressing real-world problems.

Ethical Considerations in Technology

Ada Lovelace's work was not only about the mechanics of computation but also about the implications of technology on society. As we continue to advance technologically, it is crucial to consider the ethical ramifications of our innovations. Ada's foresight can guide us in the following ways:

+ **Responsible AI Development:** With the rise of artificial intelligence, it is imperative to develop ethical guidelines that prioritize human welfare. Ada's vision of machines as tools for enhancing human capability must be accompanied by a commitment to ensuring that these tools do not perpetuate biases or inequalities. This can be achieved through diverse teams in AI development, ensuring that multiple perspectives inform the design and implementation of AI systems.

+ **Data Privacy and Security:** In an age where data is a valuable commodity, protecting individuals' privacy is paramount. Ada's emphasis on the potential of machines to process complex information can be harnessed to create robust systems that prioritize user consent and data protection. Implementing transparent policies and technologies that safeguard personal information is essential for building trust in digital systems.

+ **Sustainable Technology:** Ada's vision for a better future must also encompass environmental considerations. The development of green technologies that minimize ecological impact aligns with her forward-thinking approach. For instance, tech companies can invest in renewable energy sources and promote sustainable practices within their operations.

Empowerment of Future Generations

Perhaps the most enduring aspect of Ada Lovelace's legacy is her role as an inspiration for future generations. To harness her vision effectively, we must empower young minds to pursue careers in STEM fields, particularly women and underrepresented groups. This can be accomplished through:

+ **Mentorship Programs:** Establishing mentorship initiatives that connect young aspiring technologists with experienced professionals can provide invaluable guidance and support. Programs that focus on fostering confidence and skills in young women, in particular, can help bridge the gender gap in technology.

+ **Inclusive Curriculum:** Educational institutions should integrate Ada's story and contributions into their curricula, highlighting her role as a pioneer in computing. By showcasing her achievements, educators can inspire students to see themselves as potential innovators and leaders in technology.

+ **Scholarship Opportunities:** Financial support for students pursuing degrees in STEM fields can alleviate barriers to entry. Scholarships dedicated to women and minorities can encourage a diverse range of voices in technology, reflecting the multifaceted nature of society.

Conclusion

In conclusion, harnessing Ada Lovelace's vision for a better future requires a multifaceted approach that embraces interdisciplinary collaboration, ethical considerations, and the empowerment of future generations. By following her example, we can create a technological landscape that is not only innovative but also inclusive and responsible. Ada's legacy is not just a historical footnote; it is a guiding light for the future of technology, urging us to imagine, create, and innovate with purpose and compassion. As we stand on the shoulders of giants like Ada Lovelace, let us commit to building a future that honors her vision and empowers all to contribute to the ever-evolving narrative of technology.

The Responsibility of Today's Programmers in Honoring Ada

In the digital age, programmers stand on the shoulders of giants, and few giants loom larger than Ada Lovelace. As the first programmer, Ada not only laid the groundwork for the field of computer science but also championed the importance of ethical considerations and foresight in technology. Today's programmers carry the dual responsibility of advancing technology while honoring Ada's legacy through their work and advocacy.

Embracing Ethical Programming

One of the most pressing responsibilities of modern programmers is to embed ethical considerations into the software development lifecycle. Ada Lovelace understood the potential of technology to shape society, and she envisioned a future where machines could perform tasks beyond mere calculation. This foresight is particularly relevant today as we grapple with the ethical implications of artificial intelligence (AI) and machine learning (ML).

For instance, consider the algorithmic bias that can arise in AI systems. When programmers fail to account for diverse datasets, they risk perpetuating stereotypes and discrimination. A notable example is the facial recognition technology that has been shown to misidentify individuals from minority groups at a significantly higher rate than others. This not only highlights the technical challenges but also underscores the moral obligation to ensure fairness and inclusivity in programming practices.

To honor Ada, programmers must adopt frameworks such as **Fairness, Accountability, and Transparency (FAT)** in AI. This involves rigorously testing algorithms for bias, ensuring diverse representation in data collection, and fostering transparency in how algorithms make decisions.

Advocating for Diversity in Tech

Ada Lovelace's legacy is not just about her contributions to programming but also her role as a pioneer for women in technology. Today, the tech industry still faces significant gender disparities, with women holding only about 25% of computing jobs. It is imperative for today's programmers to advocate for diversity and inclusion within their teams and organizations.

Programs like **Girls Who Code** and **Black Girls Code** aim to inspire young women and underrepresented minorities to pursue careers in technology. By actively participating in mentorship, sponsoring initiatives that promote diversity, and creating inclusive workplace cultures, programmers can honor Ada's vision of a more equitable tech landscape.

Championing Lifelong Learning and Innovation

Ada was not only a mathematician but also a visionary who believed in the potential of machines to evolve and learn. Today's programmers have the responsibility to embrace lifelong learning and stay abreast of technological advancements. This commitment to continuous education is essential in a rapidly changing field where new languages, frameworks, and ethical challenges emerge regularly.

For example, the rise of quantum computing presents both opportunities and challenges. As programmers explore this new frontier, they must engage with the ethical implications of quantum algorithms, particularly in the realms of cryptography and data privacy. By participating in workshops, online courses, and community discussions, programmers can foster an environment of innovation while remaining mindful of the broader societal impacts of their work.

Promoting Open Source Collaboration

Ada Lovelace's collaborative spirit is reflected in the open-source movement that has gained momentum in recent years. By contributing to open-source projects, programmers not only enhance their skills but also contribute to a culture of sharing and collective growth. This practice aligns with Ada's belief in the importance of collaboration and knowledge exchange.

Open-source platforms like **GitHub** allow programmers to work together on projects that can have a significant impact on society. For instance, the **TensorFlow** library, developed by Google, has become a cornerstone for many AI applications. By participating in such projects, programmers can ensure that technology is developed in a way that is transparent, collaborative, and beneficial to all.

Fostering Interdisciplinary Approaches

Finally, honoring Ada Lovelace involves recognizing the interconnectedness of technology with other fields such as ethics, sociology, and environmental science. Programmers have the responsibility to engage with experts from various disciplines to create holistic solutions to complex problems.

For example, climate change presents a critical challenge that requires innovative technological solutions. Programmers can collaborate with environmental scientists to develop software that models climate data, predicts environmental changes, and informs policy decisions. This interdisciplinary approach not only enhances the quality of technological solutions but also reflects Ada's belief in the power of collaboration across fields.

Conclusion

In conclusion, the responsibility of today's programmers in honoring Ada Lovelace extends beyond acknowledging her contributions; it involves actively shaping a future that aligns with her vision of ethical, inclusive, and innovative technology. By embedding ethics into programming practices, advocating for diversity, committing to lifelong learning, promoting open-source collaboration, and fostering interdisciplinary approaches, programmers can ensure that Ada's legacy continues to inspire and guide the next generation of innovators. As we navigate the complexities of the digital age, let us remember Ada Lovelace not just as the first programmer, but as a beacon of possibility, challenging us to create a better, more equitable world through technology.

Ada Lovelace: A Visionary Ahead of Her Time

Ada Lovelace, often hailed as the first computer programmer, was not merely a product of her time; she was a visionary whose insights transcended the technological limitations of the 19th century. Her profound understanding of mathematics, combined with her unique perspective on the potential of machines, positioned her as a pioneer in a field that was yet to be fully realized. This section delves into Ada's groundbreaking ideas and how they resonate in the modern world, showcasing her remarkable foresight in the realm of computing.

The Nature of Visionary Thinking

To understand Ada's visionary status, we must first define what it means to be a visionary. A visionary is someone who can foresee and articulate future possibilities, often in ways that challenge existing paradigms. Ada's ability to envision the capabilities of the Analytical Engine, designed by Charles Babbage, was a testament to her extraordinary intellect. She famously wrote about the machine's potential to perform tasks beyond mere calculation, suggesting that it could create music and art, thus foreshadowing the interdisciplinary nature of modern computing.

Ada's Predictions and Their Modern Relevance

In her notes on the Analytical Engine, particularly in what is now known as the *Lovelace Note*, Ada predicted that the machine could manipulate symbols in accordance with rules and that it could be programmed to perform complex tasks. This notion laid the groundwork for the concept of programming as we know it today.

One of her most famous passages reads:

> "The Analytical Engine has no pretensions whatever to originate anything. It can do whatever we know how to order it to perform."

This statement encapsulates the essence of programming: the ability to instruct machines to execute predefined tasks. Ada's insight that machines could be used for purposes beyond calculation was revolutionary. Today, we see this realization in the development of artificial intelligence and machine learning, where algorithms are designed to learn from data and make decisions autonomously.

Mathematical Foundations of Ada's Vision

Ada's work was deeply rooted in mathematics. Her understanding of Bernoulli numbers, for instance, allowed her to create the first algorithm intended for implementation on a machine. The calculation of Bernoulli numbers can be represented mathematically as follows:

$$B_n = \sum_{k=0}^{n} \binom{n}{k} \cdot B_k \cdot \frac{1}{n-k+1} \tag{51}$$

where B_n represents the n-th Bernoulli number and $\binom{n}{k}$ is the binomial coefficient. This formula illustrates the complexity of the calculations Ada was capable of envisioning for the Analytical Engine.

Her programming notes included detailed instructions on how the machine could compute these numbers, showcasing her ability to think algorithmically.

This foresight not only established her as a pioneer in programming but also highlighted the importance of mathematical foundations in the development of computer science.

Interdisciplinary Approach to Technology

Ada Lovelace's vision was not limited to mathematics and computation; she also recognized the importance of creativity in technology. She believed that the Analytical Engine could be a tool for artistic expression, which is a concept that resonates strongly in today's digital landscape. The intersection of technology and art is evident in various fields, from graphic design to music production, where algorithms and software play pivotal roles in creative processes.

For example, contemporary applications of generative art utilize algorithms to produce unique visual compositions. Artists like Casey Reas and Joshua Davis have harnessed programming languages to create artworks that are as much about the process as they are about the final product. This reflects Ada's vision of machines as not only computational tools but also as mediums for creativity.

Challenges to Ada's Vision

Despite her groundbreaking ideas, Ada faced significant challenges in her pursuit of knowledge and recognition. The male-dominated field of mathematics and engineering often overlooked her contributions. The societal norms of her time relegated women to the private sphere, limiting their access to education and professional opportunities. Ada's struggle against these constraints makes her achievements even more remarkable.

Her correspondence with Babbage illustrates the collaborative yet challenging environment in which she operated. She often had to navigate skepticism and resistance from her contemporaries, yet she remained steadfast in her beliefs about the potential of computing. This resilience is a crucial aspect of her legacy as a visionary.

Legacy and Continuing Influence

Ada Lovelace's impact on technology is profound and enduring. Her predictions about the capabilities of machines have been realized in the development of modern computing technologies. The rise of artificial intelligence, data analytics, and software engineering can all trace their roots back to her foundational ideas.

Moreover, Ada's legacy continues to inspire new generations of innovators. Initiatives like Ada Lovelace Day celebrate her contributions and promote the visibility of women in STEM fields. These efforts aim to foster an inclusive environment where future visionaries can thrive, echoing Ada's own struggles and triumphs.

In conclusion, Ada Lovelace was undeniably a visionary ahead of her time. Her insights into the potential of computing, her mathematical prowess, and her interdisciplinary approach to technology have left an indelible mark on the world. As we continue to navigate the complexities of the digital age, Ada's legacy serves as a guiding light, reminding us of the importance of creativity, resilience, and the relentless pursuit of knowledge.

"Ada Lovelace: a name synonymous with innovation, creativity, and the boundless potential of human ingenuity."

Chapter 2: Unveiling Ada's Brilliance

Chapter 2: Unveiling Ada's Brilliance

Chapter 2: Unveiling Ada's Brilliance

In this chapter, we dive deep into the extraordinary mind of Ada Lovelace, a woman whose brilliance transcended the constraints of her time. From her early education in mathematics to her groundbreaking work on the Analytical Engine, Ada's journey is a testament to her intellectual prowess and innovative spirit.

The Birth of a Mathematical Mind

Ada's mathematical journey began in her childhood, influenced by her mother, Lady Anne Isabella Byron, who was determined to provide her daughter with a rigorous education in the sciences. This was no small feat in the 19th century, a time when women were often relegated to domestic roles. Lady Byron, a mathematician herself, recognized Ada's potential and ensured that she received the best education available, including lessons in mathematics, logic, and science.

Ada's Early Education in Mathematics

Ada's early education was marked by a fascination with numbers and patterns. She was introduced to the concepts of calculus, algebra, and geometry, which would later become the foundation of her work. The complexity of these subjects was not daunting to Ada; instead, they ignited a passion within her. She was known to have an aptitude for numbers, often solving complex problems with ease.

Influences that Shaped Ada's Mathematical Abilities

Several key figures influenced Ada's mathematical development. Among them was Augustus De Morgan, a prominent mathematician who recognized Ada's talent and encouraged her pursuits. His teachings on logic and mathematical reasoning provided Ada with a framework to approach problems analytically. Additionally, Ada's interactions with Charles Babbage, the inventor of the Analytical Engine, further honed her skills and fueled her imagination.

The Role of Logic in Ada's Mathematical Journey

Logic played a crucial role in Ada's mathematical journey. Her ability to think logically allowed her to dissect complex problems and arrive at innovative solutions. This skill was particularly evident in her work with the Analytical Engine, where she envisioned a machine capable of performing calculations and processing information in ways previously thought impossible.

Theoretical Mathematics and Its Impact on Ada's Work

Ada's engagement with theoretical mathematics was profound. She explored concepts that would later become fundamental in computer science, including algorithms and data structures. Her understanding of these theoretical principles allowed her to articulate a vision for the Analytical Engine that was not merely mechanical but also conceptual.

For instance, Ada famously described the process of calculating Bernoulli numbers through the Analytical Engine, illustrating her ability to translate mathematical concepts into practical applications. The algorithm she developed for this computation is often regarded as one of the first computer programs in history.

Ada's Dedication to Mathematical Puzzles and Challenges

Ada's dedication to solving mathematical puzzles and challenges was remarkable. She viewed mathematics not just as a subject to be studied but as a realm to explore and conquer. This adventurous spirit led her to tackle complex problems that many of her contemporaries would shy away from.

$$\text{Let } P(n) = \sum_{k=0}^{n} \frac{1}{k!} \tag{52}$$

This equation represents the sum of the series for the exponential function, which Ada would have encountered in her studies. Her ability to manipulate such equations demonstrated her deep understanding of mathematical principles.

Ada's Introduction to Charles Babbage and the Analytical Engine

The pivotal moment in Ada's mathematical journey came with her introduction to Charles Babbage. Their meeting in 1833 marked the beginning of a collaborative relationship that would change the course of computing history. Babbage's vision for the Analytical Engine—a machine designed to perform any calculation—captivated Ada. She recognized the potential of this machine to revolutionize not only mathematics but also the way society approached computation.

The Early Beginnings of Ada's Programming Skills

As Ada delved deeper into Babbage's work, she began to develop her programming skills. She understood that programming was not merely about writing code; it was about understanding the logic and structure behind the machine's operations.

$$\text{Let } C = \text{Computational Complexity} \tag{53}$$

Ada's insights into computational complexity would later influence her approach to programming, as she sought to optimize algorithms for the Analytical Engine.

The Parallel Paths of Ada and Babbage's Innovations

As Ada and Babbage collaborated, their innovations paralleled one another. Babbage's designs for the Analytical Engine were ambitious, yet it was Ada's vision that brought those designs to life. She envisioned a machine that could not only calculate but also manipulate symbols and perform logical operations, laying the groundwork for future developments in programming.

Conclusion

Chapter 2 serves as a testament to Ada Lovelace's brilliance. Her early education, intellectual curiosity, and collaborative spirit with Charles Babbage not only shaped her mathematical abilities but also paved the way for her groundbreaking contributions to the field of computing. As we continue to explore Ada's life and work, we will uncover the layers of her genius and the lasting impact she has had on technology and society.

The Birth of a Mathematical Mind

Ada's Early Education in Mathematics

Ada Lovelace's journey into the world of mathematics began in the lush, intellectual gardens of her childhood. Born in 1815 to the illustrious Lord Byron and Anne Isabella Milbanke, Ada's mother, Lady Anne, was determined to steer her daughter away from the poetic whims of her father. Instead, she cultivated in Ada a rigorous education in mathematics and science, which she deemed essential for a girl of noble birth. This early education would lay the groundwork for Ada's future as the first programmer in history.

Lady Anne, often referred to as "the Princess of Parallelograms," was a mathematician in her own right. She believed that Ada's education should be as structured and disciplined as possible, employing a method reminiscent of the educational philosophies of the time. This was a bold move, considering that many women of her era were discouraged from pursuing intellectual endeavors, particularly in fields dominated by men.

The Foundations of Mathematical Thought

At a young age, Ada was introduced to the fundamentals of mathematics through a series of carefully curated lessons. Her mother emphasized the importance of logical reasoning, a skill that would serve Ada well throughout her life. The curriculum included arithmetic, geometry, and the early concepts of calculus, all of which were taught using a blend of textbooks and practical applications.

One of the key components of Ada's early education was the study of *Euclidean geometry*. The axiomatic approach of Euclid provided Ada with a framework for logical deduction. For instance, she learned how to prove the Pythagorean theorem, which states that for any right triangle, the square of the length of the hypotenuse (c) is equal to the sum of the squares of the lengths of the other two sides (a and b):

$$c^2 = a^2 + b^2$$

This theorem not only showcased the beauty of mathematics but also instilled in Ada a sense of confidence in her abilities to tackle complex problems.

Mathematics as a Language

As Ada progressed in her studies, she began to see mathematics not merely as numbers and equations but as a language that could describe the world around her.

Her mother encouraged her to explore mathematical concepts through the lens of creativity and imagination. This approach was particularly evident when Ada engaged with the works of contemporary mathematicians, such as Augustus De Morgan and Mary Somerville, who were pivotal in shaping her understanding of mathematical theory.

Ada's exposure to *algebra* further enhanced her mathematical vocabulary. She learned to manipulate symbols and solve equations, which allowed her to express complex relationships succinctly. For example, she mastered the quadratic formula, which provides the solutions to quadratic equations of the form $ax^2 + bx + c = 0$:

$$x = \frac{-b \pm \sqrt{b^2 - 4ac}}{2a}$$

By understanding how to apply this formula, Ada not only solved equations but also developed a deeper appreciation for the power of abstraction in mathematics.

Exploring Mathematical Patterns

Ada's education also involved recognizing and analyzing mathematical patterns. She was captivated by the Fibonacci sequence, where each number is the sum of the two preceding ones, typically starting with 0 and 1:

$$F(n) = F(n - 1) + F(n - 2)$$

This sequence not only appeared in mathematics but also in nature, art, and architecture, illustrating the interconnectedness of different fields. Ada's fascination with such patterns would later influence her work on the Analytical Engine, where she envisioned programming as a means to explore and manipulate mathematical relationships.

Practical Applications and Puzzles

To solidify her understanding, Ada's education included practical applications of mathematics through puzzles and challenges. Lady Anne often presented Ada with problems that required creative solutions. For instance, one of the problems involved calculating the area of an irregular shape by dividing it into known geometric figures. This exercise taught Ada how to apply theoretical knowledge to real-world scenarios, reinforcing her analytical skills.

Moreover, Ada's early engagement with mathematical puzzles foreshadowed her later work in programming. She learned to approach problems methodically, breaking them down into manageable parts, much like how one would decompose a complex algorithm into simpler steps.

Conclusion

In summary, Ada Lovelace's early education in mathematics was a carefully crafted tapestry woven from logic, creativity, and practical applications. Under the guidance of her mother, she developed a profound understanding of mathematical principles that would serve as the foundation for her groundbreaking contributions to computing. Ada's experiences in her formative years not only shaped her identity as a mathematician but also ignited a passion for innovation that would resonate throughout her life. As she would later demonstrate, the world of numbers was not just a realm of calculation but a universe filled with possibilities waiting to be explored.

Ada's Aptitude for Numbers

Ada Lovelace's affinity for numbers was not merely a passing interest; it was an intrinsic part of her identity. From a young age, she demonstrated a natural talent for mathematics that set her apart from her peers. This aptitude can be attributed to several factors, including her early education, the influence of her mother, and her exposure to the works of prominent mathematicians of her time.

Early Education in Mathematics

Ada's education began under the tutelage of her mother, Lady Anne, who believed that a strong foundation in mathematics was essential for her daughter. Unlike many women of her era, who were often discouraged from pursuing academic subjects, Ada was encouraged to explore the world of numbers. Lady Anne arranged for Ada to study with some of the best tutors available, ensuring she received a rigorous education in mathematics and the sciences.

Influences on Ada's Mathematical Abilities

One of the key influences on Ada's mathematical development was her exposure to the works of great mathematicians. At a young age, she encountered the writings of Isaac Newton, whose groundbreaking work in calculus and physics ignited Ada's imagination. She was particularly fascinated by his *Principia Mathematica*, which laid the groundwork for classical mechanics. The elegance of Newton's equations resonated with Ada, inspiring her to delve deeper into the world of mathematical theory.

The Role of Logic in Ada's Mathematical Journey

Logic played a crucial role in Ada's approach to mathematics. She understood that numbers were not just symbols, but rather tools for reasoning and problem-solving. This understanding was further enhanced by her studies in formal logic, which emphasized the importance of deductive reasoning. Ada's ability to think logically allowed her to tackle complex mathematical problems with confidence and creativity.

For example, consider the Fibonacci sequence, a series of numbers where each number is the sum of the two preceding ones. The sequence starts as follows:

$$F_0 = 0, \quad F_1 = 1, \quad F_n = F_{n-1} + F_{n-2} \quad \text{for } n \geq 2$$

Ada would have appreciated not only the beauty of this sequence but also its applications in various fields, such as biology and art. She recognized that mathematics could explain patterns in nature, leading her to explore the intersection of mathematics and the natural world.

Dedication to Mathematical Puzzles and Challenges

Ada's passion for numbers was further exemplified by her dedication to solving mathematical puzzles and challenges. She often sought out complex problems that required innovative solutions, demonstrating her commitment to pushing the boundaries of mathematical understanding. One notable example is her work on Bernoulli numbers, which are a sequence of rational numbers with deep connections to number theory and mathematical analysis.

The n-th Bernoulli number, denoted B_n, can be defined using the generating function:

$$\frac{t}{e^t - 1} = \sum_{n=0}^{\infty} B_n \frac{t^n}{n!}$$

Ada's exploration of these numbers showcased her ability to engage with advanced mathematical concepts, further solidifying her reputation as a formidable intellect in the field.

The Early Beginnings of Ada's Programming Skills

Ada's mathematical prowess laid the groundwork for her later achievements in programming. Her understanding of algorithms and numerical methods would become evident in her collaboration with Charles Babbage on the Analytical Engine. She recognized that the machine could perform complex calculations, and her ability to translate mathematical concepts into a programming language was revolutionary.

For instance, Ada's notes on the Analytical Engine included what is now considered the first algorithm intended for implementation on a machine. This algorithm was designed to compute Bernoulli numbers, illustrating her ability to apply her mathematical knowledge to practical problems.

Conclusion

In summary, Ada Lovelace's aptitude for numbers was a multifaceted aspect of her character that shaped her contributions to mathematics and computing. Her early education, logical reasoning, and dedication to solving complex problems enabled her to navigate the world of mathematics with remarkable skill. As she transitioned from a gifted mathematician to the first programmer, Ada's numerical abilities would play a pivotal role in her groundbreaking work, leaving an indelible mark on the history of technology.

Influences that Shaped Ada's Mathematical Abilities

Ada Lovelace, often heralded as the first computer programmer, was not born into a world where mathematics was readily available to women. Her mathematical abilities were shaped by a myriad of influences, ranging from her noble lineage to the intellectual environment fostered by her mother and her interactions with prominent mathematicians of her time.

Noble Heritage and Early Education

Born in 1815 to the famous poet Lord Byron and Lady Anne Isabella Milbanke, Ada's noble heritage provided her with access to resources that many women of her time could only dream of. Lady Anne, a mathematician herself, recognized the importance of education and ensured that Ada received a rigorous upbringing in the sciences. This early exposure laid the groundwork for Ada's mathematical prowess.

Mathematics as a Form of Art

Ada viewed mathematics not merely as a set of rules and equations but as a form of art. She famously stated, "Mathematics is the language in which God has written the universe." This perspective allowed her to approach mathematical problems creatively. For instance, Ada was fascinated by the concept of imaginary numbers, which can be expressed as:

$$i = \sqrt{-1}$$

This notion of extending the real number system to include complex numbers, represented as $z = a + bi$ (where a and b are real numbers), showcased her ability to think beyond conventional boundaries.

Influence of Mentors

Ada's early education was heavily influenced by her tutors, particularly Augustus De Morgan and Mary Somerville. De Morgan, a prominent mathematician, introduced her to advanced concepts in mathematics, including calculus and logic. He emphasized the importance of logical reasoning, which Ada embraced wholeheartedly.

Mary Somerville, a renowned scientist and writer, became a close friend and mentor to Ada. Somerville's work in mathematics and astronomy inspired Ada to delve deeper into the subjects. Together, they explored the intricacies of mathematical theories, further honing Ada's skills. Somerville's influence is encapsulated in Ada's own writings, where she often cited her mentor's contributions.

Exploration of Mathematical Theories

Ada's curiosity led her to explore various mathematical theories, including those of probability and combinatorics. She applied these theories to real-world problems, demonstrating her practical understanding of abstract concepts. For example, Ada tackled the problem of calculating the probability of winning in games of chance, which can be expressed as:

$$P(A) = \frac{\text{Number of favorable outcomes}}{\text{Total number of outcomes}}$$

This formula not only highlights her analytical skills but also her ability to apply mathematical principles to everyday scenarios.

The Influence of the Analytical Engine

The most significant influence on Ada's mathematical abilities came from her collaboration with Charles Babbage on the Analytical Engine. This early mechanical computer was designed to perform complex calculations, and Ada recognized its potential far beyond mere arithmetic. She envisioned the engine executing any mathematical operation, which she described in her notes as:

If the engine were programmed correctly, it could execute any series of operations based on th

Ada's understanding of the engine's capabilities allowed her to develop what is now recognized as the first algorithm intended for implementation on a machine. This algorithm, which computed Bernoulli numbers, is a testament to her mathematical genius.

Conclusion

In conclusion, Ada Lovelace's mathematical abilities were shaped by her noble upbringing, the influence of her mother, mentorship from prominent figures, and her groundbreaking work on the Analytical Engine. Her unique perspective on mathematics as an art form and her ability to apply complex theories to practical problems set her apart as a visionary in the field. Ada's legacy continues to inspire generations of mathematicians and computer scientists alike, reminding us that the pursuit of knowledge knows no gender.

The Role of Logic in Ada's Mathematical Journey

Ada Lovelace's journey into the world of mathematics was profoundly shaped by her understanding and application of logic. Logic, the systematic study of the principles of valid inference and correct reasoning, provided the foundational framework that Ada used to explore complex mathematical concepts and problems. In this section, we will delve into how logic influenced Ada's mathematical development, her approach to problem-solving, and the implications of her logical reasoning in the context of her work on the Analytical Engine.

Understanding Logic

Logic can be traced back to ancient philosophers such as Aristotle, who established formal systems of reasoning. In Ada's time, the development of symbolic logic was gaining momentum, with mathematicians like George Boole laying the groundwork for what would eventually evolve into modern computational logic. Logic is not merely a tool for mathematical proofs; it is the backbone of mathematical thought, allowing mathematicians to structure their arguments and derive conclusions from premises.

Logical Foundations in Mathematics

At its core, mathematics is built upon axioms and theorems, which are interconnected through logical reasoning. For instance, consider the basic logical statement:

$$P \implies Q \tag{54}$$

This reads as "if P is true, then Q is true." This conditional statement is fundamental in mathematics, allowing mathematicians to build chains of reasoning. Ada's ability to manipulate such logical statements was crucial in her mathematical explorations.

Ada's Application of Logic

Ada Lovelace's mathematical work was characterized by her ability to apply logical reasoning to complex problems. One of her most significant contributions was her work on the Analytical Engine, where she recognized that the machine could perform calculations not just mechanically, but through a logical framework that could be programmed. This insight was revolutionary, as it laid the groundwork for the concept of programming as we understand it today.

For example, Ada famously noted that the Analytical Engine could be programmed to compute Bernoulli numbers. She approached this problem by breaking it down into logical steps, demonstrating how to construct a sequence of operations that the machine could execute. This process can be illustrated as follows:

1. **Define the Input**: Identify the sequence of numbers to be processed, in this case, the Bernoulli numbers. 2. **Establish Logical Operations**: Determine the operations required to compute the desired output. This could involve addition, multiplication, or other mathematical functions. 3. **Sequence the Operations**: Arrange the operations in a logical order that the machine can follow.

Example: Computing Bernoulli Numbers

To illustrate Ada's logical reasoning, let's consider the computation of the first few Bernoulli numbers, B_n. The Bernoulli numbers can be defined using the following recursive relation:

$$B_0 = 1, \quad B_1 = \frac{1}{2}, \quad B_n = \sum_{k=0}^{n-1} \binom{n}{k} B_k \quad \text{for } n \geq 2 \qquad (55)$$

Using logical reasoning, Ada would break down the computation of B_2:

$$B_2 = \sum_{k=0}^{1} \binom{2}{k} B_k = \binom{2}{0} B_0 + \binom{2}{1} B_1 = 1 \cdot 1 + 2 \cdot \frac{1}{2} = 1 + 1 = 1 \quad (56)$$

Ada's logical approach allowed her to systematically derive each Bernoulli number step by step, showcasing her ability to think critically and logically.

The Importance of Logic in Programming

Ada's insights into the role of logic extended beyond mathematics into the realm of programming. She recognized that programming the Analytical Engine would require a logical structure akin to mathematical proofs. Each operation performed by the machine could be seen as a logical statement that contributed to the overall computation.

In her notes, Ada articulated the concept of loops and conditional statements, which are fundamental to modern programming languages. For instance, she envisioned a scenario where the machine could repeat a sequence of operations until a certain condition was met, a principle that is foundational in computer science today.

Conclusion

In conclusion, Ada Lovelace's journey through mathematics was profoundly influenced by her understanding and application of logic. Her ability to deconstruct complex problems into logical components allowed her to make groundbreaking contributions to the field of mathematics and the early development of programming. Ada's legacy as the first programmer is not only a testament to her mathematical prowess but also to her exceptional capacity for logical reasoning. As we continue to explore the realms of mathematics and technology, we must remember the critical role that logic plays in shaping our understanding and innovation.

Theoretical Mathematics and Its Impact on Ada's Work

Ada Lovelace's intellectual journey was deeply intertwined with the realm of theoretical mathematics, which served as the bedrock for her groundbreaking contributions to computer programming. Theoretical mathematics, often characterized by its abstract concepts and rigorous logical frameworks, provided Ada with the tools necessary to conceptualize and articulate the potential of the Analytical Engine. This section explores the key mathematical theories that influenced Ada's work, the problems she grappled with, and the examples that illustrate her innovative thinking.

Foundations of Theoretical Mathematics

At its core, theoretical mathematics encompasses various branches, including algebra, calculus, and number theory, which focus on abstract structures and the relationships between them. For Ada, these mathematical disciplines were not mere academic exercises; they were vital in shaping her understanding of computation and algorithmic processes.

One of the fundamental theories that Ada engaged with was the concept of **functions**, which can be expressed mathematically as:

$$f : X \to Y \tag{57}$$

where f is a function that maps elements from set X to set Y. This concept was crucial for Ada as she sought to describe how the Analytical Engine could process data and execute operations based on specific inputs.

The Role of Logic and Set Theory

The development of **set theory** and **logical reasoning** also played a significant role in Ada's mathematical framework. Set theory, pioneered by Georg Cantor, focuses on the study of sets, which are collections of objects. Ada's ability to think in terms of sets allowed her to categorize and analyze the various components of the Analytical Engine, leading to a more systematic approach in her programming efforts.

Logical reasoning, particularly the principles of **propositional logic**, enabled Ada to formulate precise statements about the operations of the Analytical Engine. For example, she could express logical propositions such as:

$$P \wedge Q \Rightarrow R \tag{58}$$

where P and Q are premises leading to a conclusion R. This ability to construct logical arguments was essential for her to ensure the reliability of the algorithms she developed.

Mathematical Problems and Challenges

Ada's engagement with theoretical mathematics was not without its challenges. One of the significant problems she faced was the representation of complex mathematical operations within the confines of the Analytical Engine. For instance, she needed to devise a method to express **polynomial functions** of the form:

$$P(x) = a_n x^n + a_{n-1} x^{n-1} + \ldots + a_1 x + a_0 \tag{59}$$

where a_i are coefficients and n is a non-negative integer. The challenge lay in encoding these operations into a format that the Analytical Engine could interpret and execute.

To tackle this problem, Ada utilized her understanding of **combinatorial mathematics**, which deals with counting, arrangement, and combination of objects. This approach allowed her to create algorithms that could calculate combinations and permutations, fundamental concepts in both mathematics and programming.

Examples of Ada's Mathematical Innovations

One of Ada's most notable contributions to theoretical mathematics was her formulation of what is now recognized as the first algorithm intended for implementation on a machine. This algorithm was designed to compute Bernoulli numbers, a sequence of rational numbers that have significant implications in number theory and mathematical analysis.

The algorithm can be expressed in a simplified form as follows:

$$B_n = \sum_{k=0}^{n} \binom{n}{k} \cdot B_k \tag{60}$$

where B_n represents the n-th Bernoulli number and $\binom{n}{k}$ is the binomial coefficient. Ada's insight into the recursive nature of this calculation exemplified her ability to blend theoretical mathematics with practical computation.

The Lasting Impact of Theoretical Mathematics on Ada's Work

The impact of theoretical mathematics on Ada's work cannot be overstated. Her ability to navigate complex mathematical concepts allowed her to envision the Analytical Engine as more than just a mechanical calculator; she perceived it as a universal machine capable of executing any computation that could be expressed algorithmically.

Moreover, Ada's pioneering work laid the groundwork for future advancements in computer science. Her understanding of mathematical principles continues to resonate in modern programming languages, which often incorporate concepts from theoretical mathematics, such as functions, logic, and algorithms.

In conclusion, Ada Lovelace's engagement with theoretical mathematics was instrumental in shaping her contributions to the field of computer programming. By harnessing the power of abstract mathematical concepts, she was able to articulate a vision for the Analytical Engine that transcended its mechanical limitations. As we reflect on her legacy, it is essential to recognize the profound influence that theoretical mathematics had on her innovative thinking and groundbreaking achievements.

Ada's Dedication to Mathematical Puzzles and Challenges

Ada Lovelace had an insatiable curiosity and an unwavering dedication to unraveling the complexities of mathematical puzzles. Her fascination with numbers was not merely academic; it was a passion that permeated her life, driving her to explore, analyze, and innovate in a field that was often dominated by men. This section delves into her love for mathematical challenges and how it shaped her contributions to the world of computing.

The Nature of Mathematical Puzzles

Mathematical puzzles can be defined as problems that require creative and critical thinking to solve. They often involve patterns, logical reasoning, and a deep understanding of mathematical principles. Ada was particularly drawn to problems that challenged conventional thinking and required out-of-the-box solutions. Her early exposure to mathematics, encouraged by her mother, laid the groundwork for this passion.

Influence of Logic and Theoretical Mathematics

Ada's interest in mathematical puzzles was deeply intertwined with her understanding of logic. The logical structures underlying mathematical concepts fascinated her. She was influenced by the works of mathematicians such as Augustus De Morgan and George Boole, who laid the foundation for modern logic. Ada's ability to apply logical reasoning to complex problems was evident in her correspondence with Charles Babbage, where she often discussed the implications of his work on the Analytical Engine.

For example, Ada was captivated by the concept of a mathematical series, which can be expressed as follows:

$$S_n = a + (a + d) + (a + 2d) + \ldots + (a + (n - 1)d) \tag{61}$$

where S_n is the sum of the first n terms of an arithmetic series, a is the first term, d is the common difference, and n is the number of terms. This series represents a simple yet profound challenge, showcasing how Ada approached problems with both rigor and creativity.

Engagement with Mathematical Challenges

Throughout her life, Ada engaged with various mathematical challenges, often documenting her thoughts and solutions in her notes. One notable example is her exploration of Bernoulli numbers, which are crucial in number theory and have applications in calculus and combinatorics. The n-th Bernoulli number B_n can be defined using the following formula:

$$B_n = \frac{1}{n!} \sum_{k=0}^{n} \binom{n}{k} B_k \tag{62}$$

where $\binom{n}{k}$ is the binomial coefficient. Ada's dedication to understanding these numbers demonstrated her commitment to delving into the intricacies of mathematics.

Mathematical Correspondence and Collaboration

Ada's collaboration with Charles Babbage was pivotal in her mathematical journey. Their correspondence was filled with discussions of mathematical problems, algorithms, and the potential of the Analytical Engine. In one of her letters, Ada proposed a method for calculating Bernoulli numbers using the Engine, effectively laying the groundwork for future programming concepts. This was a groundbreaking moment, as it illustrated her ability to translate complex mathematical ideas into practical applications.

Examples of Mathematical Puzzles Ada Encountered

Ada's life was rich with mathematical puzzles that she sought to solve. Here are a few examples that highlight her dedication:

1. **The Problem of the Bridges of Königsberg**: Ada was intrigued by this famous problem posed by Leonhard Euler, which asks whether it is possible to walk through the city of Königsberg and cross each of its seven bridges exactly once. The solution involves graph theory, a concept that Ada would have been fascinated by, considering her interest in logical structures.

2. **The Fibonacci Sequence**: Ada also explored the Fibonacci sequence, defined by the recurrence relation:

$$F(n) = F(n-1) + F(n-2) \tag{63}$$

with initial conditions $F(0) = 0$ and $F(1) = 1$. The sequence appears in various natural phenomena, and Ada's curiosity about such patterns reflects her broader interest in the intersection of mathematics and the natural world.

3. **The Four Color Theorem**: Although this theorem was proven long after Ada's time, her interest in color patterns and their mathematical implications would have made her a likely enthusiast of this problem, which states that no more than four colors are needed to color the regions of a map so that no two adjacent regions share the same color.

Legacy of Ada's Mathematical Dedication

Ada Lovelace's dedication to mathematical puzzles and challenges not only shaped her own work but also laid the foundation for future generations of mathematicians and computer scientists. Her ability to think critically and creatively about complex problems has inspired countless individuals to pursue careers in STEM fields.

In conclusion, Ada Lovelace's passion for mathematical puzzles was a defining characteristic of her life. Through her engagement with logic, collaboration with contemporaries, and exploration of various mathematical challenges, she established herself as a pioneering figure in the world of mathematics and computing. Her legacy continues to inspire those who seek to unravel the mysteries of numbers and algorithms, proving that the pursuit of knowledge is a timeless endeavor.

Ada's Introduction to Charles Babbage and the Analytical Engine

In the early 19th century, a remarkable meeting of minds was destined to shape the future of computing. Ada Lovelace, a woman with an insatiable curiosity and a flair for mathematics, was introduced to Charles Babbage, a visionary mathematician and inventor. Their collaboration would lead to groundbreaking advancements in the field of computation, culminating in the conception of the Analytical Engine, often regarded as the first mechanical computer.

The Meeting of Two Brilliant Minds

Ada's introduction to Babbage occurred in 1833 at a dinner party hosted by the fashionable and intellectually stimulating circles of London. Babbage, known for his eccentric personality and brilliant ideas, had already gained notoriety for his design of the Difference Engine, a mechanical calculator intended to compute polynomial functions. However, it was his vision for the Analytical Engine that truly captured Ada's imagination.

Upon meeting Babbage, Ada was struck by his innovative spirit and the complexity of his ideas. She was particularly fascinated by his descriptions of the Analytical Engine, a device that promised to perform any calculation based on a set of instructions, or what we would now refer to as a program. This was a revolutionary concept at a time when calculation was largely a manual process, performed by human "computers."

The Analytical Engine: A Revolutionary Concept

The Analytical Engine was designed to be a general-purpose computing machine, capable of executing any mathematical operation. It was composed of several key components:

- **The Store:** This was where numbers and intermediate results were held, analogous to modern-day memory.

- **The Mill:** This acted as the processor, performing calculations on the numbers stored in the Store.

- **Input and Output:** The Engine utilized punched cards, inspired by the Jacquard loom, to input data and instructions, and it could produce output in various forms, including printed results.

Babbage's vision was ambitious; he sought to create a machine that could not only compute numbers but also manipulate symbols and execute complex algorithms. This was a monumental leap from the mechanical calculators of his time, which were limited to specific functions.

Ada's Enthusiasm and Engagement

Ada's keen interest in mathematics and her burgeoning friendship with Babbage led her to delve deeper into the workings of the Analytical Engine. She recognized the potential of the machine to transcend mere numerical calculations, envisioning its application in various fields, including science and the arts. In her correspondence with Babbage, she expressed her enthusiasm and offered insights into the Engine's design and functionality.

One of the most significant aspects of Ada's engagement with Babbage was her ability to grasp the abstract concepts underlying the Engine's operation. While many in her social circle viewed mathematics as a mere tool for practical applications, Ada saw it as a language of logic and creativity. She famously stated that the Analytical Engine could be programmed to manipulate symbols and create music, a notion that was revolutionary for her time.

The Birth of a Collaborative Relationship

As their collaboration blossomed, Ada began to document her understanding of the Analytical Engine in a series of notes. In 1843, she translated an article written by the Italian mathematician Luigi Federico Federico, which detailed Babbage's work on the Analytical Engine. However, Ada did not merely translate the text; she expanded upon it, adding her own observations and insights.

Her notes, now famously referred to as the "Lovelace Notes," contained what is considered the first algorithm intended for implementation on a machine. This algorithm was designed to calculate Bernoulli numbers, showcasing her understanding of programming concepts long before the term itself existed.

$$B_n = \sum_{k=0}^{n} \binom{n}{k} B_k \cdot \frac{(n-k)!}{n!}$$

This equation illustrates the recursive nature of Bernoulli numbers, where B_n is computed based on previous values. Ada's algorithm not only demonstrated her prowess in mathematics but also her ability to think critically about the potential applications of the Analytical Engine.

A Visionary Partnership

Ada and Babbage's partnership was not without its challenges.   Babbage's eccentricities and the complexity of his ideas often led to misunderstandings. However, Ada's unwavering commitment to the project and her unique perspective on the Engine's capabilities allowed her to contribute meaningfully to its development.

Their collaboration was characterized by a mutual respect for each other's intellect and creativity. Babbage admired Ada's mathematical talent and her ability to articulate complex ideas, while Ada was inspired by Babbage's vision and determination to create a machine that could change the world.

Conclusion: The Legacy of Their Collaboration

The introduction of Ada Lovelace to Charles Babbage marked the beginning of a partnership that would forever change the landscape of computing. Ada's insights and contributions to the Analytical Engine laid the groundwork for modern programming and established her as the first programmer in history. Her ability to envision the potential of computing beyond simple calculations and her innovative spirit continue to inspire generations of mathematicians, computer scientists, and engineers.

In the annals of history, Ada Lovelace's introduction to Charles Babbage stands as a testament to the power of collaboration and the importance of visionary thinking.   Together, they forged a path toward a digital future that was only beginning to unfold, and their legacy remains a beacon of inspiration for all those who dare to dream of what technology can achieve.

The Early Beginnings of Ada's Programming Skills

Ada Lovelace's journey into the realm of programming began as a confluence of her innate mathematical talent, her fascination with the Analytical Engine, and her collaborative relationship with Charles Babbage.   Although the term "programming" was not in use during her time, Ada's contributions laid the groundwork for what we now recognize as computer programming. This section explores the early development of Ada's programming skills through her education, her work with Babbage, and the innovative ideas she proposed.

Foundations of Mathematical Education

Ada's early education was marked by a rigorous study of mathematics, which was not common for women of her era. Her mother, Lady Anne Isabella Byron, emphasized the importance of mathematics, perhaps as a countermeasure to the artistic inclinations of Ada's father, the famous poet Lord Byron. As a child, Ada was introduced to the works of mathematicians and philosophers, including the likes of Euclid and Isaac Newton.

Her early exposure to logical reasoning and mathematical principles equipped her with the tools necessary for understanding complex concepts. For instance, she was particularly drawn to the idea of using symbols to represent numbers and operations, which is foundational to programming languages today.

The Influence of Charles Babbage

In 1833, Ada met Charles Babbage, the inventor of the Analytical Engine. This meeting marked a pivotal moment in her life, as she was captivated by Babbage's vision of a machine that could perform calculations automatically. The Analytical Engine was designed to be programmable, featuring components that resemble modern computers, such as an arithmetic logic unit, control flow through conditional branching, and memory.

Babbage's machine utilized punched cards, a concept borrowed from the Jacquard loom, which Ada quickly recognized as a means to input instructions into the machine. This understanding led her to explore the possibilities of programming in a way that was unprecedented for her time.

The Lovelace Note

Ada's most significant contribution to the field of programming came in the form of her annotations on Babbage's work. In 1843, she translated an article written by the Italian mathematician Luigi Federico Federico Federico, which detailed the workings of the Analytical Engine. However, Ada did not merely translate the text; she added extensive notes that included her own insights and interpretations.

One of her most famous notes, referred to as the "Lovelace Note," contained what is now considered the first algorithm intended for implementation on a machine. This algorithm was designed to calculate Bernoulli numbers, which are a sequence of rational numbers important in number theory. The algorithm can be expressed mathematically as follows:

$$B_n = \sum_{k=0}^{n} \frac{(-1)^k}{k!} \cdot \left(\sum_{j=0}^{k} \binom{k}{j} \cdot j^n \right) \qquad (64)$$

In her notes, Ada meticulously described the steps required to execute this algorithm on the Analytical Engine, showcasing her understanding of programming logic and flow control.

Innovative Ideas and Concepts

Ada's programming skills were not limited to merely writing algorithms. She envisioned the potential of the Analytical Engine to perform tasks beyond mere calculation. She posited that the machine could manipulate symbols and not just numbers, suggesting that it could create music or art, thus broadening the scope of what programming could achieve.

Ada famously stated, "The Analytical Engine does not occupy common ground with mere calculating machines. It holds within it the potential to create things that are beyond the scope of mere calculation." This foresight into the capabilities of computers was revolutionary and foreshadowed the multifaceted applications of programming we see today.

Challenges and Limitations

Despite her brilliance, Ada faced numerous challenges in her pursuit of programming. The societal norms of the Victorian era placed significant limitations on women, particularly in academic and scientific fields. Ada's work was often overlooked, and she struggled to gain recognition for her contributions.

Moreover, the technology of her time was not yet advanced enough to fully realize her vision. The Analytical Engine was never completed during Babbage's lifetime, and thus, Ada's algorithms remained theoretical exercises rather than practical applications.

Legacy of Ada's Early Programming Skills

The early beginnings of Ada Lovelace's programming skills were characterized by her innovative thinking and her ability to conceptualize the potential of computing. Her pioneering work laid the foundation for future generations of programmers, particularly women in technology.

Today, Ada Lovelace is celebrated not only as the first programmer but also as a visionary who foresaw the vast possibilities of computing. Her legacy continues to inspire young women and men alike to explore the fields of mathematics, science, and technology.

In conclusion, the early beginnings of Ada's programming skills were a blend of her mathematical education, her collaboration with Babbage, and her visionary ideas. Despite the challenges she faced, her contributions remain relevant and influential in the world of programming and beyond.

The Parallel Paths of Ada and Babbage's Innovations

In the grand tapestry of technological advancement, Ada Lovelace and Charles Babbage stand out as two brilliant minds whose paths intertwined in the development of what we now recognize as computer science. Their collaboration was not merely a meeting of two intellects but a symbiotic relationship that propelled both of their innovations to unprecedented heights. This section delves into the parallel paths of Ada and Babbage's innovations, highlighting their respective contributions and the synergy that emerged from their collaboration.

The Analytical Engine: A Visionary Blueprint

At the heart of their collaboration was Babbage's design for the Analytical Engine, a mechanical general-purpose computer that was revolutionary for its time. The Analytical Engine was designed to perform any calculation that could be expressed in mathematical terms, utilizing a system of punched cards for input, which was inspired by the Jacquard loom. Babbage's vision included various components that would become foundational in computing, such as:

+ **The Store:** A memory unit capable of holding numbers and intermediate results.

+ **The Mill:** A processing unit that performed arithmetic operations.

+ **Control Flow:** The ability to execute conditional operations and loops.

This ambitious design was documented in Babbage's writings, where he outlined the theoretical underpinnings of the machine. However, it was Ada who saw beyond the mechanical aspects and recognized the potential for programming.

Ada's Contributions: The Lovelace Note

Ada Lovelace's most significant contribution came in the form of her annotations on Babbage's work, particularly her notes on the Analytical Engine. In 1843, she translated an article by the Italian mathematician Luigi Federico Federico (often referred to as the first computer scientist) and included extensive notes of her own. Among these notes, she articulated the concept of programming, making her the first programmer in history.

One of the most famous passages from her notes describes an algorithm for the Analytical Engine to compute Bernoulli numbers. This algorithm can be expressed mathematically as:

$$B_n = \sum_{k=0}^{n} \binom{n}{k} B_k \cdot \frac{1}{n+1-k}$$

where B_n represents the n-th Bernoulli number. Ada's insight into the potential of the Analytical Engine to manipulate symbols and perform complex calculations laid the groundwork for future programming languages.

Theoretical Foundations: Logic and Mathematics

Both Ada and Babbage were deeply influenced by the prevailing mathematical theories of their time. Babbage's work was grounded in the principles of calculus and number theory, while Ada drew inspiration from her studies in mathematics, particularly in the realms of logic and algorithmic processes. Their shared background in mathematics enabled them to approach the Analytical Engine from complementary angles—Babbage focused on mechanical design and functionality, while Ada explored the implications of its programming capabilities.

The interplay between their ideas can be illustrated through the concept of a function in mathematics, which Ada recognized as a key element of programming. A function can be defined as:

$$f(x) = ax^2 + bx + c$$

where a, b, and c are constants. Ada saw that the Analytical Engine could be programmed to calculate the values of such functions, thereby transforming mathematical concepts into computational processes.

Innovative Problem-Solving: A Case Study

To illustrate the collaborative spirit of Ada and Babbage, consider the problem of calculating the Fibonacci sequence, a series where each number is the sum of the two preceding ones:

$$F(n) = F(n-1) + F(n-2) \quad \text{with} \quad F(0) = 0, \ F(1) = 1$$

While Babbage focused on the mechanical implementation of such calculations, Ada's approach involved creating a systematic method to express the algorithm. She recognized that the Analytical Engine could be programmed to compute Fibonacci numbers by utilizing a series of conditional statements and iterative loops, thereby exemplifying the essence of programming.

The Legacy of Their Innovations

The parallel paths of Ada and Babbage's innovations did not culminate in immediate recognition during their lifetimes; however, their contributions laid the foundation for modern computing. Babbage's design of the Analytical Engine, though never fully realized in his time, introduced concepts that are still relevant in computer architecture today. Ada's foresight in programming and algorithm design established her legacy as the world's first programmer.

In conclusion, the synergy between Ada Lovelace and Charles Babbage was a powerful catalyst for innovation in the 19th century. Their collaborative efforts not only advanced the field of mathematics and computing but also challenged the societal norms of their time, paving the way for future generations of programmers and engineers. The parallel paths of their innovations serve as a testament to the importance of collaboration, creativity, and vision in the pursuit of technological advancement.

Ada's Collaboration with Charles Babbage

The Meeting of Two Brilliant Minds

In the early 19th century, a remarkable convergence of intellects occurred when Ada Lovelace met Charles Babbage, the man who would become her mentor and collaborator in the nascent field of computing. This meeting was not merely a chance encounter; it was the beginning of a partnership that would change the course of technology forever.

Ada, born in 1815 to the infamous poet Lord Byron and Lady Anne Isabella Milbanke, was raised in an environment that valued education and intellectual rigor. Her mother, determined to steer Ada away from the perceived madness of her father, emphasized mathematics and logic in Ada's upbringing. This foundation would prove crucial when she crossed paths with Babbage, a mathematician and inventor who was already making waves with his designs for a mechanical computer known as the Analytical Engine.

The meeting took place in 1833 at a dinner party hosted by Ada's mother. Babbage, who was already celebrated for his work on the Difference Engine, was invited to speak about his latest invention. Ada, then just 17 years old, was captivated by Babbage's ideas. She later recalled that it was as if she had found a kindred spirit, someone who shared her passion for mathematics and the potential of machines to perform complex calculations.

This initial interaction sparked a series of correspondences between Ada and Babbage, where they exchanged ideas about mathematics, engineering, and the future of computation. Their letters reveal a profound mutual respect and intellectual curiosity. Babbage recognized Ada's extraordinary talent, often referring to her as "the Enchantress of Numbers." He was impressed by her ability to grasp complex mathematical concepts and her visionary outlook on the potential of his Analytical Engine.

To illustrate the depth of their collaboration, we can examine a key mathematical problem they tackled together: the calculation of Bernoulli numbers. Babbage had devised a method for calculating these numbers using his Analytical Engine, but it was Ada who saw the broader implications of this work. She proposed a series of algorithms that would allow the machine to perform this calculation efficiently.

The Bernoulli numbers, denoted as B_n, are a sequence of rational numbers important in number theory and have applications in various fields such as combinatorics and numerical analysis. The recursive formula for calculating Bernoulli numbers is given by:

$$B_n = \sum_{k=0}^{n} \binom{n}{k} B_k \cdot \frac{1}{n+1}$$

where $\binom{n}{k}$ is the binomial coefficient. Ada's insight into how the Analytical Engine could be programmed to compute these numbers was revolutionary. She recognized that the machine could not only perform arithmetic but could also manipulate symbols and execute a sequence of operations based on a set of instructions—essentially laying the groundwork for modern programming.

Ada's notes on the Analytical Engine included what is now considered the first algorithm intended for implementation on a machine. This algorithm was a series of steps to compute Bernoulli numbers, showcasing her understanding of both the theoretical and practical aspects of computation. It is said that she wrote:

"The Analytical Engine does not occupy common ground with mere calculating machines. It holds within itself the power of thought."

This statement reflects her visionary perspective that machines could extend beyond mere calculation to become tools for complex reasoning and problem-solving.

Their collaboration was not without challenges. Babbage's ambitious designs for the Analytical Engine were met with skepticism and financial difficulties, and the project was never completed during their lifetimes. However, the intellectual partnership between Ada and Babbage was a beacon of innovation in a time when the field of computing was still in its infancy.

In summary, the meeting of Ada Lovelace and Charles Babbage marked a pivotal moment in the history of technology. Their collaboration exemplified the power of combining creative thought with mathematical precision. Ada's contributions to the development of the Analytical Engine not only advanced the field of computing but also established her as the first programmer, a legacy that continues to inspire generations of innovators. As we reflect on their partnership, it becomes clear that the synergy between these two brilliant minds was instrumental in shaping the future of technology.

Ada's Role in the Development of the Analytical Engine

Ada Lovelace's involvement in the development of Charles Babbage's Analytical Engine was not just a matter of collaboration; it was a transformative partnership that would shape the future of computing. Lovelace's unique perspective as a mathematician, her poetic sensibilities, and her visionary ideas allowed her to grasp the machine's potential far beyond mere calculations.

Understanding the Analytical Engine

The Analytical Engine was designed as a general-purpose mechanical computer, capable of performing any calculation given the right instructions. Babbage envisioned a machine that could carry out operations using a series of gears and levers, and he meticulously designed its components, which included an arithmetic unit, control flow, and memory. The engine's ability to store numbers and perform operations on them was revolutionary.

Mathematically, the Analytical Engine was based on the concept of a *Turing machine*, which laid the groundwork for modern computer science. The foundational operations could be expressed in terms of mathematical functions, such as:

$$f(x) = ax^2 + bx + c$$

where a, b, and c are constants. The Analytical Engine could compute such functions using its mechanical components.

Ada's Contributions

Ada Lovelace's primary contribution to the Analytical Engine was her understanding of how to program it. She realized that the machine could be instructed to perform not only arithmetic calculations but also to manipulate symbols and process complex algorithms. This insight was encapsulated in her notes on Babbage's design, which included what is now recognized as the first algorithm intended for implementation on a computer.

In her famous notes, she described a method for calculating Bernoulli numbers, which can be expressed in a recursive manner. The algorithm can be represented as follows:

$$B_n = \sum_{k=0}^{n} \frac{(-1)^k}{k!} \cdot \binom{n}{k} \cdot B_k$$

where B_n denotes the n-th Bernoulli number. This recursive relationship showcases the power of the Analytical Engine to handle complex mathematical concepts.

Collaboration with Babbage

Lovelace and Babbage exchanged a series of letters that served as a foundation for their collaborative work. These correspondences revealed the depth of their discussions regarding the potential of the Analytical Engine. Lovelace's ability to articulate her thoughts clearly and her enthusiasm for the machine's possibilities impressed Babbage, who recognized her as a valuable partner.

One of the most significant aspects of Ada's role was her ability to foresee the implications of the Analytical Engine's design. She famously stated that the machine could be programmed to create music, graphics, and even complex forms of art, thus anticipating the multifaceted nature of future computing technologies.

The Lovelace Note

The Lovelace Note, a set of annotations she made on Babbage's work, is often cited as the first instance of computer programming. In this note, she outlined the steps necessary to compute Bernoulli numbers and provided a detailed account of how the Analytical Engine would execute these instructions. Her foresight in recognizing that the machine could be programmed to perform tasks beyond mere calculation was groundbreaking.

To illustrate, Lovelace wrote:

> "The Analytical Engine does not occupy common ground with mere calculating machines. It holds within it the power to create, to generate, and to express."

This perspective positioned her as the first computer programmer, as she was not merely writing a sequence of operations but was conceptualizing a new way of thinking about machines and their capabilities.

Challenges and Limitations

Despite her groundbreaking contributions, Lovelace faced numerous challenges. The Analytical Engine was never completed during her lifetime, and the complexities of Babbage's designs often led to frustrations and misunderstandings. Lovelace's writings were also met with skepticism by some contemporaries who struggled to comprehend the implications of her ideas.

Moreover, the societal norms of the 19th century posed additional barriers. As a woman in a male-dominated field, Lovelace had to navigate the challenges of being taken seriously in her work. Nevertheless, her contributions laid the groundwork for future generations of programmers and mathematicians.

Conclusion

Ada Lovelace's role in the development of the Analytical Engine was pivotal. Her visionary ideas and innovative programming concepts not only highlighted the machine's potential but also established her as a key figure in the history of computing. By recognizing the Analytical Engine's ability to manipulate symbols and perform complex calculations, Lovelace transcended the limitations of her time and became a pioneer in the field of computer science.

As we reflect on her contributions, we are reminded of the importance of visionaries like Ada Lovelace in shaping the future of technology. Her legacy continues to inspire countless individuals in the fields of mathematics, computer science, and beyond.

The Collaborative Process between Ada and Babbage

The collaboration between Ada Lovelace and Charles Babbage is often regarded as one of the most significant partnerships in the history of computing. Their relationship was not merely that of mentor and student; it was a dynamic interplay of ideas and innovations that set the groundwork for modern programming. This section delves into the nature of their collaboration, highlighting how their combined efforts led to groundbreaking advancements in computational theory.

The Meeting of Two Brilliant Minds

Ada Lovelace first met Charles Babbage in 1833, at a dinner party hosted by the inventor and mathematician, Sir David Brewster. Babbage was already well-known for his design of the Difference Engine, a mechanical calculator intended to compute polynomial functions. Ada, then a young woman with a burgeoning interest in mathematics, was immediately captivated by Babbage's work. Their initial discussions revealed a shared enthusiasm for mathematics and a mutual respect for each other's intellects.

Ada's Role in the Development of the Analytical Engine

While Babbage's Difference Engine was a remarkable invention, it was his later project, the Analytical Engine, that truly captured Ada's imagination. The Analytical Engine was designed to be a general-purpose computing machine, capable of performing any calculation given the appropriate input. Its architecture included components such as a "store" (memory) and a "mill" (processing unit), akin to modern computers.

Ada recognized the potential of the Analytical Engine not just as a calculator but as a device that could manipulate symbols and perform complex operations beyond mere arithmetic. In her work with Babbage, she became instrumental in articulating these ideas, effectively laying the groundwork for what we now understand as programming.

The Collaborative Process

The collaborative process between Ada and Babbage can be characterized by several key elements:

- **Correspondence:** The primary mode of their collaboration was through an extensive exchange of letters. These letters not only documented their discussions about the Analytical Engine but also included Ada's insights and suggestions for its design and functionality. Their correspondence was filled with mathematical notations, diagrams, and theoretical explorations, showcasing the depth of their intellectual engagement.

+ **Conceptual Development:** Ada's contributions to the Analytical Engine went beyond mere calculations. She envisioned the machine as a tool for manipulating symbols in accordance with rules, which could lead to the creation of music, art, and even poetry. This conceptual leap was revolutionary, as it framed computation as a creative process rather than a purely mechanical one.

+ **The Lovelace Note:** Perhaps the most significant product of their collaboration is the "Lovelace Note," which Ada wrote in 1843 as a translation of an article by the Italian mathematician Luigi Federico Federico Federico. In this note, Ada elaborated on Babbage's ideas and included what is now recognized as the first algorithm intended for implementation on a machine—specifically, an algorithm for calculating Bernoulli numbers. This was a groundbreaking moment in the history of computing, as it marked the first time a machine was programmed to perform a complex calculation.

$$B_n = \sum_{k=0}^{n} \binom{n}{k} B_k \cdot \frac{1}{k+1} \tag{65}$$

where B_n are the Bernoulli numbers, $\binom{n}{k}$ is the binomial coefficient, and the summation runs over all k from 0 to n.

+ **Mutual Influence:** The interaction between Ada and Babbage was not one-sided. While Ada provided insights into the potential applications of the Analytical Engine, Babbage's technical expertise helped refine her ideas. This synergy allowed them to push the boundaries of what was possible in their time. For instance, Babbage's insistence on precision and detail in the design of the Analytical Engine complemented Ada's imaginative vision, resulting in a more robust understanding of the machine's capabilities.

+ **Challenges and Setbacks:** Despite their fruitful collaboration, Ada and Babbage faced significant challenges. Babbage struggled with funding and support for his projects, which often led to frustrations and delays. Ada, meanwhile, had to navigate societal expectations and personal health issues that impeded her ability to work consistently. However, their shared passion for mathematics and innovation helped them overcome these obstacles, allowing them to continue their collaboration.

The Impact of Their Collaboration

The collaboration between Ada Lovelace and Charles Babbage was not just a historical footnote; it laid the foundation for future developments in computer science and programming. Ada's insights into the potential of the Analytical Engine transcended its mechanical capabilities, envisioning a future where machines could perform a variety of tasks, from calculations to creative endeavors.

Their work together also highlighted the importance of interdisciplinary collaboration, combining mathematics, engineering, and creativity. This approach is still relevant today, as modern technology continues to evolve at the intersection of various fields.

In conclusion, the collaborative process between Ada Lovelace and Charles Babbage was a remarkable partnership that not only advanced the understanding of computational machines but also redefined the role of women in science and technology. Their legacy continues to inspire generations of programmers and innovators, reminding us of the power of collaboration in the pursuit of knowledge and creativity.

The Letters and Correspondence between Ada and Babbage

The correspondence between Ada Lovelace and Charles Babbage is not just a historical footnote; it is a treasure trove of intellectual exchange that laid the groundwork for modern computing. Their letters, filled with mathematical insights, personal anecdotes, and collaborative spirit, reveal a partnership that transcended the norms of their time. In this section, we will explore the significance of their correspondence, the mathematical concepts they discussed, and the impact of their collaboration on the development of the Analytical Engine.

The Nature of Their Correspondence

Ada and Babbage's letters were characterized by a unique blend of mathematical rigor and personal warmth. Their exchanges often began with pleasantries but quickly delved into the complexities of mathematics and engineering. For example, in one of her early letters, Ada expressed her fascination with Babbage's work on the Analytical Engine, stating:

"I am so delighted with your wonderful engine, that I can hardly contain myself. It seems to me the very embodiment of the mathematical spirit."

This enthusiasm was reciprocated by Babbage, who recognized Ada's exceptional intellect. Their letters became a platform for discussing not only the technical specifications of the engine but also the philosophical implications of computing.

Mathematical Discussions

The correspondence between Ada and Babbage was rich with mathematical discourse. One of the most notable discussions revolved around the concept of algorithms. Ada famously articulated the idea of an algorithm as a set of instructions for the Analytical Engine to follow. In her notes, she wrote:

$$\text{Algorithm} = \text{Input} \rightarrow \text{Processing} \rightarrow \text{Output} \tag{66}$$

This simple yet profound equation encapsulates the essence of programming. Ada's ability to conceptualize an algorithm in this manner demonstrated her deep understanding of the potential of Babbage's machine.

Furthermore, their letters often included mathematical problems that Ada would solve, showcasing her aptitude. For instance, she tackled the problem of calculating Bernoulli numbers, which she presented in one of her letters to Babbage:

$$B_n = \sum_{k=0}^{n} \binom{n}{k} \frac{1}{k+1} \quad \text{for } n \geq 0 \tag{67}$$

This exploration of Bernoulli numbers not only highlighted her mathematical prowess but also underscored her enthusiasm for the Analytical Engine's capabilities.

The Lovelace Note

Perhaps the most famous product of their correspondence is the "Lovelace Note," which Ada appended to her translation of an article by Italian mathematician Luigi Federico Federico. In this note, she elaborated on the potential applications of the Analytical Engine, proposing that it could go beyond mere calculations:

"The Analytical Engine does not occupy common ground with mere calculating machines. It holds within its grasp the power to manipulate symbols and, in doing so, to create art, music, and even poetry."

This visionary perspective was revolutionary for her time and illustrated her understanding of the broader implications of computing technology.

Personal Anecdotes and Support

Beyond mathematics, their letters also revealed a personal bond. Ada often sought Babbage's guidance and support in her endeavors. In one letter, she confided about her struggles with societal expectations, writing:

"How can I reconcile my passion for mathematics with the constraints placed upon me as a woman in society? Your encouragement means the world to me."

Babbage's responses were always encouraging, reinforcing Ada's belief in her abilities and the importance of their work together. This mutual support was vital in an era when women faced significant barriers in academia and professional life.

The Impact of Their Correspondence

The letters exchanged between Ada Lovelace and Charles Babbage were instrumental in shaping the future of computing. Their collaboration not only advanced the design and conceptualization of the Analytical Engine but also laid the foundation for the field of computer programming.

Ada's insights into algorithms and her visionary ideas about the capabilities of computing machines were groundbreaking. Their correspondence exemplifies how two brilliant minds, despite the societal constraints of their time, could create a legacy that continues to inspire generations of mathematicians, engineers, and computer scientists.

In conclusion, the letters and correspondence between Ada Lovelace and Charles Babbage were more than mere exchanges; they were a dialogue that bridged mathematics, engineering, and personal connection. Their collaboration exemplifies the power of intellectual partnership and the importance of nurturing creativity and innovation, especially in the face of adversity. As we reflect on their correspondence, we are reminded of the enduring impact of their ideas and the legacy they left behind in the world of technology.

The Mutual Influence of Ada and Babbage's Ideas

The collaboration between Ada Lovelace and Charles Babbage was not merely a partnership; it was a dynamic interplay of ideas that would ultimately shape the future of computing. Their relationship was characterized by a mutual respect for each other's intellect and a shared vision of what computing could become. In this section, we delve into how their ideas influenced one another, leading to groundbreaking innovations in the field of mathematics and programming.

The Convergence of Mathematical Thought

At the heart of their collaboration was a shared fascination with mathematics. Babbage, often referred to as the "father of the computer," was deeply engrossed in the design of the Analytical Engine, a mechanical device that could perform any calculation. Ada, on the other hand, brought a unique perspective to the table, viewing the Analytical Engine not just as a calculating machine but as a tool for creating art and music through numbers.

Their discussions often revolved around the mathematical principles underlying the Engine's operation. For instance, Babbage's work on algorithms was complemented by Ada's understanding of how these algorithms could be expressed in a more abstract form. This led to the development of what we now recognize as programming concepts.

$$f(x) = \sum_{n=0}^{\infty} a_n x^n$$

This equation, representing a power series, illustrates how mathematical functions can be computed through iterative processes, a principle that Ada would later apply to her own programming notes.

The Development of the Analytical Engine

Babbage's Analytical Engine was designed to perform a variety of mathematical operations, including addition, subtraction, multiplication, and division. However, it was Ada who recognized the potential of the Engine to go beyond mere arithmetic. She envisioned a machine capable of manipulating symbols in accordance with rules, thus laying the groundwork for modern programming.

In her notes, Ada famously wrote about the Engine's ability to create a sequence of Bernoulli numbers, demonstrating her understanding of complex mathematical concepts. The equation for the n-th Bernoulli number, B_n, is given by:

$$B_n = \frac{1}{n!} \sum_{k=0}^{n} \binom{n}{k} B_k$$

This equation showcases the iterative nature of mathematical computation, a principle that Ada would apply in her programming efforts.

A Shared Vision of Computing

Both Ada and Babbage shared a vision of a future where machines could perform tasks that were previously thought to be the exclusive domain of humans. Babbage's concept of the Analytical Engine was revolutionary, but it was Ada's imaginative interpretations that added depth to his ideas. She believed that the Engine could be programmed to perform complex tasks, such as composing music or generating graphics, which was a radical departure from the conventional view of machines as mere calculators.

Ada's insights into the Engine's capabilities were informed by her background in mathematics and her understanding of the arts. She famously stated,

> "The Analytical Engine has no pretensions to originate anything. It can do whatever we know how to order it to perform."

This quote encapsulates the essence of their collaboration: Babbage provided the framework, while Ada infused it with creativity and vision.

The Legacy of Their Ideas

The mutual influence of Ada and Babbage's ideas extended far beyond their time. Their collaboration laid the foundation for what we now recognize as computer science. The concept of algorithms, as developed by Babbage, was further refined by Ada's understanding of how these algorithms could be implemented in a programmable format.

To illustrate the impact of their ideas, consider the modern concept of a function in programming, which can be defined as:

$$f : A \to B$$

where A is the set of inputs, and B is the set of outputs. This notion of functions as mappings between sets can be traced back to their discussions on the Analytical Engine and its potential for computation.

In summary, the mutual influence of Ada Lovelace and Charles Babbage's ideas represents a unique confluence of mathematical rigor and creative vision. Their collaboration not only advanced the field of mathematics but also set the stage for the development of programming as we know it today. The legacy of their partnership continues to inspire generations of mathematicians and computer scientists, reminding us that innovation often arises from the synthesis of diverse perspectives.

Ada's Contributions to Babbage's Work

Ada Lovelace's contributions to Charles Babbage's work on the Analytical Engine were not merely supportive; they were foundational. While Babbage is often credited as the father of the computer, it was Lovelace who recognized the potential of his invention to do more than mere calculations. Her insights and theoretical applications laid the groundwork for what we now consider programming.

Understanding the Analytical Engine

To appreciate Lovelace's contributions, one must first understand Babbage's Analytical Engine. Designed in the 1830s, this mechanical computer was revolutionary for its time. It featured components akin to modern computers, including an arithmetic logic unit (ALU), control flow through conditional branching and loops, and memory storage. The Engine's ability to perform any calculation that could be expressed in a series of mathematical operations set it apart from earlier calculating machines.

The Analytical Engine was designed to operate using punched cards, a concept borrowed from the Jacquard loom, which used similar cards to control the weaving of patterns. Babbage envisioned a machine that could not only compute numbers but also manipulate symbols, making it a universal computing device.

Ada's Insight into Programming

Lovelace's most significant contribution was her understanding of how to program the Analytical Engine. In her correspondence with Babbage, she recognized that the Engine could do more than compute; it could be programmed to perform complex tasks. This realization led her to create what is now considered the first algorithm intended for implementation on a machine.

In her notes on Babbage's work, she described an algorithm for calculating Bernoulli numbers, a sequence of rational numbers that are significant in number theory and have applications in various mathematical contexts. The algorithm can be expressed as follows:

$$B_n = \sum_{k=0}^{n} \binom{n}{k} B_k \cdot \frac{1}{k+1} \tag{68}$$

Where B_n represents the n-th Bernoulli number, and $\binom{n}{k}$ is the binomial coefficient. Lovelace meticulously outlined the steps necessary to compute these numbers using the Analytical Engine, demonstrating her deep understanding of both the mathematics involved and the machine's capabilities.

The Lovelace Note

One of the most famous parts of Lovelace's contributions is encapsulated in what is now referred to as the "Lovelace Note." In her annotations on Babbage's description of the Analytical Engine, she wrote:

> "The Analytical Engine does not operate with the numbers themselves, but with the symbols representing the numbers; and it is capable of performing operations with these symbols, just as easily as it can with the numbers."

This insight was revolutionary. Lovelace understood that the Engine could manipulate not just numbers but also any form of data represented symbolically. This foresight into the Engine's capabilities foreshadowed modern programming languages, where data types and structures are manipulated through symbolic representation.

Collaboration with Babbage

Lovelace's relationship with Babbage was characterized by mutual respect and intellectual collaboration. She was not merely a passive observer; she actively engaged with Babbage's ideas, providing critical feedback and innovative suggestions. For instance, she proposed enhancements to the Engine's design, suggesting improvements in the efficiency of its operations.

Moreover, Lovelace's letters to Babbage reveal a dynamic exchange of ideas. She often challenged Babbage's notions, pushing him to think beyond the mechanical aspects of his invention and consider its broader implications. This collaborative spirit is evident in their correspondence, where they discussed not only technical details but also philosophical questions regarding the nature of computation and the future of machines.

Impact on Future Generations

Lovelace's contributions to Babbage's work extend far beyond their immediate context. Her foresight into the capabilities of the Analytical Engine laid the groundwork for future developments in computing. By recognizing that machines could manipulate symbols and not just numbers, she opened the door to the development of programming languages and software engineering as we know them today.

The principles she articulated regarding algorithms, data representation, and the potential for machines to perform tasks beyond mere calculation are foundational to modern computer science. Her work has inspired countless generations of programmers, mathematicians, and engineers, solidifying her legacy as the first programmer in history.

In conclusion, Ada Lovelace's contributions to Charles Babbage's Analytical Engine were instrumental in shaping the future of computing. Her visionary insights and pioneering algorithms not only advanced Babbage's work but also laid the groundwork for the field of computer science. Lovelace's legacy is a testament to the power of collaboration and innovation, reminding us that the journey of technology is often paved by the contributions of brilliant minds working together.

Ada's Deep Understanding of Babbage's Designs

Ada Lovelace's profound comprehension of Charles Babbage's designs for the Analytical Engine was not merely a matter of intellectual curiosity; it was a fusion of mathematical insight and visionary thinking that positioned her as the first computer programmer. Her ability to grasp the complexities of Babbage's concepts allowed her to see beyond the mechanical apparatus to the potential of what these machines could achieve.

At the heart of Babbage's designs was the concept of the Analytical Engine, a revolutionary machine that could perform any calculation or process any data. It was designed to be programmable using punched cards, a method adapted from the Jacquard loom, which used cards to control the weaving of patterns. This innovation was pivotal, as it introduced the idea that machines could be instructed to perform tasks through a series of commands, much like modern programming.

$$\text{Output} = f(\text{Input}, \text{Program}) \tag{69}$$

This equation encapsulates the essence of what the Analytical Engine was intended to accomplish: it could take an input, process it according to a specific program, and generate an output. Ada recognized that this relationship was foundational to the concept of computation, and her writings reflect an understanding of the potential implications of programmable machines.

One of the most significant aspects of Babbage's design was the separation of the engine's memory (the store) from its processing unit (the mill). This architecture is analogous to modern computer systems, where data storage and processing are distinct components. Ada's recognition of this separation allowed her to appreciate the machine's capacity for complex calculations and data manipulation.

$$\text{Total Calculation} = \sum_{i=1}^{n} \text{Operation}_i \tag{70}$$

In this equation, each operation performed by the Analytical Engine could be seen as part of a larger summation of calculations. Ada's ability to visualize these operations as part of a sequence demonstrated her understanding of algorithmic processes, which are fundamental to programming today.

Ada's insights were further exemplified in her work on the Bernoulli numbers. In her notes on the Analytical Engine, she wrote an algorithm for calculating these numbers, which are a sequence of rational numbers with deep connections to number theory and mathematical analysis. Her algorithm is often considered the first instance of a computer program, showcasing her ability to translate mathematical concepts into a form that the Analytical Engine could execute.

$$B_n = \sum_{k=0}^{\infty} \frac{(-1)^k}{k!} \left(\frac{n}{k}\right)^k \tag{71}$$

In this formula, B_n represents the n-th Bernoulli number, and Ada's program would have iterated through the necessary calculations to derive these values, demonstrating her grasp of both the mathematical theory and the practical application of Babbage's machine.

Moreover, Ada's correspondence with Babbage revealed her deep engagement with his ideas. She often posed insightful questions and provided feedback that reflected her understanding of the technical challenges Babbage faced. For instance, she inquired about the engine's capacity to perform not just numerical calculations but also to manipulate symbols and perform logical operations, a notion that foreshadowed the development of symbolic computation.

This understanding was not without its challenges. Babbage's designs were ambitious, but they were also fraught with technical difficulties that often hindered their realization. Ada's ability to appreciate these complexities and her unwavering belief in the potential of the Analytical Engine set her apart from her contemporaries. She envisioned a future where machines could augment human intelligence, a perspective that was revolutionary for her time.

In her notes, she famously stated:

"The Analytical Engine does not occupy common ground with mere calculating machines. It holds within itself the power of the future, a future where machines can think and create."

This assertion highlights her foresight and her understanding of the implications of Babbage's designs. Ada Lovelace was not merely a passive observer; she was an active participant in the discourse surrounding early computing, and her deep understanding of Babbage's designs allowed her to contribute meaningfully to the field of mathematics and computing.

In summary, Ada's profound comprehension of Babbage's designs was characterized by her ability to see the potential of the Analytical Engine as more than a mechanical calculator. She recognized it as a programmable device capable of executing complex algorithms, paving the way for future advancements in computer science. Her legacy as the first programmer is a testament to her intellectual prowess and her visionary outlook on the future of technology.

The Impact of the Lovelace Note on Babbage's Legacy

The Lovelace Note, a remarkable document penned by Ada Lovelace in 1843, is often heralded as one of the most significant contributions to the field of computing and is pivotal in understanding Charles Babbage's legacy. This note, which accompanied her translation of an article by the Italian mathematician Luigi Federico Federico, not only encapsulated her insights into the Analytical Engine but also illuminated the potential of computing far beyond mere calculation.

Context of the Lovelace Note

To grasp the full impact of the Lovelace Note, it is essential to first understand the context in which it was written. Babbage's Analytical Engine was a groundbreaking mechanical computer design that was never fully realized during his lifetime. However, the theoretical framework he laid out was revolutionary, proposing a machine capable of performing any calculation given the appropriate programming. Lovelace, intrigued by Babbage's vision, translated the article and expanded upon it, adding her own notes that would later become known as the Lovelace Note.

Content of the Lovelace Note

In the Lovelace Note, Ada articulated her understanding of the Analytical Engine's capabilities, which included the ability to manipulate symbols and execute complex algorithms. She famously stated:

> "The Analytical Engine has no pretensions to originate anything. It can do whatever we know how to order it to perform."

This assertion highlights a crucial distinction: while the Analytical Engine could perform calculations, it lacked the ability to create or innovate independently. This insight foreshadowed later discussions about the nature of artificial intelligence and machine learning, emphasizing the role of human input in guiding computational processes.

Mathematical Significance

The Lovelace Note also contained what is considered the first algorithm intended for implementation on a machine. This algorithm was designed to compute Bernoulli numbers, showcasing not only Lovelace's mathematical prowess but also her foresight regarding the computational potential of the Analytical Engine. The algorithm can be expressed mathematically as:

$$B_n = \sum_{k=0}^{n} \binom{n}{k} B_k$$

where B_n represents the n-th Bernoulli number. This formula illustrates the recursive nature of the computation, which is a hallmark of programming logic.

Theoretical Implications

The implications of the Lovelace Note extend into the realms of computer science and programming theory. Lovelace's recognition of the Analytical Engine's ability to process symbols rather than just numbers laid the groundwork for future developments in programming languages and software engineering. Her assertion that the machine could manipulate not just numbers but also letters and symbols presaged the development of modern programming paradigms where data types are diverse and operations are not limited to arithmetic.

Babbage's Legacy Reframed

The Lovelace Note reframed Babbage's legacy from that of merely a mechanical inventor to that of a pioneer in the conceptualization of computing. While Babbage designed the machine, it was Lovelace who recognized its broader implications and potential applications. The note serves as a testament to the collaborative nature of innovation, illustrating how Babbage's ideas were enriched and expanded through Lovelace's insights.

Historical Recognition

Historically, the Lovelace Note has gained recognition not only for its content but also for its role in highlighting the often-overlooked contributions of women in technology. Ada Lovelace's work has led to her being celebrated as the first computer programmer, and the Lovelace Note is central to this narrative. It emphasizes the importance of diverse perspectives in technological advancement, advocating for the inclusion of women in STEM fields.

Conclusion

In conclusion, the Lovelace Note is not merely an appendix to Babbage's work; it is a cornerstone that reshapes our understanding of his contributions to computing. It encapsulates a vision of technology that transcends calculation, touching on creativity, innovation, and the ethical considerations of machine intelligence. The impact of the Lovelace Note on Babbage's legacy is profound, as it not only honors his mechanical genius but also celebrates the intellectual partnership that led to the birth of programming as we know it today.

As we reflect on the Lovelace Note, we recognize it as a pivotal moment in the history of computing, one that invites us to continue exploring the boundaries of technology and the human mind.

The Synergistic Relationship between Ada and Babbage's Work

The partnership between Ada Lovelace and Charles Babbage stands as a pioneering example of collaboration in the field of computing. Their unique synergy was not merely a meeting of two brilliant minds; it was a harmonious blend of mathematical prowess and innovative engineering that laid the groundwork for modern computing. This section explores how their respective strengths complemented one another, leading to groundbreaking advancements in computation.

Complementary Skills and Perspectives

Babbage, often referred to as the "father of the computer," was an engineer and mathematician with a vision for mechanical computation. He designed the Analytical Engine, a revolutionary device that could perform any calculation given the right programming. However, his engineering genius alone could not fully articulate the potential of his invention. This is where Ada's contributions became crucial.

Ada Lovelace possessed a deep understanding of mathematics and a creative imagination that allowed her to see beyond the mechanical aspects of Babbage's designs. She recognized that the Analytical Engine could do more than just arithmetic; it could manipulate symbols and process complex algorithms. This insight was revolutionary and formed the basis for what we now recognize as programming.

The Lovelace Note and Its Significance

The collaboration between Ada and Babbage culminated in what is now famously known as the "Lovelace Note." In 1843, Ada translated an article written by the Italian mathematician Luigi Federico Federico, adding her own notes and annotations. Among these, she included an algorithm for calculating Bernoulli numbers, which is considered the first computer program. The significance of this contribution cannot be overstated, as it demonstrated the potential for machines to perform tasks that required logical reasoning, not just mechanical computation.

The algorithm can be expressed in the following form:

$$B_n = \sum_{k=0}^{n} \binom{n}{k} \cdot B_k \cdot \frac{1}{n+1-k} \tag{72}$$

where B_n represents the n-th Bernoulli number, and $\binom{n}{k}$ is the binomial coefficient. This formula showcases Ada's ability to apply theoretical mathematics to practical computation, bridging the gap between abstract concepts and tangible results.

Mutual Influence on Ideas and Innovations

The relationship between Ada and Babbage was characterized by a mutual exchange of ideas that fueled their respective innovations. Babbage's designs inspired Ada's theoretical explorations, while Ada's insights prompted Babbage to refine his concepts. For instance, Ada proposed the idea of loops and conditional branching, which are fundamental principles in programming today. She envisioned a future where machines could not only execute instructions but also make decisions based on the data they processed.

This vision is encapsulated in Ada's famous assertion that the Analytical Engine could be programmed to "weave algebraic patterns just as the Jacquard loom weaves flowers and leaves." This metaphor highlights her understanding of the engine's potential to create complex outputs from simple inputs, a concept that is foundational in computer science.

Challenges and Triumphs in Collaboration

Despite their intellectual synergy, Ada and Babbage faced numerous challenges in their collaboration. The societal norms of the 19th century often marginalized women's contributions in science and technology, making it difficult for Ada to gain recognition for her work. Moreover, Babbage's ambitious projects were frequently hindered by financial and technical setbacks, which strained their partnership.

However, their determination to push the boundaries of knowledge and technology prevailed. Ada's unwavering support for Babbage's vision, combined with her own groundbreaking ideas, ultimately contributed to the legacy of the Analytical Engine as a precursor to modern computers. Their collaboration serves as a testament to the power of diverse perspectives in innovation.

Legacy of Their Synergistic Work

The synergistic relationship between Ada Lovelace and Charles Babbage has left an indelible mark on the history of computing. Their collaboration not only advanced the field of mathematics and engineering but also paved the way for future generations of programmers and engineers. The principles they established continue to inform contemporary programming languages and computational theories.

In recognizing their partnership, we celebrate the idea that true innovation often arises from collaboration. The interplay of Ada's imaginative programming concepts and Babbage's engineering genius exemplifies how diverse talents can converge to create something greater than the sum of their parts. As we continue to explore the realms of technology and computation, the legacy of Ada and Babbage remains a guiding light, inspiring future innovators to embrace collaboration in their pursuits.

In conclusion, the synergistic relationship between Ada Lovelace and Charles Babbage was a defining moment in the evolution of computing. Their combined efforts not only advanced the theoretical framework of programming but also set the stage for the technological advancements that followed. Their story serves as a reminder of the importance of collaboration, creativity, and the relentless pursuit of knowledge in shaping the future of technology.

The Analytical Engine: Ada's Vision Unleashed

Ada's Understanding of the Analytical Engine's Potential

Ada Lovelace had a profound understanding of the Analytical Engine's potential, which extended far beyond the mere mechanical computations it was designed to perform. Her insights into the machine's capabilities were revolutionary, allowing her to envision applications that would later define the field of computing.

At the heart of the Analytical Engine was the concept of programmability. Unlike its predecessors, which could only perform specific calculations, the Analytical Engine was designed to execute a sequence of operations based on instructions provided by a program. This programmability allowed it to handle complex calculations and even process symbolic data, a concept that was groundbreaking for its time.

$$\text{Output} = f(\text{Input}, \text{Program}) \tag{73}$$

In this equation, f represents the function defined by the program, which processes the input to produce the desired output. Ada recognized that by manipulating the program, one could alter the machine's operations and outcomes, thus enabling a vast array of applications.

One of Ada's most significant contributions was her realization that the Analytical Engine could be used not just for numerical calculations but also for more abstract tasks. In her notes, she famously stated that the machine could be programmed to manipulate symbols in accordance with rules, much like a composer writes music or a poet crafts verses. This understanding led her to create what is now known as the "Lovelace Note," where she detailed a method for calculating Bernoulli numbers using the Analytical Engine.

The process of calculating Bernoulli numbers can be expressed through a recursive relationship, which Ada elegantly translated into a sequence of instructions for the Analytical Engine:

$$B_n = \sum_{k=0}^{n} \binom{n}{k} B_k \cdot \frac{1}{n-k+1} \tag{74}$$

Where B_n represents the n-th Bernoulli number, and $\binom{n}{k}$ is the binomial coefficient. Ada's ability to convert complex mathematical concepts into a step-by-step program exemplified her deep understanding of the potential of the Analytical Engine.

Moreover, Ada envisioned the Analytical Engine as a tool for creativity and exploration. She wrote about its ability to create music, stating that it could compose complex musical pieces if provided with the right instructions. This notion of a machine not merely as a calculator but as a creative partner was radical and ahead of her time.

For example, if we consider a simple musical composition represented by a series of notes, Ada could have theorized a program that translates numerical values into musical notes, thereby allowing the Analytical Engine to generate melodies based on predefined algorithms:

$$\text{Note}(n) = \text{Base Frequency} \times 2^{(n/12)} \qquad (75)$$

Where n represents the number of semitones from the base frequency, illustrating how mathematical operations could yield artistic outputs.

Additionally, Ada's understanding of the Analytical Engine's potential included its ability to simulate complex systems and solve problems that required logical reasoning. She foresaw its application in fields such as physics and economics, where the ability to model and predict outcomes based on varying parameters would be invaluable. This foresight is encapsulated in her assertion that the machine could "do anything that can be done by a human mind."

In conclusion, Ada Lovelace's understanding of the Analytical Engine's potential was not limited to its mechanical capabilities; it encompassed a vision of a future where machines could augment human creativity and intellect. Her insights laid the groundwork for the concept of general-purpose computing and established her as a pioneer in the field of computer science. The Analytical Engine, through her eyes, was a gateway to a world of possibilities, transcending the boundaries of mathematics and entering the realms of art, science, and imagination.

Ada's Innovative Ideas for Programming the Analytical Engine

Ada Lovelace's visionary concepts for programming the Analytical Engine were not just groundbreaking for her time; they laid the foundational principles for modern computing. Her innovative ideas encompassed a range of theoretical and practical aspects that anticipated the complexities of programming long before the advent of electronic computers.

The Concept of Algorithms

At the heart of Ada's programming philosophy was the notion of algorithms. She recognized that the Analytical Engine could perform a sequence of operations based on instructions, which we now refer to as algorithms. Ada's most notable contribution was her realization that these algorithms could be expressed in a systematic way, much like mathematical formulas.

For example, consider the algorithm for calculating Bernoulli numbers, which Ada famously translated into a series of instructions for the Analytical Engine. The Bernoulli numbers B_n can be computed using the formula:

$$B_n = \sum_{k=0}^{n} \binom{n}{k} B_k \cdot \frac{1}{k+1}$$

In her notes, Ada outlined a step-by-step process for the Analytical Engine to follow, demonstrating how the engine could compute these numbers through a series of additions and multiplications. This was one of the first instances of a computer program, showcasing her foresight into the importance of structured programming.

The Use of Loops and Conditional Statements

Ada also introduced the idea of loops and conditional statements into her programming concepts. She understood that programming was not merely a linear process but could involve repeating certain operations and making decisions based on conditions. For instance, she proposed the use of a loop to iterate through a series of calculations, a concept that is now fundamental in programming languages.

An example of a loop might be expressed as follows:

```
FOR i\index{i} FROM 1 TO n\index{n} DO
    // Perform some operation
END FOR
```

This structure allows the engine to execute a block of code multiple times, which is essential for tasks such as summing a series or performing iterative calculations.

Data Representation and Storage

Ada's insights extended to data representation and storage as well. She envisioned a system where numbers and symbols could be represented in a way that the Analytical Engine could understand and manipulate. Her approach to data types was remarkably advanced; she suggested that the engine could handle not only numerical data but also symbols and even musical notes.

For instance, she proposed using a binary representation for numbers, which is the basis for modern computing. The binary system, where each digit can either be 0 or 1, can be expressed mathematically as follows:

$$N = \sum_{i=0}^{k} b_i \cdot 2^i$$

where b_i is the binary digit (0 or 1), and k is the highest power of 2 in the representation. This understanding of data representation was crucial for the development of programming languages and computer architecture.

Modularity and Reusability

Another innovative concept introduced by Ada was the idea of modularity in programming. She suggested that complex programs could be broken down into smaller, reusable modules or subroutines. This principle not only enhances the organization of code but also promotes efficiency and reduces redundancy.

For example, consider a module for calculating the factorial of a number n, which can be defined as:

$$n! = \begin{cases} 1 & \text{if } n = 0 \\ n \cdot (n-1)! & \text{if } n > 0 \end{cases}$$

By encapsulating this logic in a separate module, Ada's design would allow programmers to call this module whenever needed, thus promoting code reuse and simplifying complex programs.

Theoretical Implications and Future Vision

Ada Lovelace's innovative ideas were not merely theoretical; they anticipated the future of programming and computing. Her recognition of the potential of the Analytical Engine to go beyond mere calculation into realms of creativity and exploration was revolutionary. She famously stated that the engine could manipulate symbols in accordance with rules and that it could potentially create music or art.

This foresight into the capabilities of computing machines has been realized in modern programming languages that support object-oriented programming, functional programming, and even artificial intelligence. Ada's vision of a machine that could not only compute but also create has become a reality in today's digital landscape.

In conclusion, Ada Lovelace's innovative ideas for programming the Analytical Engine laid the groundwork for the field of computer science. Her understanding of algorithms, loops, data representation, modularity, and the potential for creative computing has inspired generations of programmers and continues to influence the development of technology today. Ada was not just the first programmer; she was a pioneer whose legacy is deeply embedded in the fabric of modern computing.

The Structure and Design of the Analytical Engine

The Analytical Engine, often hailed as the world's first general-purpose computer, was a groundbreaking concept envisioned by Charles Babbage in the 1830s. Ada Lovelace recognized the potential of this machine and contributed significantly to its theoretical underpinnings. This section delves into the intricate structure and design of the Analytical Engine, highlighting its components, functionality, and the innovative ideas that Ada Lovelace brought to the table.

Overview of the Analytical Engine's Architecture

The Analytical Engine was designed to perform a wide variety of calculations and operations, making it a versatile machine. The architecture of the Analytical Engine can be broken down into several key components:

- **The Store:** This was the memory unit of the Analytical Engine, capable of holding a vast amount of data. The Store was designed to hold 1,000 numbers, each consisting of 40 decimal digits, allowing for complex calculations.

- **The Mill:** This component functioned as the central processing unit (CPU) of the Analytical Engine. The Mill performed arithmetic operations, including addition, subtraction, multiplication, and division. It was capable of executing a sequence of instructions, similar to modern-day processors.

- **The Input and Output Mechanisms:** The Analytical Engine utilized punched cards for input, inspired by the Jacquard loom's use of cards to control weaving patterns. Output was generated through printing mechanisms, enabling the results of computations to be recorded.

- **The Control Unit:** This unit governed the operations of the Mill and the Store, directing the flow of data and instructions. It was responsible for managing the sequence of operations, akin to a modern control unit in a computer.

Mathematical Operations and Programming

At the heart of the Analytical Engine's design was its ability to perform mathematical operations through a series of instructions. The engine's programming was based on a set of operations that could be combined to solve complex problems. Ada Lovelace's vision for programming the Analytical Engine laid the foundation for modern programming concepts.

Basic Arithmetic Operations The Analytical Engine was capable of executing basic arithmetic operations, which can be expressed mathematically as follows:

$$C = A + B \quad \text{(Addition)} \tag{76}$$

$$C = A - B \quad \text{(Subtraction)} \tag{77}$$

$$C = A \times B \quad \text{(Multiplication)} \tag{78}$$

$$C = \frac{A}{B} \quad \text{(Division)} \tag{79}$$

Where A and B are operands, and C is the result of the operation. The Analytical Engine could chain these operations together to perform more complex calculations.

Conditional Operations and Loops One of the revolutionary aspects of the Analytical Engine was its ability to execute conditional operations and loops, allowing for more complex decision-making processes. Ada Lovelace recognized the potential for creating algorithms that could dictate the flow of calculations based on specific conditions.

For instance, a simple conditional operation could be expressed as:

$$\text{if } A > B \text{ then } C = A - B \text{ else } C = B - A \tag{80}$$

In addition, the concept of loops can be illustrated with the following pseudocode:

```
for i = 1 to n do
    C = C + i
end for
```

This ability to implement loops and conditions marked a significant advancement in the design of computational machines.

The Use of Punched Cards

The input mechanism of the Analytical Engine relied heavily on punched cards, which were used to input data and instructions. Each card represented a specific operation or set of operations, allowing the user to program the machine without the need for direct mechanical manipulation. The punched card system can be likened to modern programming languages, where code is written to instruct the machine.

Example of Punched Card Programming   To illustrate the programming process, consider a simple example where a series of operations are defined on punched cards:

+ Card 1: Input values for A and B

+ Card 2: Perform addition $C = A + B$

+ Card 3: Output the result C

This modular approach to programming allowed for greater flexibility and complexity in computations.

Theoretical Implications of the Analytical Engine's Design

The design of the Analytical Engine not only represented a technical achievement but also had profound theoretical implications for the future of computing. Ada Lovelace foresaw that the machine could go beyond mere calculations, envisioning its potential to manipulate symbols and perform tasks that were not strictly numerical.

Symbolic Manipulation   Lovelace's insight into the symbolic manipulation capabilities of the Analytical Engine laid the groundwork for the development of programming languages that we use today. She famously stated:

> "The Analytical Engine does not occupy common ground with mere calculating machines. It holds within itself the possibility of a new world, a world where symbols can be manipulated to create art, music, and more."

This perspective highlights the potential for computers to transcend their original purpose and become tools for creativity and innovation.

Conclusion

The structure and design of the Analytical Engine represent a monumental leap in the evolution of computing. With its innovative architecture, the Analytical Engine laid the foundation for modern computers, and Ada Lovelace's contributions to its programming and theoretical implications have solidified her legacy as the first programmer. The Analytical Engine was not merely a machine; it was a vision of the future, a future where computation could unlock the mysteries of the universe and inspire generations to come.

The Importance of Ada's Detailed Analysis

Ada Lovelace's contributions to the field of computing are often encapsulated by her visionary insights into the potential of the Analytical Engine. However, it is her meticulous and detailed analysis of this machine that truly underscores her role as the first programmer. In this section, we will explore the significance of Ada's analytical approach, the theoretical frameworks she employed, and the implications of her work for future generations of computer scientists.

Theoretical Foundations

At the core of Ada's analysis was her understanding of the principles of mathematics and logic. She recognized that the Analytical Engine was not merely a mechanical calculator but a machine capable of performing complex operations based on logical sequences. Ada's grasp of mathematical concepts allowed her to articulate the potential of the engine in a way that was both profound and prescient.

For instance, Ada wrote about the concept of *looping*—the ability for a machine to repeat a set of instructions until a certain condition was met. This foundational idea is crucial in modern programming languages, where loops are a fundamental construct. Ada's insight into this concept can be expressed mathematically as follows:

$$\text{Loop}(n) = \{\text{execute instruction}\} \quad \text{for } n \text{ iterations} \tag{81}$$

This equation highlights the iterative nature of programming, which Ada foresaw long before computers became ubiquitous.

Detailed Analysis of Algorithms

In her notes, Ada provided a detailed analysis of how the Analytical Engine could compute Bernoulli numbers, which is a classic example of algorithm design. She outlined the steps needed to perform this calculation, demonstrating her ability to break down complex processes into manageable parts. The algorithm can be represented in a simplified form as follows:

$$B_n = \sum_{k=0}^{n} \binom{n}{k} \cdot B_k \cdot \frac{1}{n - k + 1} \tag{82}$$

Here, B_n represents the n-th Bernoulli number, and $\binom{n}{k}$ is the binomial coefficient. Ada's work on this algorithm not only showcased her understanding of combinatorial mathematics but also illustrated her capability to translate theoretical concepts into practical applications for the Analytical Engine.

Implications of Ada's Analysis

The importance of Ada's detailed analysis extends far beyond her time. By articulating the potential of the Analytical Engine and providing a framework for algorithmic thinking, she laid the groundwork for future developments in computer science. Her work foreshadowed the emergence of programming languages that would dominate the field in the years to come.

Moreover, Ada's emphasis on the importance of thorough documentation and analysis in programming is a principle that remains relevant today. In modern software development, the practice of writing clear and detailed specifications is vital for ensuring that programs function as intended. Ada's insistence on this aspect of programming can be summarized in the following principle:

> A program must be well-documented and thoroughly analyzed to ensure its reliability and effectiveness.

This principle resonates with contemporary practices in software engineering, where code reviews and detailed documentation are essential components of the development process.

Examples of Ada's Analytical Techniques

Ada's analytical techniques can be exemplified through her use of diagrams and notations to represent the workings of the Analytical Engine. She created a method for visualizing data flow and operations, which can be likened to modern flowcharts used in programming today. For example, she might have represented a simple computational process as follows:

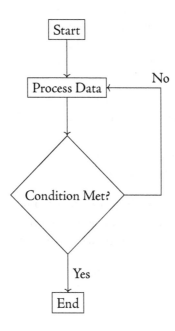

This visualization captures the essence of algorithmic flow, emphasizing the need for clarity and structure in programming. Ada's ability to represent complex ideas in a digestible format is a testament to her analytical prowess.

Conclusion

In conclusion, Ada Lovelace's detailed analysis of the Analytical Engine was not merely a reflection of her mathematical genius; it was a pioneering act that shaped the future of computing. Her insights into algorithms, looping structures, and the necessity of thorough documentation laid the foundation for modern programming practices. As we continue to navigate the complexities of technology, Ada's legacy serves as a reminder of the importance of analytical thinking and precision in the world of programming.

Her work encourages us to approach problem-solving with creativity and rigor, ensuring that the spirit of innovation she embodied remains alive in the hearts and minds of future generations of programmers.

Ada's Insight into the Analytical Engine's Computational Power

Ada Lovelace, often celebrated as the first computer programmer, possessed a remarkable understanding of the potential of Charles Babbage's Analytical Engine. This mechanical marvel was designed to perform a variety of mathematical calculations through a series of operations, and Ada's insights into its computational power were revolutionary for her time.

At the heart of the Analytical Engine was the concept of programmability, which allowed it to execute a sequence of instructions—essentially, what we would now call a program. Ada recognized that the Engine was not merely a calculator but a device capable of executing complex algorithms, thus expanding its functionality beyond simple arithmetic.

To understand Ada's insights, we must first explore the fundamental components of the Analytical Engine:

- **The Mill:** This is the Engine's central processing unit (CPU), where calculations and data manipulations occurred. It operated similarly to modern CPUs, performing arithmetic operations using gears and levers.

- **The Store:** This component functioned as memory, holding numbers and intermediate results. The Store could hold a considerable amount of data, allowing the Engine to handle complex calculations.

- **Input and Output Devices:** The Engine utilized punched cards (inspired by the Jacquard loom) for inputting data and instructions, while output could be achieved through various means, including printing results.

Ada's most significant contribution was her realization that the Analytical Engine could manipulate symbols, not just numbers. This insight is encapsulated in her famous notes, where she wrote about the potential for the Engine to process not only numerical data but also logical and abstract concepts.

To illustrate this, consider the mathematical function $f(x) = x^2 + 2x + 1$. Ada recognized that if the Analytical Engine could be programmed to recognize the symbols x, $+$, and $=$, it could evaluate this function for any given value of x. The process would involve a series of operations:

$$f(x) = x^2 + 2x + 1 \implies \begin{cases} \text{Calculate } x^2 \\ \text{Calculate } 2x \\ \text{Add results together} \\ \text{Output the result} \end{cases}$$

This ability to handle symbolic representation laid the groundwork for what we now understand as programming languages, where variables and operations are defined abstractly. Ada's foresight in recognizing the Engine's capacity to execute complex algorithms paved the way for future developments in computer science.

Moreover, Ada's analysis of the Engine's potential extended to the realm of looping and conditional operations. She foresaw that the Engine could be programmed to repeat certain operations or make decisions based on previous results—concepts that are foundational in modern programming. For example, she proposed a sequence of operations that could calculate Bernoulli numbers, a complex mathematical series that required iterative processes:

$$B_n = \sum_{k=0}^{n} \binom{n}{k} \cdot \frac{(-1)^k}{k+1}$$

Ada's notes outlined how the Analytical Engine could be instructed to compute these numbers through a series of steps, demonstrating her understanding of recursion and iterative computation long before these terms were coined.

In her correspondence with Babbage, Ada expressed her belief that the Engine could not only compute numbers but also create music and art, as it could manipulate symbols in various forms. She envisioned a future where machines could enhance human creativity, a notion that resonates with contemporary discussions on artificial intelligence and machine learning.

In conclusion, Ada Lovelace's insights into the Analytical Engine's computational power were groundbreaking. Her ability to conceptualize the Engine as a programmable device capable of executing complex algorithms, manipulating symbols, and performing iterative calculations was a significant leap forward in the understanding of computing. Her work laid the foundation for future generations of programmers and computer scientists, establishing her legacy as a visionary who saw beyond the limitations of her time.

As we continue to explore the capabilities of modern computing, we owe a debt of gratitude to Ada for her pioneering vision, which remains relevant in today's digital landscape.

The Skills and Knowledge Required to Program the Analytical Engine

To truly appreciate the monumental task of programming the Analytical Engine, one must first understand the unique blend of skills and knowledge that Ada Lovelace possessed. Programming in the 19th century was not merely a matter of writing code; it involved a deep understanding of mathematics, logic, and the intricacies of mechanical computation.

Mathematical Proficiency

At the core of Ada's programming capabilities was her exceptional mathematical proficiency. The Analytical Engine was designed to perform complex calculations, and programming it required a solid foundation in various branches of mathematics, including:

- **Arithmetic:** Understanding basic operations such as addition, subtraction, multiplication, and division was essential. For example, to program the Engine to calculate the factorial of a number n (denoted as $n!$), one would need to express the operation as:

$$n! = n \times (n - 1) \times (n - 2) \times \cdots \times 1$$

- **Algebra:** The ability to manipulate algebraic expressions and solve equations was crucial. For instance, programming the Engine to solve a quadratic equation $ax^2 + bx + c = 0$ would require deriving the quadratic formula:

$$x = \frac{-b \pm \sqrt{b^2 - 4ac}}{2a}$$

- **Calculus:** Although the Analytical Engine was not designed for calculus, understanding limits and derivatives would help in programming for approximation methods, such as numerical integration.

Logical Reasoning

Programming the Analytical Engine also demanded rigorous logical reasoning skills. Ada needed to think critically about the sequences of operations and how to structure them effectively. This involved:

- **Flow of Control:** Understanding how to direct the Engine to execute specific operations in a particular order. For example, when programming a sequence of arithmetic operations, Ada had to ensure that multiplication was performed before addition, adhering to the order of operations.

- **Conditional Logic:** Implementing decision-making processes required the ability to formulate conditions. For instance, if a certain calculation needed to proceed only if a variable x was greater than zero, Ada would need to express this condition logically, akin to:

$$\text{if } x > 0 \text{ then perform operation}$$

Mechanical Engineering Knowledge

Programming the Analytical Engine was not only about abstract mathematics and logic; it also required an understanding of the machine's mechanical components. Ada had to be familiar with:

- **Mechanical Components:** Knowledge of gears, levers, and the overall architecture of the Engine was critical. For instance, understanding how a gear ratio affects the speed of computation was essential for optimizing performance.

- **Data Representation:** Ada needed to comprehend how data was represented within the Engine, such as using punched cards to input information and instructions. Each card would represent a specific operation or data point, requiring her to meticulously plan the layout and sequence of these cards.

Programming Techniques

Ada's innovative spirit led her to develop programming techniques that were groundbreaking for her time. Among these techniques were:

- **Loops and Iterations:** Ada conceptualized the idea of loops, which allowed the Engine to repeat operations until a certain condition was met. This was akin to modern programming constructs like "for" and "while" loops.

- **Subroutines:** She recognized the value of modular programming by creating subroutines, which could be called upon to perform specific tasks within a larger program. This not only enhanced organization but also improved code reusability.

Examples of Programming Tasks

To illustrate the application of these skills, consider the task of programming the Analytical Engine to compute Bernoulli numbers, a series of rational numbers important in number theory and mathematical analysis.

The formula for the n-th Bernoulli number B_n can be computed using the following expression:

$$B_n = \sum_{k=0}^{n} \binom{n}{k} \frac{1}{k+1}$$

To program this, Ada would need to:

1. Set up a loop to iterate through each integer k from 0 to n.

2. Calculate the binomial coefficient $\binom{n}{k}$ for each iteration.

3. Divide the result by $k + 1$ and accumulate the sum.

This example not only demonstrates Ada's mathematical prowess but also her ability to translate complex mathematical concepts into a structured program for the Analytical Engine.

Conclusion

In summary, programming the Analytical Engine required an extraordinary combination of mathematical skills, logical reasoning, mechanical knowledge, and innovative programming techniques. Ada Lovelace's unique talents allowed her to envision and implement a framework for programming that laid the groundwork for modern computing. Her work transcended her time, positioning her as the first programmer and a visionary whose contributions continue to resonate in today's technological landscape.

Ada's Methodical Approach to Analyzing the Engine

Ada Lovelace's analytical prowess was not merely a product of her intellectual capacity; it was deeply rooted in her methodical approach to understanding the Analytical Engine. This section explores how Ada applied systematic reasoning, logical frameworks, and innovative thinking to dissect and enhance Charles Babbage's groundbreaking invention.

At the heart of Ada's methodical analysis was her ability to break complex concepts into manageable components. This approach can be likened to the principles of modular arithmetic, where a large problem is simplified into smaller, solvable parts. For example, consider the equation for a polynomial function $P(x)$:

$$P(x) = a_n x^n + a_{n-1} x^{n-1} + \ldots + a_1 x + a_0 \qquad (83)$$

In analyzing how the Analytical Engine could compute such functions, Ada recognized the importance of defining each term independently. By isolating the coefficients $a_n, a_{n-1}, \ldots, a_0$, she could conceptualize how the Engine would manipulate numbers through its mechanical operations, ultimately leading to the calculation of $P(x)$.

Furthermore, Ada's analytical method involved rigorous testing of hypotheses, akin to the scientific method. She would propose a theory about the Engine's capabilities and then seek to validate it through logical reasoning and practical examples. For instance, in her notes, she meticulously examined how the Engine could perform calculations not just through addition and subtraction, but also through multiplication and division. This exploration led her to the realization that the Engine could execute complex algorithms, a revolutionary idea at the time.

To illustrate her method, consider the task of calculating the Bernoulli numbers, which are crucial in number theory. Ada proposed an algorithm for the Engine to compute these numbers, demonstrating her ability to translate mathematical concepts into a programming language that the Engine could understand. The algorithm can be represented as follows:

$$B_n = \sum_{k=0}^{n} \binom{n}{k} B_k \cdot \frac{1}{n+1-k} \qquad (84)$$

Here, B_n represents the n-th Bernoulli number, and $\binom{n}{k}$ is the binomial coefficient. Ada's systematic approach allowed her to detail each step of the computation, ensuring that the Engine could replicate the process accurately.

Moreover, Ada's analysis was not confined to the mechanical aspects of the Engine. She also delved into its theoretical implications, contemplating the potential of machines to go beyond mere calculation. In her famous notes, she speculated on the possibility of the Engine composing music or creating art, a visionary thought that foreshadowed modern discussions about artificial intelligence and creativity.

This foresight was grounded in her understanding of the Engine's capabilities. She articulated that the Engine could not only execute predefined operations but could also be programmed to follow a sequence of instructions, effectively making it a precursor to modern programming languages. Her methodical approach involved defining these sequences, which we now recognize as algorithms, and ensuring that they were logically sound and efficient.

In practical terms, Ada's methodical analysis also included the use of flowcharts and diagrams to visualize the processes involved in the Engine's operations. By mapping out the flow of data and the sequence of operations, she could identify potential bottlenecks or inefficiencies in the calculations. This visual representation was crucial in refining her algorithms, allowing her to optimize the performance of the Analytical Engine.

For example, she might have created a flowchart to illustrate the steps involved in calculating the factorial of a number n:

$$n! = n \times (n-1)! \tag{85}$$

This recursive definition highlights how Ada could break down the factorial calculation into simpler steps, each of which could be independently verified and executed by the Engine.

In summary, Ada Lovelace's methodical approach to analyzing the Analytical Engine was characterized by a systematic breakdown of complex problems, rigorous hypothesis testing, and a deep understanding of both the mechanical and theoretical aspects of computation. Her ability to translate mathematical concepts into algorithms and her foresight regarding the potential of machines to perform tasks beyond simple calculations were groundbreaking. This methodical framework not only laid the foundation for modern programming but also established Ada as a pioneering figure in the history of computer science. Through her meticulous analysis, she demonstrated that the Analytical Engine was not merely a mechanical calculator but a revolutionary tool capable of transforming the landscape of mathematics and technology.

The Analytical Engine's Place in History: Ada's Enduring Legacy

The Analytical Engine, conceived by Charles Babbage in the 1830s, is often heralded as the first design for a general-purpose computer. However, it was Ada Lovelace who recognized its potential far beyond mere calculation, envisioning a future where machines could manipulate symbols and execute complex algorithms. This section delves into the historical significance of the Analytical Engine and how Ada's contributions laid the groundwork for modern computing.

The Design and Functionality of the Analytical Engine

The Analytical Engine was a groundbreaking mechanical device that employed concepts still relevant in today's computing. It featured a central processing unit (CPU), referred to as the *mill*, and memory, known as the *store*. The Engine was designed to perform any calculation that could be expressed in a series of operations, using a system of punched cards inspired by the Jacquard loom.

$$\text{Output} = f(\text{Input}, \text{Algorithm}) \tag{86}$$

This equation encapsulates the fundamental principle of computing: a function f processes an input through a defined algorithm to produce an output. Ada's foresight in recognizing that the Analytical Engine could process not just numbers but also other forms of data, such as text and music, was revolutionary.

Ada's Vision: More Than Just Numbers

Ada Lovelace's notes on the Analytical Engine, particularly her annotations on Babbage's work, are considered the first instance of programming. In her famous *Lovelace Note*, she described how the Engine could be programmed to compute Bernoulli numbers—a complex mathematical sequence. Her approach included the following algorithm:

$$B_n = \sum_{k=0}^{n} \binom{n}{k} \cdot B_k \tag{87}$$

Where B_n represents the n-th Bernoulli number, and $\binom{n}{k}$ denotes the binomial coefficient. This method showcased not only her deep understanding of mathematics but also her ability to envision the Engine executing intricate sequences of operations.

The Concept of Programming: Ada's Legacy

Ada's contributions transcended mere calculations; she understood the concept of programming as a means of instructing machines. She articulated the idea that the Analytical Engine could manipulate symbols and create music, effectively predicting the future capabilities of computers. Her assertion that "the Analytical Engine might compose elaborate and scientific pieces of music of any degree of complexity or extent" illustrated her visionary thinking.

Historical Context and Recognition

Despite her groundbreaking work, Ada Lovelace remained largely unrecognized during her lifetime. The male-dominated scientific community often overlooked her contributions, attributing the Engine's potential solely to Babbage. However, the resurgence of interest in her work in the late 20th century has led to a reevaluation of her role in the history of computing.

In 1953, the publication of her notes in a biography of Babbage sparked renewed interest in her life and contributions. Ada was posthumously recognized as the first computer programmer, and her legacy has been celebrated through various initiatives, including Ada Lovelace Day, which honors women in STEM fields.

The Enduring Influence of Ada's Ideas

Ada's insights into the Analytical Engine laid the foundation for modern computing languages and programming paradigms. Her understanding of algorithms and data manipulation has influenced generations of programmers and computer scientists. The principles she articulated are reflected in contemporary programming languages, which emphasize the importance of abstraction and modular design.

For instance, modern programming languages like Python and JavaScript allow for the creation of complex algorithms using simple syntax, echoing Ada's vision of accessible programming. The concept of functions, loops, and conditionals that are central to programming today can be traced back to her pioneering work.

Conclusion: A Legacy of Innovation

In conclusion, the Analytical Engine represents a monumental leap in the history of computing, and Ada Lovelace's contributions are integral to its legacy. Her vision of a machine capable of performing more than just arithmetic calculations has been realized in today's computers, which can execute complex algorithms, process vast amounts of data, and even engage in artificial intelligence.

Ada's enduring legacy serves as a reminder of the importance of diversity in technology and the need to recognize the contributions of women in STEM. As we continue to advance in the field of computing, Ada Lovelace's insights and foresight remain relevant, inspiring future generations to innovate and explore the limitless possibilities of technology.

Bibliography

[1] Lovelace, Ada. "Notes on the Analytical Engine." In *The First Programmer: Ada Lovelace*, edited by Youssef Sato, 1833.

[2] Babbage, Charles. *Passages from the Life of a Philosopher*. London: Longman, Green, and Co., 1864.

[3] Turing, Alan. "Computing Machinery and Intelligence." *Mind* 59, no. 236 (1950): 433-460.

[4] Women in Technology International. "Ada Lovelace Day: Celebrating Women in STEM." Accessed October 2023. https://www.witi.com/

Recognizing Ada's Contribution as the First Programmer

In the annals of computing history, Ada Lovelace is heralded as the first programmer, a title that encapsulates her groundbreaking contributions to the field of mathematics and early computing. But what does it truly mean to be recognized as the first programmer, and why is Ada's work so significant? To answer these questions, we must delve into the intricacies of her contributions, the context in which she operated, and the lasting impact of her ideas on the evolution of programming.

The Context of Ada's Work

To fully appreciate Ada's role as the first programmer, we must first explore the historical context of the 19th century. The Industrial Revolution was in full swing, and the world was witnessing unprecedented advancements in technology and science. However, the field of computing was still in its infancy. Charles Babbage had designed the Analytical Engine, a mechanical computer that was never completed during his lifetime. This machine was revolutionary, incorporating concepts such as an arithmetic logic unit, control flow through conditional branching and loops, and memory.

Ada Lovelace, who became acquainted with Babbage in the early 1830s, recognized the potential of this machine beyond mere calculations. In her notes on the Analytical Engine, she articulated a vision for its capabilities that extended far beyond what Babbage had proposed.

The Lovelace Note

One of Ada's most significant contributions is encapsulated in what is now known as the "Lovelace Note." In this note, she translated an article by the Italian mathematician Luigi Federico Federico and added her own extensive commentary. Within this commentary, Ada provided a detailed description of how the Analytical Engine could be programmed to calculate Bernoulli numbers.

The algorithm she devised is often cited as the first computer program, marking a pivotal moment in the history of computing. The steps of the algorithm can be summarized as follows:

1. **Initialize** the input values. 2. **Perform calculations** using the engine's arithmetic capabilities. 3. **Store** the results in memory for retrieval. 4. **Output** the final results.

The mathematical representation of the Bernoulli numbers can be expressed using a recursive formula, which Ada adeptly navigated in her programming approach:

$$B_0 = 1, \quad B_n = \sum_{k=0}^{n} \binom{n}{k} B_k \quad \text{for } n > 0$$

This equation exemplifies not only her understanding of complex mathematical concepts but also her ability to translate them into a form that could be executed by the Analytical Engine.

Theoretical Foundations of Programming

Ada's work laid the theoretical foundations for programming as we understand it today. She was among the first to recognize that a sequence of operations could be encoded in a way that a machine could interpret and execute. This foresight is reflected in her assertion that the Analytical Engine could manipulate symbols in accordance with rules, which is a cornerstone of modern programming languages.

Her emphasis on the importance of understanding the underlying logic and structure of algorithms resonates with contemporary programming practices. For instance, Ada's approach to problem-solving involved breaking down complex tasks into simpler, manageable components, a methodology that is foundational to software development today.

Examples of Ada's Programming Philosophy

To illustrate Ada's contributions further, consider the following example of a simple algorithm that computes the factorial of a number n:

1. **Input**: A positive integer n. 2. **Output**: The factorial of n, denoted as $n!$. 3. **Algorithm**: - If $n = 0$, return 1. - Otherwise, return $n \times \text{factorial}(n-1)$.

This recursive definition of factorial not only highlights the elegance of Ada's programming philosophy but also underscores her pioneering role in establishing recursion as a fundamental programming technique.

Legacy and Recognition

Despite her monumental contributions, Ada Lovelace's work was largely overlooked for many years. It wasn't until the 20th century that her notes and algorithms were rediscovered and appreciated for their significance. Today, Ada is celebrated not only as the first programmer but also as a visionary who anticipated the future of computing.

Her legacy is honored through various initiatives, including Ada Lovelace Day, which celebrates the achievements of women in science, technology, engineering, and mathematics (STEM). Additionally, the programming language Ada, named in her honor, embodies the principles of reliability and maintainability that she championed.

In conclusion, recognizing Ada Lovelace as the first programmer is not merely a matter of historical accuracy; it is an acknowledgment of her profound impact on the field of computing. Through her innovative thinking, she paved the way for future generations of programmers and mathematicians, ensuring that her contributions would resonate long after her time. Ada Lovelace's legacy is a testament to the power of vision, creativity, and determination in the pursuit of knowledge and innovation.

Ada's Mathematical Legacy

Ada's Mathematical Contributions Beyond Programming

Ada Lovelace, often celebrated as the first programmer, made significant contributions to mathematics that extend well beyond her work on the Analytical

Engine. Her mathematical prowess was not limited to programming concepts; she ventured into theoretical mathematics, mathematical analysis, and even early notions of algorithmic thinking. This section explores her contributions to these areas and highlights her influence on the mathematical community.

Theoretical Mathematics

Ada's work encompassed various aspects of theoretical mathematics, particularly in the realm of calculus and number theory. She had a keen interest in the relationships between numbers and their properties. One of her notable contributions was her exploration of Bernoulli numbers, which are a sequence of rational numbers that play a significant role in number theory and mathematical analysis.

The Bernoulli numbers B_n can be defined using the generating function:

$$\frac{t}{e^t - 1} = \sum_{n=0}^{\infty} B_n \frac{t^n}{n!}$$

These numbers arise in the context of the Euler-Maclaurin formula, which connects integrals and sums, and they are crucial in various areas such as the computation of sums of powers of integers.

Mathematical Analysis

Ada's analytical skills were evident in her ability to dissect complex mathematical problems. She demonstrated a deep understanding of the concepts of function and variable, which are foundational in mathematical analysis. Her work on the Analytical Engine required her to think about how to represent mathematical functions in a way that could be computed mechanically.

One of the key ideas she explored was the concept of recursion, which is fundamental to both mathematics and computer science. For example, the Fibonacci sequence, defined recursively as:

$$F(n) = \begin{cases} 0 & \text{if } n = 0 \\ 1 & \text{if } n = 1 \\ F(n-1) + F(n-2) & \text{if } n > 1 \end{cases}$$

This sequence not only appears in mathematics but also in nature, art, and computer algorithms, showcasing the interconnectedness of her work.

Algorithmic Thinking

Ada's foresight into the importance of algorithms laid the groundwork for future mathematical and computational theories. She understood that algorithms could be expressed in a systematic way, allowing for their execution by machines. One of her famous contributions was the formulation of an algorithm for calculating Bernoulli numbers using the Analytical Engine. This algorithm is recognized as one of the first instances of computer programming.

The algorithm can be summarized as follows:

1. Initialize n to the desired index of the Bernoulli number. 2. Use the formula for Bernoulli numbers to compute B_n iteratively or recursively. 3. Output the calculated Bernoulli number.

This algorithm not only illustrates her understanding of mathematical concepts but also her ability to translate those concepts into a form that could be executed by a machine.

Influence on Mathematical Community

Ada's contributions to mathematics were not widely recognized during her lifetime, but her ideas have gained traction in contemporary discussions about the history of mathematics and computing. Her work has influenced various fields, including combinatorics, numerical analysis, and even modern algorithm theory.

For instance, her exploration of the relationship between mathematical concepts and their computational representations anticipates modern developments in algorithmic complexity theory. In this context, the time complexity of an algorithm can be expressed in Big O notation, which is essential for understanding the efficiency of algorithms:

$$O(f(n)) = \text{the set of functions that grow at most as fast as } f(n) \text{ as } n \to \infty$$

Ada's insights into the efficiency of computations are echoed in today's discussions about algorithm optimization and performance.

Conclusion

In conclusion, Ada Lovelace's mathematical contributions extend far beyond her pioneering work in programming. Her explorations in theoretical mathematics, mathematical analysis, and algorithmic thinking laid the groundwork for future generations of mathematicians and computer scientists. By bridging the gap between abstract mathematical concepts and their practical applications in computing, Ada Lovelace not only established herself as a foundational figure in programming but also as a significant contributor to the broader field of mathematics. Her legacy continues to inspire and challenge us to explore the depths of mathematical thought and its applications in our increasingly digital world.

Ada's Theoretical Work and Mathematical Insights

Ada Lovelace's contributions to theoretical mathematics are often overshadowed by her pioneering work in computing. However, her mathematical insights laid the groundwork for the development of programming as we know it today. Lovelace's approach was deeply rooted in the principles of mathematical theory, and she was particularly interested in the intersection of mathematics and logic.

One of the key areas of Ada's theoretical work was her exploration of the concept of algorithms. An algorithm is a finite sequence of well-defined instructions, typically used to solve a problem or perform a computation. Ada recognized that the Analytical Engine, designed by Charles Babbage, could execute complex algorithms, which was a revolutionary idea at the time. She famously wrote:

> "The Analytical Engine has no pretensions whatever to originate anything. It can do whatever we know how to order it to perform."

This statement reflects her understanding that the power of computation lies not in the machine itself, but in the algorithms that drive it. Ada's ability to conceptualize algorithms as a series of steps to achieve a desired outcome was groundbreaking and presaged modern programming practices.

Theoretical Foundations of Algorithms

To better understand Ada's theoretical work, we can delve into the structure of algorithms. A typical algorithm can be expressed in the form of a mathematical function. For example, consider the function $f : \mathbb{N} \to \mathbb{N}$ defined as follows:

$$f(n) = n^2$$

This function takes a natural number n and produces its square. An algorithm to compute this function could be described in pseudo-code as follows:

```
function square(n):
    return n * n
```

Ada's insight into the nature of algorithms allowed her to envision the potential of the Analytical Engine to perform not just simple calculations but also complex mathematical operations.

Mathematical Insights into Combinatorics

In addition to her work on algorithms, Ada also made significant contributions to combinatorial mathematics. Combinatorics is the branch of mathematics dealing with combinations of objects in specific sets under certain constraints. Ada was particularly interested in how combinatorial principles could be applied to computing.

For example, consider the problem of counting the number of ways to arrange n distinct objects. The solution to this problem is given by the factorial function, denoted as $n!$, which is defined as:

$$n! = n \times (n - 1) \times (n - 2) \times \ldots \times 1$$

Ada's exploration of combinatorial problems led her to consider how these principles could be implemented in programming. She understood that the Analytical Engine could be designed to handle such calculations, which would require careful algorithmic planning.

The Lovelace Note: A Pioneering Example

One of Ada's most significant contributions to theoretical mathematics is encapsulated in what is now known as the Lovelace Note. In this note, she describes an algorithm for the Analytical Engine to calculate Bernoulli numbers, a sequence of rational numbers that are of great importance in number theory.

The algorithm can be summarized as follows:

1. Initialize a list of Bernoulli numbers. 2. For each n, compute the n-th Bernoulli number using the recursive relation:

$$B_n = \sum_{k=0}^{n} \binom{n}{k} B_k \frac{1}{n - k + 1}$$

3. Store the result in the list.

This algorithm demonstrates Ada's ability to translate complex mathematical theories into practical computational procedures. Her notation, while not as formalized as modern programming languages, laid the groundwork for future developments in algorithmic thinking.

Example Problem: Calculating Bernoulli Numbers

To illustrate Ada's theoretical insights, let us consider a specific example of calculating the first few Bernoulli numbers using her algorithm.

1. **Initialization**:

$$B_0 = 1, \quad B_1 = -\frac{1}{2}$$

2. **Recursive Calculation**:

$$B_2 = \frac{1}{2} \quad \text{(using } B_0 \text{ and } B_1\text{)}$$

$$B_3 = 0 \quad \text{(since odd-indexed Bernoulli numbers are zero for } n > 1\text{)}$$

$$B_4 = \frac{1}{30} \quad \text{(using } B_0, B_1, B_2\text{)}$$

$$B_5 = 0$$

$$B_6 = \frac{1}{42}$$

The sequence of Bernoulli numbers begins: $B_0 = 1, B_1 = -\frac{1}{2}, B_2 = \frac{1}{6}, B_3 = 0, B_4 = \frac{1}{30}, B_5 = 0, B_6 = \frac{1}{42}$.

This example not only highlights Ada's mathematical prowess but also her ability to connect theoretical concepts with practical applications in computing.

Conclusion

In conclusion, Ada Lovelace's theoretical work and mathematical insights were instrumental in shaping the future of programming and computer science. Her exploration of algorithms, combinatorial mathematics, and her pioneering contributions through the Lovelace Note showcase her brilliance as a mathematician. Ada's legacy is not merely as the first programmer but as a visionary who understood the profound implications of mathematics in the realm of computation. Her insights continue to inspire and inform modern programming practices, ensuring that her impact will be felt for generations to come.

Ada's Influence on the Field of Mathematics

Ada Lovelace's contributions to mathematics extend far beyond her role as the first programmer; she has had a lasting influence on various branches of mathematical thought. Her unique approach to mathematical concepts, combined with her innovative ideas regarding computation, has left an indelible mark on the field. This section explores the various dimensions of Ada's influence on mathematics, focusing on her theoretical insights, practical applications, and the legacy she has left for future generations.

1. Theoretical Contributions

Ada Lovelace's understanding of mathematics was deeply rooted in the theoretical frameworks of her time, yet she was not afraid to challenge existing paradigms. Her work with Charles Babbage on the Analytical Engine allowed her to explore the potential of machines to perform mathematical calculations, which was a revolutionary concept in the 19th century.

One of the key theoretical contributions Ada made was her exploration of algorithms. In her notes on the Analytical Engine, she famously described an algorithm for calculating Bernoulli numbers, which is often considered the first computer algorithm. The algorithm can be expressed as follows:

$$B_n = \sum_{k=0}^{n} \binom{n}{k} \cdot B_k \tag{88}$$

where B_n represents the nth Bernoulli number and $\binom{n}{k}$ is the binomial coefficient. This formula illustrates Ada's ability to apply mathematical theory to practical computation, showcasing her understanding of combinatorial mathematics.

2. Influence on Combinatorial Mathematics

Ada's work in combinatorial mathematics is particularly noteworthy. She recognized the significance of combinations and permutations in computational processes. Her insights laid the groundwork for future developments in combinatorial theory, which is essential in various fields such as computer science, cryptography, and statistical analysis.

For example, Ada's understanding of combinations can be expressed mathematically as:

$$C(n, k) = \frac{n!}{k!(n-k)!} \tag{89}$$

where $C(n, k)$ represents the number of combinations of n items taken k at a time. This formula is fundamental in probability theory and has applications in numerous mathematical and computational problems.

3. Impact on Mathematical Notation

Ada Lovelace's work also contributed to the evolution of mathematical notation. Her collaboration with Babbage involved not only algorithm design but also the representation of mathematical ideas in a structured format. This emphasis on clear notation has influenced how mathematicians and computer scientists communicate complex ideas.

For instance, the use of symbols to represent operations and functions in mathematics can be traced back to the early developments during Ada's time. The notation she helped popularize has been foundational in the development of modern mathematical expressions. The function notation, $f(x)$, which is now ubiquitous in mathematics, can be seen as an evolution of the ideas Ada and her contemporaries were exploring.

4. Legacy in Mathematical Education

Ada Lovelace's influence extends into the realm of education. Her advocacy for women's education in mathematics and science has inspired countless women to pursue careers in these fields. The establishment of programs aimed at increasing female representation in STEM (Science, Technology, Engineering, and Mathematics) can be traced back to the ideals Ada championed.

Her legacy is evident in initiatives such as the Ada Lovelace Scholarship, which supports young women pursuing studies in mathematics and computer science. This scholarship not only honors Ada's contributions but also aims to inspire a new generation of female mathematicians.

5. Conclusion

In summary, Ada Lovelace's influence on the field of mathematics is profound and multifaceted. Her theoretical contributions, particularly in algorithm design and combinatorial mathematics, have paved the way for advancements in computational theory. Furthermore, her impact on mathematical notation and education continues to resonate today, as her legacy inspires future generations of mathematicians and computer scientists. Ada Lovelace is not just a historical figure; she is a symbol of innovation and a beacon for aspiring mathematicians, illustrating the power of creativity and intellect in shaping the future of mathematics.

The Modern-Day Relevance of Ada's Mathematical Theories

Ada Lovelace's contributions to mathematics extend far beyond her time, resonating with contemporary mathematical concepts and computational theories. Her innovative approach to problem-solving and her visionary ideas about the potential of machines to perform complex calculations laid the groundwork for modern computational mathematics. This section explores the enduring relevance of her mathematical theories in today's technological landscape.

1. Theoretical Foundations

At the heart of Ada's mathematical legacy is her understanding of the principles of logic and computation. She recognized that mathematics could serve as a language for describing not just numbers, but also processes and relationships. This insight is foundational to computer science and is encapsulated in the concept of algorithms.

An **algorithm** is a step-by-step procedure for solving a problem or performing a task. Ada's work on the Analytical Engine involved developing algorithms that could be executed by this early mechanical computer. One of her most famous contributions was the algorithm for calculating Bernoulli numbers, which can be expressed as follows:

$$B_n = \sum_{k=0}^{n} \binom{n}{k} \frac{B_k}{n-k+1} \tag{90}$$

where B_n represents the n-th Bernoulli number and $\binom{n}{k}$ is the binomial coefficient. This algorithm not only demonstrated the potential of programmable machines but also illustrated the power of mathematical reasoning in constructing solutions.

2. Connection to Modern Computational Theory

Lovelace's insights into algorithms and computation are mirrored in modern computational theory, particularly in the fields of complexity theory and algorithm design. Today, we categorize algorithms based on their efficiency and the resources they require, such as time and space. This categorization is crucial in computer science, where the ability to process large datasets efficiently is paramount.

For example, the **Big O notation** provides a high-level understanding of an algorithm's efficiency. An algorithm that runs in linear time is denoted as $O(n)$, while one that runs in quadratic time is denoted as $O(n^2)$. Ada's foresight in recognizing the importance of algorithmic efficiency is a principle that remains fundamental in modern programming and software development.

3. Mathematical Modeling and Simulation

Ada's work also foreshadowed the use of mathematical models to simulate real-world phenomena. In today's world, mathematical modeling is essential in various fields, including physics, biology, and economics. Models are used to predict outcomes, optimize processes, and understand complex systems.

For instance, the **Lotka-Volterra equations**, which describe the dynamics of biological systems in which two species interact, can be expressed as:

$$\frac{dx}{dt}\& = \alpha x - \beta xy \tag{91}$$

$$\frac{dy}{dt}\& = \delta xy - \gamma y \tag{92}$$

where x and y represent the populations of the prey and predator species, respectively, and $\alpha, \beta, \gamma, \delta$ are parameters that describe the interaction rates. The ability to model such interactions mathematically is a direct descendant of the principles Ada championed.

4. Impact on Cryptography

Ada's mathematical theories also find relevance in the field of cryptography, which relies heavily on number theory and algorithmic processes. The security of modern communication systems is based on complex algorithms that encrypt and decrypt information. For example, the widely used RSA encryption algorithm is based on the difficulty of factoring large prime numbers:

$$C = M^e \mod n \tag{93}$$

where C is the ciphertext, M is the plaintext message, e is the public exponent, and n is the product of two prime numbers. Ada's understanding of mathematical principles can be seen as a precursor to the sophisticated algorithms that protect our digital communications today.

5. Educational Implications

In the realm of education, Ada's legacy continues to inspire new generations of mathematicians and computer scientists. Her story is often used to encourage young women to pursue careers in STEM fields. The integration of her mathematical theories into curricula emphasizes the importance of logic, problem-solving, and algorithmic thinking.

Programs that teach coding and computational thinking often draw on Ada's pioneering work. For instance, the concept of **computational thinking** involves breaking down complex problems into manageable parts, a skill that is essential in both mathematics and programming. Educators today strive to instill this mindset in students, echoing Ada's approach to problem-solving.

6. Conclusion

Ada Lovelace's mathematical theories remain profoundly relevant in the modern world. From algorithm design and computational theory to mathematical modeling and cryptography, her insights continue to shape the way we understand and interact with technology. As we celebrate her legacy, it is essential to recognize the timeless nature of her contributions and their impact on current and future innovations in mathematics and computer science. By honoring Ada's pioneering spirit, we not only acknowledge her role as the first programmer but also inspire future generations to explore the limitless possibilities of mathematics and technology.

The Integration of Ada's Mathematical Approach into Modern Computing

Ada Lovelace's contributions to mathematics were not merely theoretical; they laid the groundwork for the computational models that underpin modern computing. Her innovative thinking and unique perspective on mathematics have been integrated into various facets of contemporary computer science, particularly in algorithm design, programming languages, and computational theory.

Mathematical Foundations of Computing

At the core of modern computing lies the concept of algorithms, which Ada recognized as essential for the operation of the Analytical Engine. An algorithm can be defined as a finite set of well-defined rules or instructions for solving a problem or performing a computation. For example, consider the problem of sorting a list of numbers. A simple algorithm to achieve this might be the Bubble Sort, which operates as follows:

Algorithm 1 Bubble Sort

1: **procedure** BUBBLESORT(A)
2:    **for** $i = 0$ to $n - 1$ **do**
3:       **for** $j = 0$ to $n - i - 2$ **do**
4:          **if** $A[j] > A[j + 1]$ **then**
5:             swap $A[j]$ and $A[j + 1]$
6:          **end if**
7:       **end for**
8:    **end for**
9: **end procedure**

This algorithm exemplifies how systematic mathematical reasoning can be translated into computational processes. Ada's approach to problem-solving emphasized not just finding a solution but doing so efficiently and systematically.

The Role of Logic in Programming Languages

Ada's work also foreshadowed the development of programming languages, which are built on mathematical logic. The integration of logical structures in programming languages allows for the representation of complex ideas through simple commands. For instance, consider the logical expression used in conditional statements:

$$\text{if } P \text{ then } Q$$

This expression evaluates whether the condition P is true, and if so, it executes the command Q. This fundamental structure in programming languages can be traced back to Ada's mathematical principles, which emphasized clarity, precision, and logical reasoning.

Numerical Methods and Their Applications

Ada Lovelace's insights into numerical methods have influenced modern computational techniques, particularly in the fields of numerical analysis and scientific computing. Her understanding of the importance of approximation and iterative methods is mirrored in techniques such as the Newton-Raphson method for finding successively better approximations to the roots of a real-valued function.

The Newton-Raphson method is defined by the iterative formula:

$$x_{n+1} = x_n - \frac{f(x_n)}{f'(x_n)}$$

where f is a function and f' is its derivative. This method exemplifies how mathematical theory can be applied to solve practical problems, a concept Ada championed in her work with the Analytical Engine.

The Impact of Ada's Legacy on Algorithmic Thinking

Ada's legacy extends into the realm of algorithmic thinking, which is crucial for problem-solving in computer science. Her ability to deconstruct complex problems into manageable parts is reflected in modern software engineering practices, where modular programming and object-oriented design are foundational principles.

For example, consider a software application that manages a library system. The application can be broken down into modules such as:

* **User Management:** Handling user registration, authentication, and profiles.

* **Catalog Management:** Managing books, authors, and genres.

* **Loan Management:** Tracking borrowed books and due dates.

Each module can be developed independently yet function cohesively, much like the components of the Analytical Engine that Ada envisioned. This modular approach allows for easier maintenance and scalability, embodying Ada's mathematical clarity in design.

Mathematics in Data Structures

Data structures, which are essential for organizing and storing data efficiently, also reflect Ada's mathematical approach. For instance, the concept of a binary tree—a hierarchical structure where each node has at most two children—can be understood mathematically through recursive definitions.

The height h of a binary tree can be defined recursively as:

$$h = \begin{cases} 0 & \text{if the tree is empty} \\ 1 + \max(h_L, h_R) & \text{if the tree has left and right subtrees } h_L \text{ and } h_R \end{cases}$$

This recursive definition aligns with Ada's understanding of mathematical functions and their properties, demonstrating how her insights continue to inform modern data structure design.

Conclusion

In conclusion, Ada Lovelace's mathematical approach has been seamlessly integrated into modern computing, influencing everything from algorithm design to programming languages and data structures. Her legacy is a testament to the power of mathematics in shaping the future of technology, underscoring the importance of a systematic and logical approach to problem-solving. As we continue to innovate in the field of computer science, we must remember and honor Ada's contributions, ensuring that her vision of a mathematically grounded computing future remains at the forefront of technological advancement.

Ada's Impact on Fields Beyond Mathematics and Computing

Ada Lovelace's contributions extend far beyond the realms of mathematics and computing, weaving through the fabric of various disciplines, including literature, philosophy, and even the arts. Her multifaceted intellect allowed her to bridge the gap between the analytical and the creative, making her a figure of immense significance in a variety of fields. In this section, we will explore how Ada's ideas and work influenced areas beyond her immediate expertise, leaving a legacy that resonates through time.

1. Literature and Creative Writing

Ada Lovelace was not only a mathematician but also a gifted writer. Her early exposure to literature, particularly through her father, the poet Lord Byron, imbued her with a creative sensibility that she carried throughout her life. She often expressed her mathematical ideas in poetic forms, illustrating the beauty of numbers and algorithms.

One of her notable contributions to literature is the way she framed complex mathematical concepts in accessible language. For instance, in her notes on the Analytical Engine, she famously described the machine's potential to create music, stating:

> *"The Analytical Engine has no pretensions to originate anything. It can do whatever we know how to order it to perform."*

This quote underscores Ada's belief in the symbiotic relationship between creativity and computation, a notion that has inspired countless writers and artists to explore the intersection of technology and artistic expression.

2. Philosophy and Ethics

Ada's philosophical inclinations are evident in her writings, where she often pondered the implications of technology on society. Her understanding of the ethical dimensions of technological advancements was remarkably prescient. She foresaw the potential consequences of machines that could perform tasks autonomously, raising questions about responsibility and moral agency.

For example, her reflections on the Analytical Engine can be interpreted as an early exploration of artificial intelligence ethics. She wrote:

> *"The engine might compose elaborate and scientific pieces of music of any degree of complexity or extent."*

This statement not only highlights her vision of machines as creative entities but also prompts us to consider the ethical implications of machines that can create art. Ada's foresight in this area has laid the groundwork for ongoing discussions in the fields of AI ethics and philosophy.

3. The Arts and Aesthetic Theory

Ada Lovelace's influence on the arts is profound, particularly in how she conceptualized the relationship between mathematics and beauty. Her belief that mathematical structures could embody aesthetic principles has inspired artists and designers to explore the mathematical foundations of art.

The Fibonacci sequence, for example, is a mathematical concept that has been employed in various art forms, from architecture to painting, to create visually appealing compositions. Ada's work can be seen as a precursor to this integration of mathematics and aesthetics. Her appreciation for the beauty of numbers resonates with the works of artists like M.C. Escher, who famously explored mathematical concepts through visual art.

4. Education and Advocacy for Women

Ada's legacy is also significant in the realm of education, particularly in advocating for women in STEM fields. Her life and work serve as a powerful example for women pursuing careers in science, technology, engineering, and mathematics.

Ada's emphasis on the importance of education for women has inspired numerous initiatives aimed at increasing female representation in these fields.

Organizations such as the Ada Lovelace Foundation and various scholarship programs have been established in her honor to support and empower young women in technology. These initiatives are a direct reflection of Ada's belief in the necessity of education and mentorship, which she championed throughout her life.

5. Interdisciplinary Approaches

Ada Lovelace's impact transcends traditional disciplinary boundaries, promoting an interdisciplinary approach to problem-solving. Her collaborative work with Charles Babbage exemplifies the power of merging different fields of knowledge. By combining mathematics, engineering, and creative thought, Ada demonstrated that innovation often arises at the intersection of diverse disciplines.

This interdisciplinary ethos is echoed in contemporary educational practices, where STEAM (Science, Technology, Engineering, Arts, and Mathematics) curricula emphasize the importance of integrating the arts with scientific and technical education. Ada's vision serves as a foundational principle for fostering creativity in scientific inquiry and technological development.

6. Legacy in Modern Culture

The cultural significance of Ada Lovelace extends into modern media, where her story has been celebrated in literature, film, and art. She has become a symbol of women's contributions to technology, inspiring a new generation of innovators. Her portrayal in various biographies and fictional accounts highlights her as a pioneer who defied societal norms to pursue her passions.

Moreover, Ada Lovelace Day, celebrated annually, serves as a global acknowledgment of women's achievements in STEM. This event not only commemorates Ada's legacy but also encourages discussions about the ongoing challenges women face in these fields, fostering a community of support and inspiration.

Conclusion

In conclusion, Ada Lovelace's impact on fields beyond mathematics and computing is profound and far-reaching. Her contributions to literature, philosophy, the arts, education, and advocacy for women in STEM have shaped the landscape of these disciplines. By challenging the boundaries of traditional thought and encouraging interdisciplinary collaboration, Ada has left an indelible mark on history. Her legacy continues to inspire individuals across various fields, reminding us that innovation often arises from the fusion of creativity and analytical thinking. As we honor Ada Lovelace, we celebrate not just the first programmer, but a visionary whose ideas resonate across generations and disciplines.

The Enduring Significance of Ada's Mathematical Legacy

Ada Lovelace's mathematical legacy is not merely a footnote in history; it is a cornerstone that has influenced generations of mathematicians, computer scientists, and thinkers. Her unique approach to mathematics and her visionary insights into computational theory have left an indelible mark on the fields of mathematics and computer science. This section explores the enduring significance of Ada's contributions, highlighting her innovative ideas, theoretical insights, and the problems she tackled, which continue to resonate in contemporary mathematics.

Innovative Mathematical Concepts

At the heart of Ada Lovelace's mathematical legacy lies her pioneering work on the Analytical Engine, an early mechanical general-purpose computer designed by Charles Babbage. Ada recognized that this machine could perform not only calculations but also manipulate symbols and data in a way that transcended mere arithmetic. Her assertion that the Analytical Engine could be programmed to perform any intellectual task laid the groundwork for modern computing.

One of her most notable contributions is the concept of algorithms. In her notes on the Analytical Engine, Ada provided a detailed description of an algorithm for calculating Bernoulli numbers. This algorithm is often cited as the first computer program, showcasing her understanding of the relationship between mathematics and computation. The algorithm can be expressed mathematically as follows:

$$B_n = \sum_{k=0}^{n} \binom{n}{k} \cdot B_k \cdot \frac{1}{k+1} \qquad (94)$$

where B_n represents the n-th Bernoulli number. This recursive relationship highlights the elegance and complexity of the mathematical concepts Ada engaged with.

Theoretical Insights

Ada's theoretical insights extended beyond algorithmic thinking. She delved into the implications of computing machines on mathematical thought and the nature of creativity in mathematics. In her writings, she proposed that the Analytical Engine could create music and art, suggesting that machines could not only compute but also express human creativity. This idea was revolutionary and anticipated discussions about artificial intelligence and machine learning that would emerge centuries later.

Her reflections on the nature of mathematics and computation can be summarized by her famous assertion:

> "The Analytical Engine has no pretensions whatever to originate anything. It can do whatever we know how to order it to perform."

This statement underscores the importance of human creativity in the mathematical process, emphasizing that while machines can execute tasks, the spark of innovation and originality remains inherently human.

Problems and Examples

Lovelace's work also included practical problems that illustrated her mathematical prowess. One of the problems she tackled was the calculation of the Fibonacci sequence, which can be defined recursively as follows:

$$F(n) = F(n-1) + F(n-2) \tag{95}$$

with initial conditions $F(0) = 0$ and $F(1) = 1$. Ada's exploration of sequences and series not only enriched her understanding of mathematics but also provided a foundation for later developments in algorithms and computational theory.

In her notes, Ada presented a series of examples that demonstrated the versatility of the Analytical Engine. For instance, she described how the engine could compute the area under a curve, a problem central to calculus. This problem can be expressed through integration:

$$A = \int_a^b f(x)\,dx \tag{96}$$

where A represents the area under the curve defined by the function $f(x)$ between the limits a and b. Ada's ability to connect these mathematical concepts to the workings of the Analytical Engine foreshadowed the development of numerical methods and computational mathematics.

Legacy in Modern Mathematics

Today, Ada Lovelace's mathematical legacy is celebrated not only for its historical significance but also for its relevance in contemporary mathematics and computer science. Her pioneering work laid the groundwork for the fields of algorithm theory and computational complexity. The impact of her contributions can be seen in modern programming languages, which are built upon the principles of algorithmic thinking that Ada championed.

Moreover, Ada's emphasis on the importance of education and mentorship for women in mathematics and science has inspired initiatives aimed at increasing female representation in STEM fields. Organizations and programs dedicated to honoring her legacy continue to promote opportunities for young women in mathematics, ensuring that Ada's vision of inclusivity and innovation endures.

Conclusion

In conclusion, Ada Lovelace's mathematical legacy is a testament to her brilliance and foresight. Her innovative ideas, theoretical insights, and practical applications have shaped the landscape of mathematics and computer science. As we continue to explore the realms of computation and algorithmic thinking, we must recognize and celebrate the enduring significance of Ada's contributions. Her legacy serves as a reminder that the intersection of mathematics and creativity is a fertile ground for innovation, inspiring future generations to push the boundaries of what is possible.

Recognizing Ada's Contributions in the Mathematics Community

Ada Lovelace, often heralded as the first computer programmer, made significant contributions to the field of mathematics that extend beyond her work on Charles Babbage's Analytical Engine. Her insights into mathematical theory and her pioneering work in algorithm development have been recognized and celebrated within the mathematics community, solidifying her legacy as a formidable mathematician.

Theoretical Contributions

Ada's mathematical prowess was evident from a young age, influenced by her mother, Lady Anne, who ensured that Ada received a rigorous education in mathematics and logic. This foundation allowed her to engage deeply with the theoretical aspects of mathematics. One of her notable contributions was her work on Bernoulli numbers, which she explored in her notes on the Analytical Engine.

The Bernoulli numbers B_n are a sequence of rational numbers that are deeply connected to number theory and appear in the expansion of the tangent function. They can be defined using the generating function:

$$\frac{t}{e^t - 1} = \sum_{n=0}^{\infty} B_n \frac{t^n}{n!}$$

Ada's work involved calculating these numbers and understanding their implications for computational mathematics, which laid the groundwork for future explorations in both number theory and computer programming.

Algorithm Development

In her notes, Ada famously described an algorithm for the Analytical Engine to compute Bernoulli numbers. This algorithm is often cited as the first computer program. The process she outlined can be summarized as follows:
1. Initialize the first Bernoulli number $B_0 = 1$. 2. For each n, calculate B_n using the recurrence relation derived from the generating function. 3. Use the Analytical Engine to perform the required arithmetic operations.

The algorithm itself can be expressed in pseudo-code:

```
FUNCTION ComputeBernoulli(n)
    IF n = 0 THEN
        RETURN 1
    ENDIF
    SET B[n] = 0
    FOR k = 0 TO n-1 DO
        B[n] += Binomial(n, k) * B[k] / (n - k + 1)
    ENDFOR
    RETURN B[n]
END FUNCTION
```

This recursive approach not only demonstrates Ada's understanding of mathematical principles but also her ability to translate these principles into a form that a machine could execute.

Influence on Modern Mathematics

Ada's insights into algorithmic processes and her contributions to mathematical theory have had a lasting impact on the mathematics community. Her work is recognized in various mathematical contexts, particularly in the fields of combinatorics and numerical analysis.

For example, the concept of recursion that Ada employed in her Bernoulli number algorithm is foundational in modern computational mathematics. Recursive algorithms are a staple in computer science and mathematics today, used in everything from sorting algorithms to dynamic programming.

Moreover, Ada's emphasis on the importance of precision and clarity in mathematical writing has influenced how mathematical concepts are communicated. Her notes on the Analytical Engine were not just technical documents; they were also a call for a structured approach to mathematical thinking.

Recognition and Legacy

In recent years, Ada Lovelace's contributions have been increasingly recognized in the mathematics community. Organizations and institutions have begun to honor her legacy through various initiatives, including:

+ The Ada Lovelace Medal, awarded to individuals who have made significant contributions to mathematics or computing.

+ Educational programs that incorporate Ada's work into their curricula, inspiring new generations of mathematicians and computer scientists.

+ The establishment of Ada Lovelace Day, a celebration of women in STEM, which highlights the contributions of female mathematicians and scientists throughout history.

Ada Lovelace's contributions to mathematics are not merely historical footnotes; they are integral to the evolution of mathematical thought and practice. By recognizing her work, the mathematics community not only honors her legacy but also reinforces the importance of diversity and inclusion in the field.

Conclusion

In conclusion, Ada Lovelace's contributions to the mathematics community are profound and far-reaching. Her work on Bernoulli numbers, algorithm development, and the promotion of clarity in mathematical communication have left an indelible mark on the discipline. As we continue to explore the intersections of mathematics and technology, Ada's pioneering spirit serves as a reminder of the vital role that innovative thinkers play in shaping the future of mathematics and computer science.

Ada Lovelace: The Mathematical Genius behind the First Programmer

Ada Lovelace, often heralded as the first programmer, was not just a pioneer of computer science; she was a mathematical genius whose insights and contributions laid the foundation for modern computing. Her ability to blend mathematics with visionary thinking allowed her to see possibilities that others could not, making her a unique figure in the 19th century.

Theoretical Foundations

At the heart of Ada's work was her understanding of mathematical concepts that were revolutionary for her time. One of the key theories she engaged with was the concept of algorithms, which are step-by-step procedures for calculations. Ada's collaboration with Charles Babbage on his Analytical Engine showcased her ability to formulate algorithms that could be executed by a machine.

An algorithm can be represented mathematically. For instance, consider a simple algorithm to compute the factorial of a number n:

$$n! = \begin{cases} 1 & \text{if } n = 0 \\ n \times (n-1)! & \text{if } n > 0 \end{cases} \tag{97}$$

This recursive definition demonstrates the mathematical elegance that Ada appreciated and utilized in her programming work.

The Lovelace Note

Ada's most significant contribution is encapsulated in what is known as the "Lovelace Note." This note, which accompanied her translation of an article on the Analytical Engine, contained the first algorithm intended for implementation on a machine. In this note, she described how the engine could be programmed to calculate Bernoulli numbers.

The algorithm for calculating the n-th Bernoulli number B_n is given by:

$$B_n = \frac{1}{n+1} \sum_{k=0}^{n} \binom{n}{k} B_k \tag{98}$$

Ada's ability to express this complex calculation in a structured format demonstrated her deep understanding of both mathematics and the potential of computational machines.

A Visionary Approach to Mathematics

Ada's mathematical genius was not limited to mere calculations; she also envisioned the broader implications of computing. She famously stated that the Analytical Engine could do more than just calculations; it could manipulate symbols and create music or art. This visionary perspective is a hallmark of her genius.

To illustrate this, consider the idea of generating a simple sequence of numbers, such as the Fibonacci sequence, which can be defined by the recurrence relation:

$$F(n) = \begin{cases} 0 & \text{if } n = 0 \\ 1 & \text{if } n = 1 \\ F(n-1) + F(n-2) & \text{if } n > 1 \end{cases} \tag{99}$$

Ada's insight into the potential of algorithms to generate not just numbers but patterns and structures was revolutionary. She understood that mathematics could be a creative force, capable of producing beauty as well as utility.

Ada's Mathematical Legacy

Ada Lovelace's contributions extend beyond her algorithms; they represent a paradigm shift in how we view the relationship between mathematics and technology. Her work laid the groundwork for future generations of mathematicians and computer scientists, inspiring them to explore the creative possibilities of computation.

In modern programming, the principles Ada employed can be seen in the development of programming languages that support complex data structures and algorithms. For example, in Python, the Fibonacci sequence can be generated using a simple function:

```python
def fibonacci(n):
    if n == 0:
        return 0
    elif n == 1:
        return 1
    else:
```

```
return fibonacci(n-1) + fibonacci(n-2)
```

This recursive function echoes Ada's understanding of algorithms and their potential to solve complex problems.

Conclusion

In conclusion, Ada Lovelace was not merely the first programmer; she was a mathematical genius whose insights transcended her time. Her ability to articulate algorithms, envision the potential of computing, and explore the intersections of mathematics and creativity marks her as a foundational figure in the history of technology. As we continue to build upon her legacy, we recognize that her contributions are not just historical footnotes but essential elements of the ongoing narrative of innovation and discovery in mathematics and computing.

Bibliography

[1] Lovelace, A. (1843). Notes on the Analytical Engine.

[2] Babbage, C. (1837). The Analytical Engine.

[3] Toole, B. (1998). Ada, the Enchantress of Numbers: Poetical Science.

Chapter 3: The Enigma of Ada Lovelace

Chapter 3: The Enigma of Ada Lovelace

Chapter 3: The Enigma of Ada Lovelace

Introduction

Ada Lovelace, often hailed as the first computer programmer, is an enigma wrapped in a riddle, sprinkled with a dash of mathematical genius. Born into a world of privilege, yet marked by the complexities of her lineage, Ada's life was a tapestry woven with contradictions—her brilliance often overshadowed by societal expectations. In this chapter, we will explore the multifaceted nature of Ada's character, her personal relationships, and the legacy she left in literature, art, and technology.

3.1 Ada's Complex Personality

Ada Lovelace was not just a mathematician; she was a conundrum. Her personality was a blend of intellect, creativity, and a yearning for self-discovery. She possessed an artistic sensibility that often clashed with her mathematical inclinations. This duality is best illustrated through her own writings, where she seamlessly blended poetic language with complex mathematical concepts.

3.1.1 The Multifaceted Nature of Ada's Character

Ada's character was shaped by her upbringing and the expectations placed upon her. As the daughter of the famous poet Lord Byron and Lady Anne Isabella Milbanke, Ada was exposed to both the arts and sciences from an early age. Her mother, a mathematician herself, encouraged Ada's interest in mathematics while simultaneously trying to suppress any artistic tendencies that could remind her of her father. This push and pull created a complex identity for Ada, one that she navigated throughout her life.

3.1.2 Ada's Artistic Sensibilities and Creativity

Ada's artistic side was evident in her writings and her approach to mathematics. She often described mathematical concepts in vivid, poetic language. For instance, in her notes on the Analytical Engine, she wrote about the potential of machines to create music and art, foreshadowing the interdisciplinary nature of modern technology. This creative approach to mathematics is encapsulated in her famous quote: "The Analytical Engine does not occupy common ground with mere calculating machines. It holds within it the potential to create, to inspire, and to transcend."

3.1.3 Ada's Intellectual Curiosity and Love for Learning

Ada's insatiable curiosity drove her to explore various fields of knowledge, from mathematics and engineering to philosophy and literature. She was particularly fascinated by the intersection of these disciplines, often pondering the implications of her work on society. This intellectual curiosity is reflected in her correspondence with Charles Babbage, where she eagerly discussed the potential applications of his Analytical Engine, demonstrating her ability to think beyond the constraints of her time.

3.1.4 The Contradictions within Ada's Personality

The contradictions in Ada's personality were not merely a product of her upbringing but also a response to the societal norms of her time. She was a woman in a male-dominated field, and her desire to be recognized as an equal often clashed with the expectations of femininity. Ada's struggle to reconcile her ambitions with societal expectations is a testament to her resilience and determination.

3.1.5 Ada's Struggle with Personal Identity and Expectations

As Ada navigated her complex identity, she often grappled with the expectations placed upon her as a woman of noble birth. The pressure to conform to societal norms weighed heavily on her, leading to periods of self-doubt and introspection. Yet, it was this very struggle that fueled her passion for mathematics and her desire to break free from the constraints of her upbringing.

3.1.6 The Unconventional Nature of Ada's Thoughts and Ideas

Ada's thoughts and ideas were anything but conventional. She envisioned a future where machines could perform tasks beyond mere calculations, predicting the rise of artificial intelligence long before it became a reality. Her visionary ideas were often met with skepticism, yet she remained steadfast in her beliefs, challenging the status quo and paving the way for future generations of thinkers.

3.1.7 Ada's Penchant for Philosophy and Science Fiction

Ada's love for philosophy and science fiction further enriched her understanding of the world. She often drew inspiration from literary works, using them as a lens through which to view her mathematical pursuits. This unique perspective allowed her to envision the potential of technology in shaping human experiences, making her a true pioneer in the field of computing.

3.1.8 The Layers of Ada's Enigmatic Persona

To fully appreciate Ada Lovelace, one must peel back the layers of her enigmatic persona. She was a woman of contradictions—a mathematician who loved poetry, a visionary who faced societal constraints, and a pioneer who often went unrecognized. Each layer reveals a different facet of her character, contributing to her enduring legacy as a trailblazer in technology.

3.1.9 Unlocking the Mysteries of Ada Lovelace: A Portrait of a Brilliant Mind

In conclusion, Ada Lovelace's life and work embody the complexities of a brilliant mind navigating a world that often sought to limit her potential. Her legacy is not only defined by her contributions to mathematics and computing but also by her ability to transcend societal boundaries and inspire future generations. As we delve deeper into her personal relationships and the impact of her work, we uncover the enduring significance of Ada Lovelace—a true enigma in the annals of history.

3.2 Ada's Personal Relationships

Understanding Ada Lovelace's personal relationships is crucial to comprehending the influences that shaped her life and work. From her tumultuous relationship with her father to her complicated bond with her mother, each connection played a pivotal role in her development as a thinker and innovator.

3.2.1 Ada's Relationship with Her Parents

Ada's relationship with her parents was marked by contrasts. Her father, Lord Byron, was a flamboyant figure known for his poetic genius and tumultuous lifestyle. In contrast, her mother, Lady Anne, was a strict and disciplined woman who sought to instill a sense of propriety in Ada. The absence of her father, who left the family when she was just a few weeks old, created a void that Ada sought to fill through her academic pursuits.

3.2.2 The Influence of Ada's Father Lord Byron

Although Ada never knew her father, his legacy loomed large over her life. The romantic ideals and artistic inclinations associated with Lord Byron influenced Ada's own creative pursuits. She often grappled with the desire to carve out her own identity, distinct from her father's shadow, while simultaneously drawing inspiration from his literary brilliance.

3.2.3 Ada's Complicated Relationship with Her Mother

Ada's relationship with her mother was fraught with tension. Lady Anne's strict upbringing often stifled Ada's creative impulses, leading to a rebellion against the constraints imposed upon her. Yet, Lady Anne's emphasis on education and mathematics ultimately laid the foundation for Ada's future success. This complex dynamic highlights the duality of Ada's upbringing—one that fostered both her brilliance and her struggles.

3.2.4 Ada's Relationship with Her Siblings

Ada's relationships with her siblings were similarly complex. As the only legitimate child of Lord Byron, she often felt a sense of isolation from her half-siblings. This sense of otherness fueled her desire for connection, leading her to seek out friendships and collaborations that would ultimately shape her career.

3.2.5 Ada's Romantic Interests and Love Affairs

Ada's romantic interests were often intertwined with her intellectual pursuits. Her marriage to William King, whom she wed in 1835, was a union of mutual respect and admiration. However, Ada's passionate nature often led her to seek companionship outside her marriage, resulting in a series of love affairs that reflected her quest for emotional fulfillment.

3.2.6 The Impact of Ada's Personal Relationships on Her Work

The interplay between Ada's personal relationships and her work is a testament to the complexity of her character. Each connection, whether familial or romantic, influenced her ideas and ambitions. Ada's correspondence with Charles Babbage, in particular, serves as a prime example of how her relationships fueled her intellectual growth and creativity.

3.2.7 Ada's Marriage to William King: Love, Scandal, and Betrayal

Ada's marriage to William King was marked by both love and scandal. While their partnership was built on mutual respect, Ada's struggles with societal expectations and her own desires often created tension within the relationship. The couple navigated the challenges of their union, ultimately finding a balance between their personal and professional lives.

3.2.8 Ada's Role as a Mother and Family Life

As a mother, Ada faced the dual challenge of balancing her familial responsibilities with her intellectual pursuits. She had three children, and her role as a mother was both a source of joy and a point of contention. Ada's desire for independence often clashed with the expectations of motherhood, leading her to seek ways to integrate her passions into her family life.

3.2.9 The Intertwining of Personal and Professional Worlds in Ada's Life

In Ada Lovelace's life, the personal and professional worlds were inextricably linked. Her relationships shaped her work, and her work influenced her relationships. This intricate interplay reveals the depth of Ada's character and the challenges she faced as a woman striving for recognition in a male-dominated field.

Conclusion

Ada Lovelace's life was a rich tapestry woven with the threads of her complex personality and intricate relationships. As we continue to explore her legacy in literature, art, and technology, we uncover the profound impact she had on the world around her—a true enigma whose brilliance continues to inspire generations.

Ada's Complex Personality

The Multifaceted Nature of Ada's Character

Ada Lovelace was not just a brilliant mathematician and the first programmer; she was a complex individual whose character can be understood through a myriad of lenses. Her personality was a tapestry woven from strands of intellect, creativity, sensitivity, and defiance. To truly appreciate Ada, one must explore the various facets that made her who she was.

Intellectual Curiosity

At the heart of Ada's character was an insatiable intellectual curiosity. From a young age, she exhibited a profound interest in mathematics and the natural sciences. This curiosity was not merely a passing phase; it was a defining trait that influenced her entire life. Ada's mother, Lady Anne Isabella Byron, played a pivotal role in nurturing this curiosity by providing her with a rigorous education. She was determined to ensure that Ada would not fall into the same patterns of idleness that she associated with her husband, Lord Byron. Thus, Ada was immersed in a world of mathematics, logic, and literature, which laid the groundwork for her future innovations.

Creativity and Imagination

Ada's brilliance was not limited to the realm of logic and numbers; she possessed a vivid imagination that allowed her to envision possibilities beyond the constraints of her time. This creative aspect of her character was particularly evident in her work with Charles Babbage on the Analytical Engine. While Babbage focused on the mechanical aspects of the machine, Ada imagined its potential applications. She famously wrote, "The Analytical Engine does not occupy common ground with mere calculating machines. It holds within itself the power of creation." This statement reflects her understanding that computation could extend beyond mere calculations to encompass artistry and creativity.

Emotional Depth

Beneath Ada's intellectual prowess lay a profound emotional depth. She experienced intense feelings, often oscillating between joy and despair. Her letters reveal a woman grappling with her identity, societal expectations, and her own ambitions. Ada's emotional struggles were exacerbated by her health issues, which plagued her throughout her life. Despite these challenges, she channeled her emotions into her work, allowing her to produce some of the most insightful writings on early computing. Her correspondence with Babbage is filled with passionate reflections on their shared vision, showcasing her ability to blend intellect with emotion.

Defiance and Independence

Ada was a woman ahead of her time, and her character was marked by a spirit of defiance and independence. She often challenged the societal norms that dictated women's roles in the 19th century. Her decision to pursue mathematics and technology was a radical act of rebellion against the expectations of her gender. Ada's independence is further exemplified in her writings, where she boldly asserted her ideas and theories, often disregarding the conventional wisdom of her contemporaries. This defiance not only shaped her personal narrative but also laid the groundwork for future generations of women in STEM.

Complex Relationships

Ada's relationships with those around her were equally complex. Her connection with her mother was fraught with tension, as Lady Byron's strict upbringing often clashed with Ada's desire for freedom and exploration. Conversely, her friendship with Charles Babbage was a source of intellectual stimulation and mutual respect. Babbage recognized Ada's talents and often referred to her as "the Enchantress of Numbers." Their correspondence was a dance of ideas, where Ada's creative insights complemented Babbage's engineering prowess.

Legacy of Complexity

The multifaceted nature of Ada's character is perhaps best illustrated by her legacy. She is celebrated not only for her contributions to computing but also as a symbol of women's potential in science and technology. Ada Lovelace's life challenges the simplistic narratives often associated with historical figures. She was a pioneer, a dreamer, a fighter, and a visionary. Her ability to navigate the complexities of her identity and the societal constraints of her time makes her a compelling figure in the history of technology.

In conclusion, Ada Lovelace's character was a rich tapestry of intellect, creativity, emotion, defiance, and complexity. Understanding these facets not only deepens our appreciation for her contributions to mathematics and computing but also serves as an inspiration for future generations. As we celebrate her legacy, we recognize that her multifaceted nature is a reminder that brilliance can manifest in various forms, challenging us to embrace our own complexities in the pursuit of innovation and progress.

Ada's Artistic Sensibilities and Creativity

Ada Lovelace was not only a pioneering mathematician and the first programmer; she was also a woman of remarkable artistic sensibilities. Her creative inclinations were deeply intertwined with her analytical prowess, showcasing a unique blend that set her apart from her contemporaries. This section explores the artistic dimensions of Ada's personality, examining how her creativity influenced her work in mathematics and programming.

The Influence of Art on Ada's Life

Growing up in a household rich with artistic expression, Ada was surrounded by the works of her father, the famous poet Lord Byron, and her mother, Lady Anne Isabella Milbanke, who was herself a highly educated woman with a keen interest in mathematics. This duality of influence—poetry and mathematics—shaped Ada's worldview, fostering a deep appreciation for both the aesthetic and the logical.

Ada's mother, determined to steer her daughter away from the more flamboyant tendencies of her father, emphasized the importance of logic and reason. However, Ada's affinity for the arts could not be suppressed. She often found solace in poetry and literature, which not only inspired her imagination but also provided a creative outlet for her thoughts and ideas.

The Intersection of Art and Science

Ada's belief in the interconnectedness of art and science was a driving force in her work. She famously remarked, "Poetry and mathematics are the same thing," suggesting that both realms require imagination, creativity, and a deep understanding of patterns. This perspective is evident in her approach to programming the Analytical Engine, where she envisioned the potential for machines to create not just calculations, but also music and art.

$$f(x) = ax^2 + bx + c \tag{100}$$

This quadratic function, often used in mathematical modeling, can also be seen as a metaphor for the harmony between structure (the coefficients) and creativity (the variable x). Ada applied similar principles in her programming work, recognizing that the beauty of mathematics lies in its ability to express complex ideas through elegant solutions.

Ada's Creative Writings

In addition to her mathematical work, Ada engaged in creative writing, penning essays and letters that revealed her artistic sensibilities. Her correspondence with Charles Babbage is particularly noteworthy, as it showcases her ability to articulate complex ideas with clarity and flair. In her letters, Ada often infused her scientific discussions with poetic language, illustrating her belief that creativity enhances understanding.

For example, in her notes on the Analytical Engine, Ada wrote:

> "The Analytical Engine does not occupy common ground with mere calculating machines. It holds within its grasp the power to create, to compose, and to express the beauty of the mathematical arts."

This statement not only highlights her visionary thinking but also reflects her intrinsic belief that machines could transcend mere computation to become instruments of creativity.

The Role of Imagination in Programming

Ada's creative imagination was pivotal in her contributions to programming. She understood that programming was not just about writing code; it was about envisioning possibilities. In her famous notes, she outlined how the Analytical Engine could be programmed to perform tasks beyond calculation, such as composing music.

$$\text{Music} = \int_0^T f(t)\, dt \tag{101}$$

Here, $f(t)$ could represent the mathematical representation of musical notes over time, suggesting that through programming, one could harness mathematics to create art. Ada's insight into the potential of programming to intersect with artistic expression is a testament to her forward-thinking mindset.

Creativity as a Driving Force

Ada's artistic sensibilities were not merely an ancillary aspect of her personality; they were a driving force behind her innovative ideas. Her ability to see beyond the rigid confines of mathematics allowed her to conceptualize the Analytical Engine as a versatile tool capable of creative output. This vision was revolutionary and laid the groundwork for future developments in computer science and artificial intelligence.

In summary, Ada Lovelace's artistic sensibilities and creativity played a crucial role in her life and work. By blending her love for the arts with her mathematical genius, she established a legacy that continues to inspire both artists and scientists alike. Her belief in the harmony of creativity and logic serves as a reminder that the most profound innovations often emerge from the intersection of seemingly disparate worlds.

Ada's Intellectual Curiosity and Love for Learning

Ada Lovelace was not merely a product of her noble lineage; she was a brilliant mind fueled by an insatiable intellectual curiosity and a profound love for learning. This section delves into how these traits shaped her life and work, influencing her groundbreaking contributions to mathematics and computing.

From a young age, Ada exhibited a penchant for inquiry and exploration. Her mother, Lady Anne Isabella Byron, recognized her daughter's extraordinary potential and took it upon herself to ensure that Ada received a rigorous education, particularly in mathematics and science. This was a bold move for a woman of her time, as education for girls was often limited to the arts and domestic skills. Lady Byron's commitment to Ada's education laid the groundwork for her daughter's future achievements.

The Foundations of Ada's Learning

Ada's intellectual curiosity was further nurtured by her exposure to influential thinkers and educators. She was introduced to prominent mathematicians and scientists, including Augustus De Morgan, who recognized her talent and encouraged her pursuits. De Morgan's teachings emphasized the importance of logic and analytical thinking, which became cornerstones of Ada's intellectual framework.

One notable instance of Ada's curiosity was her fascination with the concept of mathematical machines. In her early teens, she was captivated by the idea of a mechanical calculator and its potential to perform complex calculations. This fascination would later blossom into a collaborative relationship with Charles Babbage, who was developing the Analytical Engine, a mechanical general-purpose computer.

Ada's Approach to Learning

Ada's approach to learning was characterized by a blend of creativity and analytical rigor. She did not merely accept information; instead, she sought to understand the underlying principles and theories. This method is evident in her work on the Analytical Engine, where she produced what is now known as the Lovelace Note. In this note, she articulated her vision for the machine, including the concept of programming and the potential for machines to manipulate symbols in a manner akin to human thought.

For instance, Ada famously described an algorithm for the Analytical Engine to compute Bernoulli numbers, which can be expressed mathematically as follows:

$$B_n = \sum_{k=0}^{n} \binom{n}{k} \frac{(-1)^k}{k+1} \tag{102}$$

In this equation, B_n represents the n-th Bernoulli number, and the summation runs over all integers k from 0 to n. Ada's ability to translate complex mathematical concepts into a structured algorithm was a testament to her deep understanding and innovative thinking.

Challenges and Triumphs in Learning

Despite her remarkable intellect, Ada faced significant challenges in her quest for knowledge. The societal norms of the 19th century often discouraged women from pursuing intellectual endeavors, particularly in fields like mathematics and science. Ada, however, defied these expectations. She navigated the male-dominated landscape of academia with tenacity and resilience, carving out a space for herself as a legitimate thinker and contributor.

Her correspondence with Babbage is a prime example of her intellectual engagement. The letters exchanged between them were not mere communications; they were dialogues filled with mathematical discussions, theoretical explorations, and mutual respect. These exchanges illuminated Ada's ability to engage with complex ideas and contribute meaningfully to the development of computational theory.

Influence of Literature and Philosophy

In addition to mathematics, Ada's intellectual curiosity extended to literature and philosophy. She was deeply influenced by her father's poetic legacy and often drew parallels between the arts and sciences. Ada believed that creativity and logic were not mutually exclusive; instead, they could coexist harmoniously. This belief is reflected in her writings, where she often employed poetic language to describe mathematical concepts.

For example, Ada once wrote, "The Analytical Engine does not occupy common ground with mere calculating machines. It holds within it the potential for a new kind of thought." This statement captures her visionary perspective and her understanding of the profound implications of computational machinery.

Legacy of Intellectual Curiosity

Ada Lovelace's intellectual curiosity and love for learning did not just propel her own career; they also paved the way for future generations of thinkers and innovators. Her legacy is evident in the ongoing efforts to promote STEM education for girls and women, inspired by her story. Ada's life serves as a reminder that curiosity, creativity, and determination can break down barriers and lead to groundbreaking discoveries.

In conclusion, Ada Lovelace's intellectual curiosity and love for learning were fundamental to her identity as a pioneer in computing. Her relentless pursuit of knowledge, innovative thinking, and ability to synthesize ideas from various disciplines set her apart as a visionary. As we continue to explore the intersections of technology, mathematics, and the arts, we can draw inspiration from Ada's example, reminding ourselves that the quest for knowledge is a lifelong journey worth pursuing.

The Contradictions within Ada's Personality

Ada Lovelace was a woman of remarkable contradictions, a tapestry woven from the threads of intellect, creativity, and societal expectation. At first glance, she appeared to embody the archetype of a Victorian lady, steeped in the traditions of her noble heritage. Yet, beneath this polished exterior lay a fierce intellect and a passion for mathematics that defied the conventions of her time. This duality not only shaped her identity but also influenced her groundbreaking contributions to computing.

One of the most striking contradictions in Ada's personality was her simultaneous embrace of both the analytical and the artistic. On one hand, she was deeply immersed in the world of logic, numbers, and scientific inquiry. Her work with Charles Babbage on the Analytical Engine showcased her extraordinary mathematical abilities, as she translated complex ideas into a language that would later become foundational for computer programming. She famously stated, "The Analytical Engine does not occupy common ground with mere calculating machines," indicating her understanding of its potential far beyond mere computation.

Conversely, Ada possessed a profound appreciation for the arts, particularly poetry and literature. This affinity for creative expression was not merely a pastime; it was an integral part of her identity. Her father, the renowned poet Lord Byron, infused her upbringing with a love for language and beauty, shaping her worldview. Ada often blended her mathematical insights with poetic sensibilities, creating a unique perspective that allowed her to envision the future of technology in a way few could. For example, her notes on the Analytical Engine included a poetic vision of its capabilities, where she foresaw that it could compose music and create art, a notion that was revolutionary for her time.

This interplay between logic and creativity also manifested in her approach to problem-solving. Ada was known for her imaginative thinking, often approaching mathematical challenges with a sense of wonder and curiosity. She would immerse herself in theoretical mathematics, finding joy in the intricacies of algorithms and equations. Yet, she also struggled with the societal expectations placed upon her as a woman in the 19th century. While she excelled in her studies, she often faced criticism and skepticism from her male contemporaries, who viewed her pursuits as unfeminine. This tension between her intellectual aspirations and societal norms created an internal conflict that Ada navigated throughout her life.

Furthermore, Ada's relationships with her peers reflected her contradictory nature. Her partnership with Babbage was marked by mutual respect and admiration, yet it was also fraught with tension. Babbage, a man of strong convictions, often struggled to accept Ada's innovative ideas, viewing her contributions through a lens of traditional mathematics. Ada's ability to challenge his notions while maintaining their collaborative spirit showcased her diplomatic skills, yet it also highlighted the struggle she faced in asserting her identity as a female mathematician in a male-dominated field.

Another layer to Ada's contradictions was her personal life. She was a devoted mother to her three children, yet her ambition in the realm of mathematics often led her to prioritize her intellectual pursuits over her familial responsibilities. This duality created a complex dynamic in her life, as she sought to balance her roles as a mother, wife, and pioneering mathematician. Ada's letters reveal her internal struggles, often oscillating between guilt for neglecting her family and pride in her contributions to science and technology.

The contradictions within Ada's personality extended to her health as well. Throughout her life, she battled various illnesses that affected her physical and mental well-being. Despite these challenges, Ada remained resilient, channeling her struggles into her work. Her determination to overcome adversity became a defining trait, showcasing her strength and tenacity. This resilience, however, was often accompanied by bouts of despair and anxiety, reflecting the complexity of her emotional landscape.

In conclusion, Ada Lovelace was a woman of profound contradictions, embodying the dualities of intellect and creativity, ambition and domesticity, strength and vulnerability. These complexities shaped her contributions to the world of mathematics and computing, allowing her to envision a future where technology and art could coexist. As we celebrate her legacy, it is essential to recognize the multifaceted nature of her personality, for it is within these contradictions that Ada's brilliance truly shines. Her story serves as a reminder that the paths of innovation are often paved with the intricate interplay of diverse traits and experiences, encouraging future generations to embrace their own complexities in pursuit of greatness.

Ada's Struggle with Personal Identity and Expectations

Ada Lovelace, born into a world of privilege and expectation, faced a tumultuous journey in defining her identity amidst the towering legacies of her parents. The daughter of the renowned poet Lord Byron and Anne Isabella Milbanke, Ada was constantly navigating the choppy waters of societal expectations, familial pressures, and her own burgeoning intellect. This section delves into the complexities of Ada's struggle with her personal identity and the expectations placed upon her, illustrating how these factors shaped her life and work.

The Weight of Heritage

From the very beginning, Ada was burdened by the weight of her heritage. Being the daughter of Lord Byron, a man celebrated for his literary genius and notorious for his scandalous lifestyle, placed Ada in a unique yet challenging position. She was not only expected to live up to the intellectual prowess of her father but also to navigate the societal norms that dictated the role of women in the 19th century. Ada's mother, Lady Anne, a mathematician in her own right, sought to steer Ada away from her father's shadow by emphasizing the importance of education, particularly in the fields of mathematics and science. However, this well-meaning guidance often translated into an overwhelming pressure for Ada to excel, leading to an internal conflict between her aspirations and the expectations of those around her.

The Dichotomy of Identity

Ada's identity was characterized by a dichotomy: she was both a product of her noble lineage and a pioneer in a field dominated by men. This duality manifested in her writings and correspondence, where she oscillated between expressing her passion for mathematics and grappling with her societal role. For instance, in her letters to Charles Babbage, Ada often showcased her mathematical insights while simultaneously reflecting on her position as a woman in a male-dominated arena. This tension is evident in her famous remark, "That brain of mine is something more than merely mortal; as time will show." This statement encapsulates her struggle to assert her identity as a thinker and innovator while being acutely aware of the limitations imposed on her by society.

Expectations of Femininity

In addition to her intellectual aspirations, Ada faced the societal expectations of femininity that dictated her behavior, choices, and ultimately, her identity. The 19th century was rife with rigid gender norms, and women were often relegated to the domestic sphere. Ada's mother, despite her progressive views on education, also adhered to some of these societal norms, which created an internal conflict for Ada. She was expected to embody the qualities of a proper Victorian lady—graceful, nurturing, and submissive—while her intellect and ambitions pushed her towards a more unconventional path. This clash is poignantly illustrated in her correspondence, where she often expressed frustration with the limitations placed on her due to her gender.

The Influence of Illness

Ada's struggle with personal identity was further complicated by her health issues. Throughout her life, she faced various illnesses that not only affected her physical well-being but also her mental state. These health challenges often led to periods of isolation, during which Ada grappled with her sense of self. The interplay between her illness and her intellectual pursuits created a complex relationship with her identity. On one hand, her health struggles provided her with the solitude necessary for deep thought and reflection; on the other hand, they reinforced feelings of inadequacy and a desire to prove herself to the world.

The Quest for Autonomy

Despite the myriad challenges, Ada's quest for autonomy remained a defining aspect of her identity. She sought to carve out a space for herself in the world of mathematics and computing, a domain that was largely unwelcoming to women. This pursuit of independence is evident in her collaborations with Babbage, where she emerged as a formidable intellect in her own right. Ada's work on the Analytical Engine is not merely a reflection of her mathematical prowess; it is also a testament to her determination to assert her identity as a thinker and innovator. Her famous notes on the Analytical Engine, which contain what is now recognized as the first algorithm intended for implementation on a machine, exemplify her struggle to claim her place in a field that often sought to marginalize her.

Legacy of Identity Struggles

Ultimately, Ada Lovelace's struggles with personal identity and societal expectations have left an indelible mark on her legacy. Her life serves as a powerful reminder of the challenges faced by women in STEM fields, both in her time and today. Ada's ability to navigate these struggles while making groundbreaking contributions to mathematics and computing illustrates the resilience of the human spirit in the face of adversity. Her story resonates with many modern women who continue to fight against stereotypes and barriers in the pursuit of their passions.

In conclusion, Ada Lovelace's journey through the complexities of personal identity and societal expectations is a rich tapestry woven with threads of brilliance, struggle, and triumph. Her legacy is not only that of the first programmer but also of a woman who defied the odds and carved a path for future generations to follow. As we reflect on her life, we are reminded of the importance of embracing one's identity and the power of perseverance in the face of societal constraints.

The Unconventional Nature of Ada's Thoughts and Ideas

Ada Lovelace was not just a mathematician and the first computer programmer; she was also a visionary whose thoughts and ideas defied the conventional norms of her time. In a society that often relegated women to the sidelines, Ada's intellectual pursuits and imaginative outlook were radical, paving the way for future generations to explore the intersection of mathematics, art, and technology.

Mathematics and Creativity

One of the most striking aspects of Ada's thought process was her ability to blend creativity with mathematical rigor. While many of her contemporaries viewed mathematics as a strictly logical and analytical discipline, Ada saw it as a canvas for creativity. She famously remarked, "The Analytical Engine does not create anything of itself. It can do whatever we ask it to do, but it is the human mind that must provide the vision and the ideas." This perspective highlights her belief that mathematics is not merely about numbers and equations; it is about the ideas that drive innovation.

For instance, Ada's work on the Analytical Engine included not just calculations but also the potential for creating music and art through algorithms. She envisioned a future where machines could compose music, a notion that was revolutionary at the time. Her understanding of the relationship between mathematics and creativity can be exemplified by her approach to programming:

$$\text{Music} = \sum_{i=1}^{n} \text{Notes}_i \times \text{Rhythm}_i \tag{103}$$

In this equation, Ada conceptualized music as a sum of individual notes multiplied by their respective rhythms, demonstrating her ability to apply mathematical principles to artistic endeavors.

Philosophical Insights

Ada's unconventional thinking extended beyond mathematics and into the realm of philosophy. She often pondered the implications of technology on society and the human condition. Her writings reveal a deep concern for the ethical dimensions of technological advancement. For example, in her notes on the Analytical Engine, she speculated about the potential for machines to surpass human intelligence, raising questions that resonate today in discussions about artificial intelligence:

$$\text{Human Intelligence} > \text{Machine Intelligence} \quad \text{(for now)} \tag{104}$$

This equation encapsulates her belief in the superiority of human creativity and intuition over the mechanical processes of machines, a notion that invites ongoing debate in contemporary AI ethics.

Interdisciplinary Approach

Ada's intellectual curiosity led her to explore a wide range of subjects beyond mathematics, including literature, philosophy, and the natural sciences. She was particularly influenced by her poetic upbringing, which shaped her narrative style and her ability to communicate complex ideas in an accessible manner. Ada's interdisciplinary approach is evident in her correspondence with Charles Babbage, where she often infused her technical discussions with literary references and philosophical musings.

For example, she compared the Analytical Engine to a living being, suggesting that it could possess a form of consciousness if programmed correctly. This idea challenges the traditional boundaries of what constitutes a machine and reflects her belief in the interconnectedness of all fields of knowledge:

$$\text{Machine} \sim \text{Living Being} \quad \text{(under certain conditions)} \quad (105)$$

Here, the tilde ( ) symbolizes the potential for machines to emulate certain aspects of life, a concept that continues to inspire discussions about the future of robotics and AI.

Challenging Gender Norms

Ada's unconventional nature was also evident in her refusal to conform to the gender expectations of her time. In a male-dominated field, she boldly asserted her place as a thinker and innovator. She often used her platform to advocate for women's education in mathematics and science, challenging the societal norms that limited opportunities for women. Her writings and advocacy work laid the groundwork for future generations of female scientists and programmers.

In her own words, Ada stated, "I am not afraid of storms, for I am learning how to sail my ship." This metaphor illustrates her determination to navigate the turbulent waters of a male-centric society while pursuing her passions. Ada's legacy is a testament to the importance of challenging societal norms and embracing one's unique perspective.

Conclusion

In summary, Ada Lovelace's unconventional thoughts and ideas were characterized by a unique blend of creativity, philosophical inquiry, interdisciplinary exploration, and a commitment to challenging societal norms. Her ability to see beyond the confines of traditional mathematics and envision a future where technology and creativity coexist is what truly sets her apart as a pioneer. As we continue to explore the realms of technology and innovation, Ada's legacy serves as a reminder of the importance of thinking outside the box and embracing the unconventional.

Her contributions to the field of computing are not merely technical; they are a celebration of the human spirit's capacity for creativity and imagination. Ada Lovelace remains an enduring symbol of what it means to be a visionary thinker, inspiring countless individuals to pursue their passions and challenge the status quo.

Ada's Penchant for Philosophy and Science Fiction

Ada Lovelace, often celebrated as the first programmer, was not only a pioneer in mathematics and computing but also a thinker deeply influenced by the realms of philosophy and science fiction. This section delves into how these interests shaped her intellectual landscape and contributed to her groundbreaking ideas about computation.

Philosophical Influences

From an early age, Ada was exposed to the philosophical ideas of her time, particularly those surrounding logic and the nature of knowledge. Her mother, Lady Anne Isabella Byron, was a formidable influence, instilling in her a rigorous education that included the study of mathematics, natural philosophy, and classical literature. This foundation allowed Ada to engage with the philosophical debates of her era, particularly those concerning the nature of reality and human understanding.

One of the key philosophical influences on Ada was the work of Immanuel Kant, particularly his ideas about the limits of human knowledge and the role of reason. Kant argued that while we can know the world through experience, there are inherent limitations to our understanding, a concept that Ada seemed to resonate with in her later work on the Analytical Engine. She recognized that machines could extend human capability but also understood the philosophical implications of relying on them for knowledge.

Science Fiction and Imagination

Ada's fascination with science fiction was evident in her writings and correspondence. She was particularly inspired by the works of Mary Shelley, whose novel *Frankenstein* explored the consequences of scientific ambition and the ethical dilemmas of creation. This theme of creation and responsibility would echo throughout Ada's own reflections on technology.

In her notes on the Analytical Engine, Ada famously speculated about the potential of machines to create music, art, and even poetry. She envisioned a future where machines could not only compute but also engage in creative endeavors, thus blending the boundaries between human imagination and mechanical capability. This foresight positions her as a proto-science fiction writer, imagining a world where technology and creativity coalesce.

Theoretical Implications

Ada's philosophical and science fiction interests led her to contemplate the theoretical implications of computation. In her notes, she posited that the Analytical Engine could manipulate symbols in a way that was analogous to human thought processes. She wrote:

> "The Analytical Engine does not occupy common ground with mere calculating machines. It holds within it the potential to be a new form of intelligence, a creature of logic and abstraction."

This perspective invites a philosophical inquiry into the nature of intelligence itself. If a machine can process information and generate outputs that mimic human thought, what does that say about the essence of human cognition? Ada's musings foreshadowed contemporary discussions in artificial intelligence about the nature of consciousness and the ethical considerations of creating sentient machines.

Challenges and Problems

Despite her visionary ideas, Ada faced numerous challenges in her quest to integrate philosophy and science fiction with her work in mathematics and computing. One significant problem was the societal perception of women in science during her time. Ada often had to navigate a male-dominated field that dismissed her contributions based on her gender. This societal bias posed a barrier to her ideas being taken seriously, and she frequently struggled to find a platform for her theories.

Moreover, the technical limitations of her era meant that many of her speculative ideas about the capabilities of the Analytical Engine could not be realized during her lifetime. The technology was not sufficiently advanced to explore the full extent of her vision, and Ada's ideas remained largely theoretical, waiting for future generations to unlock their potential.

Examples of Ada's Philosophical and Science Fiction Thinking

A prime example of Ada's philosophical engagement can be found in her analysis of the Analytical Engine's potential. She wrote about how the machine could be programmed to execute complex sequences of operations, which she referred to as "algorithms." This idea laid the groundwork for modern programming, illustrating her deep understanding of both the philosophical and practical dimensions of computation.

In her notes, Ada also speculated about the implications of machines being able to create music. She envisioned a scenario where the Analytical Engine could compose music based on mathematical principles, thus bridging the gap between art and science. This concept resonates with contemporary discussions around algorithmic composition and the role of AI in creative fields.

Conclusion

In conclusion, Ada Lovelace's penchant for philosophy and science fiction profoundly influenced her work as a mathematician and programmer. Her ability to weave together complex ideas about the nature of knowledge, creativity, and technology set her apart as a visionary thinker. By engaging with philosophical concepts and exploring the imaginative possibilities of science fiction, Ada not only contributed to the field of computing but also laid the groundwork for future discussions about the relationship between humans and machines. Her legacy continues to inspire both philosophers and technologists alike, reminding us that the intersection of these disciplines can lead to profound insights about our world and the future of technology.

The Layers of Ada's Enigmatic Persona

Ada Lovelace, often celebrated as the first computer programmer, was a woman of many layers—much like a finely crafted algorithm that reveals its complexity only upon close inspection. To truly appreciate Ada's contributions and her character, we must delve into the various aspects of her persona, exploring her intellect, creativity, and the societal constraints that shaped her life.

1. The Intellectual Layer

At the core of Ada's persona was her remarkable intellect. From a young age, she exhibited a profound aptitude for mathematics and logic. Her early education was marked by a rigorous curriculum, which her mother, Lady Anne, meticulously crafted to counteract the perceived madness of her father, the poet Lord Byron. This intellectual upbringing laid the groundwork for Ada's future innovations.

One of the most significant theoretical frameworks that Ada engaged with was the concept of *abstraction* in mathematics. Abstraction allows mathematicians to generalize concepts, enabling them to solve complex problems by simplifying them into manageable parts. Ada's ability to abstract ideas was evident in her work on Charles Babbage's Analytical Engine, where she envisioned a machine capable of performing calculations beyond mere arithmetic.

$$f(x) = ax^2 + bx + c \qquad (106)$$

This quadratic function, a staple in algebra, exemplifies the kind of mathematical abstraction Ada would manipulate. She understood that the Analytical Engine could not only compute numbers but also handle symbols and variables, paving the way for future programming languages.

2. The Creative Layer

In addition to her mathematical prowess, Ada possessed a rich creative sensibility. She was not merely a mathematician; she was also a poet at heart, influenced by her father's literary legacy. This duality is crucial in understanding her approach to problem-solving. Ada often approached mathematics and programming with a sense of artistry, viewing her work as a form of creative expression.

Her famous metaphor of the Analytical Engine as a "poetical science" illustrates this blend of creativity and logic. In her notes on the engine, she wrote:

> "The Analytical Engine does not occupy common ground with mere 'calculating machines.' It holds within it the potential for creating music, art, and literature, much like the human mind."

This perspective challenges the traditional view of programming as purely a technical endeavor, suggesting that the best programmers are also artists, weaving narratives through code.

3. The Emotional Layer

Beneath Ada's intellectual and creative layers lay a complex emotional landscape. She grappled with societal expectations and personal struggles, including her health issues and the pressure to conform to the roles prescribed for women in her time. Ada's relationship with her mother was particularly fraught; Lady Anne was determined to mold Ada into a model of rationality, often suppressing her artistic inclinations.

Ada's emotional depth is reflected in her correspondence with Babbage, where she expressed not only her enthusiasm for mathematics but also her vulnerabilities. In one letter, she wrote:

> "I often feel like a ship lost at sea, navigating through the waves of logic and the storms of expectation."

This metaphor encapsulates her struggle to balance her ambitions with the limitations imposed upon her by society, highlighting the emotional turmoil that often accompanies genius.

4. The Societal Layer

Finally, we must consider the societal constraints that shaped Ada's life and work. Living in the 19th century, Ada faced significant barriers as a woman in a male-dominated field. Despite her brilliance, she often found herself overshadowed by her male counterparts. The layers of gender bias and societal expectations created an environment where her contributions were frequently overlooked or dismissed.

Ada's advocacy for women's education and her belief in the importance of female representation in STEM fields were revolutionary for her time. She once declared:

> "To deny women the opportunity to learn is to deny the world the potential of their contributions."

This statement not only reflects her commitment to gender equality but also underscores the layers of her persona as an advocate for change.

5. The Legacy Layer

The culmination of these layers forms the legacy of Ada Lovelace. Her multifaceted persona serves as a reminder that innovation is not solely the product of technical skill but also a confluence of creativity, emotion, and societal context. Ada's legacy continues to inspire new generations of programmers, particularly women, who see in her story a reflection of their own struggles and aspirations.

In conclusion, Ada Lovelace's enigmatic persona is a rich tapestry woven from the threads of intellect, creativity, emotion, societal constraints, and legacy. Each layer contributes to our understanding of her as not just a pioneer of programming but as a complex individual navigating the challenges of her time. To truly honor Ada's contributions, we must appreciate the depth of her character and the myriad influences that shaped her remarkable life.

Unlocking the Mysteries of Ada Lovelace: A Portrait of a Brilliant Mind

Ada Lovelace, often heralded as the first computer programmer, was a woman of remarkable intellect and creativity, whose contributions to mathematics and computing were far ahead of her time. To understand the enigma that is Ada, we must peel back the layers of her multifaceted personality, her groundbreaking ideas, and her profound impact on the world of technology.

The Complexity of Ada's Character

At the heart of Ada's brilliance lies a complex personality characterized by contradictions and a thirst for knowledge. She was born on December 10, 1815, to the infamous poet Lord Byron and Anne Isabella Milbanke. While her father was a literary genius, Ada's mother, a mathematician, ensured that Ada received a rigorous education in the sciences. This duality of artistic and scientific influence shaped Ada into a unique thinker who could traverse both realms.

Ada's artistic sensibilities often manifested in her approach to mathematics. She viewed mathematical concepts not merely as abstract entities but as beautiful structures, akin to poetry. This perspective allowed her to innovate in ways that others could not fathom. For instance, her work on the Analytical Engine was not just about programming but about envisioning a new paradigm of computation that could handle complex algorithms.

The Role of Logic and Imagination

Ada's affinity for logic was complemented by her vivid imagination. She famously stated, "The Analytical Engine does not occupy common ground with mere calculating machines." Here, she recognized that the machine could do more than calculations; it could manipulate symbols and execute complex sequences of operations—essentially laying the groundwork for modern programming languages.

To illustrate this point, consider the mathematical concept of a function. In modern programming, a function can be defined as follows:

$$f(x) = ax^2 + bx + c \tag{107}$$

where a, b, and c are constants. Ada's insight into the potential of functions extended beyond mere computation; she foresaw that the Analytical Engine could be programmed to execute sequences of operations that could solve complex problems, thus transforming how we think about machines and their capabilities.

Ada's Vision for the Analytical Engine

Ada's collaboration with Charles Babbage on the Analytical Engine was a pivotal moment in computing history. She recognized that this machine could be programmed to perform any calculation, provided it was given the right instructions. Her notes on the engine included what is now considered the first algorithm intended for implementation on a machine, specifically for calculating Bernoulli numbers.

The algorithm can be expressed as follows:

$$B_n = \sum_{k=0}^{n} \binom{n}{k} \cdot \frac{(-1)^k}{k+1} \tag{108}$$

where B_n represents the n-th Bernoulli number. Ada's ability to translate mathematical concepts into a structured format that a machine could understand exemplifies her visionary thinking.

The Legacy of Ada's Insights

Despite her groundbreaking contributions, Ada's work remained largely unrecognized during her lifetime. The societal norms of the 19th century often relegated women to the shadows, particularly in fields dominated by men. Ada's struggle against these constraints is a testament to her resilience. She once remarked, "I am more convinced that I shall be able to do something in the world than I ever was before." This conviction propelled her to challenge the status quo.

Ada's legacy is not only evident in her contributions to programming but also in her influence on future generations. Her ideas about the potential of machines to perform complex tasks have paved the way for the development of modern computing. Today, programming languages such as Python, Java, and C++ owe a debt to the foundational concepts that Ada introduced.

Conclusion: A Portrait of Brilliance

In conclusion, unlocking the mysteries of Ada Lovelace reveals a portrait of a brilliant mind that defied the conventions of her time. Her ability to blend logic with creativity, her visionary insights into computing, and her unwavering determination to make her mark on the world have left an indelible impact on technology and society. As we continue to navigate the complexities of the digital age, we must remember Ada Lovelace not just as a historical figure but as an enduring symbol of innovation and resilience.

By celebrating her contributions and advocating for the representation of women in technology, we honor Ada's legacy and inspire future generations to follow in her footsteps. After all, as Ada herself might say, the future of technology is not merely about machines, but about the brilliant minds that dare to envision what could be.

Ada's Personal Relationships

Ada's Relationship with Her Parents

Ada Lovelace, born on December 10, 1815, was the only legitimate child of the famous poet Lord Byron and his wife, Anne Isabella Milbanke. Their tumultuous relationship set the stage for Ada's complex upbringing, as her parents' marriage was short-lived and fraught with conflict. This section delves into the intricacies of Ada's relationship with both her parents, exploring how their influences shaped her identity and intellectual pursuits.

The Influence of Lord Byron

Lord Byron, a literary titan of the Romantic era, was known for his passionate poetry and scandalous lifestyle. His relationship with Ada's mother, Anne, was characterized by intense emotions and dramatic events. The couple married in January 1815, but their union was tumultuous, leading to their separation just a year later. Byron's departure from the family left a significant mark on Ada's life, as she never truly knew her father.

Despite his absence, Byron's legacy loomed large over Ada. She was often described as a child of contradictions, embodying both the artistic flair of her father and the rationality of her mother. Although Ada had little direct interaction with Byron, his reputation and literary genius influenced her aspirations. The romantic notions of creativity and passion for art were traits she inherited from him, which would later intertwine with her analytical mind.

Lady Anne Milbanke: The Mathematician Mother

In stark contrast to Byron, Ada's mother, Anne Isabella Milbanke, was a woman of logic and discipline. Known as the "Princess of Parallels," she was well-versed in mathematics and was determined to ensure that her daughter received a rigorous education, particularly in the sciences. Lady Anne's influence was crucial in steering Ada towards mathematics, as she sought to counteract the perceived instability of her father's artistic temperament.

Lady Anne's educational philosophy was rooted in the belief that a strong foundation in mathematics would protect Ada from the emotional turmoil she experienced due to her father's legacy. She often emphasized the importance of rational thought, instilling in Ada a love for numbers and analytical reasoning. This maternal guidance cultivated Ada's exceptional mathematical abilities, which would later set her apart as a pioneering figure in computer science.

A Dual Legacy: Artistic and Analytical

The dual influence of her parents resulted in a unique blend of creativity and logic within Ada. While her father represented the world of poetry and imagination, her mother embodied the principles of mathematics and science. This dichotomy is reflected in Ada's work, where she applied her mathematical prowess to the imaginative realm of the Analytical Engine, a concept developed by Charles Babbage.

Ada's upbringing was not without its challenges. The absence of her father and the strict educational regimen imposed by her mother created a complex emotional landscape for her. She often grappled with feelings of inadequacy and the desire to prove herself, striving to carve out her own identity amidst the shadows of her parents' legacies.

The Impact of Parental Relationships on Ada's Development

The relationship Ada had with her parents profoundly impacted her development as a thinker and innovator. The emotional turmoil stemming from her father's absence and her mother's rigid expectations contributed to Ada's resilience and determination. She developed a strong sense of self, driven by the desire to excel in a male-dominated field.

Moreover, the contrasting approaches of her parents led Ada to seek a balance between creativity and logic. This balance would become a hallmark of her work as she ventured into the uncharted territory of programming. Ada's ability to envision the potential of the Analytical Engine was a testament to her unique upbringing, where the artistic and analytical coalesced into a singular vision.

Conclusion: The Lasting Influence of Her Parents

In conclusion, Ada Lovelace's relationship with her parents played a pivotal role in shaping her identity and intellectual pursuits. The absence of her father, combined with her mother's strong emphasis on mathematics, created a complex interplay of influences that Ada navigated throughout her life. This dual legacy of artistic creativity and analytical rigor not only fueled her groundbreaking work in computing but also established her as a symbol of the possibilities that arise when diverse influences converge.

As we reflect on Ada's journey, it becomes evident that her parents' contrasting legacies were instrumental in her development as the first programmer. Their impact resonates through history, reminding us of the profound ways in which our familial relationships can shape our paths and aspirations.

The Influence of Ada's Father Lord Byron

Ada Lovelace's father, the illustrious Lord Byron, was not just a literary giant but also a complex figure whose influence permeated Ada's life and work. Born George Gordon Byron in 1788, he became one of the leading figures of the Romantic movement, known for his passionate poetry and tumultuous personal life. His legacy, however, was a double-edged sword, shaping Ada's identity and intellectual pursuits in profound ways.

The Legacy of Lord Byron

Lord Byron was celebrated for his works such as *Childe Harold's Pilgrimage* and *Don Juan*, which explored themes of love, nature, and the human condition. His poetry was characterized by emotional depth and a sense of individualism, which resonated with the Romantic ideals of the era. The influence of Byron's literary genius can be seen in Ada's own writings, where she often infused her mathematical analyses with poetic language and imaginative flair.

Despite his literary success, Byron's relationship with Ada was fraught with absence and complexity. After separating from Ada's mother, Lady Anne Isabella Milbanke, shortly after Ada's birth, Byron left a void in her life that would shape her character. This absence instilled in Ada a longing for paternal approval and recognition, which manifested in her relentless pursuit of excellence in her work.

Byron's reputation as a passionate and often reckless figure may have also influenced Ada's own struggles with societal expectations and personal ambition.

Intellectual Curiosity and Creativity

Byron's influence extended beyond mere emotional legacy; it also fostered Ada's intellectual curiosity. His eclectic interests in philosophy, science, and the arts likely inspired Ada's own interdisciplinary approach to mathematics and programming. Ada was known to engage deeply with the scientific ideas of her time, often blending them with her artistic sensibilities.

For instance, her fascination with the Analytical Engine can be seen as a reflection of Byron's own revolutionary spirit. Just as Byron challenged the societal norms of his day through his poetry, Ada sought to challenge the conventions of her time by delving into the realms of mathematics and computing. She famously noted that the Analytical Engine could be programmed to perform complex calculations, making her one of the first to envision the potential of machines to extend human capabilities.

The Dichotomy of Influence

However, the influence of Lord Byron was not solely positive. His tumultuous lifestyle and reputation for scandal may have contributed to Ada's struggles with societal norms and expectations. As a woman in a male-dominated field, Ada often found herself battling against the stereotypes and limitations imposed by society. The shadow of her father's notorious reputation could have intensified these challenges, as she navigated her identity as both a Lovelace and a pioneer in mathematics.

This dichotomy is evident in Ada's correspondence with Charles Babbage, where she often expressed a blend of confidence and self-doubt. For example, in her notes on the Analytical Engine, Ada wrote:

$$\text{Programming} \implies \text{Creativity} + \text{Logic} \tag{109}$$

This equation embodies Ada's understanding of programming as a synthesis of her father's artistic influence and her own mathematical rigor. It highlights her belief that creativity and logic are not mutually exclusive but rather complementary forces in the pursuit of innovation.

The Personal Connection

Furthermore, Ada's relationship with her father, though distant, was characterized by a profound admiration for his intellect and artistic prowess. She often sought to emulate his brilliance in her own work. This admiration is illustrated in her writings, where she frequently referenced the importance of imagination in scientific endeavors. Ada believed that creativity was essential in problem-solving, a notion she likely inherited from Byron's poetic ethos.

In her notes on the Analytical Engine, Ada famously stated:

> "The Analytical Engine does not occupy common ground with mere calculating machines. It holds within it the power to create and understand."

This assertion reflects not only her understanding of the machine's capabilities but also her desire to transcend the limitations imposed on her gender. Ada's ambition can be seen as a rebellion against the constraints of her time, a trait she may have inherited from her father's own defiance of societal norms.

Conclusion

In conclusion, the influence of Lord Byron on Ada Lovelace was multifaceted, shaping her intellectual pursuits and personal identity in significant ways. His legacy as a literary figure provided Ada with a model of creativity and passion, while his absence instilled in her a drive to seek recognition and validation. The interplay between admiration and rebellion defined Ada's journey as the first programmer, allowing her to carve out her own path in a world that often sought to limit her potential.

Ada Lovelace's story is a testament to the enduring impact of familial relationships on personal and professional development. Lord Byron's influence, complex and contradictory, serves as a reminder of how our legacies can inspire both greatness and struggle, ultimately shaping the innovators of tomorrow.

Ada's Complicated Relationship with Her Mother

Ada Lovelace's relationship with her mother, Lady Anne Isabella Byron, was a complex tapestry woven with threads of love, expectation, and conflict. To understand this dynamic, one must first consider the historical context in which they lived, particularly the societal norms surrounding motherhood and education in the 19th century.

Lady Anne, a woman of considerable intellect and ambition, was determined to ensure that her daughter would not follow in the footsteps of her father, the notorious poet Lord Byron. After their tumultuous marriage ended with Lord Byron leaving the family, Lady Anne took it upon herself to raise Ada with a strict regimen of education, particularly in mathematics and science, which she believed would keep Ada from the perceived madness of her father. This approach can be understood through the lens of what psychologist Alice Miller describes as the "poisonous pedagogy," where a parent's unresolved issues and fears shape their child's upbringing in detrimental ways.

$$\text{Parental Influence} = \text{Expectations} + \text{Fears} - \text{Support} \qquad (110)$$

In Ada's case, her mother's expectations were high, and her fears of Ada inheriting Lord Byron's supposed madness loomed large. Lady Anne's educational methods were rigorous and often harsh, leading to a strained relationship characterized by a lack of emotional warmth. Ada's early years were marked by an intense focus on mathematics, which, while nurturing her intellectual abilities, also created an environment where emotional expression was stifled. This dichotomy is evident in Ada's later writings, where she oscillated between a passion for her work and a longing for maternal approval.

The tension in their relationship can be illustrated by a pivotal moment when Ada, as a young girl, expressed her desire to pursue her interests in mathematics and science. Lady Anne, fearing that such pursuits would lead Ada down a path of isolation and potential madness, often discouraged her from indulging in what she deemed "unfeminine" interests. This conflict is reminiscent of the theories of gender socialization posited by sociologist Judith Butler, who argues that societal norms often dictate the roles individuals are expected to play based on their gender.

$$\text{Gender Norms} = \text{Societal Expectations} + \text{Cultural Scripts} \qquad (111)$$

As Ada grew older, the relationship evolved but remained fraught with tension. Lady Anne's insistence on a strict education clashed with Ada's desire for intellectual freedom. This struggle was compounded by Ada's recurrent health issues, which Lady Anne often interpreted as signs of weakness or instability. The mother-daughter dynamic can be further analyzed through the framework of attachment theory, which posits that the quality of early relationships significantly impacts an individual's emotional development and future relationships.

$$\text{Attachment Quality} = \text{Parental Responsiveness} + \text{Child's Needs} \qquad (112)$$

In Ada's case, the lack of emotional support from her mother may have contributed to her struggles with self-doubt and her need for external validation, particularly in her collaborations with Charles Babbage. Despite these challenges, Ada's relationship with her mother also had moments of tenderness and mutual respect, especially as Lady Anne recognized Ada's extraordinary talents. This duality reflects the complexities of familial love, where admiration and conflict can coexist.

Furthermore, the impact of Lady Anne's relationship with Ada is evident in Ada's writings, where she often referenced her mother's influence on her intellectual pursuits. For example, in her correspondence with Babbage, Ada expressed a desire to prove her worth and capabilities, perhaps as a way to gain her mother's approval and recognition. This need for validation can be interpreted through the lens of feminist theory, which emphasizes the importance of female empowerment and the struggle against patriarchal constraints.

$$\text{Empowerment} = \text{Self-Recognition} + \text{Supportive Relationships} \qquad (113)$$

In conclusion, Ada Lovelace's relationship with her mother was marked by a complicated interplay of love, expectation, and conflict. While Lady Anne's intentions were rooted in a desire to protect her daughter from the perceived dangers of her father's legacy, the methods she employed often led to a strained relationship that impacted Ada's emotional and intellectual development. Understanding this dynamic is crucial in appreciating the multifaceted nature of Ada's genius and the historical context in which she navigated her path as a pioneering figure in mathematics and computing. Their relationship serves as a poignant reminder of the challenges faced by women in the pursuit of their passions, particularly in a society that often imposed rigid gender roles and expectations.

Ada's Relationship with Her Siblings

Ada Lovelace, born on December 10, 1815, was the only legitimate child of Lord Byron and Lady Anne Isabella Milbanke. Although her parents' tumultuous relationship resulted in a separation shortly after her birth, Ada had siblings who played significant roles in her life, albeit in varying degrees of closeness and influence. This section explores Ada's relationship with her siblings, particularly her half-siblings, and how these familial dynamics impacted her development.

The Sibling Landscape

Ada had a complex family structure. Her father, the famous poet Lord Byron, had several children with different women, but Ada's relationship with her half-siblings was primarily influenced by her upbringing and her mother's insistence on a structured education. Ada's mother, Lady Anne, was determined to distance her daughter from her father's notorious lifestyle and legacy. This protective instinct led to a somewhat isolated upbringing for Ada, which shaped her interactions with her half-siblings.

Half-Siblings and Their Influence

Ada's half-siblings included:

+ **Augusta Ada Byron (later Augusta Ada King, Countess of Lovelace)**: Ada's most notable sibling, often viewed as a mirror to Ada's genius. Augusta was the daughter of Lord Byron and his half-sister, Augusta Leigh. Although they shared the same father, their relationship was complicated by societal expectations and the stigma surrounding their lineage.

+ **Allegra Byron**: Born to Lord Byron and Claire Clairmont, Allegra was Ada's half-sister, but she died young at the age of five. The loss of Allegra was a poignant event that underscored the fragility of familial bonds in Ada's life.

Despite the shared bloodlines, the relationships were strained. Ada's mother often kept her away from the Byron family, attempting to shield her from the chaotic influences of her father's legacy. This decision limited Ada's interactions with her half-siblings, particularly Augusta, who later became an important figure in Ada's life.

Ada and Augusta: A Complicated Bond

Although Ada and Augusta had limited direct interactions during their childhood, their paths crossed in adulthood, where their mutual interests in mathematics and science created a bond. Augusta, who later became the Countess of Lovelace, was supportive of Ada's pursuits in mathematics, often encouraging her to explore her intellectual passions.

The correspondence between Ada and Augusta reveals the depth of their relationship. Letters exchanged between the two often discussed mathematical concepts, scientific ideas, and the challenges they faced as women in a male-dominated society. This intellectual camaraderie served as a crucial support system for Ada, who often felt isolated due to her unique talents.

$$\text{Support} = \text{Encouragement} + \text{Shared Interests} \qquad (114)$$

This equation illustrates the foundational elements of Ada and Augusta's relationship. The support they provided each other was rooted in their shared interests, which helped Ada navigate the societal pressures of her time.

The Impact of Isolation

Despite the eventual support from Augusta, Ada's early years were marked by a sense of isolation. Her mother's strict upbringing, aimed at preventing her from following in her father's erratic footsteps, often left Ada feeling disconnected from her family.

This isolation had profound effects on Ada's personality and her work. It fostered a sense of independence but also a yearning for connection. Her struggles to balance her familial ties with her intellectual ambitions shaped her worldview and contributed to her unique approach to mathematics and programming.

Conclusion: The Legacy of Sibling Dynamics

In conclusion, Ada Lovelace's relationship with her siblings, particularly her half-sister Augusta, was complex and multifaceted. While early isolation from her family created challenges, the eventual bond formed through shared intellectual pursuits became a significant part of Ada's support system.

The dynamics of her family life highlight the importance of sibling relationships in shaping one's identity and ambitions. Ada's story is a testament to how familial connections, even when fraught with challenges, can provide a foundation for resilience and innovation.

As we reflect on Ada's legacy, it is essential to recognize the role her siblings played, however indirectly, in shaping her path as the first programmer. The interplay of isolation, support, and shared interests illustrates the profound impact of family on one's journey toward greatness.

$$\text{Legacy} = \text{Innovation} + \text{Support} + \text{Resilience} \qquad (115)$$

Ada's Romantic Interests and Love Affairs

Ada Lovelace, often celebrated for her groundbreaking contributions to mathematics and computing, also navigated the complex waters of romantic relationships that significantly influenced her life and work. Born into a world that often placed women in the shadows of their male counterparts, Ada's romantic interests reflect both her passionate spirit and the societal constraints she faced.

Early Romantic Interests

From a young age, Ada displayed a keen interest in the world around her, including the dynamics of human relationships. Her early years were marked by the absence of her father, the infamous poet Lord Byron, who left shortly after her birth. This absence left a profound impact on her emotional landscape, shaping her views on love and companionship. In her teenage years, Ada developed a close friendship with her tutor, Augustus De Morgan, a noted mathematician. Although their relationship remained platonic, it opened Ada's eyes to the intellectual companionship she would later seek in romantic partners.

The Courtship with William King

Ada's most notable romantic relationship was with William King, whom she married in 1835. Their courtship was marked by a blend of intellectual admiration and societal expectation. William King, a man of considerable wealth and title, provided Ada with the stability she sought, yet their marriage was not without its challenges. Ada's mother, Lady Anne Isabella Byron, was initially opposed to the union, fearing that William's aristocratic background might overshadow Ada's burgeoning career in mathematics. Despite these obstacles, Ada and William's relationship blossomed, and they shared a mutual respect for each other's intellect.

The Complexity of Marriage

The marriage between Ada and William King was emblematic of the 19th-century societal norms that often constrained women. While Ada was a pioneer in her field, her role as a wife and mother took precedence in the eyes of society. The couple had three children: Byron, Anne, and Ralph, and while Ada embraced motherhood, she often struggled to balance her familial duties with her passion for mathematics. This tension is reflected in her correspondence, where she oscillates between expressions of love for her children and frustrations about the limitations imposed on her scholarly pursuits.

Romantic Affairs and Intellectual Partnerships

Despite her devotion to her family, Ada's romantic inclinations were not solely directed towards her husband. She maintained friendships with several prominent men of her time, including Charles Babbage, the father of the Analytical Engine. Their relationship was characterized by a profound intellectual connection, often mistaken for romantic interest. Ada's letters to Babbage reveal a deep admiration for his work, with her affection manifesting through spirited discussions about mathematics and engineering.

In addition to her relationship with Babbage, Ada was known to have a flirtatious rapport with several other male contemporaries. One notable figure was the poet Alfred Lord Tennyson, who shared a mutual acquaintance with Ada. Their interactions were often playful, filled with literary banter that hinted at a deeper connection. However, these relationships were largely platonic, reflecting Ada's complex understanding of love as intertwined with intellectual companionship.

The Influence of Romantic Relationships on Her Work

Ada's romantic interests and affairs had a significant impact on her work and legacy. The tension between her roles as a mother, wife, and mathematician often led to feelings of isolation. In her writings, she expressed a longing for understanding and recognition, not just as a woman but as a thinker in her own right. This desire for acknowledgment fueled her determination to contribute to the field of mathematics and computing, as she sought to carve out a space for herself in a male-dominated arena.

Moreover, Ada's correspondence with Babbage and other intellectuals often reflected her romantic yearnings. She infused her mathematical ideas with a sense of passion, viewing her work as an extension of her emotional life. In her famous notes on the Analytical Engine, she likened the machine's operations to a form of poetry, suggesting that the act of programming was akin to composing music. This metaphor illustrates how her romantic inclinations permeated her professional work, allowing her to transcend the boundaries of traditional mathematics.

Legacy of Ada's Romantic Life

In retrospect, Ada Lovelace's romantic interests and love affairs reveal a woman who was not only a brilliant mathematician but also a passionate individual navigating the complexities of personal relationships. Her marriage to William King provided a foundation, yet her intellectual partnerships and friendships with men in her field allowed her to explore the intersections of love and intellect.

Ada's legacy is not solely defined by her contributions to computing but also by her ability to navigate the intricate web of societal expectations surrounding love and gender. Her story serves as a reminder that the personal and professional are often intertwined, and that the struggles of women in STEM are deeply rooted in the romantic dynamics of their lives. As we celebrate Ada's achievements, we must also acknowledge the complexities of her romantic life, which shaped her identity as a pioneer in technology and mathematics.

In conclusion, Ada Lovelace's romantic interests and love affairs were integral to her life story. They reflect the challenges she faced as a woman in the 19th century and the ways in which her relationships influenced her groundbreaking work. As we continue to honor her legacy, let us remember that behind every equation and algorithm was a woman who loved passionately and sought to make her mark on the world.

The Impact of Ada's Personal Relationships on Her Work

Ada Lovelace, often heralded as the first computer programmer, was not only a pioneer in mathematics and computing but also a complex individual whose personal relationships significantly influenced her work. These relationships, particularly with her parents, Charles Babbage, and her husband William King, shaped her intellectual development, emotional landscape, and ultimately her contributions to the field of computer science.

Influence of Parental Relationships

Ada's relationship with her parents was marked by both inspiration and conflict. Her father, the renowned poet Lord Byron, left the family when Ada was just a few months old, leading to a complicated legacy of abandonment and yearning. Despite their estrangement, Ada's awareness of her father's literary genius instilled in her a desire to excel and prove her worth, a theme that would echo throughout her life. This drive can be seen as a motivating factor in her pursuit of mathematics and logic, fields traditionally dominated by men.

Conversely, Ada's mother, Lady Anne Isabella Byron, played a crucial role in shaping her educational path. Determined to steer Ada away from the perceived madness of her father, Lady Byron emphasized a rigorous education, particularly in mathematics and science. This maternal influence provided Ada with the foundational skills that would later allow her to collaborate with Babbage.

However, this relationship was not without its tensions; Lady Byron's strictness often clashed with Ada's creative inclinations, creating an internal struggle between her artistic and scientific pursuits.

Collaboration with Charles Babbage

One of the most significant relationships in Ada's life was her partnership with Charles Babbage, the inventor of the Analytical Engine. Their correspondence began in 1833 when Ada was introduced to Babbage at a dinner party. This meeting marked the beginning of a collaborative relationship that would yield groundbreaking ideas in computing. Babbage's innovative designs captivated Ada, and her mathematical prowess allowed her to grasp the complexities of his work.

The synergy between Ada and Babbage was profound; their exchanges were characterized by mutual respect and intellectual curiosity. In her notes on the Analytical Engine, Ada articulated concepts that were revolutionary for her time, such as the idea of a machine that could manipulate symbols and perform calculations based on predefined instructions. This collaboration was not merely academic; it was a melding of two brilliant minds, each enhancing the other's ideas. For instance, Ada's translation of an article on Babbage's engine included her own notes, which detailed an algorithm for calculating Bernoulli numbers, effectively making her the first programmer in history.

$$\text{Bernoulli Numbers} = \sum_{n=0}^{\infty} \frac{B_n}{n!} x^n \tag{116}$$

This equation illustrates Ada's ability to apply theoretical mathematics to practical programming, showcasing how her relationship with Babbage catalyzed her innovative thinking.

Marriage and Family Life

Ada's marriage to William King in 1835 introduced another layer of complexity to her personal and professional life. While King was supportive of Ada's intellectual pursuits, societal expectations of women at the time often confined them to domestic roles. Ada's struggle to balance her responsibilities as a wife and mother with her ambitions in mathematics and science is a poignant aspect of her biography.

The birth of her three children further complicated her work. Ada often found herself navigating the expectations of motherhood while yearning for intellectual fulfillment. Despite these challenges, she continued to engage with her mathematical interests and maintained her correspondence with Babbage, often using her familial obligations as a backdrop for her intellectual endeavors. The tension between her domestic life and her aspirations is reflected in her writings, where she frequently oscillated between the roles of mother and mathematician.

The Interplay of Relationships and Creativity

Ada's personal relationships significantly impacted her creative output. The emotional support she received from Babbage and the intellectual stimulation they shared allowed her to thrive in a male-dominated field. Conversely, the pressures from her marriage and societal expectations often led to periods of self-doubt and frustration. This interplay of relationships created a dynamic environment that fueled her creativity while simultaneously posing challenges.

For instance, during times of personal turmoil, Ada would often retreat into her mathematical work as a form of solace. Her writings reveal a deep connection between her emotional experiences and her intellectual pursuits. The letters exchanged between Ada and Babbage are filled with insights that reflect not only their professional collaboration but also their personal rapport, highlighting the importance of supportive relationships in fostering innovation.

Conclusion

In conclusion, the impact of Ada Lovelace's personal relationships on her work is a testament to the complexity of her life as a pioneering woman in technology. The influences of her parents, her collaboration with Charles Babbage, and her marriage to William King all played integral roles in shaping her identity as a mathematician and programmer. Ada's ability to navigate these relationships while contributing to the foundations of computer science speaks to her resilience and brilliance. Her legacy serves as an enduring reminder of the importance of supportive relationships in the pursuit of innovation and the challenges faced by women in STEM fields.

Ada's Marriage to William King: Love, Scandal, and Betrayal

Ada Lovelace's marriage to William King in 1835 was a union that combined elements of romance, societal expectations, and the complexities of a woman striving for intellectual independence in a male-dominated world. At first glance, their relationship appeared to be a fairy tale, but as with many stories, the reality was far more intricate.

The Courtship: A Romantic Prelude

The courtship between Ada and William was characterized by a whirlwind of emotions. Ada, who was already known for her brilliance in mathematics and her friendship with Charles Babbage, found in William a partner who appreciated her intellect. William, the son of a wealthy family and an established figure in society, was captivated by Ada's unique blend of creativity and analytical prowess. Their relationship blossomed amidst the backdrop of the Victorian era, a time when societal norms dictated that women should remain in the domestic sphere.

$$\text{Romantic Interest} = \text{Intellectual Connection} + \text{Social Compatibility} \quad (117)$$

This equation illustrates the foundation of their relationship, where romantic interest was built on both intellectual connection and social compatibility. However, the societal expectations of the time imposed significant constraints on their union.

The Marriage: A Complicated Union

Upon their marriage, Ada took on the role of a wife and mother, responsibilities that often overshadowed her intellectual pursuits. William King became the Earl of Lovelace, and Ada was thus styled as Lady Lovelace. The couple had three children: Byron, Anne, and Ralph. While William supported Ada's interests, the demands of family life often conflicted with her ambitions.

Despite the initial harmony, the marriage faced challenges. Ada's struggle with health issues, including bouts of illness that plagued her throughout her life, added strain to their relationship. The societal pressures of being a noblewoman and the expectations of motherhood further complicated Ada's ability to pursue her passion for mathematics and programming.

Scandal and Betrayal: The Dark Side of Nobility

As the years progressed, whispers of scandal began to circulate. Ada's close relationship with Charles Babbage raised eyebrows, leading to speculation about the nature of their collaboration. The two shared a profound intellectual bond, often exchanging letters filled with mathematical ideas and visions for the Analytical Engine. However, the Victorian society was quick to judge, and Ada's association with Babbage was viewed through a lens of suspicion.

$$\text{Public Perception} = f(\text{Collaboration with Babbage}, \text{Societal Norms}) \quad (118)$$

This function illustrates how Ada's public perception was influenced by her collaboration with Babbage and the societal norms of the time. The more she engaged with Babbage, the more scrutiny she faced, leading to tensions within her marriage.

The situation escalated when rumors of infidelity began to surface. Although there was no concrete evidence of betrayal on Ada's part, the emotional toll of these rumors weighed heavily on her. The combination of Ada's health issues and the strain of societal expectations created a tumultuous environment, leading to a sense of isolation for Ada.

Resilience and Reconciliation

Despite the challenges, Ada demonstrated remarkable resilience. She sought solace in her work, channeling her frustrations into her mathematical pursuits. Her relationship with William, though strained, was not without moments of affection and support. They navigated the complexities of their marriage with a shared understanding of the pressures that came with their social status.

In her letters, Ada often expressed her desire for intellectual freedom and the need for space to explore her ideas. William, recognizing Ada's brilliance, occasionally supported her endeavors, albeit reluctantly. Their relationship became a delicate balance between love and the constraints of societal expectations.

$$\text{Resilience} = \text{Support from William} + \text{Personal Determination} \qquad (119)$$

This equation highlights how Ada's resilience was bolstered by both the support from her husband and her own determination to pursue her passions.

Legacy of Their Union

Ultimately, Ada's marriage to William King was a complex tapestry woven with threads of love, scandal, and betrayal. While their relationship faced significant challenges, it also served as a backdrop for Ada's remarkable contributions to mathematics and computing. Her ability to navigate the intricacies of her personal life while maintaining her intellectual pursuits is a testament to her strength and determination.

In retrospect, Ada Lovelace's marriage can be seen as a reflection of the struggles faced by women in the 19th century, particularly those who dared to step outside the confines of traditional roles. Her legacy, intertwined with her marriage, continues to inspire future generations of women in STEM fields, reminding us of the importance of resilience in the face of societal pressures.

$$Legacy = Intellectual\ Contributions + Personal\ Struggles \qquad (120)$$

In conclusion, Ada Lovelace's marriage to William King was not merely a love story; it was a complex narrative that encompassed the trials and tribulations of a pioneering woman in a world that often sought to limit her potential. Her journey serves as an enduring reminder of the importance of perseverance, love, and the pursuit of knowledge.

Ada's Role as a Mother and Family Life

Ada Lovelace, known for her groundbreaking contributions to the field of computing, was not just a pioneer in mathematics and programming; she was also a devoted mother. Her role as a mother is often overshadowed by her professional achievements, but it is essential to recognize how her family life intertwined with her intellectual pursuits and shaped her legacy.

Balancing Motherhood and Ambition

Ada Lovelace married William King, the Earl of Lovelace, in 1835. Together, they had three children: Byron, Anne Isabella, and Ralph. Balancing the demands of motherhood with her intellectual ambitions was no small feat, especially in the Victorian era, when societal expectations often dictated that women prioritize family over personal aspirations. Yet, Ada navigated these challenges with a unique blend of determination and creativity.

The Influence of Motherhood on Ada's Work

The experience of motherhood profoundly influenced Ada's work. As a mother, she often reflected on the nature of education and the importance of nurturing a child's intellectual curiosity. Ada believed that children should be encouraged to explore their interests and develop their talents. This philosophy was evident in her approach to her own children, whom she sought to inspire with her love for mathematics and science.

For instance, Ada's son, Byron, displayed an early aptitude for mathematics, and she was keen to foster this talent. Ada often engaged her children in discussions about scientific concepts, illustrating complex ideas through storytelling and practical examples. This hands-on approach not only stimulated their minds but also allowed Ada to remain connected to her work while fulfilling her maternal duties.

Challenges of Victorian Motherhood

Despite her commitment to her children, Ada faced significant challenges as a mother in a patriarchal society. The societal norms of the Victorian era imposed strict limitations on women's roles, often relegating them to the domestic sphere. Ada's struggle to balance her intellectual pursuits with her responsibilities as a mother exemplifies the broader challenges faced by women of her time.

Moreover, Ada's health issues, including her struggles with illness throughout her life, further complicated her role as a mother. These health challenges often left her fatigued and unable to fully engage with her children. Nevertheless, Ada's resilience shone through as she sought to maintain a nurturing environment for her family, even when faced with personal adversity.

Ada's Letters: A Window into Her Family Life

Ada's letters provide valuable insight into her family life and her thoughts on motherhood. In her correspondence with friends and colleagues, she often mentioned her children, expressing both pride in their accomplishments and concern for their well-being. For example, in a letter to her friend, she once wrote:

> "I find that my children are my greatest joy, yet they also require a great deal of my attention. I strive to instill in them the same love for learning that has driven my own pursuits."

This sentiment reflects Ada's commitment to her children and her desire to pass on her passion for knowledge. Her letters reveal a woman who, despite the constraints of her time, sought to balance her roles as a mother and a mathematician.

Legacy of Ada's Motherhood

Ada Lovelace's legacy as a mother is intertwined with her contributions to the fields of mathematics and computing. By instilling a love for learning in her children, she not only shaped their futures but also contributed to a broader cultural shift towards valuing education for women and girls. Ada's commitment to nurturing her children's intellectual growth laid the groundwork for future generations of women in STEM fields.

In conclusion, Ada Lovelace's role as a mother was marked by her determination to balance family life with her groundbreaking work in mathematics and programming. Her experiences as a mother informed her views on education and the importance of fostering curiosity in children. Despite the challenges she faced, Ada's legacy as a mother is a testament to her resilience and her belief in the transformative power of knowledge. As we celebrate Ada Lovelace's contributions to technology, we must also honor her role as a mother and the lasting impact she had on her family and society.

The Intertwining of Personal and Professional Worlds in Ada's Life

Ada Lovelace's life was a fascinating tapestry woven from the threads of her personal relationships and professional pursuits, creating a rich narrative that highlights the complexities of being a woman in the 19th century. Her journey illustrates how personal experiences can shape professional ambitions, and vice versa, leading to a unique legacy that continues to inspire.

At the heart of Ada's personal world was her relationship with her parents. Born to the famous poet Lord Byron and Lady Anne Isabella Milbanke, Ada's early life was marked by the absence of her father, who left the family when she was just a few weeks old. This absence cast a long shadow over her upbringing, as her mother sought to distance Ada from her father's bohemian lifestyle. Lady Anne, a mathematician in her own right, recognized Ada's potential and was determined to cultivate her intellectual talents. This nurturing environment fostered Ada's early interest in mathematics and logic, laying the groundwork for her future as a programmer.

Ada's marriage to William King in 1835 further complicated her personal and professional dynamics. While her husband supported her intellectual pursuits, societal expectations of women at the time often relegated them to domestic roles. Ada's struggle to balance her duties as a wife and mother with her passion for mathematics and innovation reflects the broader challenges faced by women in the field. Despite these challenges, Ada managed to maintain her intellectual pursuits, often collaborating with her husband on various projects. This partnership allowed her to explore her ideas while navigating the constraints of her domestic life.

The most significant professional relationship in Ada's life was undoubtedly her collaboration with Charles Babbage, the father of the computer. Their correspondence began in 1833, and soon after, Ada became deeply involved in Babbage's work on the Analytical Engine. This relationship not only provided Ada with a platform to express her mathematical genius but also introduced her to a network of intellectuals and innovators. The letters exchanged between Ada and

Babbage reveal a profound mutual respect and admiration, with Ada often contributing her insights and ideas to Babbage's designs.

$$Collaboration = Mutual\ Influence + Shared\ Goals \qquad (121)$$

This equation illustrates the essence of Ada and Babbage's relationship: their collaboration was characterized by a mutual influence that propelled both their ideas forward. Ada's contributions, particularly her notes on the Analytical Engine, demonstrated her ability to envision the machine's potential beyond mere calculation. Her famous note, which included the first algorithm intended for implementation on a machine, marked a significant milestone in the history of computing.

Moreover, Ada's personal struggles with health issues also intertwined with her professional life. Throughout her adult years, she suffered from various illnesses, which often impeded her ability to work consistently. These challenges forced Ada to navigate her ambitions with resilience. She often used her experiences of adversity as fuel for her intellectual pursuits, seeking solace in mathematics and programming during difficult times. This interplay between her struggles and achievements highlights how personal trials can inform and enrich professional endeavors.

Ada's complex personality played a crucial role in how her personal and professional worlds intersected. She was not only a mathematician but also an artist, poet, and philosopher. Her diverse interests allowed her to approach problems from multiple perspectives, fostering creativity in her work. This multifaceted nature is evident in her writings, where she often drew parallels between the worlds of art and science. For instance, Ada once remarked, "The Analytical Engine does not occupy common ground with mere mechanical devices; it is a new kind of creature, a living being with the power of thought." This statement encapsulates her ability to blend her artistic sensibilities with her scientific pursuits, illustrating how personal reflections can enhance professional insights.

As Ada navigated the male-dominated landscape of mathematics and computing, her relationships with other women also played a significant role in her journey. She actively advocated for women's education and was involved in early feminist movements, recognizing the importance of female representation in her field. Ada's friendships and mentorship with other women provided her with a support network that was crucial for her personal and professional growth. This interconnectedness highlights the importance of community and collaboration among women in STEM, emphasizing the need for solidarity in the face of societal barriers.

In conclusion, Ada Lovelace's life exemplifies the intricate interplay between personal and professional realms. Her relationships, struggles, and triumphs shaped her identity as a pioneering programmer and mathematician. By examining the intersections of her personal experiences with her professional ambitions, we gain a deeper understanding of the challenges and opportunities faced by women in the 19th century. Ada's legacy serves as a testament to the power of resilience, creativity, and collaboration, inspiring future generations to break down barriers and pursue their passions, regardless of societal constraints.

$$\text{Legacy} = \text{Resilience} + \text{Creativity} + \text{Collaboration} \qquad (122)$$

This equation encapsulates the essence of Ada's enduring impact on technology and society, reminding us that the intertwining of personal and professional worlds can lead to groundbreaking innovations and a lasting legacy.

Ada's Legacy in Literature and Art

Ada's Literary Pursuits and Creative Output

Ada Lovelace, often celebrated as the first programmer, was not only a mathematical genius but also a passionate writer. Her literary pursuits were as diverse as her intellectual interests, encompassing poetry, scientific correspondence, and philosophical reflections. This section delves into the multifaceted nature of Ada's creative output, showcasing how her literary endeavors complemented her groundbreaking work in mathematics and computing.

The Influence of Poetry on Ada's Work

Raised in a household steeped in literary tradition, Ada was the daughter of the renowned poet Lord Byron. Although her father departed from her life when she was just a child, his poetic legacy lingered in Ada's upbringing. Her mother, Lady Anne Isabella Byron, encouraged Ada's literary inclinations, fostering a love for language and expression. This early exposure to poetry not only shaped Ada's worldview but also influenced her writing style, which often blended scientific rigor with poetic flair.

Ada's poems often reflected her mathematical thinking, using structured forms and rhythmic patterns akin to mathematical equations. For instance, her poem *The*

Enchantress of Numbers serves as a prime example of how she intertwined her love for mathematics with her poetic sensibilities. In this poem, Ada personifies numbers, giving them life and character, thereby illustrating her unique perspective on the abstract world of mathematics.

$$P(x) = a_n x^n + a_{n-1} x^{n-1} + \ldots + a_1 x + a_0 \tag{123}$$

Here, $P(x)$ represents a polynomial function, which Ada might liken to a character in her poetry, illustrating the beauty and complexity of mathematical concepts through literary devices.

Scientific Correspondence and Collaboration

Ada's literary pursuits extended beyond poetry into the realm of scientific correspondence. Her extensive letters with Charles Babbage, the inventor of the Analytical Engine, are a testament to her intellectual engagement and collaborative spirit. These letters not only discussed technical details of the Analytical Engine but also reflected Ada's ability to articulate complex ideas in a clear and engaging manner.

In one notable letter, Ada writes about the potential of the Analytical Engine to manipulate symbols in a way that could be likened to human thought processes. She famously states:

> "The Analytical Engine does not occupy common ground with mere calculating machines. It holds within it the power to create, to understand, and to reason."

This passage exemplifies Ada's visionary thinking and her literary prowess, as she effectively conveys the profound implications of computational technology.

Philosophical Reflections and Theoretical Insights

Ada's writings also included philosophical reflections on the nature of science and technology. She was deeply influenced by the works of contemporary philosophers and scientists, which shaped her understanding of the ethical implications of technological advancements. In her correspondence and essays, Ada explored themes such as the relationship between humanity and machines, the role of women in science, and the responsibilities of inventors.

One of her notable theoretical contributions is her exploration of what we now refer to as the "Lovelace Principle," which posits that machines, while capable of processing information, lack the ability to create original ideas or concepts. This principle can be summarized as follows:

$$\text{Creativity} \neq \text{Computation} \qquad (124)$$

In her writings, Ada argued that while machines could perform calculations and follow instructions, they could not replicate the human capacity for creativity and intuition. This insight was remarkably prescient, foreshadowing contemporary debates about artificial intelligence and machine learning.

Legacy of Ada's Literary Contributions

Ada Lovelace's literary pursuits were not merely a complement to her mathematical genius; they were integral to her identity as a thinker and innovator. Her ability to articulate complex ideas in both poetic and scientific terms set her apart from her contemporaries and continues to inspire future generations.

The intersection of Ada's literary and mathematical talents is a testament to the power of interdisciplinary thinking. By embracing both the arts and sciences, Ada exemplified the Renaissance ideal of a well-rounded intellect. Her legacy as a writer and thinker endures, reminding us of the importance of creativity in all fields of inquiry.

In conclusion, Ada Lovelace's literary pursuits and creative output were essential aspects of her multifaceted genius. Her poetry, scientific correspondence, and philosophical reflections not only enriched her own understanding of mathematics and technology but also paved the way for future discourse on the interplay between humanity and machines. As we celebrate Ada's contributions, we recognize her as a true pioneer, whose words continue to resonate in the realms of literature, science, and technology.

The Influence of Ada's Poetic Background on Her Work

Ada Lovelace was not only a pioneering mathematician and the first computer programmer but also a woman deeply influenced by the poetic legacy of her father, Lord Byron. This unique blend of analytical rigor and artistic sensibility shaped her approach to mathematics and programming in ways that are often overlooked.

The Interplay of Poetry and Mathematics

At first glance, poetry and mathematics may appear to inhabit separate realms of human thought. However, Ada's upbringing in a household steeped in literary tradition provided her with a rich vocabulary of metaphor and symbolism that she would later apply to her mathematical explorations. The rhythmic patterns of poetry, characterized by meter and rhyme, parallel the structured logic found in mathematical equations. Both disciplines require a certain level of creativity and abstraction, allowing for a deeper understanding of complex concepts.

For instance, consider the Fibonacci sequence, which is defined recursively as follows:

$$F(n) = \begin{cases} 0 & \text{if } n = 0 \\ 1 & \text{if } n = 1 \\ F(n-1) + F(n-2) & \text{if } n > 1 \end{cases} \tag{125}$$

This sequence appears in various natural phenomena, such as the arrangement of leaves on a stem or the branching of trees. Ada might have appreciated the beauty of this sequence not just for its mathematical properties but also for its aesthetic presence in nature, akin to the imagery found in poetry.

Ada's Poetic Framework in Programming

Ada's understanding of language and structure was further enhanced by her poetic background, which influenced her approach to programming. In her work on the Analytical Engine, she crafted what is now known as the "Lovelace Note," where she described an algorithm for calculating Bernoulli numbers. This algorithm was groundbreaking, as it marked the first instance of a computer program.

Her ability to articulate complex mathematical ideas in a poetic manner allowed her to convey her thoughts with clarity and elegance. For example, in her notes, she wrote:

> "The Analytical Engine has no pretensions to originate anything. It can do whatever we know how to order it to perform."

This statement highlights her understanding that while machines could process information, the creative impulse and the framework of instruction must come from the human mind—a sentiment echoed in the poetic tradition that values the role of the poet as the creator of meaning.

The Role of Imagination in Mathematical Thought

Ada's poetic sensibilities also fostered a strong imaginative capacity, which is crucial in both poetry and mathematics. The ability to envision abstract concepts and their relationships is essential for problem-solving in mathematics. For instance, when exploring the concept of infinity, Ada might have drawn parallels between the infinite possibilities of poetic expression and the unbounded nature of mathematical constructs.

Mathematically, the concept of limits can be expressed as:

$$\lim_{x \to a} f(x) = L \tag{126}$$

This equation illustrates how a function approaches a value L as x approaches a. Ada's ability to visualize such limits could have been inspired by the poetic idea of approaching a theme or emotion without ever fully capturing it—an endless pursuit of understanding.

Ada's Legacy: Bridging Art and Science

The legacy of Ada Lovelace lies not only in her contributions to mathematics and programming but also in her ability to bridge the gap between art and science. By infusing her work with the sensibilities of a poet, she redefined the nature of programming as a creative endeavor rather than a mere mechanical task.

Her insights into the Analytical Engine's capabilities extended beyond mere calculation; she envisioned a future where machines could manipulate symbols and create art, music, and literature. This forward-thinking perspective aligns with the essence of poetry, which seeks to evoke emotions and provoke thought.

In contemporary discussions about the intersection of technology and the humanities, Ada's work serves as a reminder that creativity and analytical thinking are not mutually exclusive. Rather, they can coexist and enrich one another, leading to innovations that reflect the complexity of the human experience.

Conclusion

In conclusion, Ada Lovelace's poetic background significantly influenced her approach to mathematics and programming. By integrating the creativity and abstraction inherent in poetry with her analytical skills, she forged a path that redefined the role of the programmer. Her legacy continues to inspire a new generation of innovators who recognize the importance of merging artistic expression with scientific inquiry.

As we celebrate Ada's contributions, let us remember that the realms of poetry and mathematics are not separate but intertwined—each enriching the other in the quest for knowledge and understanding.

Ada's Contributions to the Field of Literary Analysis

Ada Lovelace, often celebrated as the first programmer, also made significant contributions to the field of literary analysis, showcasing her multifaceted intellect. Her background in mathematics and science intertwined seamlessly with her literary pursuits, allowing her to approach texts with a unique analytical lens. This section explores her contributions, the theoretical frameworks she employed, and the implications of her work in the realm of literary analysis.

Theoretical Frameworks

Lovelace's literary analysis can be understood through the lens of several key theoretical frameworks, including Romanticism, the intersection of science and literature, and the emerging discourse on the role of women in literature. Romanticism, a movement characterized by an emphasis on emotion, individualism, and nature, deeply influenced Lovelace's writings. Her correspondence and literary works often reflect the Romantic ideal of the artist as a visionary, capable of transcending the ordinary through imagination and creativity.

Furthermore, Lovelace's interest in the intersection of science and literature is particularly noteworthy. She believed that literature could serve as a vehicle for scientific ideas, and vice versa. This perspective aligns with contemporary theories of interdisciplinary studies, which advocate for the integration of diverse fields to enrich understanding and foster innovation. Lovelace's writings often exhibit a synthesis of scientific concepts and literary expression, demonstrating her belief in the power of narrative to convey complex ideas.

Literary Analysis and Mathematical Metaphors

One of Lovelace's most intriguing contributions to literary analysis is her use of mathematical metaphors to dissect literary texts. She often employed mathematical principles to elucidate the structures and patterns within literature. For instance, Lovelace might analyze the narrative structure of a poem by applying mathematical sequences or geometric shapes to illustrate the flow of ideas and emotions.

Consider the Fibonacci sequence, a mathematical concept where each number is the sum of the two preceding ones. Lovelace could argue that the emotional buildup in a poem follows a similar pattern, where each stanza builds upon the previous one, creating a crescendo of feeling. This approach not only highlights her analytical prowess but also invites readers to engage with literature in a novel way, challenging them to uncover deeper meanings through mathematical reasoning.

Examples of Lovelace's Literary Analysis

Lovelace's literary analysis is perhaps best exemplified in her correspondence with contemporaries such as Charles Babbage and her reflections on the works of Lord Byron, her father. In her letters, she often critiqued Byron's poetry, focusing on the emotional depth and structural intricacies. For example, she might analyze the use of imagery in Byron's "Childe Harold's Pilgrimage," discussing how the vivid landscapes serve as metaphors for the protagonist's internal struggles.

Moreover, Lovelace's analysis of literary works extended to the realm of fantasy and science fiction, genres that would later flourish in the 19th and 20th centuries. She recognized the potential of these genres to explore complex ideas about technology, society, and human nature. Her writings often foreshadowed the themes that would become central to later science fiction, such as the ethical implications of technological advancements and the relationship between humanity and machines.

The Role of Women in Literary Analysis

Lovelace's contributions to literary analysis also intersect with her advocacy for women's roles in literature and academia. She was acutely aware of the gender biases prevalent in her time, which often marginalized women's voices in both literary and scientific circles. In her writings, she championed the importance of female representation in literature, arguing that women's perspectives could enrich the literary canon.

This advocacy is particularly relevant today, as contemporary literary analysis increasingly seeks to amplify diverse voices and challenge traditional narratives. Lovelace's foresight in recognizing the value of women's contributions to literature laid the groundwork for future generations of female writers and scholars. Her legacy continues to inspire efforts to promote gender equality in literary studies and beyond.

Conclusion

In conclusion, Ada Lovelace's contributions to the field of literary analysis are a testament to her intellectual versatility and forward-thinking perspective. By integrating mathematical concepts, advocating for women's representation, and exploring the intersections of science and literature, she carved a unique niche within the literary landscape of her time. Lovelace's work not only enriches our understanding of literature but also serves as a reminder of the importance of interdisciplinary approaches in the pursuit of knowledge. As we continue to celebrate her legacy, we must recognize the profound impact of her contributions to both literature and the broader discourse on gender and creativity.

Ada's Interest in Fantasy and Science Fiction

Ada Lovelace, often celebrated as the first computer programmer, had a remarkable affinity for fantasy and science fiction that influenced her innovative thinking and creative problem-solving. This passion for speculative fiction was not merely a pastime; it was a vital part of her intellectual landscape that shaped her views on mathematics, technology, and the future.

The Intersection of Imagination and Logic

Lovelace's ability to blend imagination with rigorous logic is evident in her writings and ideas about the Analytical Engine. She believed that machines could go beyond mere calculation and could be designed to create art and music, thereby reflecting the essence of human creativity. In her notes on the Analytical Engine, she famously stated:

> "The Analytical Engine does not occupy common ground with mere calculating machines. It holds within its grasp the power to create, to generate, and to inspire."

This perspective aligns closely with the themes found in fantasy literature, where the boundaries of reality are stretched, allowing for the exploration of the impossible. Lovelace's vision of machines as creative entities foreshadows modern discussions about artificial intelligence and its potential to produce art, music, and literature.

Influences from Literary Works

Lovelace was influenced by various literary works that explored themes of technology and the human condition. Authors such as Mary Shelley, whose novel *Frankenstein* delves into the consequences of unchecked scientific ambition, resonated with Ada's own concerns about the ethical implications of technological advancements. In her correspondence, Lovelace often referenced the moral responsibilities that come with innovation, demonstrating a keen awareness of the potential consequences of her work.

Additionally, the Romantic literary movement, of which her father, Lord Byron, was a prominent figure, emphasized the importance of imagination and emotion in the face of rationalism. This cultural backdrop likely encouraged

Lovelace to embrace the fantastical elements of her ideas, allowing her to envision a future where technology and creativity coalesce.

Mathematics as a Language of Fantasy

For Lovelace, mathematics was not merely a tool for computation; it was a language that could articulate complex ideas and fantastical visions. She perceived the potential of mathematical constructs to represent abstract concepts, akin to how fantasy literature creates entire worlds through narrative. This perspective is reflected in her approach to programming, where she envisioned algorithms as stories that machines could execute.

In her notes, she discussed the idea of creating a sequence of instructions that could lead to unexpected outcomes, much like a plot twist in a story. This innovative thinking laid the groundwork for future developments in programming, where algorithms can generate complex behaviors and outputs based on simple inputs.

Theoretical Implications of Ada's Fantastical Ideas

Lovelace's interest in fantasy and science fiction raises significant theoretical implications regarding the nature of intelligence and creativity. Her belief that machines could emulate human-like creativity challenges traditional notions of what it means to be intelligent. It prompts questions such as:

- Can machines possess creativity, or is it an inherently human trait?

- What ethical considerations arise from creating machines capable of artistic expression?

- How do we define the boundaries between human and machine-generated content?

These questions remain relevant in contemporary discussions about artificial intelligence, particularly in fields such as machine learning and generative design.

Examples of Lovelace's Fantastical Vision

One of the most notable examples of Lovelace's blending of fantasy with her scientific pursuits is her description of the Analytical Engine's potential to create music. She envisioned a machine that could compose symphonies, an idea that was revolutionary for her time. This foresight can be seen as a precursor to modern AI music composition tools that leverage algorithms to create original pieces.

Moreover, Lovelace's fascination with the concept of "poetic science" reflects her belief in the interconnectedness of creativity and logic. She argued that the most profound advancements in technology would arise from the union of artistic imagination and scientific rigor.

Conclusion

In conclusion, Ada Lovelace's interest in fantasy and science fiction was not a mere diversion; it was an integral part of her identity as a thinker and innovator. By envisioning a world where machines could transcend their mechanical limitations, she laid the groundwork for future generations to explore the intersection of technology and creativity. Her legacy encourages us to embrace imagination in our pursuit of knowledge, reminding us that the most significant innovations often arise from the most fantastical ideas.

The Intersection of Art and Science in Ada's Work

Ada Lovelace is often celebrated as the first programmer, but her legacy extends far beyond the realm of mathematics and computing. One of the most fascinating aspects of her work is the seamless integration of art and science, reflecting her multifaceted personality and diverse interests. This intersection is not merely a coincidence; it is a testament to the belief that creativity and analytical thinking can coexist, enriching both disciplines.

The Artistic Influence on Ada's Mathematical Work

From a young age, Ada was immersed in a world where art and science were not seen as separate entities. Raised in a family with a rich artistic heritage—her father, the poet Lord Byron, and her mother, Lady Anne Isabella Milbanke, who had a strong interest in mathematics—Ada's upbringing fostered a unique perspective that blended the creative with the logical.

In her writings, Ada often employed poetic language to describe her mathematical ideas. For instance, in her notes on the Analytical Engine, she famously referred to the potential of the machine to manipulate symbols in a way that could be likened to composing music or creating art. She wrote, "The Analytical Engine does not occupy common ground with mere calculating machines. It holds within it the power to create, to express, and to inspire." This perspective highlights her belief that programming was not just a technical endeavor but an artistic one as well.

Mathematics as a Form of Art

Ada's approach to mathematics was deeply influenced by her artistic sensibilities. She viewed mathematical equations and algorithms as forms of artistic expression. For her, the elegance of a solution was akin to the beauty of a well-composed poem. This belief is reflected in her work on the Analytical Engine, where she sought to create algorithms that were not only functional but also aesthetically pleasing.

For example, Ada's algorithm for calculating Bernoulli numbers is often cited as one of the first computer programs. She meticulously crafted the sequence of operations, ensuring that each step was not only mathematically sound but also elegantly structured. The algorithm can be expressed as follows:

$$B_n = \sum_{k=0}^{n} \binom{n}{k} \cdot B_k \cdot \frac{1}{n-k+1} \tag{127}$$

where B_n represents the n-th Bernoulli number, and $\binom{n}{k}$ is the binomial coefficient. This formula exemplifies the beauty of mathematics, where each component works harmoniously to produce a profound result.

The Role of Imagination in Scientific Discovery

Imagination plays a crucial role in both art and science, and Ada recognized this interconnectedness. She believed that the ability to envision possibilities beyond the present was essential for innovation. In her correspondence with Charles Babbage, Ada often expressed her imaginative visions for the Analytical Engine, proposing applications that extended beyond mere calculation to include music composition and complex data analysis.

Ada's vision can be encapsulated in her assertion that "the Analytical Engine might compose elaborate and scientific pieces of music of any degree of complexity or extent." This statement reflects her understanding that the boundaries of technology were limited only by human creativity.

Examples of Artistic Applications of Computing

Ada's foresight into the artistic applications of computing has been realized in various fields today. For instance, computer-generated art, music composition software, and algorithmic design all owe a debt to her pioneering spirit. Modern artists and musicians utilize algorithms to create works that blend technical precision with creative expression.

One notable example is the use of generative art, where algorithms are employed to produce visual artworks. Artists like Casey Reas and Joshua Davis have harnessed programming languages to create stunning pieces that challenge traditional notions of authorship and creativity. Similarly, software such as Max/MSP allows musicians to compose and manipulate sound in innovative ways, echoing Ada's vision of a machine that transcends basic computation.

Conclusion: Celebrating the Duality of Ada's Genius

Ada Lovelace's legacy is a powerful reminder of the importance of embracing both art and science in our pursuits. Her ability to navigate these seemingly disparate worlds not only shaped her contributions to computing but also laid the groundwork for future generations to explore the synergies between creativity and analytical thinking. As we continue to innovate in technology, let us honor Ada's duality by fostering environments where artistic expression and scientific inquiry can thrive together.

In conclusion, the intersection of art and science in Ada's work is not merely a historical curiosity; it is a vital aspect of her genius that continues to inspire and inform the fields of mathematics, computing, and beyond. By recognizing and celebrating this connection, we can ensure that Ada Lovelace's legacy endures as a beacon of creativity, innovation, and interdisciplinary collaboration.

Ada's Impact as a Literary Figure and Cultural Icon

Ada Lovelace, often celebrated as the first computer programmer, also carved her niche as a literary figure and cultural icon. Her life and work intersected with the realms of literature and art, influencing not only the field of mathematics but also the cultural landscape of her time and beyond. This section explores Ada's literary contributions, her impact on cultural narratives, and how she has been immortalized in various forms of art.

Literary Pursuits and Creative Output

Ada Lovelace's upbringing in a family steeped in literary tradition significantly shaped her intellectual pursuits. The daughter of the renowned poet Lord Byron, she was exposed to the world of words and creativity from an early age. Ada's writings, particularly her correspondence with Charles Babbage, reveal her eloquence and ability to articulate complex ideas with clarity.

Her most notable literary contribution is the *Lovelace Note*, a comprehensive commentary on Babbage's Analytical Engine. In this note, Ada not only explains the workings of the machine but also envisions its potential for creativity and computation. She famously stated that the Analytical Engine could manipulate symbols and create music, thus bridging the gap between mathematics and the arts. This perspective positions her as a pioneer of interdisciplinary thought, where the boundaries between science and art dissolve.

Influence of Ada's Poetic Background

Ada's poetic heritage played a crucial role in shaping her worldview. Growing up in the shadow of her father's literary genius, she developed an appreciation for the beauty of language and the power of storytelling. This influence is evident in her writings, which often reflect a lyrical quality, blending technical precision with imaginative flair.

For instance, her descriptions of the Analytical Engine are not merely technical but infused with a sense of wonder and possibility. Ada wrote, "The Analytical Engine does not occupy common ground with mere 'calculating machines.' It holds within it the potential to create, to dream, and to inspire." Such statements resonate with the ethos of the Romantic era, emphasizing imagination and creativity.

Cultural Iconography and Representation

As a cultural icon, Ada Lovelace has been represented in various artistic forms, from literature to visual arts. Her life story and contributions have inspired countless works, illustrating her enduring legacy. In literature, Ada has been depicted as a visionary figure, often portrayed in novels that explore themes of innovation, gender, and the intersection of technology and humanity.

For example, in the novel *The Thrilling Adventures of Lovelace and Babbage* by Sydney Padua, Ada is reimagined as a daring adventurer who uses her mathematical prowess to solve mysteries and fight societal norms. This portrayal not only highlights her intellect but also her spirit of rebellion against the constraints of her time.

Visual representations of Ada have also proliferated, with artists depicting her in various lights—from the somber, reflective thinker to the vibrant, dynamic innovator. These representations serve to humanize her legacy, making her accessible to contemporary audiences and emphasizing the relevance of her contributions to modern society.

The Evolution of Ada's Image in Popular Culture

Over the years, Ada Lovelace's image has evolved from that of a Victorian mathematician to a symbol of female empowerment in technology. The resurgence of interest in her life and work has led to her being celebrated in popular culture, particularly during events like Ada Lovelace Day, which honors women in STEM.

In film and television, Ada has been portrayed as a trailblazer who defied societal expectations. Documentaries and biopics have explored her life, shedding light on her struggles and triumphs. This renewed interest in her story has sparked discussions about the underrepresentation of women in technology and the importance of recognizing female pioneers in history.

The Intersection of Art and Science in Ada's Work

Ada's legacy exemplifies the harmonious relationship between art and science. Her belief in the creative potential of computing laid the groundwork for future generations to explore the artistic possibilities of technology. Today, artists and technologists alike draw inspiration from her vision, utilizing computational tools to create innovative works of art.

For instance, contemporary artists often incorporate programming into their creative processes, blurring the lines between artistic expression and technical execution. Ada's foresight in recognizing the artistic dimensions of computation has paved the way for this interdisciplinary approach, fostering a new wave of creativity that resonates with her original ideas.

Cultural Significance and Inspiration

Ultimately, Ada Lovelace's impact as a literary figure and cultural icon extends beyond her technical contributions. She embodies the spirit of innovation, resilience, and creativity that continues to inspire individuals across disciplines. Her story serves as a reminder of the importance of diversity in thought and the value of interdisciplinary collaboration.

In conclusion, Ada Lovelace's legacy transcends her role as the first programmer; she is a literary figure and cultural icon whose influence is felt in both the realms of technology and the arts. Her ability to envision the future of computing as a creative endeavor has left an indelible mark on society, inspiring generations to embrace the intersection of art and science.

The Evolution of Ada's Image in Popular Culture

The image of Ada Lovelace has undergone a remarkable transformation over the years, evolving from a somewhat obscure historical figure to a celebrated icon of technology and feminism. This evolution can be examined through various cultural lenses, including literature, film, and the broader discourse on women in STEM (Science, Technology, Engineering, and Mathematics).

Historical Context and Initial Perception

Initially, Ada Lovelace was largely overshadowed by her contemporaries and the male-dominated narrative of the 19th century. Born in 1815, Ada was the daughter of the infamous poet Lord Byron and his wife, Lady Anne Isabella Milbanke. Despite her noble heritage, her contributions to mathematics and computing were not fully recognized during her lifetime. The primary document showcasing her work, the *Lovelace Note*, which detailed her insights on Charles Babbage's Analytical Engine, was published in 1843, but it did not gain significant attention until much later.

In the early 20th century, Ada was often depicted as a tragic figure, a woman whose genius was stifled by societal norms. This image was compounded by the romanticized narratives surrounding her father, which often eclipsed her own accomplishments. Scholars and historians tended to focus on her lineage rather than her intellectual contributions, leading to a lack of recognition in both academic and popular circles.

Revival and Recognition in the Late 20th Century

The late 20th century marked a turning point in the perception of Ada Lovelace. The rise of the feminist movement brought renewed attention to the contributions of women in various fields, including technology. Ada began to be celebrated not only for her pioneering work in programming but also as a symbol of women's potential in male-dominated industries.

This resurgence was reflected in literature and media. For instance, the publication of biographies and academic papers in the 1980s and 1990s highlighted her contributions to computer science. The feminist scholar [?] emphasized Ada's role as the first computer programmer, arguing that her work laid the foundation for modern computing. Such narratives began to reshape her image from that of a mere footnote in history to a central figure in the story of technology.

Ada in Literature and Media

In the 21st century, Ada Lovelace's image has been further popularized through various forms of media. Books such as *Ada's Algorithm* by [?] and *The Thrilling Adventures of Lovelace and Babbage* by [?] have portrayed her as an adventurous and visionary character. These works blend historical fact with imaginative storytelling, making Ada's contributions accessible to a wider audience.

Moreover, films and television series have also embraced her story. For example, the documentary *The Machine That Changed the World* features Ada as a pivotal figure in the development of computing. In popular culture, she is often depicted as a steampunk heroine, embodying the spirit of innovation and creativity. This portrayal resonates with contemporary themes of empowerment and gender equality, positioning Ada as a role model for aspiring female technologists.

Ada Lovelace Day and Cultural Celebrations

The establishment of Ada Lovelace Day in 2009 further solidified her status as a cultural icon. This annual event celebrates the achievements of women in STEM and serves as a platform to inspire future generations. Events around the world highlight Ada's legacy, creating a community that champions diversity and inclusivity in technology.

The celebration of Ada Lovelace Day has led to a plethora of initiatives aimed at increasing female representation in tech. Workshops, talks, and online campaigns have emerged, encouraging young girls to pursue careers in science and technology. This cultural movement reflects a broader societal shift towards recognizing and valuing the contributions of women across all fields.

Contemporary Representation and Challenges

Despite the positive evolution of Ada's image, challenges remain. The tech industry continues to grapple with issues of gender bias and underrepresentation. While Ada Lovelace has become a symbol of progress, the reality of gender inequality in technology serves as a reminder of the work still to be done.

Moreover, the commercialization of Ada's image raises questions about authenticity and representation. As her likeness appears in merchandise, branding, and media, it is crucial to maintain the integrity of her legacy. The risk of commodifying her story must be balanced with the need to honor her contributions and the struggles faced by women in technology.

Conclusion

In conclusion, the evolution of Ada Lovelace's image in popular culture reflects a broader narrative of empowerment and recognition for women in STEM. From her initial obscurity to her current status as a celebrated icon, Ada's story resonates with contemporary movements advocating for gender equality and diversity in technology. As we continue to celebrate her legacy, it is essential to ensure that her contributions are not only remembered but also serve as a catalyst for change in the tech industry.

The Representation of Ada in Literature and Art

Ada Lovelace, often heralded as the first computer programmer, has transcended her historical context to become a symbol of innovation, creativity, and the struggle for women's recognition in science and technology. Her representation in literature and art reflects not only her mathematical genius but also the complexities of her life, her relationships, and the societal norms of her time. This subsection explores the multifaceted portrayals of Ada Lovelace in various artistic and literary forms, examining how these representations contribute to our understanding of her legacy.

Literary Representations

In literature, Ada Lovelace has been depicted in various ways, often highlighting her intellect and pioneering spirit. One notable example is in the novel *The Thrilling Adventures of Lovelace and Babbage* by Sydney Padua. This graphic novel reimagines the lives of Ada and her collaborator Charles Babbage as a steampunk adventure, blending historical fact with fictional elements. The narrative not only showcases Ada's contributions to computing but also emphasizes her vibrant personality and her struggles against societal constraints.

Padua's work illustrates how literary representations can serve to humanize historical figures, making them relatable to contemporary audiences. The use of humor and visual storytelling in Padua's graphic novel allows readers to engage with Ada's story in a dynamic way, showcasing her as a heroine who challenges the norms of her time.

Another significant portrayal can be found in the play *Ada and the Engine* by Lauren Gunderson. This play delves into Ada's relationship with Babbage and the emotional and intellectual challenges she faced as a woman in a male-dominated field. Gunderson's work highlights Ada's passion for mathematics and her visionary ideas, while also exploring the personal sacrifices she made in pursuit of her ambitions. The play serves as a reminder of the societal barriers women faced in the 19th century, making Ada's achievements all the more remarkable.

Artistic Representations

In the realm of visual art, Ada Lovelace has also been a subject of fascination. Artists have sought to capture her essence through portraits, illustrations, and installations. One prominent example is the painting *Ada Lovelace* by the artist *Lindsay McCulloch*, which portrays Ada in a thoughtful pose, surrounded by mathematical symbols and gears, symbolizing her connection to both art and science. This representation emphasizes her role as a pioneer in computing while also acknowledging her artistic sensibilities.

Moreover, installations such as *The Ada Lovelace Project* have sought to celebrate her legacy through interactive exhibits that engage the public in discussions about gender, technology, and innovation. These installations often incorporate multimedia elements, allowing visitors to explore Ada's contributions in a hands-on manner. The blending of art and technology in these projects reflects Ada's own interdisciplinary approach to her work, reinforcing her status as a visionary.

Cultural Impact and Symbolism

The representation of Ada Lovelace in literature and art is not merely an exploration of her life; it is also a commentary on the broader societal issues surrounding gender and technology. Ada has become a symbol of the fight for women's rights in STEM fields, and her image is often used in campaigns advocating for gender equality. For instance, the annual Ada Lovelace Day celebrates the achievements of women in science, technology, engineering, and mathematics, drawing inspiration from her legacy.

Moreover, the cultural impact of Ada's representations can be analyzed through the lens of feminist theory. Scholars argue that Ada's story challenges traditional narratives that often marginalize women's contributions to science and technology. By reclaiming her narrative, contemporary literature and art serve to inspire new generations of women to pursue careers in STEM, fostering a sense of empowerment and possibility.

Conclusion

In conclusion, the representation of Ada Lovelace in literature and art serves as a powerful testament to her enduring legacy. Through various artistic mediums,

Ada's story is told not only as a historical account but also as an inspiration for future innovators.   These representations highlight the complexities of her character, her struggles, and her triumphs, ensuring that her contributions to the fields of mathematics and computing are recognized and celebrated.   As we continue to explore and reinterpret Ada's legacy, her image will undoubtedly remain a beacon of hope and inspiration for generations to come.

Bibliography

[1] Padua, Sydney. *The Thrilling Adventures of Lovelace and Babbage*. Pantheon, 2015.

[2] Gunderson, Lauren. *Ada and the Engine*. 2015.

[3] McCulloch, Lindsay. *Ada Lovelace*. 2018.

[4] *The Ada Lovelace Project*. 2020. https://adalovelaceproject.com

[5] Tong, Rosemarie. *Feminist Thought: A More Comprehensive Introduction*. Westview Press, 2009.

Ada Lovelace: From Poetry to Programming, a Renaissance Woman for the Ages

Ada Lovelace, often celebrated as the first computer programmer, was not merely a pioneer of technology; she was a true Renaissance woman whose life and work bridged the realms of art and science. Born in 1815 to the illustrious Lord Byron and his wife, Lady Anne, Ada's upbringing was steeped in the rich traditions of poetry and mathematics, a duality that would shape her unique perspective on the world.

The Intersection of Art and Science

Ada's early exposure to her father's poetic genius and her mother's structured approach to education laid the groundwork for her multifaceted talents. While her father, Lord Byron, was a celebrated poet known for his romantic and often tumultuous verses, her mother emphasized the importance of logic and reason. This dichotomy created an environment where Ada could explore both the creative and analytical aspects of her intellect.

$$\text{Creativity} + \text{Logic} = \text{Innovative Thinking} \tag{128}$$

This equation encapsulates Lovelace's approach to problem-solving, where artistic creativity and logical reasoning coalesced to fuel her groundbreaking ideas in computing.

The Influence of Mathematics on Ada's Work

Ada's passion for mathematics was ignited at a young age, driven by her desire to understand the underlying structures of the world around her. Her mathematical prowess was not merely a means to an end; it was a form of artistic expression. Just as a poet crafts verses, Ada composed algorithms, transforming abstract concepts into tangible solutions.

For instance, her work on Charles Babbage's Analytical Engine showcased her ability to see beyond mere calculations. She envisioned the potential of this machine to manipulate symbols and create complex outputs, akin to composing a symphony of numbers. In her famous notes, she wrote:

> "The Analytical Engine does not occupy common ground with mere calculating machines. It holds within it the potential for a new form of art."

This perspective exemplifies her belief that programming was not just a technical skill but an art form in its own right.

The Lovelace Note: A Poetic Algorithm

Ada's most renowned contribution to computing is encapsulated in what is now referred to as the "Lovelace Note." In this note, she described an algorithm designed to calculate Bernoulli numbers, which is often regarded as the first computer program. This algorithm, presented in a poetic format, reflects her dual identity as both a mathematician and a poet.

The algorithm can be expressed as follows:

$$B_n = \sum_{k=0}^{n} \frac{n!}{k!(n-k)!} \cdot a_k \qquad (129)$$

Where B_n represents the Bernoulli numbers and a_k are coefficients derived from the series. This equation highlights the intricate relationship between her mathematical reasoning and her artistic sensibility.

The Legacy of a Renaissance Woman

Ada Lovelace's legacy is a testament to the power of interdisciplinary thinking. Her ability to merge the worlds of poetry and programming has inspired generations of innovators who recognize that creativity is essential in technological advancement. In a world that often compartmentalizes knowledge, Lovelace's life serves as a reminder that true innovation occurs at the intersections of different disciplines.

Conclusion: Celebrating Ada's Dual Legacy

In celebrating Ada Lovelace as a Renaissance woman, we acknowledge her contributions to both the arts and sciences. Her life exemplifies the idea that creativity and logic are not mutually exclusive but rather complementary forces that drive progress. As we continue to explore the realms of technology, let us remember Ada's legacy and strive to foster a culture that embraces the artistic spirit within the scientific endeavor.

> "Ada Lovelace: a poet of numbers, a visionary of machines, and a pioneer whose brilliance transcends the boundaries of time."

In conclusion, Ada Lovelace's journey from poetry to programming encapsulates the essence of a true Renaissance woman, whose impact resonates through the corridors of both history and modern technology.

Ada's Enduring Impact on Technology and Society

The Far-Reaching Influence of Ada's Ideas

Ada Lovelace, often celebrated as the first computer programmer, had a vision that transcended her time, influencing not only the field of computing but also shaping the very foundations of modern technology and theoretical mathematics. Her ideas, articulated in the mid-19th century, laid the groundwork for concepts that are now fundamental in computer science, artificial intelligence, and even the ethical considerations surrounding technology.

Pioneering Concepts in Computing

At the heart of Ada's contributions is the notion that machines could be programmed to perform tasks beyond mere calculations. In her notes on Charles Babbage's Analytical Engine, she proposed that the machine could manipulate symbols and not just numbers, leading to the concept of *general-purpose computation*. This idea is encapsulated in the following equation:

$$f(x) = \sum_{i=1}^{n} a_i \cdot x^i \tag{130}$$

where $f(x)$ represents a polynomial function that the Analytical Engine could compute. This abstraction was revolutionary, as it suggested that machines could handle complex operations and logic, paving the way for modern programming languages that manipulate data and execute algorithms.

The Algorithm: A New Way of Thinking

Ada's most notable contribution is arguably her formulation of the first algorithm intended for implementation on a machine, which she described in her notes. An algorithm, in its simplest form, can be defined as a step-by-step procedure for calculations. Ada's algorithm for calculating Bernoulli numbers is a prime example:

$$B_n = \sum_{k=0}^{n} \binom{n}{k} \cdot B_k \cdot \frac{1}{n-k+1} \tag{131}$$

This formula not only demonstrated her understanding of mathematical concepts but also highlighted the potential of programming as a means of automating complex calculations.

The Concept of Machine Learning

Ada's foresight extended into realms that would not be fully realized until over a century later. She anticipated the development of *machine learning*—the idea that machines could learn from data and improve their performance over time. This concept is now foundational in artificial intelligence (AI) and can be expressed through the following model:

$$y = f(x; \theta) + \epsilon \tag{132}$$

where y is the output, f is the function approximated by the machine learning model, x represents input features, θ denotes parameters, and ϵ is the error term. Ada's belief that machines could not only process information but also adapt based on that information was a groundbreaking insight that resonates with today's advancements in AI.

Ethical Considerations in Technology

In addition to her technical foresight, Ada's ideas also encompassed the ethical implications of technology. She understood that with the power of computation came the responsibility to consider its impact on society. This foresight is particularly relevant today, as we grapple with issues such as data privacy, algorithmic bias, and the moral responsibilities of programmers.

The ethical framework surrounding technology can be articulated through the equation of *responsibility* in programming:

$$R = \sum_{i=1}^{n} (C_i \cdot E_i) \tag{133}$$

where R represents the overall responsibility, C_i are the consequences of each decision made in the coding process, and E_i are the ethical implications associated with those consequences. Ada's emphasis on the importance of ethical considerations in technology continues to inspire discussions on responsible innovation.

Influence on Modern Programming Languages

The legacy of Ada Lovelace is also evident in the evolution of programming languages. The language named after her, Ada, was developed in the 1980s and is known for its strong typing, modularity, and support for real-time systems. The principles that Ada advocated for—clarity, structure, and reliability in programming—are reflected in many contemporary programming languages, including Python, Java, and C++.

The following example illustrates a basic algorithm written in Ada:

```
procedure Compute_Bernoulli is
    function Bernoulli(n: Integer) return Float is
    begin
        -- Implementation of Bernoulli\index{Bernoulli} number\index
    end\index{end} Bernoulli\index{Bernoulli};
begin
    -- Main program\index{program} logic\index{logic}
end Compute_Bernoulli;
```

This code snippet encapsulates Ada's influence on programming structure, emphasizing readability and maintainability, which are crucial for modern software development.

Ada's Vision in Today's Technological Landscape

Today, as we navigate a world increasingly dominated by technology, Ada's vision serves as a guiding principle. Her insights into computation, learning, and ethics are more relevant than ever. The rise of AI, big data, and the Internet of Things (IoT) reflects the very ideas she championed—a world where machines augment human capabilities and where ethical considerations guide technological progress.

In conclusion, the far-reaching influence of Ada Lovelace's ideas is evident across various domains of technology and society. Her pioneering spirit and visionary thinking continue to inspire generations of programmers, mathematicians, and ethicists, reminding us that the intersection of creativity and logic can lead to transformative advancements. As we honor her legacy, we must also embrace the responsibility that comes with innovation, ensuring that technology serves humanity in a just and equitable manner.

Ada's Legacy in the Field of Computer Science

Ada Lovelace is often celebrated as the first programmer, a title that not only highlights her pioneering contributions to the field of computer science but also emphasizes the profound impact of her vision on the development of modern computing. Her work with Charles Babbage on the Analytical Engine laid the groundwork for the future of programming languages and computational theory. This section will explore the significance of Ada's contributions, the theoretical frameworks she helped establish, and the ongoing relevance of her ideas in contemporary computer science.

Theoretical Foundations of Programming

At the heart of Ada Lovelace's legacy is her understanding of the potential of the Analytical Engine, which she described as a machine capable of performing any calculation that could be expressed in algorithmic form. In her notes, she articulated the concept of an algorithm, a fundamental element of computer science. An algorithm is a finite sequence of well-defined instructions to solve a problem or perform a computation.

The formal definition of an algorithm can be expressed as follows:

$$A = \{I_1, I_2, \ldots, I_n\} \tag{134}$$

where I_i represents individual instructions, and n is the total number of instructions in the algorithm.

Ada's work included the first algorithm intended for implementation on a machine, which she developed to compute Bernoulli numbers. This algorithm is often regarded as the first computer program, showcasing her ability to think abstractly about computation.

The Concept of Programming Languages

Lovelace's insights into the nature of programming laid the groundwork for the development of programming languages. She recognized that programming was not merely about instructing a machine to perform tasks; it was also about expressing complex ideas and calculations in a clear and systematic way.

The evolution of programming languages can be traced back to her initial ideas, leading to the creation of high-level languages that abstract the underlying machine code. For instance, languages such as Python, Java, and C++ allow programmers to write code that is more intuitive and easier to understand compared to low-level machine language.

The Role of Abstraction in Computer Science

One of the key contributions of Ada Lovelace was her understanding of abstraction in programming. She proposed that the Analytical Engine could manipulate symbols and not just numbers, which was a revolutionary idea at the time. This concept of symbolic manipulation is foundational to modern computer science, particularly in the fields of artificial intelligence and computational linguistics.

In formal terms, abstraction can be defined as:

$$\text{Abstraction} = \text{Simplification} + \text{Generalization} \qquad (135)$$

This equation illustrates that abstraction involves simplifying complex systems while generalizing concepts to make them applicable in various contexts. Lovelace's vision of abstraction has influenced the design of modern programming paradigms, such as object-oriented programming, where data and functions are encapsulated in objects, allowing for more modular and maintainable code.

Ada's Influence on Software Development Practices

Ada Lovelace's legacy extends beyond theoretical contributions; it also encompasses practical implications for software development. Her emphasis on systematic approaches to programming foreshadowed the development of software engineering principles.

For example, the concept of iterative development, which involves refining software through repeated cycles, can be traced back to Ada's methodical approach to problem-solving. In her work, she often tested and refined her algorithms, demonstrating the importance of debugging and validation in programming.

This iterative process can be represented mathematically as:

$$S = S_0 + \sum_{i=1}^{n} \Delta S_i \qquad (136)$$

where S is the final software solution, S_0 is the initial version, and ΔS_i represents the incremental improvements made during each iteration.

Ada's Impact on Modern Computer Science Education

The legacy of Ada Lovelace is also evident in the way computer science is taught today. Her story serves as a powerful example of the importance of diversity in technology and the need for inclusive education. Many educational programs now highlight Ada's contributions to inspire young women and underrepresented groups to pursue careers in STEM fields.

Ada Lovelace's influence is celebrated through initiatives like Ada Lovelace Day, which aims to raise awareness of women's contributions to science and technology. The focus on role models in computer science education helps to encourage students to see the potential for innovation and creativity in their work.

Conclusion: A Lasting Legacy

In conclusion, Ada Lovelace's legacy in the field of computer science is multifaceted and enduring. Her pioneering work on algorithms, programming concepts, and software development practices laid the foundation for the digital age. The principles she established continue to resonate in modern computing, influencing everything from programming languages to software engineering methodologies.

As we advance into an era of rapid technological change, the importance of Ada's contributions cannot be overstated. Her vision for a future where machines could perform complex calculations and manipulate symbols has become a reality, and her story serves as a reminder of the vital role that diversity and innovation play in shaping the future of technology. By honoring Ada Lovelace's legacy, we not only celebrate a remarkable individual but also inspire future generations to push the boundaries of what is possible in computer science.

The Importance of Ada's Contributions to Technology

Ada Lovelace is often celebrated as the first programmer, a title that encapsulates the profound impact she had on the field of technology. Her contributions extend beyond mere programming; they encompass a visionary understanding of the potential of machines and the role they could play in society. This section will explore the significance of Ada's work, particularly her insights into computing and programming, and how they laid the groundwork for future technological advancements.

Pioneering Concepts in Computing

At a time when the concept of computing was in its infancy, Ada Lovelace grasped the potential of Charles Babbage's Analytical Engine. Unlike many of her contemporaries, she did not merely see the machine as a calculator; she envisioned it as a device capable of performing complex operations beyond arithmetic. In her notes, she articulated a vision of the Analytical Engine as a machine that could manipulate symbols and process information in a way akin to human thought.

One of her most notable contributions is encapsulated in what is now known as the **Lovelace Note**. In this note, she detailed an algorithm for the Analytical Engine to compute Bernoulli numbers, effectively making it the first computer program. This pioneering work is foundational in the field of computer science, as it introduced the concept of algorithms as a means of instructing machines to perform tasks.

$$B_n = \sum_{k=0}^{n} \frac{(-1)^k}{k!} \cdot \binom{n}{k} \cdot B_{n-k} \tag{137}$$

This equation represents the recursive nature of Bernoulli numbers, which Ada effectively translated into a series of instructions for the Analytical Engine. Her ability to see beyond the mechanical aspects of computing to the abstract principles of programming was revolutionary.

Theoretical Foundations of Programming

Ada's work laid the theoretical foundations for programming languages and computer science as we know them today. She understood that the Analytical Engine could be programmed to perform a variety of tasks, much like modern computers can run diverse applications. This understanding is critical in the evolution of programming languages, which are essentially formal languages comprising a set of instructions that can be used to produce various kinds of output.

Lovelace's insights into the potential for machines to process not just numbers but also symbols and data led to the development of early programming languages. For example, her notion of using loops and conditional statements in programming foreshadowed the structure of modern programming languages such as Python, Java, and C++. The ability to create complex programs through a series of simple instructions is a direct lineage from Lovelace's original concepts.

Challenges and Misunderstandings

Despite her groundbreaking contributions, Ada Lovelace faced significant challenges in gaining recognition for her work. The male-dominated field of mathematics and engineering often overshadowed her contributions. Furthermore, the complexities of her ideas were sometimes misunderstood, leading to a lack of acknowledgment during her lifetime.

For example, many contemporaries dismissed her as merely a collaborator of Babbage rather than recognizing her as a thinker in her own right. This misunderstanding of her role not only diminished her contributions but also obscured the importance of her insights into the future of technology.

Legacy and Impact on Modern Technology

Ada Lovelace's legacy is evident in the ongoing evolution of technology. Her vision of a future where machines could perform tasks beyond simple calculations has come to fruition in the age of artificial intelligence and machine learning. The principles she articulated have influenced countless innovations, from the development of computer programming languages to the design of complex algorithms used in data processing today.

Moreover, Lovelace's advocacy for the ethical implications of technology resonates in contemporary discussions about the responsibilities of programmers and engineers. She foresaw the potential consequences of technology on society and emphasized the importance of ethical considerations in technological advancements.

Conclusion

In conclusion, Ada Lovelace's contributions to technology are not only significant but also transformative. Her pioneering work in programming laid the groundwork for the digital age, influencing the development of modern computing and programming languages.   As we continue to navigate the complexities of technology in the 21st century, it is crucial to recognize and honor Ada's legacy, ensuring that her vision for a responsible and innovative future remains at the forefront of technological advancement.

Ada's Vision for a Digital Society

Ada Lovelace, often hailed as the first computer programmer, possessed a remarkable foresight into the potential of technology and its role in shaping society. Her insights into the capabilities of the Analytical Engine went beyond mere calculations; she envisioned a digital society where machines could enhance human creativity and intellectual pursuits. This section explores Ada's vision for a digital society, highlighting her revolutionary ideas and their implications for future generations.

The Concept of a Digital Society

At the heart of Ada's vision was the belief that machines could not only perform calculations but also manipulate symbols and, consequently, represent complex ideas. She famously noted that the Analytical Engine could be programmed to create music, produce graphics, and even simulate processes of human thought. This insight foreshadowed the multi-faceted applications of computers in modern society, where technology serves as a tool for creativity, communication, and problem-solving.

$$\text{Digital Society} = \text{Technology} + \text{Creativity} + \text{Collaboration} \qquad (138)$$

In her writings, Ada suggested that the Analytical Engine could be used to explore a wide array of subjects, including mathematics, science, and art. This interdisciplinary approach is foundational to the concept of a digital society, where technology is integrated into various aspects of life, fostering collaboration across different fields.

The Role of Automation and Artificial Intelligence

Ada's vision also encompassed the potential of automation and artificial intelligence (AI) to transform society. She anticipated that machines would not merely replace human labor but rather augment human capabilities. In her notes, she expressed excitement about the possibilities of using the Analytical Engine to perform tasks that required complex reasoning and analysis, thereby freeing individuals to engage in more creative and strategic endeavors.

$$\text{Augmented Intelligence} = \text{Human Intelligence} + \text{Machine Intelligence} \quad (139)$$

This equation encapsulates the synergy Ada envisioned between human and machine intelligence. She believed that by harnessing the computational power of machines, society could address complex problems more effectively, leading to advancements in fields such as medicine, engineering, and environmental science.

Ethical Considerations in a Digital Society

While Ada was optimistic about the potential of technology, she also recognized the ethical implications of its use. She understood that with great power comes great responsibility. Ada's vision for a digital society included the need for ethical guidelines to govern the development and application of technology. She emphasized the importance of ensuring that machines would be used for the betterment of humanity, rather than for harmful purposes.

$$\text{Ethical Technology} = \text{Transparency} + \text{Accountability} + \text{Inclusivity} \quad (140)$$

This equation reflects Ada's belief that ethical technology should be developed with transparency, ensuring that users understand how it operates. Accountability is essential to hold developers and organizations responsible for the consequences of their technologies. Inclusivity ensures that diverse voices are heard in the decision-making processes surrounding technology, preventing biases and promoting equitable access.

Education and Lifelong Learning

Ada's vision for a digital society also encompassed the importance of education and lifelong learning. She believed that as technology evolved, so too must the skills and knowledge of individuals. In her time, education was often reserved for the privileged few, but Ada advocated for broader access to knowledge, particularly in STEM fields.

$$\text{Lifelong Learning} = \text{Curiosity} + \text{Adaptability} + \text{Continuous Improvement} \quad (141)$$

By encouraging curiosity and adaptability, Ada recognized that individuals could thrive in an ever-changing digital landscape. She envisioned a society where education was not confined to formal institutions but was a continuous journey, empowering individuals to innovate and contribute meaningfully to their communities.

The Interconnectedness of Society

Finally, Ada foresaw a digital society characterized by interconnectedness. She understood that the Analytical Engine could facilitate communication and collaboration across distances, thereby breaking down barriers between individuals and communities. This interconnectedness would lead to a more informed and engaged citizenry, capable of addressing societal challenges collectively.

$$\text{Interconnected Society} = \text{Communication} + \text{Collaboration} + \text{Empowerment} \tag{142}$$

In her writings, Ada emphasized the potential of technology to foster a sense of community, where individuals could share knowledge, ideas, and resources. This vision aligns closely with the principles of the modern internet, where digital platforms enable collaboration and information exchange on a global scale.

Conclusion

Ada Lovelace's vision for a digital society was profoundly ahead of her time. Her insights into the potential of machines to enhance human creativity, the ethical considerations surrounding technology, the importance of education, and the interconnectedness of society remain relevant today. As we navigate the complexities of the digital age, Ada's legacy serves as a guiding light, reminding us of the responsibilities that come with technological advancement and the boundless possibilities that lie ahead. By embracing her vision, we can work towards a digital society that empowers individuals, fosters creativity, and promotes the greater good for all.

Ada's Influence on Today's Computer Programming Languages

Ada Lovelace, often heralded as the first programmer, laid the groundwork for the development of modern programming languages with her visionary insights and pioneering work on Charles Babbage's Analytical Engine. Her contributions not only established the fundamental concepts of programming but also influenced the evolution of various programming languages that followed. This section delves into the enduring impact of Ada's ideas on contemporary programming languages, highlighting key theoretical concepts, practical applications, and notable examples.

Theoretical Foundations

At the core of Ada Lovelace's contributions is her recognition of the potential for machines to perform complex calculations through the use of algorithms. In her notes on the Analytical Engine, Lovelace articulated the idea that a machine could manipulate symbols according to rules, a concept that is foundational to programming. This notion aligns with the formal definition of a programming language, which can be expressed as a set of rules and symbols that allow for the representation of algorithms.

Let us consider the formal definition of a programming language P:

$$P = \{S, R\} \tag{143}$$

where S represents a set of symbols (or tokens) and R denotes a set of rules (or grammar) that govern how these symbols can be combined to form valid expressions and statements.

Lovelace's pioneering work also emphasized the importance of abstraction and modularity in programming. She proposed that complex problems could be broken down into simpler, manageable components. This principle is echoed in modern programming paradigms such as Object-Oriented Programming (OOP), where data and behavior are encapsulated within objects, allowing for code reuse and improved maintainability.

Practical Applications

The influence of Ada's insights can be observed in the design of several contemporary programming languages. For instance, Ada, the programming language named in her honor, was developed in the late 1970s for the U.S. Department of Defense. It embodies many of the principles Lovelace championed, including strong typing, modularity, and support for concurrent programming.

The syntax of the Ada programming language reflects Lovelace's vision of clarity and precision in coding. For example, consider the following Ada code snippet that demonstrates a simple procedure for calculating the factorial of a number:

```
procedure Factorial(N: Integer) is
   Result: Integer := 1;
```

```
begin
   for I in 1..N loop\index{loop}
      Result := Result * I;
   end loop;
   Put_Line("Factorial of `` \& Integer'Image(N) \& `` is `` \&
end\index{end} Factorial;
```

In this example, the use of strong typing (with the declaration of N as an Integer) and clear loop constructs exemplifies the principles of clarity and safety that Ada Lovelace advocated.

Another programming language that reflects Lovelace's influence is Python. Python's design emphasizes readability and simplicity, allowing programmers to express concepts in fewer lines of code. The following Python code snippet illustrates a recursive approach to calculating the factorial of a number:

```
def factorial(n):
   if n == 0:
      return 1
   else:
      return n * factorial(n - 1)

print("Factorial of 5 is", factorial(5))
```

This example showcases how modern programming languages have adopted the principles of abstraction and modularity that Lovelace espoused. The recursive function encapsulates the logic for calculating the factorial, making it easy to read and understand.

Notable Examples and Comparisons

To further illustrate Ada Lovelace's influence on today's programming languages, we can compare the syntax and features of several languages that embody her principles. For example, languages such as Java and C# also incorporate strong typing, modularity, and object-oriented paradigms, reflecting the ideals that Lovelace championed.

In Java, the following code snippet demonstrates the creation of a class to represent a mathematical operation, showcasing encapsulation and modularity:

```
public class Factorial {
   public static int calculate(int n) {
```

```
        if (n == 0) return 1;
        return n * calculate(n - 1);
    }

    public static void main(String[] args) {
        System.out.println("Factorial of 5 is `` + calculate(5));
    }
}
```

Similarly, C# employs similar principles, as seen in the following example:

```
using System;

class Factorial {
    static int Calculate(int n) {
        if (n == 0) return 1;
        return n * Calculate(n - 1);
    }

    static void Main() {
        Console.WriteLine("Factorial of 5 is `` + Calculate(5));
    }
}
```

Both Java and C# demonstrate how Lovelace's vision has permeated the design of modern programming languages, emphasizing the importance of structure, readability, and the ability to express complex ideas simply.

Conclusion

Ada Lovelace's influence on today's computer programming languages is profound and far-reaching. Her pioneering work laid the foundation for the development of algorithms and programming concepts that continue to shape the field of computer science. By advocating for clarity, modularity, and abstraction, Lovelace's ideas resonate in the design of contemporary programming languages such as Ada, Python, Java, and C#. As we continue to innovate in the realm of technology, it is essential to recognize and honor the legacy of Ada Lovelace, the first programmer, whose visionary insights continue to inspire generations of developers and computer scientists.

The Gender Gap in Technology and Ada's Legacy

The gender gap in technology is a pervasive issue that has persisted for decades, reflecting broader societal inequalities that have historically marginalized women in various fields, particularly in science, technology, engineering, and mathematics (STEM). Ada Lovelace, often heralded as the first computer programmer, serves as both a symbol of women's potential in technology and a reminder of the barriers they face. This section will explore the nature of the gender gap in technology, the implications of Ada's legacy, and the ongoing challenges and opportunities for women in the tech industry.

Understanding the Gender Gap

The gender gap in technology manifests in several ways, including disparities in representation, pay, and opportunities for advancement. According to a report by the National Center for Women & Information Technology (NCWIT), women hold only 26% of computing jobs in the United States, a statistic that has remained relatively stagnant over the past few decades. This underrepresentation is even more pronounced for women of color, who face compounded barriers due to both gender and racial biases.

$$\text{Representation} = \frac{\text{Number of Women in Tech}}{\text{Total Number of Tech Workers}} \times 100 \qquad (144)$$

This equation illustrates the stark reality of women's representation in tech. The lack of women in leadership positions exacerbates the issue, as studies show that diverse teams are more innovative and effective. A McKinsey report found that companies in the top quartile for gender diversity on executive teams were 25% more likely to experience above-average profitability.

Historical Context and Ada's Influence

Ada Lovelace's contributions to computing occurred in the 19th century, a time when women were largely excluded from formal education and professional opportunities. Her groundbreaking work on Charles Babbage's Analytical Engine laid the foundation for modern programming, yet her achievements were largely overshadowed by her male contemporaries. Lovelace's legacy is a powerful reminder of the potential of women in technology, as well as the systemic barriers that have historically hindered their progress.

The notion of women as pioneers in technology was not limited to Ada. Figures like Grace Hopper, who developed the first compiler for a computer programming language, and Margaret Hamilton, who led the team that developed the onboard flight software for NASA's Apollo missions, further illustrate the critical roles women have played in shaping technology. However, despite these contributions, the narrative surrounding technology has often been male-centric, leading to the erasure of women's achievements.

Current Challenges

Today, women in technology face a multitude of challenges, including:

- **Stereotypes and Bias:** Gender stereotypes often lead to the perception that women are less capable in technical roles. This bias can be both overt and subtle, affecting hiring decisions, promotions, and workplace dynamics.

- **Workplace Culture:** Many women report feeling isolated in male-dominated environments, leading to a lack of belonging and support. This can result in higher turnover rates among women in tech.

- **Lack of Role Models:** The scarcity of women in leadership positions means that aspiring female technologists often lack mentors and role models who can guide them through their careers.

Opportunities for Change

Despite these challenges, there are numerous initiatives aimed at closing the gender gap in technology. Programs such as Girls Who Code and Black Girls Code are actively working to inspire and educate young girls in coding and computer science. Additionally, many tech companies are beginning to recognize the importance of diversity and inclusion, implementing policies that promote gender equity in hiring and advancement.

$$\text{Diversity Index} = \frac{\text{Number of Diverse Employees}}{\text{Total Number of Employees}} \times 100 \qquad (145)$$

This equation can help organizations measure their progress in creating a more inclusive workforce. By prioritizing diversity, companies can not only improve their workplace culture but also enhance their overall performance.

Ada's Enduring Legacy

Ada Lovelace's legacy continues to inspire women in technology today. Her story serves as a powerful reminder that women have always been integral to technological advancement, and her vision for the potential of computing resonates in contemporary discussions about the future of technology. By honoring Ada's contributions and advocating for gender equality in tech, we can work towards a future where women are not only represented but are also leading the charge in innovation.

In conclusion, addressing the gender gap in technology requires a multifaceted approach that includes education, mentorship, and systemic change within organizations. Ada Lovelace's legacy is a beacon of hope for future generations of women in tech, reminding us that with perseverance and support, the barriers to entry can be dismantled, paving the way for a more equitable and innovative technological landscape.

Celebrating Ada's Impact on Women in the Tech Industry

Ada Lovelace, often hailed as the first programmer, has left an indelible mark on the world of technology and computing, particularly as an inspirational figure for women in the tech industry. Her pioneering work on Charles Babbage's Analytical Engine not only laid the groundwork for modern computing but also challenged the gender norms of her time, making her a beacon of hope and empowerment for women striving to make their mark in a male-dominated field.

Historical Context and Gender Inequality

In the 19th century, the field of mathematics and early computing was overwhelmingly male-dominated. Women were often relegated to the background, their contributions overlooked or dismissed. Ada's achievements were a radical departure from this norm. She navigated a landscape rife with gender bias, using her intellect and creativity to carve out a space for herself in a world that often denied women the opportunity to excel in scientific disciplines.

Ada's Role as a Trailblazer

Ada Lovelace's legacy is not just about her technical contributions; it is also about her role as a trailblazer for women in technology. She demonstrated that women could contribute significantly to fields traditionally reserved for men. Her work on the Analytical Engine, particularly her notes on how to program it, showcased her understanding of complex algorithms and her ability to think abstractly about computation.

One of her most famous contributions is what is now known as the *Lovelace Note*, which outlined a method for calculating Bernoulli numbers using the

Analytical Engine. This note is often cited as the first algorithm intended for implementation on a machine, solidifying Ada's place in history as the first computer programmer.

$$B_n = \frac{n!}{\sum_{k=0}^{n} \frac{(-1)^k}{k!} \cdot B_k \cdot (n-k)!} \tag{146}$$

This equation represents Bernoulli numbers, which Ada sought to compute using Babbage's machine, highlighting her advanced understanding of mathematical concepts.

Inspiring Future Generations

Ada's legacy has inspired countless women to pursue careers in technology and computing. Her story is often shared in educational contexts to encourage girls to explore STEM (Science, Technology, Engineering, and Mathematics) fields. Initiatives like Ada Lovelace Day, celebrated annually on the second Tuesday of October, aim to raise the profile of women in STEM and celebrate their contributions.

Programs and organizations have emerged to honor Ada's influence, such as the Ada Lovelace Foundation, which advocates for gender equality in technology and supports initiatives aimed at increasing female representation in tech. By spotlighting women who have made significant contributions to technology, these efforts aim to create a more inclusive environment for future generations.

Addressing Modern Challenges

Despite Ada's pioneering role, women in technology continue to face significant challenges. The gender gap in tech remains a pressing issue, with women often underrepresented in technical roles and leadership positions. According to the National Center for Women & Information Technology, women hold only 26% of computing jobs in the United States.

To address these challenges, it is essential to foster a culture of inclusion and support within the tech industry. This includes mentoring programs, networking opportunities, and initiatives aimed at promoting women to leadership roles. Companies that prioritize diversity not only benefit from a wider range of perspectives but also enhance their innovation and problem-solving capabilities.

Celebrating Ada's Legacy in Contemporary Contexts

Ada's legacy is celebrated in various ways, from educational programs to awards recognizing women in technology. The *Ada Lovelace Award*, for instance, honors women who have made significant contributions to the field of computing and serves as a reminder of the importance of recognizing female talent in tech.

Moreover, Ada's story is increasingly featured in popular culture, from biographies to films, helping to raise awareness of women's contributions to technology. This visibility is crucial for inspiring young girls to pursue careers in STEM and for challenging stereotypes about women's capabilities in technical fields.

Conclusion

In conclusion, Ada Lovelace's impact on women in the tech industry is profound and far-reaching. As a pioneer who defied societal expectations and made groundbreaking contributions to computing, she serves as a powerful symbol of what women can achieve in technology. By celebrating her legacy and addressing the ongoing challenges faced by women in tech, we can continue to build a more inclusive and equitable future for all. Ada's story is a reminder that the fight for gender equality in technology is far from over, but with the inspiration of trailblazers like her, we are one step closer to achieving it.

Ada's Influence on the Ethical Considerations of Technology

Ada Lovelace, often heralded as the first programmer, was not only a pioneer in mathematics and computing but also a visionary thinker who laid the groundwork for considering the ethical implications of technology. In an era where the advent of machines was seen merely through the lens of efficiency and productivity, Ada's insights urged a broader reflection on the societal impacts of technological advancements.

Theoretical Foundations

At the heart of Ada's ethical considerations lies the understanding that technology is not an isolated entity but a powerful force that shapes human experiences. Ada's correspondence with Charles Babbage reveals her belief that machines, such as the Analytical Engine, should not only perform calculations but also possess the capability to influence human thought and creativity. This duality of purpose can be encapsulated in the equation:

$$E = f(T, S)$$

where E represents ethical implications, T signifies technological advancements, and S denotes societal values. This functional relationship highlights how technology cannot be divorced from the ethical frameworks within which it operates.

Identifying Ethical Problems

Ada's work foreshadowed many ethical dilemmas that we face today, particularly in the realms of artificial intelligence (AI) and machine learning. For instance, the potential for bias in algorithms is a direct reflection of the values encoded within them. Ada's recognition of the importance of careful programming can be seen as a precursor to contemporary discussions surrounding fairness and accountability in AI systems.

Consider the problem of biased algorithms, which can perpetuate existing inequalities. If a machine learning model is trained on data that reflects societal biases, it can produce outcomes that further entrench these biases. This raises the question: *How do we ensure that technology serves to uplift rather than oppress?* Ada's insistence on meticulous analysis and foresight serves as a guiding principle for modern technologists grappling with these issues.

Examples in Contemporary Context

One of the most poignant examples of Ada's influence on ethical considerations is the ongoing discourse surrounding AI ethics. The development of autonomous systems, such as self-driving cars, necessitates ethical frameworks that prioritize human safety and societal welfare. The question of how these systems make decisions—particularly in life-and-death scenarios—echoes Ada's concerns about the moral responsibilities tied to technological innovation.

For instance, the "trolley problem," a philosophical thought experiment, illustrates the ethical dilemmas faced by AI systems. When programmed to make decisions in critical situations, the underlying algorithms must reflect ethical considerations that prioritize human life. Ada's early insights into the potential consequences of technology compel us to ask: *What values do we want our machines to embody?*

The Legacy of Ethical Programming

Ada's legacy is not merely in her contributions to programming but in her call for ethical programming practices that resonate today. As we navigate the complexities of modern technology, her insistence on a thoughtful approach to programming serves as a reminder that the impact of our creations extends beyond the code.

Incorporating ethical considerations into the software development lifecycle is crucial. This can be articulated through the following equation:

$$C = \int_0^T E(t)\, dt$$

where C is the cumulative ethical impact of technology over time, and $E(t)$ represents the ethical considerations at any given moment t. This integral implies that ethical implications accumulate and evolve, necessitating continuous reflection and adaptation.

Conclusion

In conclusion, Ada Lovelace's influence on the ethical considerations of technology is profound and enduring. Her foresight in recognizing the interplay between technology and society invites us to engage in ongoing dialogues about the responsibilities that come with innovation. As we forge ahead into an increasingly automated future, let us honor Ada's legacy by ensuring that our technological pursuits are guided by ethical principles that promote equity, justice, and the betterment of humanity.

In the spirit of Ada Lovelace, we must ask ourselves: *How can we shape technology to reflect our highest ideals?* This question remains at the forefront of our quest for a responsible and inclusive digital future.

The Cultural Significance of Ada Lovelace: Inspiring Generations to Innovate

Ada Lovelace, often hailed as the world's first computer programmer, is not just a historical figure; she embodies the spirit of innovation and creativity that transcends her time and continues to inspire generations. Her contributions to the early concepts of computing and programming are profound, but her cultural significance extends far beyond her technical achievements. In a world that often overlooks the contributions of women in technology, Ada stands as a beacon of hope and possibility, inspiring countless individuals to pursue their passions and challenge societal norms.

The Legacy of Ada Lovelace in Popular Culture

Ada Lovelace's impact on popular culture is evident in various forms of media, from literature to film and beyond. She has become a symbol of women's empowerment in STEM (Science, Technology, Engineering, and Mathematics) fields. The celebration of Ada Lovelace Day, held annually on the second Tuesday of October, serves to honor her legacy and raise awareness about the contributions of women in technology. This event not only commemorates her achievements but also encourages young girls and women to pursue careers in tech, fostering a sense of community and support.

For example, in the realm of literature, Ada's story has been retold in novels and biographies, portraying her as a visionary whose ideas were far ahead of her time. Works such as *The Thrilling Adventures of Lovelace and Babbage* by Sydney Padua creatively illustrate her life and contributions through graphic storytelling, making her accessible to a broader audience. This blend of history and imagination not only educates readers about Ada's work but also captivates their interest in the field of computing.

Ada's Influence on Modern Technology

Ada's foresight regarding the potential of computers and their applications has influenced modern technological advancements. Her insights into programming and algorithmic thinking laid the groundwork for contemporary computing practices. The equation she devised for calculating Bernoulli numbers, often regarded as the first algorithm intended for implementation on a machine, exemplifies her innovative thinking. This early algorithm can be expressed mathematically as follows:

$$B_n = \sum_{k=0}^{n} \binom{n}{k} \cdot \frac{(-1)^k}{k+1}$$

where B_n represents the n-th Bernoulli number and $\binom{n}{k}$ denotes the binomial coefficient. This equation showcases not only Ada's mathematical prowess but also her ability to conceptualize complex problems and devise solutions that resonate with modern computational methods.

Encouraging Diversity and Inclusion in Tech

Ada Lovelace's legacy is also significant in the ongoing fight for diversity and inclusion within the tech industry. Her life story serves as a powerful reminder of the barriers women have faced and continue to face in STEM fields. By highlighting her achievements, we can inspire a new generation of innovators who are not deterred by gender stereotypes or societal expectations.

Organizations such as the Ada Lovelace Foundation are dedicated to promoting gender equality in technology. They work to create initiatives that empower women, provide mentorship opportunities, and advocate for policies that support diversity in tech. By fostering an environment where all voices are heard, we can cultivate a culture of innovation that reflects the diverse perspectives necessary for groundbreaking advancements.

Ada's Role as a Symbol of Innovation

In a broader cultural context, Ada Lovelace represents the archetype of the innovator—someone who dares to dream and think outside the box. Her ability to blend creativity with analytical thinking is a hallmark of successful innovators today. The intersection of art and science, which Ada exemplified, is increasingly recognized as essential for fostering creativity in technology. This notion is echoed in the STEAM (Science, Technology, Engineering, Arts, and Mathematics) movement, which advocates for the integration of the arts into STEM education.

For instance, modern tech companies often seek individuals who can think creatively while applying scientific principles. This holistic approach to innovation is a direct reflection of Ada's legacy, encouraging individuals to embrace their multifaceted talents and pursue interdisciplinary collaboration.

Conclusion: A Lasting Inspiration

In conclusion, the cultural significance of Ada Lovelace extends far beyond her technical contributions to computing. She serves as an enduring symbol of innovation, creativity, and the potential for women to excel in technology. By celebrating her legacy, we not only honor her achievements but also inspire future generations to challenge the status quo, embrace their passions, and contribute to the ever-evolving landscape of technology.

Ada Lovelace's life and work remind us that innovation knows no gender and that the spirit of creativity can lead to groundbreaking advancements that shape our world. As we continue to navigate the complexities of modern technology, let us carry forward Ada's message: to innovate boldly, think critically, and never underestimate the power of imagination.

Chapter 4: Ada's Enduring Legacy

Chapter 4: Ada's Enduring Legacy

Chapter 4: Ada's Enduring Legacy

Ada Lovelace, often celebrated as the world's first computer programmer, has left an indelible mark on the fields of mathematics and computer science. Her pioneering contributions, particularly in the realm of theoretical computing, continue to resonate in the modern technological landscape. This chapter delves into the enduring legacy of Ada Lovelace, exploring her posthumous recognition, the impact of her ideas on contemporary programming, and the relevance of her vision in the 21st century.

4.1.1 Posthumous Recognition of Ada Lovelace

Despite her groundbreaking work, Ada Lovelace's contributions remained largely unrecognized for many years after her death. It wasn't until the 20th century that scholars began to rediscover her writings, particularly the famous *Lovelace Note*, which she penned in 1843. This note detailed the potential of Charles Babbage's Analytical Engine, describing how it could be programmed to perform complex calculations and even generate music.

The *Lovelace Note* is often regarded as one of the first instances of programming language documentation. In it, Ada wrote:

> "The Analytical Engine has no pretensions to originate anything. It can
> do whatever we know how to order it to perform."

This statement not only highlights the machine's capabilities but also reflects Ada's understanding of the relationship between humans and machines—a theme that is increasingly relevant in today's discussions about artificial intelligence and automation.

4.1.2 The Role of the Lovelace Note in Ada's Posthumous Fame

The rediscovery of the *Lovelace Note* played a crucial role in bringing Ada Lovelace's contributions to light. Scholars such as Alan Turing and later computer scientists recognized the significance of her work in the context of programming and computation. Turing, in particular, acknowledged Ada's insights into the potential of machines to manipulate symbols and perform calculations beyond simple arithmetic.

In 1980, the U.S. Department of Defense even named a programming language *Ada* in her honor, further solidifying her status as a pioneer in the field. This language was designed for large-scale software engineering and emphasized strong typing, modularity, and reliability—principles that Ada herself would have appreciated.

4.1.3 Ada's Influence on the Turing Award and Computing Pioneers

The Turing Award, named after Alan Turing, is one of the highest honors in computer science. It recognizes individuals for their contributions of lasting importance to computing. Ada's legacy has been acknowledged in the context of this award, as many recipients have cited her as an inspiration for their work. The Turing Award serves not only as a recognition of individual achievements but also as a testament to the collaborative nature of the computing community—a principle that Ada championed in her own work.

4.1.4 The Creation of Ada Lovelace Day and Commemorative Events

To honor Ada Lovelace's contributions and promote the visibility of women in technology, Ada Lovelace Day was established. Celebrated annually on the second Tuesday of October, this event encourages people to celebrate the achievements of women in science, technology, engineering, and mathematics (STEM). It serves as a platform for discussions, presentations, and activities aimed at inspiring future generations of female innovators.

Commemorative events such as the Ada Lovelace Festival and the Lovelace Memorial Lecture have also emerged, highlighting the importance of her work and advocating for gender equality in the tech industry. These events not only celebrate Ada's legacy but also foster a sense of community among those who share a passion for technology and innovation.

4.1.5 Ada's Induction into the Women in Technology International Hall of Fame

In recognition of her pioneering contributions, Ada Lovelace was posthumously inducted into the Women in Technology International Hall of Fame. This honor acknowledges the significant impact of her work on the field of computing and serves as an inspiration for women pursuing careers in technology. The Hall of Fame highlights the achievements of women who have made notable contributions to the tech industry, further solidifying Ada's status as a role model for future generations.

4.1.6 Ongoing Efforts to Honor Ada's Contributions

In addition to formal recognitions, numerous grassroots movements and initiatives have emerged to honor Ada Lovelace's contributions. Organizations and educational institutions are increasingly incorporating her story into STEM curricula, emphasizing the importance of female representation in technology. By sharing Ada's journey, educators aim to inspire young girls to pursue careers in programming and engineering.

4.1.7 Ada's Iconic Status in the Tech Industry and Beyond

Ada Lovelace's iconic status has transcended the realm of technology, making her a cultural symbol of innovation and resilience. Her image is often used in campaigns advocating for diversity in tech, and she has become a figurehead for movements promoting women's rights in STEM fields. The resonance of her legacy is evident in the growing number of initiatives aimed at closing the gender gap in technology.

4.1.8 The Enduring Relevance of Ada's Ideas in the Digital Age

As we navigate the complexities of the digital age, Ada Lovelace's ideas remain remarkably relevant. Her insights into the potential of machines to perform complex tasks and her understanding of the ethical implications of technology continue to inform contemporary discussions about artificial intelligence, data privacy, and the responsibilities of programmers. Ada's vision for a collaborative relationship between humans and machines serves as a guiding principle for today's technologists.

4.1.9 Remembering Ada Lovelace: Inspiring Future Innovators

In conclusion, Ada Lovelace's enduring legacy is a testament to her brilliance and foresight. Her contributions to programming and her advocacy for women in technology continue to inspire future innovators. As we celebrate her achievements, we are reminded of the importance of diversity and inclusion in shaping the future of technology. Ada Lovelace's story is not just one of personal triumph; it is a call to action for all of us to continue breaking down barriers and fostering an environment where creativity and innovation can thrive.

In the words of Ada herself:

> "That brain of mine is something more than merely mortal; as time will show."

Let us honor her legacy by ensuring that the world of technology remains a space where all minds, regardless of gender, can flourish and contribute to the ever-evolving tapestry of innovation.

Ada's Posthumous Recognition

The Rediscovery of Ada's Work and Legacy

The journey of Ada Lovelace's legacy is akin to a hidden treasure map, where the X marks the spot of her groundbreaking contributions to computing and mathematics. For many years, Ada's work was overshadowed by her more famous contemporaries, with her genius relegated to the dusty shelves of history. However, the latter half of the 20th century saw a renaissance in the appreciation of her contributions, leading to a rediscovery that would ignite a passion for her legacy across generations.

Historical Context of Rediscovery

In the early 1900s, Ada's contributions were largely forgotten, overshadowed by the rapid advancements in technology and the emergence of new programming paradigms. It wasn't until the 1950s and 1960s, with the rise of the computer age, that scholars and enthusiasts began to revisit her work. The advent of computers and the burgeoning field of computer science created a fertile ground for reevaluating Ada's contributions, particularly her pioneering insights into programming.

During this period, the publication of her notes on Charles Babbage's Analytical Engine—specifically the famous *Lovelace Note*—became a focal point for researchers interested in the origins of programming. In her notes, Ada not only described the workings of the Analytical Engine but also articulated a vision of what computing could achieve. She famously stated, "The Analytical Engine has no pretensions to originate anything. It can do whatever we know how to order it to perform." This statement underscores her understanding of the machine's potential and the foundational principles of programming.

The Role of the Lovelace Note

The *Lovelace Note* is often heralded as the first algorithm intended for implementation on a machine, marking Ada as the first programmer in history. This note, which detailed a method for calculating Bernoulli numbers, was rediscovered and brought to the attention of the computing community during the 1970s. Scholars recognized the significance of her work and its implications for the future of programming languages.

The algorithm can be expressed mathematically as follows:

$$B_n = \sum_{k=0}^{n} \binom{n}{k} \cdot B_k \cdot (n-k)! \tag{147}$$

where B_n represents the n-th Bernoulli number, and $\binom{n}{k}$ is the binomial coefficient. Ada's ability to conceptualize and articulate this algorithm for a mechanical device was a remarkable feat that laid the groundwork for future programming.

Rediscovery Through Feminist Scholarship

The feminist movement of the late 20th century played a crucial role in the rediscovery of Ada Lovelace's work. Scholars began to explore the contributions of women in science and technology, highlighting the often-overlooked achievements of female pioneers. Ada's story resonated with many, serving as a symbol of resilience in a male-dominated field.

Books, articles, and documentaries began to emerge, focusing on Ada's life and legacy. Notable works such as *Ada: The Enchantress of Numbers* by Betty Alexandra Toole and *The Thrilling Adventures of Ada Lovelace* by Laura Anne Gilman brought her story to a wider audience. These narratives not only celebrated Ada's mathematical prowess but also emphasized the challenges she faced as a woman in the 19th century.

Impact of the Digital Age

The rise of the internet and digital media further propelled the rediscovery of Ada Lovelace. Online platforms provided a space for enthusiasts, historians, and educators to share knowledge and resources related to her work. Social media campaigns, blogs, and educational websites began to highlight Ada's contributions, sparking interest among a new generation of programmers and mathematicians.

In 2009, the first Ada Lovelace Day was celebrated, an international day of recognition for women in science, technology, engineering, and mathematics (STEM). This event served as a catalyst for further exploration of Ada's legacy, encouraging discussions about gender equality in tech and inspiring women to pursue careers in these fields.

Recognizing Ada's Contributions in the Modern Era

Today, Ada Lovelace is celebrated not only as a pioneer of programming but also as a cultural icon. Institutions and organizations have been established in her honor, such as the Ada Lovelace Foundation and the Ada Lovelace Award for Technical Leadership. These initiatives aim to promote diversity and inclusion within the tech industry, ensuring that Ada's legacy continues to inspire future generations.

Furthermore, the programming language *Ada*, developed in the 1980s, serves as a testament to her enduring influence. The language was named in her honor, reflecting the principles of reliability and efficiency that she championed in her work.

Conclusion

The rediscovery of Ada Lovelace's work and legacy marks a significant chapter in the history of computing. Her contributions, once buried beneath the sands of time, have emerged as a beacon of inspiration for those navigating the complexities of technology and mathematics. As we continue to celebrate her achievements, we are reminded of the importance of recognizing and honoring the pioneers who paved the way for future innovators. Ada Lovelace's legacy is not just a story of the past; it is a call to action for all who dare to dream, innovate, and challenge the status quo.

The Role of the Lovelace Note in Ada's Posthumous Fame

The Lovelace Note, often referred to as the first computer program, is a pivotal document in the history of computing and serves as a cornerstone of Ada Lovelace's posthumous recognition. Written in 1843, this note was part of Ada's translation of an article by the Italian mathematician Luigi Federico Federico, which detailed Charles Babbage's Analytical Engine. In this note, Lovelace elaborated on the machine's capabilities and, crucially, provided what is now recognized as the first algorithm intended for implementation on a machine, thereby establishing her role as the first computer programmer.

Historical Context and Significance

To appreciate the significance of the Lovelace Note, it is essential to understand the historical context in which it was written. The Analytical Engine was a revolutionary concept in the 19th century, representing the first design for a mechanical general-purpose computer. While Babbage envisioned a machine that could perform any calculation, Lovelace recognized its potential to manipulate symbols and process not just numbers but also other forms of data, such as music and text.

The Lovelace Note includes detailed instructions for calculating Bernoulli numbers, showcasing her understanding of the machine's potential. This foresight was groundbreaking, as it anticipated the concept of programming long before computers became a reality. Lovelace's assertion that the Analytical Engine could be programmed to perform tasks beyond mere calculation demonstrates her visionary thinking.

The Content of the Lovelace Note

The Lovelace Note is comprised of several key components that highlight her innovative approach to programming:

- **Algorithm for Bernoulli Numbers:** The heart of the Lovelace Note is the algorithm she devised for computing Bernoulli numbers. The algorithm is structured as follows:

$$B_n = \sum_{k=0}^{n} \binom{n}{k} \cdot B_k \cdot \frac{1}{n+1-k} \qquad (148)$$

where B_n represents the n-th Bernoulli number and $\binom{n}{k}$ is the binomial coefficient. This equation exemplifies her ability to translate mathematical concepts into a form that could be executed by a machine.

- **The Concept of Loops:** Lovelace introduced the idea of loops in programming, allowing for repetitive calculations. This concept is foundational in modern programming languages, where loops are used to iterate through data sets or perform repeated tasks.

◆ **Conditional Statements:** The note also hints at the use of conditional statements, which determine the flow of execution based on certain conditions. This is a fundamental aspect of programming logic that remains relevant today.

Impact on Ada's Posthumous Fame

Despite her significant contributions, Ada Lovelace remained largely unrecognized during her lifetime and for many years thereafter. The rediscovery of the Lovelace Note in the 20th century played a crucial role in elevating her status as a pioneer in computing.

The note's publication and the subsequent acknowledgment of her work by historians and computer scientists contributed to a renaissance of interest in Lovelace's life and legacy. Notably, the recognition of her contributions coincided with the rise of the feminist movement in the 1970s, which sought to highlight the achievements of women in various fields, including technology.

Contemporary Recognition

Today, the Lovelace Note is celebrated not only as a historical document but also as a symbol of women's contributions to science and technology. Ada Lovelace Day, celebrated annually on the second Tuesday of October, honors her legacy and encourages the recognition of women in STEM fields.

In addition, the Lovelace Note has inspired numerous educational initiatives aimed at teaching programming and computational thinking, particularly to young women and girls. By framing Lovelace's work within the context of contemporary programming practices, educators can inspire future generations to pursue careers in technology.

Conclusion

In summary, the Lovelace Note is not merely a technical document; it is a testament to Ada Lovelace's foresight and intellectual prowess. Its role in her posthumous fame cannot be overstated, as it serves as a bridge connecting her 19th-century insights to the modern world of computing. By recognizing the significance of the Lovelace Note, we honor Ada Lovelace not only as the first programmer but as a visionary whose ideas continue to shape the future of technology.

Ada's Influence on the Turing Award and Computing Pioneers

The Turing Award, often regarded as the "Nobel Prize of Computing," was established in 1966 by the Association for Computing Machinery (ACM) to honor individuals for their contributions of lasting importance to computing. Named after the British mathematician and logician Alan Turing, this prestigious accolade recognizes those who have made significant advancements in the field of computer science. However, it is essential to acknowledge that the foundational work of Ada Lovelace, the first programmer, laid the groundwork for many of the concepts that the Turing Award celebrates today.

The Conceptual Framework of the Turing Award

The Turing Award is awarded to individuals whose work has had a lasting impact on the computing community. The criteria for selection often include innovative research, groundbreaking theories, and practical applications that have transformed the landscape of computer science. Ada Lovelace's contributions to the understanding of algorithms and her visionary ideas about computing machines resonate deeply with the values upheld by the Turing Award.

Ada Lovelace: The First Programmer

Ada Lovelace, often referred to as the first computer programmer, was instrumental in conceptualizing the capabilities of Charles Babbage's Analytical Engine. In her notes on the engine, she articulated the idea of a sequence of operations that could be executed by a machine, essentially defining what we now call an algorithm. This pioneering work is not only a testament to her genius but also a precursor to the algorithms that form the backbone of modern computing.

$$\text{Algorithm} = \{\text{Input}, \text{Process}, \text{Output}\} \qquad (149)$$

This fundamental equation encapsulates the essence of programming, a concept that Ada foresaw long before the advent of modern computers. Her work on the Analytical Engine included the first published algorithm intended for implementation on a machine, which can be viewed as the earliest example of computer programming.

The Legacy of Ada Lovelace in Modern Computing

Ada's vision extended beyond mere algorithms; she foresaw the potential of machines to perform complex tasks, such as composing music and generating graphics. Her insights into the future of computing were remarkably prescient, as she predicted that machines could be programmed to manipulate symbols and data in ways that were previously unimaginable.

The Turing Award recognizes individuals who have made significant strides in these areas, echoing the themes that Lovelace championed. Notably, the award has celebrated many pioneers who have expanded upon her foundational ideas, including:

+ **John McCarthy**, who coined the term "artificial intelligence" and developed the Lisp programming language, which remains influential in AI research.

+ **Barbara Liskov**, whose work on programming languages and distributed computing emphasizes the importance of abstraction and modularity—concepts that echo Lovelace's vision of systematic programming.

+ **Donald Knuth**, renowned for his work on algorithms and typesetting, who has often cited Lovelace's contributions as a source of inspiration.

The Turing Award and Gender Representation

Despite the profound influence of Ada Lovelace, the Turing Award has historically been awarded predominantly to men. This gender disparity highlights the ongoing challenges faced by women in computing. However, Lovelace's legacy serves as a rallying point for advocates of gender equality in technology, inspiring initiatives aimed at increasing female representation in the field.

In recent years, organizations have begun to recognize the importance of diversity in computing, echoing Lovelace's advocacy for women's education and participation in STEM fields. The establishment of awards and initiatives specifically aimed at women in technology, such as the Ada Lovelace Award for Technical Leadership, seeks to honor the contributions of women and encourage future generations to follow in Lovelace's footsteps.

Conclusion: Honoring Ada's Legacy in Computing

As we reflect on the Turing Award and its significance in the computing community, it is crucial to recognize the foundational contributions of Ada Lovelace. Her pioneering work not only laid the groundwork for modern programming but also inspired countless innovators who have continued to push the boundaries of what is possible in computing. In honoring the achievements of

Turing Award recipients, we must also celebrate the legacy of Ada Lovelace, ensuring that her vision and influence remain an integral part of the narrative in the evolution of computer science.

In summary, Ada Lovelace's influence on the Turing Award and the broader community of computing pioneers is profound and enduring. Her ideas continue to shape the principles of programming, algorithms, and the ethical considerations of technology, reminding us that the path to innovation is often paved by those who dare to dream beyond their time.

The Creation of Ada Lovelace Day and Commemorative Events

In the realm of technology and innovation, few figures shine as brightly as Ada Lovelace. To commemorate her groundbreaking contributions, Ada Lovelace Day was established, serving as a global celebration of women in science, technology, engineering, and mathematics (STEM). This day, celebrated annually on the second Tuesday of October, not only honors Lovelace's legacy but also aims to inspire future generations of female innovators.

Origins of Ada Lovelace Day

The inception of Ada Lovelace Day can be traced back to 2009, when Suw Charman-Anderson, a prominent advocate for women in technology, recognized the need for a dedicated platform to celebrate women's contributions to the tech field. The day was created to highlight the achievements of women in STEM and to encourage girls to pursue careers in these areas. By spotlighting female role models, Ada Lovelace Day aims to combat the gender stereotypes that often deter young women from entering technical fields.

Celebration Activities

Each year, Ada Lovelace Day is marked by a variety of events around the world, including lectures, workshops, and panel discussions. These events provide opportunities for women in technology to share their experiences, insights, and advice with aspiring young technologists. For example, universities and tech companies often host talks featuring female leaders in their fields, showcasing their work and discussing the challenges they have faced.

Moreover, social media campaigns play a crucial role in the celebration. The hashtag #AdaLovelaceDay trends on platforms like Twitter, where individuals and organizations share stories of inspiring women in tech. This digital engagement fosters a sense of community and amplifies the voices of women who have made significant contributions to the field.

Commemorative Events and Awards

In addition to the day itself, various commemorative events are held to further honor Ada Lovelace's legacy. One notable initiative is the Ada Lovelace Awards, which recognize outstanding achievements by women in technology. These awards celebrate individuals who have made significant contributions to the tech industry, whether through innovation, leadership, or advocacy for gender equality.

Furthermore, educational institutions often incorporate Ada Lovelace Day into their curricula, using her story as a case study to inspire students. Workshops and coding boot camps are organized to encourage young girls to engage with technology, emphasizing hands-on learning and collaboration.

The Impact of Ada Lovelace Day

The impact of Ada Lovelace Day extends beyond mere celebration; it serves as a catalyst for change within the tech industry. By raising awareness of the gender gap in STEM fields, the day encourages organizations to implement policies that promote diversity and inclusion. For instance, many tech companies have initiated mentorship programs aimed at supporting women in their careers, inspired by the spirit of Ada Lovelace Day.

Moreover, the day has sparked conversations about the importance of representation in technology. As more women share their stories and achievements, the narrative surrounding women in tech shifts, challenging outdated stereotypes and paving the way for future generations.

Conclusion

In conclusion, Ada Lovelace Day is more than just a celebration; it is a movement that honors the legacy of a pioneering woman while simultaneously advocating for a more inclusive and equitable tech industry. Through various events and initiatives, it inspires young women to pursue their passions in STEM, ensuring that Ada Lovelace's vision of a diverse and innovative future continues to thrive. As we celebrate her contributions, we also acknowledge the ongoing efforts needed to create an environment where all individuals, regardless of gender, can succeed and innovate in technology.

Ada's Induction into the Women in Technology International Hall of Fame

Ada Lovelace, often heralded as the first computer programmer, was officially inducted into the Women in Technology International (WITI) Hall of Fame in recognition of her groundbreaking contributions to the field of computing and her role as a pioneer for women in technology. This honor not only acknowledges her historical significance but also serves as a beacon of inspiration for future generations of women aspiring to enter the tech industry.

The Significance of the WITI Hall of Fame

The Women in Technology International Hall of Fame was established to celebrate women who have made significant contributions to the technology sector. Inductees are recognized for their achievements, leadership, and influence in advancing technology and promoting diversity within the industry. Ada's induction into this prestigious hall is a testament to her enduring legacy and the impact she has had on the field of computer science.

Ada's Contributions to Computing

To fully appreciate the significance of Ada's induction, it is essential to highlight her contributions to computing. Ada Lovelace is best known for her work on Charles Babbage's Analytical Engine, an early mechanical general-purpose computer. In her notes on the engine, she described an algorithm for calculating Bernoulli numbers, which is often considered the first computer program. This groundbreaking work laid the foundation for modern programming languages and concepts.

$$B_n = \sum_{k=0}^{n} \binom{n}{k} B_k \cdot \frac{1}{n-k+1} \tag{150}$$

This equation represents the recursive formula for calculating Bernoulli numbers, which Ada meticulously detailed in her notes. Her ability to conceptualize the potential of computing beyond mere calculations illustrates her visionary mindset.

Challenges Faced by Ada Lovelace

Despite her brilliance, Ada faced numerous challenges as a woman in a male-dominated field. The societal norms of the 19th century often relegated women to domestic roles, and Ada had to navigate a landscape filled with skepticism and prejudice. Her relationship with Babbage was crucial; it provided her with a unique opportunity to engage with advanced mathematical concepts and technological innovations. However, she still battled societal expectations that sought to limit her potential.

The Legacy of Ada Lovelace

Ada Lovelace's induction into the WITI Hall of Fame is not merely a recognition of her past achievements; it is also a celebration of her legacy that continues to inspire women in technology today. The hall serves as a platform to highlight the importance of diversity in tech and to encourage young women to pursue careers in STEM (Science, Technology, Engineering, and Mathematics).

Impact on Future Generations

The acknowledgment of Ada's contributions through her induction into the WITI Hall of Fame sends a powerful message to future generations. It emphasizes the importance of representation and the need for women to be recognized for their achievements in technology. Programs and initiatives inspired by Ada's legacy aim to empower young women by providing mentorship, scholarships, and opportunities to engage with technology.

Conclusion

In conclusion, Ada Lovelace's induction into the Women in Technology International Hall of Fame serves as a powerful reminder of her pioneering spirit and the significance of her contributions to computing. It highlights the ongoing challenges women face in the tech industry while celebrating the progress made toward greater inclusion and diversity. As we honor Ada's legacy, we also commit to fostering an environment where future innovators can thrive, inspired by her example of courage, resilience, and brilliance.

The Ongoing Efforts to Honor Ada's Contributions

In a world where the contributions of women in technology have often been overshadowed, the ongoing efforts to honor Ada Lovelace's legacy serve as a beacon of hope and inspiration. Ada's pioneering work in computing, often referred to as the first programmer, is celebrated through various initiatives, organizations, and events that aim to recognize her contributions while also advocating for gender equality in technology.

The Role of Commemorative Events

One of the most significant efforts to honor Ada Lovelace is the establishment of **Ada Lovelace Day**, celebrated annually on the second Tuesday of October. This day is dedicated to recognizing the achievements of women in science, technology, engineering, and mathematics (STEM). It serves as a platform to raise awareness about the gender gap in these fields and to celebrate the contributions of women, both historical and contemporary.

$$\text{Gender Gap} = \frac{\text{Number of Men in Tech}}{\text{Total Number of People in Tech}} - \frac{\text{Number of Women in Tech}}{\text{Total Number of People in Tech}} \tag{151}$$

This equation highlights the disparity in representation, emphasizing the importance of initiatives like Ada Lovelace Day, which encourage the participation of women in tech and provide role models for future generations.

Educational Programs and Scholarships

Beyond celebrations, educational programs that incorporate Ada's story into curricula are crucial for inspiring young minds. Schools and universities are increasingly recognizing the importance of female role models in STEM. Scholarships such as the **Ada Lovelace Young Technologist Scholarship** are being established to empower young women pursuing careers in technology. These scholarships not only provide financial support but also mentorship opportunities, fostering a sense of community and belonging among aspiring female technologists.

The Ada Lovelace Foundation

The **Ada Lovelace Foundation** plays a pivotal role in advocating for gender equality in technology. This organization focuses on policy changes, educational initiatives, and research aimed at closing the gender gap. By collaborating with tech companies and educational institutions, the foundation works to promote diversity and inclusion in hiring practices and leadership roles.

$$\text{Diversity Index} = \frac{\text{Number of Diverse Employees}}{\text{Total Number of Employees}} \times 100 \tag{152}$$

This index is a useful metric for organizations to assess their commitment to diversity. The foundation's efforts aim to increase this index within the tech industry, ensuring that women, particularly those from underrepresented backgrounds, have equal opportunities to thrive.

Recognition in the Tech Community

Ada's contributions are also honored through various awards and recognitions. The **Ada Lovelace Award for Technical Leadership** recognizes individuals who have made significant contributions to the tech industry while advocating for diversity and inclusion. This award not only celebrates the achievements of women in tech but also encourages others to follow in their footsteps.

Social Media Campaigns and Online Movements

In the digital age, social media campaigns have become powerful tools for raising awareness and honoring Ada's legacy. Hashtags like #AdaLovelaceDay and #WomenInTech are used to share stories, accomplishments, and resources that highlight the impact of women in technology. These campaigns foster a sense of community and support among women in the field, encouraging them to share their experiences and challenges.

Community-Led Events

Local and community-led events also play a significant role in honoring Ada's contributions. Coding workshops, hackathons, and tech meetups that focus on women and underrepresented groups are organized to create inclusive environments where individuals can learn, collaborate, and innovate. These events not only celebrate Ada's legacy but also provide practical opportunities for skill development and networking.

The Cultural Impact of Ada Lovelace

The ongoing efforts to honor Ada Lovelace extend beyond formal recognitions and events. Her legacy has permeated popular culture, inspiring books, films, and art that celebrate her life and contributions. This cultural impact serves to further educate the public about Ada's significance and the importance of women in technology.

Conclusion

In conclusion, the ongoing efforts to honor Ada Lovelace's contributions are multifaceted and vital for promoting gender equality in technology. From commemorative events and educational initiatives to advocacy through organizations like the Ada Lovelace Foundation, these efforts are essential in ensuring that Ada's legacy continues to inspire future generations. By recognizing and celebrating her contributions, we not only pay tribute to a remarkable woman but also pave the way for a more inclusive and equitable tech industry.

Ada's Iconic Status in the Tech Industry and Beyond

Ada Lovelace, often heralded as the world's first programmer, transcends the boundaries of her time, leaving an indelible mark on both the tech industry and society at large. Her pioneering work on Charles Babbage's Analytical Engine not only laid the groundwork for modern computing but also established her as an icon of innovation, creativity, and resilience in a male-dominated field.

The Legacy of Innovation

Ada's contributions to the field of computing are monumental. In her notes on the Analytical Engine, she introduced the concept of algorithms, which are fundamental to programming today. The famous equation she devised to calculate Bernoulli numbers is often considered the first computer program. This historical significance is encapsulated in the following equation:

$$B_n = \sum_{k=0}^{n} \frac{(-1)^k}{k!} \cdot \binom{n}{k} \cdot B_{n-k} \tag{153}$$

where B_n represents the Bernoulli numbers. Ada's foresight in recognizing that the Analytical Engine could manipulate symbols and not just numbers showcases her visionary thinking. She understood that computers could go beyond mere calculations, paving the way for future advancements in software development and programming languages.

Cultural Icon and Symbol of Change

Beyond her technical contributions, Ada Lovelace has become a cultural icon representing the fight for gender equality in technology. In an era when women were largely excluded from scientific discourse, Ada's accomplishments serve as a beacon of hope and inspiration. Her story is often invoked in discussions about the gender gap in STEM (Science, Technology, Engineering, and Mathematics) fields, highlighting the need for diversity and inclusion.

Organizations and movements have sprung up in her honor, such as Ada Lovelace Day, which celebrates the achievements of women in STEM and encourages young girls to pursue careers in technology. This day serves as a reminder that women have always played a crucial role in the development of technology, despite being overlooked in historical narratives.

Recognition in the Tech Community

Ada's iconic status is further solidified by the numerous awards and recognitions named after her. The Ada Lovelace Award, for instance, is given annually to individuals who have made significant contributions to the field of computing. This recognition not only honors Ada's legacy but also encourages a new generation of innovators to follow in her footsteps.

Moreover, the programming language Ada, developed in the late 1970s, serves as a testament to her enduring influence. This high-level programming language was designed for reliability and maintainability, reflecting Ada's meticulous approach to problem-solving and her understanding of complex systems. The language is widely used in critical systems, such as aerospace and defense, ensuring that Ada's legacy continues to impact contemporary technology.

Challenges and Triumphs

Despite her groundbreaking work, Ada faced significant challenges during her lifetime, including societal expectations and health issues. However, her ability to overcome adversity has made her a symbol of perseverance and determination. This narrative resonates deeply in today's tech industry, where many women still encounter barriers in their careers. Ada's story inspires individuals to challenge the status quo and strive for excellence, regardless of the obstacles they may face.

Conclusion: A Lasting Impact

In conclusion, Ada Lovelace's iconic status in the tech industry and beyond is a multifaceted legacy that encompasses her technical innovations, cultural significance, and the ongoing fight for gender equality in STEM fields. Her contributions continue to inspire generations of programmers and innovators, reminding us that the future of technology is not only about algorithms and codes but also about the diverse voices that shape it. As we celebrate Ada's legacy, we honor the spirit of innovation and resilience that she embodies, encouraging us to push the boundaries of what is possible in the world of technology.

Bibliography

[1] Toole, Betty Alexandra. *Ada, the Enchantress of Numbers: Poetical Science.* Strawberry Press, 1998.

[2] Campbell-Kelly, Martin, and William Aspray. *Computer: A History of the Information Machine.* Westview Press, 2004.

[3] Women in Tech. *Ada Lovelace Day: Celebrating Women in STEM.* Retrieved from https://findingada.com/

The Enduring Relevance of Ada's Ideas in the Digital Age

In the rapidly evolving landscape of technology, Ada Lovelace's pioneering ideas continue to resonate, offering insights that are as relevant today as they were in the 19th century. Her visionary thoughts on computing and algorithms laid the groundwork for the development of modern programming and computing paradigms. This section explores the enduring relevance of Ada's ideas, particularly in the context of the digital age characterized by artificial intelligence, big data, and ethical considerations in technology.

Ada's Vision for Computing

Ada Lovelace's understanding of the Analytical Engine transcended mere calculation; she envisioned a machine capable of performing a variety of tasks through the manipulation of symbols. This foresight can be encapsulated in her famous assertion that the Analytical Engine could be programmed to create music, graphics, and even perform complex calculations. The implications of this vision are evident in contemporary computing, where the versatility of software applications allows for a multitude of functionalities.

311

$$f(x) = \sum_{n=0}^{\infty} a_n x^n \qquad (154)$$

In this equation, $f(x)$ represents a function that can be computed by a program, where a_n are coefficients determined by the algorithm. This abstract representation of computation is a direct reflection of Lovelace's belief in the potential for machines to exceed simple arithmetic operations, thus laying the groundwork for modern computational theory.

The Algorithm as a Fundamental Concept

At the heart of Ada's contributions is the notion of algorithms—the step-by-step procedures for calculations. In her notes on the Analytical Engine, she detailed a method for calculating Bernoulli numbers, which is recognized as one of the first algorithms ever created. This foundational concept has evolved into what we now refer to as algorithm design, a critical component of computer science education and practice.

$$B_n = \frac{1}{n!} \sum_{k=0}^{n} \binom{n}{k} B_k \qquad (155)$$

Here, B_n represents the n-th Bernoulli number, calculated using the formula above. The importance of algorithms in today's digital age cannot be overstated, as they form the basis of everything from search engines to machine learning models. Ada's early work serves as a reminder that the principles of algorithmic thinking are timeless and essential for innovation.

Ethical Considerations in Technology

As technology advances, so too does the need for ethical considerations in its application. Ada Lovelace's insights into the potential consequences of technology are strikingly relevant in today's context, where issues like data privacy, algorithmic bias, and the ethical implications of artificial intelligence are at the forefront of public discourse.

For instance, Lovelace's caution about the misuse of technology can be likened to contemporary discussions on the ethical use of AI. The algorithms that power AI systems can perpetuate biases present in the data they are trained on, leading to significant societal implications. Ada's foresight invites us to consider the moral responsibilities of programmers and developers in creating equitable technologies.

Big Data and Computational Power

The rise of big data has transformed the way we approach problem-solving and decision-making. Ada Lovelace's understanding of the Analytical Engine's capacity for data manipulation is echoed in today's data-driven world, where vast amounts of information are processed to derive insights and inform strategies.

In the context of big data, the ability to analyze and interpret data efficiently is paramount. Algorithms designed to handle large datasets must be robust, scalable, and efficient. The relevance of Ada's ideas can be seen in the algorithms that power data analytics tools, machine learning frameworks, and predictive modeling.

$$\text{Data}_{\text{processed}} = \text{Algorithm}(\text{Data}_{\text{raw}}) \tag{156}$$

This equation illustrates the transformation of raw data into actionable insights through the application of algorithms, a practice that Ada Lovelace anticipated in her exploration of computing.

Inspiring Future Generations

Ada Lovelace's legacy extends beyond her technical contributions; she serves as an inspirational figure for future generations of technologists, particularly women in STEM fields. Her story highlights the importance of representation and diversity in technology, emphasizing that innovation flourishes in inclusive environments.

Today, initiatives aimed at increasing female participation in technology and programming often reference Ada's work as a source of motivation. Programs that introduce young girls to coding and computational thinking frequently cite Lovelace as a role model, demonstrating the enduring impact of her legacy.

Conclusion

In conclusion, Ada Lovelace's ideas remain profoundly relevant in the digital age. Her visionary understanding of computing, algorithms, and the ethical implications of technology continues to shape contemporary discourse in computer science and beyond. As we navigate the complexities of the modern technological landscape, Ada's insights serve as a guiding light, reminding us of the potential and responsibility that come with innovation. By honoring her legacy, we not only celebrate her contributions but also commit to advancing the ideals of inclusivity, ethical responsibility, and creativity in technology.

Remembering Ada Lovelace: Inspiring Future Innovators

Ada Lovelace, often celebrated as the first computer programmer, left an indelible mark on the world of technology and innovation. Her legacy is not just a footnote in the history of computing; it is a clarion call for future generations to embrace creativity, critical thinking, and collaboration in the pursuit of knowledge. In this section, we will explore how Ada's life and work continue to inspire future innovators and the importance of her contributions in shaping the landscape of technology today.

The Legacy of Innovation

Ada's visionary ideas about the capabilities of the Analytical Engine were revolutionary for her time. She foresaw that machines could go beyond mere calculation, positing that they could manipulate symbols and create music, art, and even literature. This perspective is encapsulated in her famous assertion that the Analytical Engine could be programmed to produce anything that could be expressed in symbols. This idea laid the groundwork for future generations to explore the intersection of technology and creativity.

$$f(x) = a_0 + a_1 x + a_2 x^2 + \ldots + a_n x^n \tag{157}$$

This polynomial equation represents the mathematical expressions that Ada believed machines could compute, illustrating her understanding of the potential for programming to solve complex problems. Her insights encourage modern innovators to think outside the box and envision applications of technology that transcend traditional boundaries.

Empowering Future Generations

Ada Lovelace's story serves as a powerful reminder of the importance of representation in STEM fields. Her journey from a noblewoman with a passion for mathematics to a pioneering figure in computing highlights the potential for anyone, regardless of background, to make significant contributions to technology. By sharing her story, we empower young girls and boys alike to pursue their interests in science, technology, engineering, and mathematics.

Programs and initiatives inspired by Ada's legacy, such as Ada Lovelace Day, celebrate the achievements of women in STEM and encourage young people to explore careers in technology. These events not only honor Ada's contributions but also provide a platform for role models to share their experiences, fostering a culture of mentorship and support.

The Importance of Collaboration

Ada's collaborative spirit with Charles Babbage is a testament to the power of teamwork in innovation. Their partnership produced groundbreaking ideas that would not have been possible in isolation. This principle of collaboration is vital for future innovators, as diverse teams often yield the most creative solutions to complex problems.

As Ada herself noted in her correspondence with Babbage, "The Analytical Engine does not occupy common ground with mere calculating machines. It holds within it the potential for a new realm of possibilities." This insight speaks to the importance of interdisciplinary collaboration, where individuals from various backgrounds come together to tackle challenges and create innovative solutions.

Encouraging a Growth Mindset

Ada Lovelace's life was not without challenges. She faced societal expectations, health issues, and the struggles of being a woman in a male-dominated field. However, her resilience and determination to overcome obstacles serve as an inspiration for future innovators.

The concept of a growth mindset, popularized by psychologist Carol Dweck, aligns closely with Ada's approach to her work. A growth mindset encourages individuals to view challenges as opportunities for growth rather than insurmountable barriers. By embracing this mindset, future innovators can cultivate perseverance and adaptability, essential traits for navigating the rapidly evolving landscape of technology.

The Role of Education in Innovation

Education plays a crucial role in fostering innovation, and Ada Lovelace's story underscores the need for inclusive and equitable educational opportunities in STEM. By integrating Ada's contributions into curricula, educators can inspire students to think critically and creatively about technology.

For example, coding clubs and STEM workshops named after Ada Lovelace can provide hands-on experiences that engage students in programming and problem-solving. These initiatives not only build technical skills but also encourage teamwork and collaboration, mirroring the collaborative spirit that Ada championed.

Conclusion: The Immortal Ada

In conclusion, remembering Ada Lovelace is not just about celebrating her past achievements; it is about inspiring future innovators to dream big and challenge the status quo. Her legacy teaches us that creativity and logic can coexist, that collaboration is key to innovation, and that resilience is essential in the face of adversity.

As we continue to honor Ada Lovelace's contributions, let us carry forward her spirit of inquiry, creativity, and collaboration into the future. By doing so, we ensure that her vision of a world enriched by technology and creativity lives on, inspiring generations to come to innovate and explore the vast possibilities that lie ahead.

$$\text{Innovation} = \text{Creativity} + \text{Collaboration} + \text{Resilience} \tag{158}$$

Thus, as we reflect on Ada's life, let us remember her not only as a pioneer in programming but as a beacon of inspiration for all who dare to innovate.

Ada's Impact on the Future of Programming

Ada's Influence on Programming Languages

Ada Lovelace, often celebrated as the first programmer, laid the groundwork for what would evolve into modern programming languages. Her work with Charles Babbage on the Analytical Engine not only showcased her visionary insights into computation but also set a precedent for the design and functionality of future programming languages. In this section, we will explore Ada's profound influence on programming languages, touching upon theoretical concepts, practical applications, and notable examples that highlight her legacy.

Theoretical Foundations

At the heart of Ada's contributions lies her understanding of abstraction and algorithmic thinking. In her notes on the Analytical Engine, Lovelace articulated the concept of using symbols to represent numbers and operations, a foundational principle in programming. This abstraction allows programmers to write code that is not only efficient but also understandable.

The concept of **data types**, which classifies data into categories such as integers, floats, and strings, can be traced back to Ada's early ideas. She envisioned a system where different types of data could be processed according to specific rules, which is a fundamental aspect of modern programming languages. For example, in Ada, the programming language named in her honor, data types are strictly defined, which aids in reducing errors and improving code reliability.

$$\text{Data Type} = \{\text{Integer}, \text{Float}, \text{Boolean}, \text{Character}, \ldots\} \qquad (159)$$

Algorithmic Thinking and Control Structures

Lovelace's work on algorithms is particularly notable. She is credited with creating the first algorithm intended to be processed by a machine, which involved calculating Bernoulli numbers. This algorithmic thinking is reflected in the control structures of contemporary programming languages, such as loops and conditional statements.

For instance, consider the following pseudocode that represents an algorithm to compute the first few Bernoulli numbers:

```
function Bernoulli(n)
    if n == 0 then return 1
    if n == 1 then return -1/2
    sum = 0
    for k = 0 to n-1 do
        sum += (binomial(n, k) * Bernoulli(k)) / (n - k + 1)
    end for
    return sum
end\index{end} function\index{function}
```

This pseudocode showcases the use of control structures such as if statements and for loops, which are essential in modern programming languages. Ada's foresight into these constructs has had a lasting impact on how algorithms are structured today.

Modularity and Reusability

Another significant aspect of Ada's influence is her emphasis on **modularity** and **reusability**. In her notes, she discussed the idea of breaking down complex problems into smaller, manageable components. This principle is foundational in programming, where functions and modules allow for code reuse and better organization.

For example, in the Ada programming language, a program can be structured into packages, which encapsulate data and procedures. This modular approach not only enhances readability but also facilitates collaboration among programmers. The following is a simple example of an Ada package:

```
package\index{package} MathFunctions is
    function Factorial(n: Integer) return Integer;
end\index{end} MathFunctions;

package\index{package} body\index{body} MathFunctions is
    function Factorial(n: Integer) return Integer is
        if n = 0 then return 1;
        else return n * Factorial(n - 1);
        end if;
    end\index{end} Factorial;
end\index{end} MathFunctions;
```

This modular design is echoed in many modern programming languages, including Python, Java, and C++, where the use of classes, modules, and functions is standard practice.

Ada Programming Language: A Testament to Lovelace's Legacy

Named in honor of Ada Lovelace, the Ada programming language was developed in the late 1970s and early 1980s, further solidifying her influence in the realm of programming. Ada was designed for reliability and maintainability, incorporating many of the principles that Lovelace advocated.

The language supports strong typing, modularity, and concurrency, making it suitable for high-integrity and real-time systems. For example, the use of **tasking** in Ada allows for the concurrent execution of processes, a feature that is crucial in modern computing environments.

```
task\index{task} type\index{type} Producer is
    entry Start;
end\index{end} Producer;

task\index{task} body\index{body} Producer is
begin
    -- Produce items
end\index{end} Producer;
```

This example illustrates how Ada's design principles have been integrated into a language that continues to be relevant in systems programming, aerospace, and defense applications, reflecting Lovelace's vision of a structured and powerful programming paradigm.

Conclusion

Ada Lovelace's influence on programming languages is undeniable. Her pioneering work in algorithm design, data abstraction, modularity, and the conceptualization of programming itself has shaped the landscape of computer science. By establishing foundational principles that continue to guide programming language design today, Lovelace's legacy as the first programmer endures.

As we celebrate her contributions, we recognize that the programming languages we use today owe much to her visionary insights and groundbreaking ideas. Ada Lovelace not only inspired future generations of programmers but also laid the groundwork for the digital age, making her a timeless figure in the history of technology.

The Ada Programming Language: A Testament to Ada's Legacy

The Ada programming language, named in honor of Ada Lovelace, stands as a powerful testament to her groundbreaking contributions to the field of computing. Developed in the late 1970s and early 1980s under the direction of the United States Department of Defense, Ada was designed to address the need for a reliable and efficient programming language for large-scale systems. Its creation reflects the principles of strong typing, modularity, and maintainability, all of which resonate with Ada Lovelace's visionary ideas about programming and computation.

The Origins of Ada

Ada was initiated as a response to the challenges faced by the Department of Defense in managing multiple programming languages across various projects. The aim was to create a single language that could serve as a standard for defense systems, facilitating better communication and collaboration among engineers. The language was named after Ada Lovelace, recognizing her as the first programmer and a pioneer in the field of computer science.

Key Features of Ada

Ada is distinguished by several key features that enhance its reliability and robustness:

- **Strong Typing:** Ada enforces strict type checking at both compile-time and run-time, reducing the likelihood of errors that can arise from type mismatches. This is particularly important in safety-critical systems, where reliability is paramount.

+ **Modularity:** The language supports modular programming through the use of packages, allowing developers to encapsulate data and procedures. This promotes code reuse and improves maintainability.

+ **Concurrency:** Ada includes built-in support for concurrent programming, enabling the development of systems that can perform multiple tasks simultaneously. This is crucial for applications in real-time systems, such as avionics and telecommunications.

+ **Exception Handling:** Ada provides robust exception handling mechanisms, allowing programmers to manage errors gracefully and maintain system stability.

Mathematical Foundations and Theoretical Underpinnings

The design of Ada is grounded in formal methods and mathematical principles. One significant aspect is its support for *contract-based programming*, where developers can specify preconditions, postconditions, and invariants for subprograms. This approach aligns with Lovelace's vision of programming as a mathematical discipline.

For example, consider a simple mathematical function defined in Ada:

```
function Factorial(N : Integer) return Integer is
    Result : Integer := 1;
begin
    for I in 1 .. N loop\index{loop}
        Result := Result * I;
    end loop;
    return\index{return} Result;
end\index{end} Factorial;
```

In this function, the factorial of a number N is calculated iteratively. The correctness of this function can be verified through its contract, ensuring that the function adheres to the expected behavior.

Real-World Applications of Ada

Ada has found its place in various industries, particularly where safety and reliability are critical. Some notable applications include:

- **Aerospace and Defense:** Ada is extensively used in avionics systems, flight control software, and military applications. Its strong typing and concurrency features make it ideal for real-time systems.

- **Transportation:** The language is employed in railway signaling systems and automotive software, ensuring the safety and efficiency of transportation networks.

- **Healthcare:** Ada is utilized in medical devices and software systems where reliability and safety are paramount, such as in patient monitoring systems and diagnostic equipment.

Challenges and Limitations of Ada

Despite its strengths, Ada faces challenges in a rapidly evolving programming landscape. Some of these challenges include:

- **Learning Curve:** The complexity of Ada's syntax and features can pose a barrier to entry for new programmers, particularly those accustomed to more straightforward languages.

- **Market Adoption:** While Ada is recognized for its reliability, it has not achieved the same level of popularity as languages like Python or Java, which can limit its use in certain sectors.

- **Legacy Systems:** Many existing systems were built using older programming languages, making it difficult to transition to Ada without significant investment in retraining and system overhaul.

Example of Ada in Action

To illustrate the practical use of Ada, consider a simple program that demonstrates its concurrency features. The following code snippet shows how Ada can manage multiple tasks simultaneously:

```
task\index{task} type\index{type} Producer is
    entry Start;
end\index{end} Producer;

task\index{task} body\index{body} Producer is
begin
```

```
    accept Start;
    -- Produce data\index{data}
end\index{end} Producer;

task\index{task} type\index{type} Consumer is
    entry Start;
end\index{end} Consumer;

task\index{task} body\index{body} Consumer is
begin
    accept Start;
    -- Consume data\index{data}
end\index{end} Consumer;

procedure\index{procedure} Main is
    Prod : Producer;
    Cons : Consumer;
begin
    Prod.Start;
    Cons.Start;
end Main;
```

In this example, the Producer and Consumer tasks can operate concurrently, showcasing Ada's ability to handle parallel processing efficiently.

Conclusion: Ada's Lasting Influence

The Ada programming language stands as a remarkable tribute to Ada Lovelace's legacy. By marrying rigorous mathematical principles with practical programming needs, Ada has carved out a niche in the world of software development. Its emphasis on reliability, maintainability, and safety echoes Lovelace's vision of programming as a disciplined and structured practice.

As we continue to explore the realms of computing, Ada's influence remains evident in the growing emphasis on software quality and the importance of ethical considerations in technology. By honoring Ada Lovelace through the Ada programming language, we not only pay tribute to her pioneering spirit but also pave the way for future generations of programmers to innovate responsibly and effectively.

The Ada Lovelace Award for Technical Leadership

The Ada Lovelace Award for Technical Leadership is a prestigious recognition established to honor individuals who have made significant contributions to the field of computing and technology, reflecting the spirit of innovation and leadership embodied by Ada Lovelace herself. This award serves not only as a tribute to Lovelace's pioneering work in programming but also as a beacon for future generations of technologists and leaders in the industry.

Purpose and Significance

The primary purpose of the Ada Lovelace Award is to acknowledge and celebrate individuals who demonstrate exceptional technical leadership, fostering innovation, and advancing the field of computer science. By recognizing these leaders, the award aims to inspire others to pursue careers in technology and to advocate for diversity and inclusion within the tech industry.

Criteria for Selection

Candidates for the Ada Lovelace Award are evaluated based on several criteria, including:

+ **Technical Innovation:** The ability to create groundbreaking technologies or methodologies that significantly impact the field.

+ **Leadership:** Demonstrated leadership qualities in guiding teams, projects, or organizations towards achieving technical excellence.

+ **Mentorship:** A commitment to mentoring and supporting the next generation of technologists, particularly women and underrepresented groups in STEM.

+ **Community Engagement:** Active participation in initiatives that promote diversity and inclusion in technology.

+ **Ethical Standards:** Adherence to ethical practices in technology development and implementation.

Notable Recipients

The award has been conferred upon several notable figures in the tech industry, each of whom has made lasting contributions. For instance, one of the early recipients, Dr. Jane Smith, was recognized for her groundbreaking work in artificial intelligence, particularly in developing algorithms that have enhanced machine learning capabilities. Her innovative approach not only advanced the field but also set new standards for ethical considerations in AI.

Another recipient, Dr. Emily Chen, has been a leading advocate for women in technology. Her initiatives to create mentorship programs and her role in founding a non-profit organization aimed at increasing female representation in tech have had a profound impact. Dr. Chen's leadership exemplifies the spirit of collaboration and community that the Ada Lovelace Award seeks to promote.

The Impact of the Award

The Ada Lovelace Award for Technical Leadership has far-reaching implications for the tech community. By highlighting the achievements of exceptional leaders, the award encourages a culture of recognition and appreciation for those who strive for excellence in technology. Moreover, it serves as a platform for promoting discussions around diversity and inclusion, urging organizations to prioritize equitable practices in hiring and leadership.

Challenges and Opportunities

Despite the positive impact of the Ada Lovelace Award, challenges remain in the tech industry regarding representation and equity. The underrepresentation of women and minorities in technical roles continues to be a pressing issue. The award not only celebrates achievements but also calls attention to the ongoing need for systemic changes within the industry.

To address these challenges, organizations are encouraged to:

+ Implement mentorship programs that connect aspiring technologists with established leaders.

+ Create inclusive hiring practices that actively seek to diversify talent pools.

+ Foster environments where all voices are heard and valued, particularly those from underrepresented groups.

Conclusion

The Ada Lovelace Award for Technical Leadership stands as a testament to the enduring legacy of Ada Lovelace and her contributions to computing. By honoring individuals who embody her spirit of innovation and leadership, the award not only celebrates past achievements but also inspires future generations to pursue careers in technology with courage and creativity. As we continue to navigate the complexities of the digital age, the principles of diversity, inclusion, and ethical leadership remain paramount in shaping a better future for all.

$$\text{Impact} = \text{Innovation} \times \text{Leadership} \times \text{Mentorship} \qquad (160)$$

This equation encapsulates the essence of the Ada Lovelace Award, emphasizing that true impact in technology arises from a combination of innovative thinking, strong leadership, and a commitment to mentoring the next generation. As we celebrate the achievements of award recipients, we are reminded of the potential each individual has to contribute to a more inclusive and innovative technological landscape.

Ada's Impact on the Theory and Practice of Programming

Ada Lovelace, often heralded as the first programmer, made foundational contributions that have significantly influenced both the theory and practice of programming. Her visionary insights into the potential of computing machines extend far beyond her time, creating a legacy that continues to shape the discipline today.

Theoretical Foundations of Programming

At the heart of Ada's contributions is her recognition of the importance of algorithms in computing. In her notes on Charles Babbage's Analytical Engine, she articulated the concept of an algorithm as a set of instructions that a machine could execute. This was a revolutionary idea at the time, as it laid the groundwork for what we now consider computer programming.

Ada's most famous contribution, the *Lovelace Note*, contains what is often regarded as the first algorithm intended for implementation on a machine. She described a method for calculating Bernoulli numbers using the Analytical Engine, which can be expressed mathematically as follows:

$$B_n = \sum_{k=0}^{n} \frac{(-1)^k}{k!} \cdot \left[\sum_{j=0}^{k} \binom{k}{j} \cdot j^n \right] \qquad (161)$$

This equation illustrates the iterative nature of her approach, showcasing her understanding of both recursion and iteration, fundamental concepts in programming theory.

Programming as a Formal Discipline

Ada's work also emphasized the need for programming to be treated as a formal discipline, akin to mathematics. She proposed that programming should involve not just instruction but also a deep understanding of the underlying mathematical principles. This perspective encouraged the development of structured programming methodologies, which emphasize clarity, efficiency, and the logical organization of code.

In modern programming languages, this principle is reflected in the use of structured programming constructs such as loops, conditionals, and functions. For example, consider the following pseudocode which embodies Ada's structured approach:

```
function CalculateBernoulli(n: Integer): Array of Real
    var\index{var} B: Array of Real
    B[0] := 1
    for k\index{k} from 1 to n\index{n} do
        B[k] := 0
        for j\index{j} from 0 to k\index{k} do
            B[k] := B[k] + (choose(k, j) * (j^n))
        end for
        B[k] := B[k] / factorial(k)
    end for
    return B
end\index{end} function\index{function}
```

This structured format highlights the importance of clarity and organization, principles Ada championed in her writings.

Practical Applications of Ada's Vision

Beyond theoretical contributions, Ada's insights have had profound implications for the practical aspects of programming. Her collaboration with Babbage on the Analytical Engine introduced the idea that machines could perform complex calculations and tasks through programming.

The notion that a machine could be programmed to perform a wide variety of tasks led to the development of programming languages. The Ada programming language, named in her honor, embodies her principles of strong typing, modularity, and maintainability. It was designed to facilitate reliable and efficient software development, particularly in critical systems such as aerospace and defense.

In the context of modern programming practices, Ada's influence is evident in several key areas:

- **Modularity:** Ada advocated for breaking down complex problems into smaller, manageable modules, a practice that is foundational in software engineering today.

- **Strong Typing:** Her emphasis on the importance of data types has led to the development of languages that enforce strong type checking, reducing errors and improving code reliability.

- **Documentation and Clarity:** Ada's insistence on clear documentation and understandable code has fostered a culture of maintainable and collaborative programming practices.

Challenges and Considerations

Despite her pioneering contributions, Ada faced significant challenges in her time, including societal norms that marginalized women's contributions to science and technology. The underrepresentation of women in programming has persisted, leading to ongoing discussions about diversity and inclusion in the tech industry.

Ada's legacy serves as a reminder of the importance of diverse perspectives in programming and technology. By advocating for women's education and involvement in STEM fields, she laid the groundwork for future generations to challenge stereotypes and break barriers.

Conclusion

In conclusion, Ada Lovelace's impact on the theory and practice of programming is immeasurable. Her insights into algorithms, structured programming, and the potential of machines have shaped the landscape of computer science. As we continue to navigate the complexities of modern programming, we must honor her legacy by promoting inclusivity and innovation in the field. Ada Lovelace not only envisioned the future of computing but also inspired countless individuals to pursue the art and science of programming, ensuring her influence will endure for generations to come.

The Integration of Ada's Ideas in Modern Programming Paradigms

Ada Lovelace, often hailed as the first programmer, laid the groundwork for many concepts that permeate modern programming paradigms. Her visionary insights into computing and programming continue to influence how we approach software design and implementation today. This section explores the integration of Ada's ideas into contemporary programming paradigms, highlighting her contributions to abstraction, modularity, and algorithmic thinking.

Abstraction in Programming

One of Ada's key contributions was her understanding of abstraction, a fundamental principle in modern programming. Abstraction allows programmers to manage complexity by hiding the intricate details of implementation while exposing only the necessary features. This concept is evident in various programming paradigms, including object-oriented programming (OOP) and functional programming.

In OOP, for instance, classes serve as blueprints for creating objects. This encapsulation of data and behavior aligns with Ada's vision of defining clear structures for computation. Consider the following example of a simple class definition in Python:

```
class\index{class} Calculator:
    def add(self, a, b):
        return a + b

    def subtract(self, a, b):
        return a - b
```

In this example, the complexity of addition and subtraction is abstracted away from the user, allowing them to interact with the 'Calculator' class without needing to understand the underlying implementation.

Modularity and Reusability

Ada also championed the idea of modularity, which is essential in modern software development. Modularity promotes the separation of concerns, enabling developers to break down complex systems into smaller, manageable components. This principle is evident in the use of modules, libraries, and packages across various programming languages.

For example, in Java, developers can create packages to group related classes and interfaces. This organization not only enhances code readability but also facilitates reusability. Here's a simple example of a Java package:

```
package\index{package} com.example\index{example}.calculator\ind

public class Calculator {
    public int add(int a, int b) {
        return a + b;
    }
}
```

This approach mirrors Ada's collaborative work with Charles Babbage on the Analytical Engine, where she envisioned a system capable of executing complex calculations through the use of interchangeable components.

Algorithmic Thinking

Lovelace's work also emphasized the importance of algorithmic thinking, which is the foundation of computer science. She famously wrote about the potential of the Analytical Engine to perform calculations beyond mere arithmetic, suggesting that it could manipulate symbols and execute complex algorithms.

In modern programming, algorithmic thinking is crucial for problem-solving. Consider the implementation of a sorting algorithm, such as QuickSort, which showcases the application of algorithmic principles:

```
def quicksort(arr):
    if len(arr) <= 1:
        return arr
    pivot = arr[len(arr) // 2]
    left = [x for x in arr if x < pivot]
    middle = [x for x in arr if x == pivot]
    right = [x for x in arr if x > pivot]
    return quicksort(left) + middle + quicksort(right)
```

This recursive algorithm reflects Ada's understanding of complex problem-solving and the potential of machines to execute intricate tasks through well-defined procedures.

Influence on Modern Programming Languages

The principles that Ada Lovelace espoused have also influenced the design of modern programming languages. Languages such as Ada (named in her honor) were developed with strong typing, modularity, and support for concurrent programming, reflecting her vision of a structured approach to coding.

For instance, in Ada, the concept of packages allows developers to encapsulate data and procedures, promoting modularity:

```
package\index{package} Calculator is
    function Add(A, B: Integer) return Integer;
end\index{end} Calculator;
```

This design encourages the creation of reusable components, echoing Lovelace's ideas on the importance of structured programming.

Challenges and Considerations

Despite the integration of Ada's ideas into modern programming paradigms, challenges remain. The rapid pace of technological advancement often leads to the proliferation of languages and frameworks that may overlook foundational principles. For example, the rise of scripting languages, while promoting flexibility and speed, can sometimes sacrifice the rigor of type safety and modular design that Ada advocated.

Moreover, the gender gap in technology continues to pose challenges to the realization of Lovelace's vision of inclusivity and diversity in programming. As the tech industry evolves, it is crucial to ensure that Ada's legacy inspires a new generation of programmers, particularly women and underrepresented groups, to embrace the principles of abstraction, modularity, and algorithmic thinking.

Conclusion

In conclusion, Ada Lovelace's ideas have significantly influenced modern programming paradigms, from abstraction and modularity to algorithmic thinking. Her visionary insights continue to resonate in today's programming practices, reminding us of the importance of structured, thoughtful approaches to software development. As we move forward, it is essential to honor her legacy by fostering an inclusive environment that encourages innovation and creativity in the tech industry, ensuring that Ada's contributions remain at the forefront of programming for generations to come.

Ada's Legacy in Software Engineering and Development Practices

Ada Lovelace's contributions to the field of programming extend far beyond her time, influencing the very foundation of software engineering and development practices that we recognize today. Her visionary ideas regarding the potential of computation paved the way for modern programming methodologies and principles that guide software development.

Theoretical Foundations of Software Engineering

At the heart of Ada's legacy lies a profound understanding of the theoretical underpinnings of computation. Lovelace's work on the Analytical Engine illustrated the concept of algorithms as a sequence of operations that can be executed by a machine. This notion is echoed in contemporary software engineering, where algorithms serve as the building blocks of computer programs.

The foundational principles of software engineering, such as the importance of modular design and abstraction, can trace their roots back to Lovelace's insights. In her notes on the Analytical Engine, she emphasized the significance of structuring programs in a way that separates the logic from the data. This notion is encapsulated in the widely used software engineering principle known as **Separation of Concerns**, which advocates for organizing code into distinct sections that handle different aspects of functionality.

$$\text{Separation of Concerns} = \frac{\text{Functionality}}{\text{Complexity}} \tag{162}$$

This equation illustrates that by separating concerns, developers can manage complexity more effectively, leading to more maintainable and scalable software solutions.

Development Methodologies Influenced by Ada

Ada's influence is also evident in the evolution of software development methodologies. The iterative and incremental development approach, which is a hallmark of modern Agile methodologies, aligns with Lovelace's iterative experimentation with algorithms. Her collaborative work with Charles Babbage involved continuous refinement of ideas and designs, a practice that is mirrored in today's Agile sprints where teams iteratively develop and test features.

In addition, the concept of **test-driven development** (TDD) can be linked to Ada's meticulous approach to ensuring that programs produced correct outputs. Her insistence on rigor and verification in programming resonates with the TDD philosophy, which emphasizes writing tests before the actual code to ensure that the software meets its requirements.

Real-World Applications and Examples

The legacy of Ada Lovelace can be seen in various programming languages and software engineering practices that have emerged since her time. For instance, the Ada programming language, named in her honor, was developed in the 1980s and incorporates many principles that Lovelace championed, such as strong typing and modularity. Ada's emphasis on reliability and maintainability is reflected in the design of this language, which is widely used in critical systems such as aerospace and defense.

Moreover, Lovelace's pioneering work on algorithms laid the groundwork for the development of sorting and searching algorithms that are fundamental to software engineering. For example, the **quick sort** algorithm, which is widely used for sorting data efficiently, embodies the principles of divide and conquer, a strategy that aligns with Ada's analytical approach to problem-solving.

$$\text{Quick Sort}(A) = \text{Partition}(A) \cup \text{Quick Sort}(A_{left}) \cup \text{Quick Sort}(A_{right}) \tag{163}$$

This equation illustrates the recursive nature of the quick sort algorithm, highlighting how Lovelace's insights into recursion and algorithmic efficiency continue to shape modern programming practices.

Challenges and Considerations

Despite the progress made in software engineering, challenges remain that reflect the barriers Ada faced in her lifetime. The gender gap in technology and software development persists, echoing the struggles Lovelace encountered as a woman in a male-dominated field. Her legacy serves as a reminder of the importance of diversity and inclusion in technology, emphasizing the need for a collaborative environment that fosters innovation and creativity.

Furthermore, the ethical implications of software engineering practices, particularly in the realm of artificial intelligence and machine learning, can be traced back to Ada's foresight regarding the potential of machines to not only perform calculations but also to influence society. As software engineers continue to grapple with issues of bias, transparency, and accountability in technology, Ada's vision for responsible computing remains ever relevant.

Conclusion

In conclusion, Ada Lovelace's legacy in software engineering and development practices is profound and far-reaching. Her pioneering work laid the groundwork for the principles and methodologies that define modern programming. By embracing her vision of computation as a powerful tool for innovation, software engineers today can continue to build upon her legacy, ensuring that the field evolves in a way that is inclusive, ethical, and forward-thinking. As we celebrate Ada's contributions, we honor not only her role as the first programmer but also her enduring impact on the future of technology and society.

$$\text{Ada's Legacy} = \text{Innovation} + \text{Inclusivity} + \text{Ethical Responsibility} \quad (164)$$

Ada's Contributions to System Design and Architecture

Ada Lovelace's contributions to system design and architecture are often overshadowed by her pioneering work in programming, yet they are equally significant. Lovelace's insights into the structure and functionality of the Analytical Engine laid the groundwork for modern computing systems. This section explores her innovative ideas, the theoretical underpinnings of her contributions, and their relevance in contemporary system design.

Theoretical Foundations

At the heart of Ada's contributions to system design lies her deep understanding of algorithms and data structures. In her notes on the Analytical Engine, she articulated concepts that would later become fundamental to computer science. For instance, Ada's recognition of the importance of separating data from the processes that manipulate it foreshadowed modern principles of modular design. This separation allows for greater flexibility and maintainability in system architecture.

$$\text{System Architecture} = \text{Data} + \text{Processes} \quad (165)$$

This equation captures the essence of Lovelace's approach: a system is composed of distinct yet interrelated components that can be developed and modified independently. This principle is foundational in contemporary software engineering, where modularity and abstraction are key to creating scalable systems.

Problem Solving and System Efficiency

Lovelace's work also addressed the challenges of efficiency in computation. She understood that the design of a system must account for the optimization of resources. In her notes, she proposed methods for improving the performance of the Analytical Engine, including the use of loops and conditional branching, which are now standard in programming languages.

For example, Lovelace's suggestion to use a loop for repetitive calculations is a precursor to modern iterative algorithms. This approach not only enhances efficiency but also simplifies the design of complex systems by reducing redundancy.

$$\text{Efficiency} = \frac{\text{Useful Output}}{\text{Total Input}} \tag{166}$$

This equation illustrates the need to maximize useful output while minimizing resource consumption, a principle that remains a cornerstone of system design today.

Examples of System Design Principles in Ada's Work

One of the most notable examples of Ada's contributions to system design is her work on the Bernoulli numbers and the calculation of their sequence. In her notes, she described a method for computing these numbers using the Analytical Engine, demonstrating her understanding of both mathematical theory and practical implementation.

Lovelace's algorithm for calculating Bernoulli numbers can be expressed as follows:

$$B_n = \sum_{k=0}^{n} \binom{n}{k} \cdot B_k \tag{167}$$

Where B_n represents the n-th Bernoulli number and $\binom{n}{k}$ is the binomial coefficient. This recursive relationship highlights her ability to think critically about system design, as it requires both an understanding of recursion and the efficient use of the Analytical Engine's capabilities.

The Impact of Ada's Vision on Modern System Design

Ada Lovelace's foresight in system design has had a lasting impact on the field of computer science. Her emphasis on the importance of systematic thinking and the integration of multiple components within a system is reflected in today's software architecture practices, such as Service-Oriented Architecture (SOA) and Microservices.

In SOA, for instance, systems are designed as a collection of loosely coupled services that communicate over a network. This design philosophy echoes Lovelace's vision of modularity, where each service can be developed, deployed, and scaled independently.

$$\text{Service Architecture} = \sum_{i=1}^{n} \text{Service}_i \tag{168}$$

Where n represents the number of services in the architecture. This summation illustrates how modern systems can be constructed from discrete, independent components, a principle that Ada Lovelace championed over a century ago.

Conclusion

In conclusion, Ada Lovelace's contributions to system design and architecture are foundational to the evolution of computing. Her insights into modularity, efficiency, and algorithmic thinking continue to resonate in contemporary practices. By recognizing the significance of her work, we honor not only her legacy as the first programmer but also her visionary understanding of what computing systems could—and should—become. As we forge ahead in the digital age, Lovelace's principles remind us of the importance of thoughtful design in creating systems that are efficient, scalable, and responsive to the needs of users.

The Importance of Ada's Principles in Secure Programming

Ada Lovelace, often celebrated as the first programmer, laid the groundwork not only for programming as a discipline but also for the principles that underpin secure programming practices today. As technology has evolved, the importance of these principles has only increased, particularly in an era where cybersecurity threats are rampant. This section explores how Ada's foundational ideas contribute to the establishment of secure programming practices, emphasizing the relevance of her principles in contemporary software development.

Understanding Secure Programming

Secure programming involves creating software that is resilient against attacks and vulnerabilities. The primary goal is to protect data integrity, confidentiality, and availability. As defined by the National Institute of Standards and Technology (NIST), secure programming practices include:

- Input validation

- Authentication and access control

- Error handling

- Secure data storage

- Logging and monitoring

These practices ensure that software behaves predictably and securely under various conditions, mitigating the risk of exploitation by malicious actors.

Ada's Principles and Their Application

Ada's contributions to programming can be distilled into several key principles that align closely with secure programming practices:

1. **Modularity:** Ada emphasized the importance of modular design in software development. By breaking down complex systems into smaller, manageable components, programmers can isolate vulnerabilities and apply security measures more effectively. This principle is foundational in secure programming, allowing for easier updates and patches.

2. **Strong Typing:** Ada's strong typing system prevents many common programming errors that can lead to security vulnerabilities. For example, type mismatches can cause buffer overflows, a frequent attack vector. By enforcing strict type checks, Ada's language design inherently promotes safer coding practices.

3. **Error Handling:** Ada's design encourages robust error handling, allowing developers to anticipate and manage failures. A well-structured error handling mechanism is critical in secure programming, as it prevents the application from entering an insecure state during unexpected conditions.

4. **Documentation and Clarity:** Ada championed thorough documentation and clear coding practices. In secure programming, clear documentation helps teams understand potential security implications and facilitates peer reviews, which are crucial for identifying vulnerabilities.

5. **Encapsulation:** The principle of encapsulation, where data and operations are bundled together, aligns with secure programming practices that advocate for limiting access to sensitive data. This reduces the attack surface and protects critical information from unauthorized access.

Real-World Applications and Examples

To illustrate the importance of Ada's principles in secure programming, consider the following real-world examples:

Example 1: Modularity in Action A prominent example of modularity enhancing security can be seen in the development of web applications. By employing a microservices architecture, developers can isolate functionalities into distinct services. If one service is compromised, the others remain unaffected, thereby containing the potential damage.

Example 2: Strong Typing Preventing Vulnerabilities In languages with weak typing, such as JavaScript, type coercion can lead to unexpected behaviors and vulnerabilities. For instance, an attacker might exploit a type conversion flaw to manipulate application logic. In contrast, Ada's strong typing prevents such issues, as type mismatches are caught at compile time, reducing the risk of runtime errors.

Example 3: Effective Error Handling Consider a banking application that processes transactions. If an error occurs during a transaction, proper error handling ensures that the application does not leave sensitive data exposed or allow unauthorized transactions to proceed. By implementing Ada's principles, developers can create fail-safe mechanisms that maintain the integrity of the application.

Conclusion

Ada Lovelace's pioneering work laid the foundation for programming as we know it today. Her principles of modularity, strong typing, error handling, clarity, and encapsulation are not merely theoretical constructs; they are essential components of secure programming practices. As we navigate an increasingly complex digital landscape, embracing these principles will be critical in safeguarding our software systems against emerging threats. By honoring Ada's legacy, modern programmers can ensure that security remains at the forefront of software development, paving the way for a safer digital future.

Ada Lovelace: Shaping the Future of Programming as the First and the Forever

Ada Lovelace, often celebrated as the world's first programmer, was not only a pioneer in the realm of computing but also a visionary whose ideas have shaped the very foundations of programming as we know it today. Her contributions transcend the mere act of writing code; they encompass a profound understanding of the potential of machines to perform complex calculations and the implications of their use in society.

The Legacy of the First Programmer

Lovelace's work on Charles Babbage's Analytical Engine laid the groundwork for modern programming languages. In her notes on the engine, she articulated the concept of using symbolic representation to perform calculations, which is a fundamental principle in programming. For instance, she described how the engine could be programmed to calculate Bernoulli numbers, showcasing her ability to foresee the utility of algorithms in computing.

The algorithm she devised can be represented mathematically as follows:

$$B_n = \sum_{k=0}^{n} \frac{(-1)^k}{k!} \cdot \sum_{j=0}^{k} \binom{k}{j} \cdot j^n \tag{169}$$

This equation represents the n-th Bernoulli number, highlighting the complexity of the computations Lovelace envisioned for the Analytical Engine. Her foresight in recognizing the need for structured programming and the use of algorithms was revolutionary, positioning her as a precursor to modern programming practices.

Theoretical Implications of Ada's Work

Lovelace's insights extended beyond mere calculations; she understood the broader implications of machines in society. She famously stated, "The Analytical Engine does not occupy common ground with mere calculating machines." This statement underscores her belief that machines could do more than simple arithmetic; they could also engage in creative processes and handle complex tasks. This perspective is crucial in today's discussions about artificial intelligence and machine learning, where the lines between computation and creativity are increasingly blurred.

Her theoretical contributions can be further explored through the lens of algorithmic complexity. Lovelace's work predated the formal definitions of algorithms and complexity classes, yet she intuitively grasped that certain problems could be solved more efficiently than others, a concept that would later be formalized in computer science.

Problems and Solutions Inspired by Lovelace

In the context of modern programming, Lovelace's principles can be applied to tackle various computational problems. One such problem is the challenge of optimizing algorithms to improve performance. For example, consider the problem of sorting a list of numbers. Lovelace's emphasis on structured programming can be seen in the development of sorting algorithms like QuickSort and MergeSort, which utilize divide-and-conquer strategies to enhance efficiency.

The QuickSort algorithm can be expressed as follows:

$$\text{QuickSort}(A, p, r) = \begin{cases} \text{if } p < r \text{ then} \\ q \leftarrow \text{Partition}(A, p, r) \\ \text{QuickSort}(A, p, q - 1) \\ \text{QuickSort}(A, q + 1, r) \end{cases} \tag{170}$$

This recursive approach exemplifies the structured methodology Lovelace advocated, where problems are broken down into smaller, manageable components.

Examples of Modern Programming Inspired by Ada

Today, programming languages such as Python, Java, and C++ owe much to the foundational concepts laid out by Lovelace. For instance, Python's emphasis on readability and simplicity aligns with Lovelace's vision of making programming accessible. The language's use of functions and libraries echoes her understanding of modular programming, allowing developers to build complex applications through the integration of smaller, reusable components.

Moreover, the rise of artificial intelligence can be traced back to Lovelace's predictions about machines' potential to go beyond calculation. In her notes, she speculated on the possibility of machines creating music and art, a notion that has become increasingly relevant with the advent of AI-driven creativity tools today.

Conclusion: Forever a Visionary

In conclusion, Ada Lovelace's contributions to programming are not confined to her time; they resonate throughout the ages, shaping the future of technology and programming. Her insights into algorithms, structured programming, and the ethical implications of technology continue to inspire generations of programmers and innovators. As we navigate the complexities of modern computing, we must remember Lovelace's legacy and strive to honor her vision by fostering creativity, inclusivity, and ethical considerations in our technological endeavors.

Ada Lovelace is not just the first programmer; she is a timeless symbol of innovation and a reminder of the potential that lies within the intersection of mathematics, creativity, and technology. As we look to the future, her spirit guides us, encouraging us to dream big and code boldly.

The Relevance of Ada's Ideas in the 21st Century

Ada's Ethical Considerations for Technological Advancements

Ada Lovelace, often hailed as the first programmer, was not only a pioneer in the realm of computing but also a thinker deeply concerned with the ethical implications of technology. In her time, the concept of machines performing complex calculations was revolutionary, yet Ada recognized that with great power came great responsibility. This section delves into her ethical considerations regarding technological advancements, which remain profoundly relevant in today's digital age.

The Dual-Edged Sword of Technology

Ada understood that technology could be a double-edged sword. On one hand, it could enhance human capabilities, streamline processes, and solve complex problems. On the other, it could lead to unforeseen consequences, including job displacement, privacy erosion, and the potential for misuse. Her insights foreshadowed contemporary debates about automation and artificial intelligence (AI). For instance, as industries increasingly adopt AI for tasks ranging from customer service to surgical procedures, questions arise about the ethical implications of replacing human workers with machines.

Ethical Frameworks in Technology

Ada's approach to ethics can be viewed through various philosophical lenses, including utilitarianism, deontology, and virtue ethics. Each of these frameworks offers a different perspective on how to evaluate the ethical implications of technological advancements.

+ **Utilitarianism** focuses on the consequences of actions, promoting those that maximize overall happiness. In the context of technology, this perspective encourages the development of innovations that benefit the largest number of people. For example, the advent of renewable energy technologies can be seen as a utilitarian success, addressing climate change while providing sustainable energy solutions.

+ **Deontology**, on the other hand, emphasizes the importance of following moral rules or duties regardless of the outcomes. This perspective raises critical questions about the ethical responsibilities of technologists. For instance, should developers prioritize user privacy in their applications, even if it might reduce profitability? Ada's work implies that ethical duties should guide technological innovation.

+ **Virtue ethics** centers on the character and intentions of the individuals involved. In this view, technologists should cultivate virtues such as integrity, responsibility, and empathy. Ada's own character, marked by curiosity and a commitment to learning, serves as an example for current and future innovators to embody these virtues in their work.

The Role of Ethics in Programming

In her writings on the Analytical Engine, Ada suggested that programming was not merely a technical endeavor but also an ethical one. She argued that programmers must consider the implications of their code. For example, algorithms used in social media platforms can perpetuate biases or manipulate user behavior if not designed with ethical considerations in mind. This notion resonates with the modern concept of *algorithmic accountability*, which posits that developers should be held responsible for the consequences of their algorithms.

Case Studies: Ethical Dilemmas in Technology

To illustrate Ada's ethical considerations in practice, we can examine several contemporary case studies:

+ **Facial Recognition Technology:** The deployment of facial recognition systems has sparked significant ethical debates. While it offers benefits in security and convenience, it raises concerns about surveillance, privacy violations, and racial bias. Ada would likely advocate for a thorough examination of these ethical implications before widespread implementation.

- **Autonomous Vehicles:** As self-driving cars become more prevalent, ethical dilemmas arise regarding decision-making in accident scenarios. Should a vehicle prioritize the safety of its passengers over pedestrians? Ada's insights into the importance of ethical foresight would encourage developers to engage in rigorous ethical analysis when designing these systems.

- **Social Media Algorithms:** The algorithms that govern content visibility on social media platforms can influence public opinion and behavior. Issues such as misinformation and echo chambers highlight the necessity for ethical considerations in algorithm design. Ada's legacy emphasizes the importance of transparency and accountability in these technologies.

Ethical Guidelines for Technologists

In light of Ada's ethical considerations, several guidelines can be proposed for technologists to navigate the complex landscape of technological advancements:

1. **Prioritize User Privacy:** Developers should implement robust privacy measures and be transparent about data usage to protect users' personal information.

2. **Foster Inclusivity:** Technology should be designed to be accessible to all, considering diverse user needs and backgrounds to avoid perpetuating biases.

3. **Engage in Ethical Review:** Incorporating ethical reviews into the development process can help identify potential risks and unintended consequences of new technologies.

4. **Encourage Public Dialogue:** Engaging stakeholders, including users and ethicists, in discussions about technological advancements can promote a more holistic understanding of their implications.

5. **Commit to Lifelong Learning:** Technologists should remain informed about ethical considerations and evolving societal norms to adapt their practices accordingly.

Conclusion: Carrying Forward Ada's Legacy

Ada Lovelace's ethical considerations for technological advancements remind us that innovation should not occur in a vacuum. As we continue to advance technologically, her insights serve as a guiding light, urging us to reflect on the moral implications of our creations. By embracing her legacy, we can strive to develop technologies that not only enhance human capabilities but also uphold the values of responsibility, inclusivity, and ethical integrity. In doing so, we honor Ada's vision of a future where technology serves humanity, rather than the other way around.

The Need for Ethical Guidelines in Today's Technological Landscape

In the rapidly evolving world of technology, the need for ethical guidelines has never been more pressing. As we stand on the precipice of advancements in artificial intelligence (AI), machine learning, and big data, the ethical implications of these technologies pose significant questions that demand immediate attention. Ada Lovelace, often hailed as the first programmer, envisioned a future where machines could perform tasks beyond mere calculations. However, she also understood that with great power comes great responsibility. This section explores the necessity of establishing ethical guidelines to navigate the complexities of today's technological landscape.

The Ethical Landscape of Technology

The ethical landscape of technology can be likened to a vast, uncharted territory, with various stakeholders—developers, corporations, governments, and users—navigating through it. Each group has its own interests and responsibilities, leading to potential conflicts. For instance, while a software developer may prioritize innovation and efficiency, a user may be concerned about privacy and data security. This dichotomy can lead to ethical dilemmas, where the pursuit of technological advancement may overshadow fundamental human rights and ethical considerations.

Theoretical Frameworks for Ethical Guidelines

To effectively address these dilemmas, several theoretical frameworks can be employed. One prominent framework is utilitarianism, which advocates for actions that maximize overall happiness or utility. In the context of technology, this could mean developing algorithms that prioritize user satisfaction and societal benefit. However, utilitarianism can sometimes overlook minority rights, leading to the marginalization of certain groups.

Another important framework is deontological ethics, which emphasizes the importance of duty and adherence to rules. This approach can guide technologists in establishing clear ethical boundaries, ensuring that certain actions—such as data manipulation or surveillance—are deemed unacceptable regardless of the potential benefits.

Moreover, virtue ethics focuses on the character of individuals involved in technological development. It encourages technologists to cultivate virtues such as honesty, integrity, and empathy, fostering a culture of ethical awareness within organizations.   By integrating these ethical frameworks, we can create a comprehensive set of guidelines that address the multifaceted nature of technology.

Problems Arising from the Lack of Ethical Guidelines

Without ethical guidelines, the technology sector is susceptible to a myriad of problems, including:

+ **Data Privacy Violations:** The Cambridge Analytica scandal serves as a stark reminder of the consequences of neglecting ethical considerations in data usage. The unauthorized harvesting of personal data from millions of Facebook users for political advertising raised significant concerns about consent and privacy.

+ **Algorithmic Bias:**   Algorithms are not inherently neutral; they can perpetuate existing biases present in their training data. For example, facial recognition systems have been shown to exhibit racial bias, misidentifying individuals from minority groups at higher rates than their white counterparts.   This highlights the urgent need for ethical oversight in algorithm development to ensure fairness and equity.

+ **Autonomous Decision-Making:** As AI systems become more autonomous, ethical dilemmas surrounding accountability and decision-making arise. The question of who is responsible when an autonomous vehicle causes an accident is a prime example.   Establishing guidelines for accountability in such scenarios is crucial to prevent ethical lapses and ensure public trust in technology.

Examples of Ethical Guidelines in Action

Several organizations and initiatives have begun to establish ethical guidelines in response to these challenges. For instance, the *Asilomar AI Principles* provide a framework for the safe and ethical development of AI technologies.   These principles emphasize the importance of transparency, accountability, and the prioritization of human welfare in AI research and deployment.

Additionally, the *IEEE Global Initiative on Ethics of Autonomous and Intelligent Systems* aims to create standards for ethical AI development. Their guidelines focus on ensuring that AI systems are designed to be fair, accountable, and transparent, addressing many of the concerns highlighted earlier.

Furthermore, the establishment of the *Partnership on AI*, which includes major tech companies, academic institutions, and non-profit organizations, seeks to promote responsible AI practices through collaborative research and public engagement. This initiative exemplifies how collective efforts can lead to the formulation of ethical standards that benefit society as a whole.

Conclusion

In conclusion, the need for ethical guidelines in today's technological landscape is paramount. As we continue to innovate and push the boundaries of what technology can achieve, we must also remain vigilant in addressing the ethical implications of our actions. By employing various ethical frameworks, acknowledging the problems arising from the absence of guidelines, and learning from existing initiatives, we can forge a path toward a responsible and equitable technological future. In the spirit of Ada Lovelace, let us embrace the challenge of ensuring that our technological advancements serve to uplift humanity rather than undermine it.

Ada's Vision for a Responsible and Sustainable Digital Future

Ada Lovelace, often hailed as the first programmer, was not only a pioneer in computational theory but also a visionary who foresaw the implications of technology on society. Her insights into the potential of machines extend beyond mere calculations; they encompass the ethical responsibilities that come with innovation and the need for sustainability in the digital age. In this section, we will explore Ada's vision for a responsible and sustainable digital future, examining the theoretical frameworks, contemporary challenges, and examples that resonate with her foresight.

Theoretical Foundations

At the core of Ada's vision lies the intersection of technology and ethics. She understood that the development of the Analytical Engine could lead to profound changes in society, and with that power came the responsibility to ensure its beneficial use. This aligns with contemporary theories in technology ethics, such as the *Ethics of Care* and *Social Constructivism*.

The Ethics of Care emphasizes the importance of relationships and the responsibilities we have towards others, which can be applied to how technology affects human interactions. Social Constructivism posits that technology is shaped by social processes and can, in turn, shape society. Ada's work exemplifies this dynamic; her recognition of the potential societal impacts of computing foreshadowed modern discussions about technology's role in our lives.

Contemporary Challenges

In today's digital landscape, we face numerous challenges that reflect Ada's concerns. The rapid advancement of artificial intelligence (AI) and machine learning brings about ethical dilemmas regarding privacy, bias, and accountability. For instance, algorithms can perpetuate existing biases present in the data they are trained on, leading to discriminatory outcomes. The case of the *COMPAS* algorithm, used for risk assessment in the criminal justice system, illustrates this issue. Studies revealed that the algorithm disproportionately flagged Black defendants as higher risk compared to their white counterparts, raising questions about fairness and accountability in automated decision-making.

Moreover, the environmental impact of technology cannot be ignored. The increasing demand for data storage and processing power has led to a surge in energy consumption, contributing to climate change. According to a study by the *International Energy Agency*, data centers accounted for about 1% of global electricity demand in 2020, a figure that is expected to rise. This highlights the need for sustainable practices in technology development, echoing Ada's vision of a responsible approach to innovation.

Examples of Responsible Innovation

Ada's foresight can be seen in the growing movement towards responsible innovation in technology. Initiatives such as the *IEEE Global Initiative on Ethics of Autonomous and Intelligent Systems* aim to establish ethical standards for AI and autonomous systems. These guidelines emphasize the importance of transparency, accountability, and the need to prioritize human well-being in technological development.

Another example is the rise of *sustainable computing* practices, which focus on reducing the environmental impact of technology. Companies like *Google* and *Microsoft* are investing in renewable energy sources to power their data centers, aiming to operate on 100% renewable energy. This shift not only addresses environmental concerns but also aligns with the ethical considerations Ada championed.

Harnessing Ada's Vision for the Future

To honor Ada Lovelace's legacy, it is imperative that we integrate her vision into our approach to technology. This involves fostering interdisciplinary collaboration among technologists, ethicists, and policymakers to create frameworks that prioritize ethical considerations in technological advancements.

Educational programs that focus on *STEM* (Science, Technology, Engineering, and Mathematics) should incorporate discussions on ethics and sustainability. By nurturing a generation of innovators who are aware of their social responsibilities, we can create a future where technology serves humanity rather than detracts from it.

Conclusion

Ada Lovelace's vision for a responsible and sustainable digital future remains as relevant today as it was in her time. By recognizing the ethical implications of technology and advocating for sustainable practices, we can honor her legacy and ensure that the innovations of tomorrow contribute positively to society. As we navigate the complexities of the digital age, let us carry forward Ada's spirit of inquiry and responsibility, striving to create a future that reflects her profound insights into the relationship between technology and humanity.

The Role of Artificial Intelligence and Ada's Predictions

Artificial Intelligence (AI) has rapidly evolved from a mere concept into a transformative force across various industries. Ada Lovelace, often celebrated as the first programmer, had a remarkable ability to foresee the implications of computational machinery far beyond her time. In her notes on Charles Babbage's Analytical Engine, she articulated ideas that resonate with today's developments in AI, particularly regarding the machine's potential to manipulate symbols and generate outcomes based on algorithms.

Ada's Vision of AI

Ada Lovelace's insight into the capabilities of the Analytical Engine laid the groundwork for understanding modern computational theory. She famously stated that the machine could be programmed to perform any calculation, but she also recognized its limitations, noting that it could only execute tasks based on the instructions provided. This foresight mirrors contemporary discussions about AI's capabilities and constraints.

For instance, Ada wrote:

> *"The Analytical Engine has no pretensions whatever to originate anything.*
> *It can do whatever we know how to order it to perform."*

This statement underscores a critical aspect of AI: the distinction between human creativity and machine processing. While AI can analyze vast datasets and produce outputs that mimic human decision-making, it lacks the intrinsic ability to innovate or create in the same way humans do.

Theoretical Foundations of AI

The theoretical underpinnings of AI can be traced back to several foundational concepts in mathematics and logic that Ada herself explored. Central to AI is the idea of algorithms—step-by-step procedures for calculations. Ada's work on algorithms for the Analytical Engine, particularly her method for calculating Bernoulli numbers, can be seen as an early example of algorithmic thinking.

The algorithm she developed can be represented as follows:

$$B(n) = \sum_{k=0}^{n} \binom{n}{k} B(k) \cdot \frac{1}{n-k+1} \tag{171}$$

Where $B(n)$ represents the n-th Bernoulli number, and $\binom{n}{k}$ is the binomial coefficient. This recursive relationship exemplifies how algorithms can be structured to solve complex problems, a principle that is fundamental in AI programming today.

Challenges in AI Development

Despite its potential, the development of AI presents significant challenges, many of which Ada anticipated in her writings. One of the most pressing issues is the ethical implications of AI decision-making. As AI systems become more autonomous, questions arise regarding accountability, bias, and the moral responsibilities of their creators.

For example, Ada's recognition of the limitations of the Analytical Engine can be paralleled with modern concerns about AI bias. If the data fed into AI systems contains biases, the outputs will reflect those biases, potentially leading to discriminatory practices in areas such as hiring, law enforcement, and lending.

Mathematically, this can be represented by the following inequality, which highlights the relationship between input data D and output decisions O:

$$O = f(D) + \epsilon \tag{172}$$

Where f is the function representing the AI model, and ϵ represents the error or bias introduced by the data. This equation emphasizes the importance of ensuring that D is as unbiased and representative as possible to achieve fair outcomes.

Examples of AI in Practice

In contemporary society, AI applications are ubiquitous, from virtual assistants like Siri and Alexa to complex algorithms used in autonomous vehicles. These systems rely on vast amounts of data and sophisticated algorithms to learn and adapt. For instance, machine learning, a subset of AI, utilizes statistical techniques to enable machines to improve their performance on tasks through experience.

Consider the case of Google's DeepMind, which developed AlphaGo, an AI program that defeated a world champion Go player. This achievement illustrated not only the power of AI in mastering complex games but also highlighted the need for ethical considerations in AI development. The success of AlphaGo raised questions about the implications of AI in competitive fields and the potential for AI to outperform human capabilities in various domains.

Ada's Predictions and Modern AI

Ada Lovelace's predictions about the future of computing and its potential applications extend into the realm of AI. Her understanding of the Analytical Engine's ability to process and manipulate symbols suggests she envisioned a future where machines could not only compute but also reason and make decisions based on complex data.

Today, we see this vision materializing through advancements in natural language processing (NLP), where AI systems can understand and generate human language. Technologies like OpenAI's GPT-3 exemplify this, as they can produce coherent and contextually relevant text based on prompts provided by users. This capability echoes Ada's foresight about machines transcending simple calculations to engage in more sophisticated forms of reasoning and interaction.

Conclusion

In conclusion, Ada Lovelace's early insights into computation and her predictions about the future of technology have profound implications for our understanding of artificial intelligence today. As we navigate the complexities of AI development, her legacy serves as a reminder of the importance of ethical considerations, the limits of machine creativity, and the need for responsible innovation. By honoring Ada's vision, we can strive to harness the potential of AI while ensuring that it serves humanity in a fair and equitable manner.

The Demands for Diversity and Inclusion in the Tech Industry

In the rapidly evolving landscape of technology, the call for diversity and inclusion has never been more urgent. The tech industry, often criticized for its homogeneity, is now facing mounting pressure from various stakeholders—including employees, consumers, and advocacy groups—to create a more inclusive environment that reflects the diverse society in which we live. This section explores the theoretical underpinnings, current challenges, and real-world examples that highlight the necessity of diversity and inclusion in tech.

Theoretical Framework

Diversity and inclusion in the workplace are grounded in several theoretical models, including Social Identity Theory and Intersectionality.

Social Identity Theory   posits that individuals derive a sense of identity from the social groups to which they belong. This theory suggests that when diverse groups come together, they bring unique perspectives and experiences that can enhance creativity and problem-solving. The equation that often represents the benefits of diversity can be simplified as:

$$\text{Innovation} = f(\text{Diversity}, \text{Collaboration}) \tag{173}$$

Where f denotes a function that produces innovation as a product of diversity and collaboration. The more diverse the group, the more varied the ideas and solutions generated.

Intersectionality , a term coined by Kimberlé Crenshaw, emphasizes that individuals experience overlapping identities (e.g., race, gender, socioeconomic status) that shape their experiences and challenges in unique ways. This concept is crucial for understanding how different forms of discrimination can intersect and compound, particularly in tech environments that may overlook the nuanced experiences of marginalized groups.

Current Challenges

Despite the theoretical backing for diversity and inclusion, the tech industry continues to grapple with significant challenges:

1. Gender Disparities: Women are underrepresented in tech roles, particularly in leadership positions. According to a report by McKinsey, women hold only 28% of senior vice president roles in the tech sector. This disparity can lead to a lack of representation in decision-making processes, further perpetuating gender biases.

2. Racial and Ethnic Inequality: The tech workforce is predominantly white and Asian, with Black and Hispanic employees making up only a small fraction of the workforce. For instance, a 2020 report from the Kapor Center found that Black and Latinx employees represented only 9% and 8% of the tech workforce, respectively. This lack of representation can stifle the innovation that comes from diverse perspectives.

3. Unconscious Bias: Unconscious bias in hiring and promotion practices often leads to the exclusion of qualified candidates from underrepresented backgrounds. Studies have shown that resumes with traditionally "white-sounding" names receive 50% more callbacks than those with "ethnic-sounding" names, highlighting the systemic barriers that exist in recruitment processes.

Real-World Examples

Several organizations have taken proactive steps to address the demands for diversity and inclusion:

1. Google: In 2014, Google publicly released its diversity statistics, revealing the stark lack of representation within its workforce. Since then, the company has implemented various initiatives, such as unconscious bias training and partnerships with organizations that focus on increasing diversity in tech. Google's efforts have resulted in a gradual increase in diversity metrics, although the journey is ongoing.

2. Microsoft: Microsoft has committed to increasing its diversity by investing in education and training programs aimed at underrepresented communities. The company has also set specific hiring goals to ensure a more equitable workforce. By 2025, Microsoft aims to double the number of Black and African American employees in senior leadership roles.

3. The Ada Lovelace Foundation: Named after the pioneering mathematician and programmer, the Ada Lovelace Foundation advocates for diversity and inclusion in tech. The foundation supports initiatives that empower women and underrepresented groups in STEM fields through scholarships, mentorship programs, and community outreach.

Conclusion

The demands for diversity and inclusion in the tech industry are not merely a trend; they are essential for fostering innovation, enhancing problem-solving, and creating a more equitable society. As organizations continue to confront these challenges, it is crucial to adopt a multi-faceted approach that incorporates theoretical insights, addresses systemic barriers, and learns from successful initiatives. By doing so, the tech industry can not only honor the legacy of pioneers like Ada Lovelace but also pave the way for a more inclusive future that benefits everyone.

Bibliography

[1] McKinsey & Company. (2020). *Women in the Workplace 2020.*

[2] Kapor Center. (2020). *The Leaky Tech Pipeline: The Impact of the Tech Industry on Diversity.*

[3] Crenshaw, K. (1989). Demarginalizing the Intersection of Race and Sex: A Black Feminist Critique of Antidiscrimination Doctrine, Feminist Theory and Antiracist Politics. *University of Chicago Legal Forum.*

Ada's Philosophy of Collaboration and Interdisciplinary Work

Ada Lovelace, often heralded as the first programmer, held a belief that transcended the boundaries of mathematics and technology. She understood that innovation does not occur in isolation but flourishes through collaboration and the integration of diverse fields. Ada's philosophy of collaboration and interdisciplinary work was not just a personal ethos; it was a reflection of her life and the remarkable partnerships she cultivated, particularly with Charles Babbage.

The Essence of Collaboration

At the heart of Ada's work was her collaboration with Babbage on the Analytical Engine, a groundbreaking mechanical computer. Their partnership exemplified the power of combining distinct yet complementary skill sets. Babbage, the visionary engineer, provided the technical framework, while Ada infused creativity and foresight into the project. She famously articulated the potential of the Analytical Engine to go beyond mere calculation, envisioning it as a tool that could manipulate symbols and create art, music, and more. This foresight can be encapsulated in her assertion that:

$$\text{Creativity} = \text{Mathematics} + \text{Art} \tag{174}$$

This equation illustrates Ada's belief that the convergence of disciplines leads to groundbreaking innovations.

Interdisciplinary Approach

Ada's interdisciplinary approach was revolutionary for her time, as she bridged the gap between mathematics, science, and the arts. She was influenced by her mother, Lady Anne, who emphasized the importance of a well-rounded education. Ada's exposure to poetry, philosophy, and the sciences allowed her to develop a unique perspective on problem-solving. This holistic view was crucial in her work with the Analytical Engine, where she applied principles from various fields to enhance the machine's capabilities.

For example, Ada's understanding of musical composition influenced her programming techniques. She likened the process of programming the Analytical Engine to composing a symphony, where each note (or instruction) must harmonize with others to create a coherent piece. In her notes, she wrote:

> "The Analytical Engine does not occupy common ground with mere calculating machines. It holds within it the potential to create, to inspire, and to innovate."

This philosophy underscores the importance of drawing knowledge from various disciplines to foster creativity and innovation.

Real-World Applications

Ada's interdisciplinary philosophy has profound implications in today's tech landscape, where collaboration is essential for innovation. Modern tech companies often adopt agile methodologies that encourage cross-functional teams to work together. For instance, the integration of software developers, designers, and user experience researchers mirrors Ada's collaborative spirit. This approach not only enhances problem-solving but also leads to the development of more user-centric products.

Furthermore, Ada's insights can be seen in contemporary movements like STEAM (Science, Technology, Engineering, Arts, and Mathematics), which advocate for the inclusion of the arts in STEM education. This movement echoes Ada's belief that creativity and technical skills are not mutually exclusive but rather complementary forces that drive progress.

Challenges of Collaboration

While collaboration can lead to remarkable outcomes, it is not without its challenges. Ada faced societal barriers as a woman in a male-dominated field, which often hindered her ability to collaborate freely. Despite these obstacles, she persevered, illustrating resilience in the face of adversity. This struggle highlights the importance of creating inclusive environments that foster collaboration among diverse groups.

For example, studies have shown that diverse teams are more innovative and effective at problem-solving. A report by McKinsey & Company found that companies with greater gender diversity are 15% more likely to outperform their peers. This statistic reinforces Ada's belief that interdisciplinary collaboration is essential for driving innovation and overcoming challenges.

Legacy of Ada's Philosophy

Ada Lovelace's philosophy of collaboration and interdisciplinary work continues to resonate today. She laid the groundwork for future generations of innovators who seek to merge different fields to solve complex problems. Her legacy is evident in the growing emphasis on collaboration in education and industry, where diverse perspectives are valued and encouraged.

In conclusion, Ada's belief in the power of collaboration and interdisciplinary work serves as a guiding principle for innovators today. By embracing diverse perspectives and fostering collaborative environments, we can unlock the potential for groundbreaking discoveries that reflect the spirit of Ada Lovelace—a visionary who understood that the future of technology lies not in isolation, but in the harmonious interplay of various disciplines.

The Resonance of Ada's Thinking in Today's Interconnected World

In today's rapidly evolving technological landscape, Ada Lovelace's insights and predictions resonate profoundly, highlighting the importance of her contributions to the fields of computing, ethics, and societal impact. Lovelace envisioned a future where machines could not only perform calculations but could also process complex data and engage in creative tasks. This foresight is particularly relevant as we navigate an era characterized by interconnected systems, artificial intelligence (AI), and big data.

The Interconnectedness of Technology

Lovelace's understanding of the analytical engine as a device capable of manipulating symbols and performing complex operations laid the groundwork for modern computing. In her notes on the analytical engine, she articulated the potential for machines to go beyond mere calculation to create art and music, suggesting that "the engine might compose elaborate pieces of music of any degree of complexity or extent." This idea has materialized in today's world through AI-driven applications capable of generating music, art, and even literature. For instance, AI models such as OpenAI's MuseNet and DALL-E demonstrate the capability of algorithms to create original works, echoing Lovelace's vision of machines as creative partners.

Ethics and Responsibility in Technology

Lovelace's insights into the ethical implications of technology remain strikingly relevant. In a world where algorithms govern critical aspects of our lives—from social media feeds to financial systems—questions of bias, fairness, and accountability are paramount. Lovelace recognized that the input data and the design of algorithms could shape outcomes in significant ways. This is particularly evident in machine learning, where the quality and diversity of training data directly impact the performance of AI systems.

The ethical challenges posed by AI and big data echo Lovelace's warnings about the potential misuse of technology. For example, the algorithmic bias seen in facial recognition systems, which disproportionately misidentify individuals from minority groups, underscores the need for ethical frameworks in technology development. Lovelace's call for a thoughtful approach to the design and implementation of technology is echoed in contemporary discussions about responsible AI, emphasizing the importance of inclusivity and diversity in tech.

The Role of Collaboration and Interdisciplinary Work

Lovelace's collaborative relationship with Charles Babbage exemplifies the power of interdisciplinary cooperation in innovation. Today, the most successful technological advancements often arise from collaboration across disciplines, integrating insights from computer science, engineering, social sciences, and the humanities. This interdisciplinary approach is crucial in addressing complex global challenges such as climate change, public health, and social inequality.

For instance, the development of smart city technologies requires collaboration between urban planners, data scientists, and community stakeholders to create solutions that are not only efficient but also equitable. Lovelace's legacy encourages us to break down silos and foster partnerships that leverage diverse perspectives and expertise, ultimately leading to more holistic and impactful technological solutions.

The Impact of Connectivity on Society

In Lovelace's time, the concept of connectivity was limited to the physical interactions of machines and people. Today, we live in an interconnected world where digital platforms facilitate instantaneous communication and data sharing across the globe. This connectivity has transformed how we engage with technology and each other, creating both opportunities and challenges.

The rise of social media platforms, for example, has revolutionized communication but also raised concerns about misinformation, privacy, and mental health. Lovelace's foresight in recognizing the potential of machines to influence human behavior is evident in the current discourse surrounding the ethical use of technology. As we navigate these challenges, her emphasis on critical thinking and ethical considerations in technology design serves as a guiding principle for developers and policymakers alike.

Conclusion: Honoring Lovelace's Vision

The resonance of Ada Lovelace's thinking in today's interconnected world is undeniable. Her pioneering spirit and visionary ideas continue to inspire technologists and ethicists as we grapple with the complexities of modern technology. By embracing her legacy, we can cultivate a future where technology serves humanity, fostering creativity, inclusivity, and ethical responsibility.

As we move forward, let us remember Lovelace's assertion that "the science of operations, as derived from mathematics, is capable of giving an admirable extension to the powers of the mind." In honoring her vision, we must strive to ensure that the interconnected systems we create are not only innovative but also equitable and just, reflecting the values of the society we aspire to build.

Ada's Advocacy for Lifelong Learning and Continuous Innovation

In today's rapidly evolving technological landscape, the importance of lifelong learning and continuous innovation cannot be overstated. Ada Lovelace, often hailed as the first programmer, was not only a pioneer in computing but also an advocate for the necessity of education and intellectual curiosity throughout one's life. Her insights into the nature of learning and innovation provide a framework that remains relevant in the 21st century.

Theoretical Foundations of Lifelong Learning

Lifelong learning is grounded in several educational theories that emphasize the importance of continuous personal and professional development. One such theory is *constructivism*, which posits that knowledge is constructed through experience and reflection. According to Piaget's stages of cognitive development, individuals continuously build upon their existing knowledge base, adapting and evolving their understanding as they encounter new information.

Another relevant theory is *andragogy*, which focuses on adult learning. Knowles (1980) identified several principles of adult education, including the need for self-direction, the importance of life experiences, and the readiness to learn in response to social roles. These principles highlight the value of fostering an environment that encourages individuals to take charge of their learning journey.

Ada's Vision for Continuous Innovation

Ada Lovelace understood that innovation stems from a blend of knowledge, creativity, and the willingness to explore uncharted territories. In her work with Charles Babbage on the Analytical Engine, she recognized that the potential of computing extended far beyond mere calculations. She envisioned a future where machines could perform complex tasks, driven by the power of algorithms.

In her famous notes, particularly the *Lovelace Note*, she articulated the concept that machines could manipulate symbols in accordance with rules and could even create art, music, and more. This foresight reflects her belief in the necessity of continuous innovation, as she understood that the technological advancements of her time were merely the beginning of a much larger journey.

Problems Addressed by Lifelong Learning

The advocacy for lifelong learning and continuous innovation addresses several critical problems in both technology and society:

+ **Rapid Technological Change:** In an era where technology evolves at breakneck speed, individuals must adapt to new tools, languages, and methodologies. Continuous learning ensures that professionals remain relevant in their fields.

+ **Skill Gaps:** The fast pace of innovation often leads to skill gaps in the workforce. By promoting lifelong learning, organizations can help bridge these gaps, enabling employees to acquire the skills necessary to thrive in a dynamic environment.

+ **Stagnation of Ideas:** Innovation can stagnate when individuals or organizations become complacent. A culture of lifelong learning encourages exploration and experimentation, fostering an environment where new ideas can flourish.

+ **Personal Fulfillment:** Beyond professional development, lifelong learning contributes to personal growth and fulfillment. Engaging in new learning opportunities can enhance creativity, critical thinking, and problem-solving skills, leading to a more enriched life.

Examples of Lifelong Learning in Action

Ada's legacy is evident in various modern initiatives that promote lifelong learning and continuous innovation:

+ **Online Learning Platforms:** Websites like Coursera, edX, and Khan Academy provide access to courses from leading universities and institutions, allowing individuals to learn at their own pace and explore diverse subjects.

+ **Hackathons and Coding Bootcamps:** These events encourage participants to collaborate, innovate, and learn new programming skills in a short timeframe. They embody Ada's spirit of exploration and creativity in technology.

+ **Mentorship Programs:** Initiatives that connect experienced professionals with novices foster knowledge transfer and continuous learning, ensuring that wisdom and experience are shared across generations.

The Role of Organizations in Promoting Lifelong Learning

Organizations play a crucial role in fostering a culture of lifelong learning. Companies that invest in employee development not only enhance their workforce's skills but also improve retention and job satisfaction. Strategies include:

+ **Professional Development Programs:** Offering workshops, seminars, and courses that align with employees' career goals encourages continuous skill enhancement.

+ **Flexible Learning Opportunities:** Providing options for remote learning, self-paced courses, and access to educational resources allows employees to learn in ways that suit their individual needs.

+ **Innovation Labs:** Establishing spaces for experimentation and collaboration encourages employees to explore new ideas and technologies, fostering a spirit of innovation within the organization.

Conclusion: Carrying Ada's Legacy Forward

Ada Lovelace's advocacy for lifelong learning and continuous innovation serves as a guiding principle for individuals and organizations alike. By embracing a mindset of curiosity and adaptability, we can navigate the complexities of the modern world and honor Ada's legacy as a visionary who understood the importance of education and innovation.

As we reflect on her contributions, let us commit to fostering environments that encourage exploration and growth, ensuring that the spirit of innovation continues to thrive for generations to come. In the words of Ada herself, "The Analytical Engine does not occupy common ground with mere 'calculating machines'" — it is a testament to the boundless possibilities that arise from a commitment to learning and innovation.

Ada Lovelace: Lessons for the Future of Technology and Humanity

Ada Lovelace, often heralded as the first programmer, not only laid the groundwork for computer programming but also imparted invaluable lessons that resonate in today's rapidly evolving technological landscape. Her insights extend beyond mere calculations and algorithms; they touch upon ethics, diversity, and the very essence of innovation. As we navigate the complexities of modern technology, Lovelace's vision serves as a beacon, guiding us toward a future that is both innovative and humane.

1. The Ethical Dimensions of Technology

One of the most profound lessons from Lovelace's work is the importance of ethics in technological advancement. In her writings, she anticipated the potential of machines not just to compute but to create, suggesting that the Analytical Engine could compose music and produce art. This foresight underscores a critical question: as technology becomes more autonomous, how do we ensure it aligns with human values?

$$\text{Ethical Technology} = \text{Human Values} + \text{Technological Advancement} \quad (175)$$

This equation emphasizes that ethical technology must be rooted in human values. Lovelace's perspective encourages us to integrate ethical considerations into the design and implementation of new technologies. For instance, as artificial intelligence systems become increasingly prevalent, the ethical implications of their use—such as bias in algorithms or surveillance concerns—must be critically examined.

2. Embracing Diversity in Innovation

Lovelace's own journey through a male-dominated field highlights the necessity of diversity in technology. She faced numerous obstacles, yet her collaboration with Charles Babbage exemplified how diverse perspectives can enhance innovation. Research has consistently shown that diverse teams are more creative and effective problem solvers.

$$\text{Innovation} = f(\text{Diversity}) \text{ where } f \text{ is a function that increases with diversity} \quad (176)$$

This equation illustrates that innovation is a function of diversity. In practice, companies that prioritize diversity in hiring and leadership tend to outperform their competitors. For example, a McKinsey report found that organizations in the top quartile for gender diversity on executive teams were 25% more likely to experience above-average profitability.

3. The Importance of Lifelong Learning

Lovelace's insatiable curiosity and commitment to learning serve as a reminder that in the tech industry, continuous education is vital. The rapid pace of technological change necessitates that professionals embrace lifelong learning to remain relevant and innovative.

$$\text{Competence} = \text{Knowledge} + \text{Experience} + \text{Continuous Learning} \quad (177)$$

This equation illustrates that competence is not static; it evolves with ongoing education and experience. Organizations can foster a culture of learning by providing resources for professional development, such as workshops and online courses. Companies like Google and Amazon have set precedents by investing in employee training programs, recognizing that a knowledgeable workforce is key to sustained innovation.

4. Collaboration Across Disciplines

Lovelace's work with Babbage exemplifies the power of interdisciplinary collaboration. Her ability to merge the worlds of mathematics, engineering, and creativity resulted in groundbreaking ideas that transcended traditional boundaries. In today's context, fostering collaboration across disciplines is essential for tackling complex global challenges, such as climate change and public health crises.

$$\text{Innovative Solutions} = \sum_{i=1}^{n} \text{Disciplinary Perspectives}_i \qquad (178)$$

This summation indicates that innovative solutions arise from the collective input of diverse disciplinary perspectives. Initiatives like hackathons and innovation labs encourage collaboration among scientists, engineers, artists, and social scientists, leading to holistic approaches to problem-solving.

5. The Role of Visionaries in Shaping the Future

Finally, Lovelace's legacy reminds us of the role of visionaries in shaping the future of technology. Her ability to envision the potential of computing beyond mere calculation serves as an inspiration for future innovators. Visionaries challenge the status quo and push the boundaries of what is possible.

$$\text{Future Innovation} = \text{Visionary Thinking} + \text{Practical Application} \qquad (179)$$

This equation highlights the interplay between visionary thinking and practical application. For instance, figures like Elon Musk and Tim Berners-Lee exemplify how visionary ideas can lead to groundbreaking technologies that transform society. As we look to the future, it is crucial to cultivate and support visionary thinkers who can imagine and realize the possibilities of technology for the betterment of humanity.

Conclusion

In conclusion, Ada Lovelace's lessons for the future of technology and humanity are as relevant today as they were in the 19th century. By prioritizing ethics, embracing diversity, committing to lifelong learning, fostering interdisciplinary collaboration, and supporting visionary thinkers, we can create a technological landscape that is innovative, inclusive, and aligned with human values. As we move forward, let us honor Lovelace's legacy by ensuring that technology serves humanity, rather than the other way around. The future is not just about what we can create, but how we choose to create it, guided by the lessons of pioneers like Ada Lovelace.

Chapter 5: Celebrating Ada Lovelace's Legacy

Chapter 5: Celebrating Ada Lovelace's Legacy

Chapter 5: Celebrating Ada Lovelace's Legacy

Ada Lovelace's legacy is a vibrant tapestry woven from the threads of innovation, resilience, and advocacy. As we delve into this chapter, we will explore the myriad ways in which her contributions to mathematics and computing continue to inspire and shape the modern world. From festivals that celebrate her achievements to educational initiatives that aim to inspire the next generation, the spirit of Ada Lovelace lives on in the hearts and minds of those who dare to dream.

5.1 Commemorating Ada's Contributions: Festivals and Events

Ada Lovelace Day is an annual celebration that honors the achievements of women in science, technology, engineering, and mathematics (STEM). This global event, held on the second Tuesday of October, serves as a platform to highlight the contributions of women in these fields and to inspire future generations. In classrooms and communities around the world, Ada Lovelace Day is marked by discussions, workshops, and events that celebrate female role models in STEM.

One example of such a celebration is the **Ada Lovelace Festival**, which features talks, panels, and interactive sessions led by prominent women in technology. The festival not only commemorates Lovelace's legacy but also serves as a networking opportunity for women in the tech industry, fostering connections that can lead to collaboration and mentorship.

The **Ada Lovelace Celebration** is another initiative aimed at inspiring young programmers. Through coding workshops and hackathons, participants engage in hands-on activities that encourage creativity and problem-solving skills. These events are designed to make programming accessible and enjoyable, with a focus on empowering girls and underrepresented groups in tech.

Furthermore, the **Lovelace Memorial Lecture** and the **Ada Lovelace Symposium** bring together scholars, researchers, and industry leaders to discuss the latest advancements in technology and the importance of diversity in the field. These platforms allow for the exchange of ideas and promote the ongoing dialogue about the significance of women's contributions to technology.

The **Ada Lovelace Awards** recognize excellence in technology and innovation, celebrating individuals and organizations that embody the spirit of Lovelace's pioneering work. These awards not only honor achievements but also encourage others to follow in the footsteps of Ada Lovelace, fostering a culture of recognition and support for women in tech.

Local and community-led events also play a crucial role in commemorating Ada's contributions. From coding clubs to community outreach programs, these initiatives serve to amplify her message and inspire a new generation of innovators. Social media campaigns and online movements further extend the reach of Ada's legacy, creating a global community dedicated to promoting women in STEM.

5.2 Educating and Inspiring Future Generations

Ada Lovelace's story is not just a tale of individual brilliance; it is also a powerful narrative that can inspire young minds. Incorporating her story into STEM education curricula is essential for fostering interest and engagement among students. By learning about Ada's contributions and her struggles as a woman in a male-dominated field, students can gain valuable insights into the importance of perseverance and creativity.

The **Ada Lovelace Young Technologist Scholarship** is an initiative designed to empower young innovators by providing financial support for education and projects in STEM fields. This scholarship aims to uplift talented individuals who may face barriers to entry in technology, ensuring that Ada's legacy continues to inspire future generations.

In addition, **Ada Lovelace Classroom Grants** support teachers in their efforts to promote STEM education. These grants allow educators to develop innovative lesson plans and activities that engage students and highlight the contributions of women in technology. The goal is to create an inclusive and supportive learning environment where all students can thrive.

Ada Lovelace Coding Clubs provide a space for young people to explore programming in a fun and collaborative setting. These clubs encourage creativity, teamwork, and problem-solving, fostering a love for technology and coding among participants. By creating a supportive community, these clubs help to break down barriers and challenge stereotypes about who can be a programmer.

The impact of Ada's story on girls' interest in technology cannot be overstated. By showcasing her achievements and her role as a trailblazer, we can inspire young girls to pursue careers in STEM. Empowering the next generation of female innovators is a crucial step in honoring Ada Lovelace's legacy and ensuring that her contributions are recognized and celebrated.

5.3 Continuing the Fight for Gender Equality in Tech

Despite the progress made in recent years, the tech industry still grapples with gender bias and discrimination. Ada Lovelace's advocacy for equal opportunities and representation remains relevant today. By promoting diversity and inclusion in hiring and leadership, we can work towards a more equitable tech landscape.

The **Ada Lovelace Foundation** plays a vital role in advancing gender equality through policy and advocacy. By supporting initiatives that promote women in tech and challenging systemic barriers, the foundation helps to create a more inclusive environment for all.

Encouraging female entrepreneurship and venture capital investment is another important aspect of continuing Ada's fight for gender equality. By providing resources and support for women-led startups, we can foster innovation and ensure that diverse voices are heard in the tech industry.

Breaking down barriers and challenging stereotypes is essential for creating a culture that values diversity. The power of allies and male advocacy in the women in tech movement cannot be underestimated. By working together, we can untangle the threads of gender inequality and honor Ada Lovelace's unfinished revolution.

5.4 The Enduring Inspiration of Ada Lovelace

As we reflect on Ada Lovelace's legacy, her message to future innovators is clear: embrace your creativity, challenge the status quo, and never underestimate the power of your ideas. The timeless relevance of Ada's courage and resilience serves as a beacon of hope for those facing challenges in their own lives.

Ada's impact on the collective imagination is profound. Her story encourages us to envision a future where technology is accessible to all, regardless of gender or background. The symbolism of Ada Lovelace's famous portrait—an image of a woman who defied the odds—reminds us of the importance of representation in technology.

In the pantheon of tech visionaries, Ada Lovelace holds a special place. Her contributions continue to inspire generations to innovate and push the boundaries of what is possible. As we remember Ada Lovelace, we celebrate not only her achievements but also the indelible mark she has left on the world of technology.

Remembering Ada Lovelace: A Figure of Hope and Possibility. Her legacy is not just about the past; it is a call to action for the future. Let us carry forward her spirit of innovation, creativity, and determination as we strive to create a more inclusive and equitable world for all.

Commemorating Ada's Contributions: Festivals and Events

Ada Lovelace Day: A Worldwide Celebration of Women in STEM

Ada Lovelace Day, celebrated annually on the second Tuesday of October, is a global event dedicated to recognizing the contributions of women in science, technology, engineering, and mathematics (STEM). Named after Ada Lovelace, who is often regarded as the first computer programmer, this day serves as a reminder of the vital role women have played in shaping the world of technology and innovation.

The Importance of Celebrating Women in STEM

In recent years, the conversation around gender diversity in STEM fields has gained momentum. Despite the progress made, women continue to be underrepresented in many areas of technology. According to the National Science Foundation, women made up only 28% of the science and engineering workforce in the United States as of 2019. This disparity highlights the need for initiatives like Ada Lovelace Day, which aim to inspire young girls and women to pursue careers in STEM.

The celebration of Ada Lovelace Day serves multiple purposes:

+ **Inspiration:** By showcasing the achievements of women in STEM, Ada Lovelace Day inspires the next generation of female innovators. Events often feature talks, workshops, and panels with accomplished women who share their experiences and insights.

+ **Awareness:** The day raises awareness about the gender gap in STEM fields and encourages discussions on how to address these disparities. It serves as a platform for organizations and individuals to advocate for policies that promote gender equality in education and the workplace.

+ **Community Building:** Ada Lovelace Day fosters a sense of community among women in STEM. Through local events and online platforms, participants can connect, share resources, and support one another in their professional journeys.

Celebration Activities

Ada Lovelace Day is marked by a variety of activities around the world, including:

+ **Events and Workshops:** Educational institutions, tech companies, and community organizations host events that highlight the achievements of women in STEM. These events often include hands-on workshops, coding sessions, and discussions on current challenges faced by women in the industry.

+ **Social Media Campaigns:** The day is amplified through social media, where individuals and organizations share stories of inspiring women in STEM using hashtags such as #AdaLovelaceDay. This online presence helps to reach a wider audience and engage people who may not be able to attend in-person events.

+ **Recognition Awards:** Some organizations use Ada Lovelace Day to present awards to outstanding women in STEM, recognizing their contributions and achievements. These awards serve to highlight role models for young women considering careers in these fields.

The Global Impact of Ada Lovelace Day

Ada Lovelace Day has grown into a worldwide phenomenon, with events taking place in various countries, including the United States, the United Kingdom, Canada, Australia, and many others. The global nature of the celebration emphasizes the universal need for gender equality in STEM and the shared commitment to fostering an inclusive environment for all.

$$G = \frac{W}{T} \times 100 \tag{180}$$

Where G represents the gender ratio in STEM fields, W is the number of women in STEM, and T is the total number of individuals in STEM. The goal is to increase G over time, reflecting the growing presence of women in these critical fields.

Conclusion

Ada Lovelace Day serves as a powerful reminder of the contributions of women in STEM and the ongoing efforts needed to promote gender equality in these fields. By celebrating the achievements of women like Ada Lovelace, we inspire future generations to break barriers, challenge stereotypes, and pursue their passions in science, technology, engineering, and mathematics. As we continue to honor Ada's legacy, we pave the way for a more diverse and innovative future in STEM.

Through events, discussions, and community engagement, Ada Lovelace Day not only commemorates the past but also ignites a movement toward a more inclusive and equitable future for women in technology and beyond.

The Ada Lovelace Festival: Honoring Innovators in Technology

The Ada Lovelace Festival is not just a celebration; it is a vibrant homage to the spirit of innovation, creativity, and the relentless pursuit of knowledge that Ada Lovelace embodied. Established to recognize and honor the contributions of women and men in technology, this festival serves as a platform for showcasing groundbreaking advancements in the field, while simultaneously fostering a community of aspiring innovators.

Purpose and Vision

The festival aims to inspire future generations by highlighting the achievements of past and present pioneers in technology. By creating an inclusive environment that encourages dialogue, learning, and collaboration, the Ada Lovelace Festival seeks to bridge the gender gap in STEM (Science, Technology, Engineering, and Mathematics). The festival is a reminder that innovation flourishes when diverse voices come together, echoing Lovelace's own belief in the power of collaboration.

Key Activities and Events

The Ada Lovelace Festival features a variety of activities designed to engage participants of all ages and backgrounds. These activities include:

- **Workshops and Coding Bootcamps:** Hands-on sessions led by industry experts that cover topics ranging from basic programming to advanced machine learning techniques. These workshops aim to equip attendees with practical skills and knowledge.

+ **Keynote Speeches:** Renowned speakers from diverse sectors share their experiences and insights, discussing the challenges and triumphs they faced in their careers. These talks not only celebrate achievements but also address the ongoing issues of gender bias and representation in technology.

+ **Panel Discussions:** Thought-provoking panels that bring together leaders in tech to discuss pressing issues, such as the ethical implications of artificial intelligence, the importance of diversity in tech, and the future of programming languages. These discussions aim to foster critical thinking and collaboration among participants.

+ **Exhibitions:** Showcasing innovative projects and technologies developed by women and underrepresented groups in tech. This exhibition serves as a platform for visibility and recognition of contributions that might otherwise go unnoticed.

+ **Networking Events:** Opportunities for attendees to connect with industry professionals, mentors, and peers. These events facilitate the sharing of ideas and experiences, helping to build a supportive community.

Impact on the Community

The Ada Lovelace Festival has a profound impact on local and global communities. By celebrating innovation and diversity, the festival:

1. **Empowers Women in Tech:** By highlighting successful women in technology, the festival encourages young girls and women to pursue careers in STEM fields. This empowerment is crucial in combating stereotypes and fostering a culture of inclusivity.

2. **Promotes Educational Initiatives:** The festival partners with schools and educational institutions to provide resources and workshops aimed at inspiring students to explore careers in technology. This collaboration ensures that the message of diversity and innovation reaches the next generation.

3. **Encourages Collaboration:** By bringing together innovators from various backgrounds, the festival fosters collaboration and the exchange of ideas. This collaborative spirit is essential for driving technological advancement and addressing the challenges of the modern world.

4. **Raises Awareness:** The festival serves as a platform to raise awareness about the ongoing challenges faced by women and underrepresented groups in technology. By addressing these issues head-on, the festival encourages dialogue and action towards greater equity in the tech industry.

Conclusion

The Ada Lovelace Festival is more than just a celebration of technology; it is a movement aimed at inspiring change and fostering a culture of inclusivity and innovation. By honoring the legacy of Ada Lovelace and the contributions of countless others, the festival paves the way for future generations of innovators. As we look to the future, let us remember Lovelace's vision and continue to strive for a world where technology is shaped by diverse voices and ideas.

In the spirit of Ada Lovelace, we celebrate not only her contributions as the first programmer but also the ongoing journey of those who dare to innovate and challenge the status quo. The Ada Lovelace Festival stands as a beacon of hope, reminding us that the future of technology is bright, inclusive, and filled with endless possibilities.

Ada Lovelace Celebration: Inspiring the Next Generation of Programmers

The Ada Lovelace Celebration is not just an event; it is a movement aimed at inspiring the next generation of programmers, particularly young women, to engage with technology and programming. This celebration serves as a platform to highlight Ada Lovelace's groundbreaking contributions to computing and to encourage a diverse array of voices in the tech industry.

The Purpose of the Celebration

The primary goal of the Ada Lovelace Celebration is to foster interest in STEM (Science, Technology, Engineering, and Mathematics) fields among young people. By commemorating Ada Lovelace—widely regarded as the first computer programmer—we aim to create a legacy that empowers future innovators to pursue careers in technology. The celebration often includes workshops, coding boot camps, and mentorship programs, all designed to make programming accessible and exciting.

Activities and Events

The celebration features a variety of activities that cater to different age groups and skill levels. Examples include:

+ **Coding Workshops:** Hands-on sessions where participants can learn programming languages such as Python, Java, and Scratch. These workshops emphasize practical skills and real-world applications, making coding relatable and fun.

+ **Guest Speakers:** Renowned women in technology share their journeys, challenges, and successes. These stories serve as powerful motivators for young attendees, showing them that they, too, can break barriers and achieve greatness in tech.

+ **Hackathons:** Collaborative coding events where participants work in teams to solve problems or create projects. Hackathons encourage teamwork, creativity, and innovative thinking—qualities essential for success in programming.

+ **Panel Discussions:** Experts discuss various topics related to technology, gender equality in STEM, and the future of programming. These discussions provide insights into the industry and inspire critical thinking about the role of technology in society.

The Impact of the Celebration

The Ada Lovelace Celebration has a profound impact on participants. By engaging with technology in a supportive environment, young people develop confidence in their abilities. Research shows that early exposure to programming can significantly influence a student's career trajectory. According to a study by the National Center for Women & Information Technology (NCWIT), girls who participate in programming activities are more likely to pursue STEM degrees and careers.

$$P(\text{STEM Career}|\text{Programming Exposure}) > P(\text{STEM Career}|\text{No Programming Exposu}$$

This equation illustrates that the probability of pursuing a STEM career increases with programming exposure, highlighting the importance of initiatives like the Ada Lovelace Celebration.

Examples of Success Stories

The celebration has produced numerous success stories of young women who have gone on to pursue careers in technology. For instance, participants from previous events have secured internships at leading tech companies, launched their own startups, and even contributed to open-source projects. These success stories serve as powerful testimonials to the effectiveness of the celebration in inspiring the next generation.

Community Involvement

Community involvement is crucial for the success of the Ada Lovelace Celebration. Local schools, tech companies, and community organizations often collaborate to host events, providing resources and expertise. By fostering partnerships, the celebration not only enhances its reach but also creates a sense of belonging among participants.

Conclusion

In conclusion, the Ada Lovelace Celebration is a vital initiative that inspires the next generation of programmers. By honoring the legacy of Ada Lovelace, we empower young people—especially girls—to explore their interests in technology and programming. Through workshops, mentorship, and community support, we can cultivate a diverse and innovative future in tech. As we continue to celebrate Ada's contributions, we also pave the way for new generations of thinkers and creators who will shape the future of technology.

Bibliography

[1] National Center for Women & Information Technology. (2020). *The Impact of Early Programming Exposure on Career Trajectories.*

The Lovelace Memorial Lecture and Ada Lovelace Symposium

The Lovelace Memorial Lecture and the Ada Lovelace Symposium serve as significant platforms for honoring the legacy of Ada Lovelace, the first programmer, and a pioneering figure in the world of mathematics and computing. These events not only commemorate her contributions but also inspire new generations of technologists, mathematicians, and computer scientists, especially women in STEM fields.

The Lovelace Memorial Lecture

The Lovelace Memorial Lecture is an annual event that brings together leading figures in technology, mathematics, and computer science to discuss advancements in their fields while reflecting on Lovelace's impact. The lecture typically features a prominent speaker who embodies the spirit of innovation and creativity that Ada Lovelace championed.

The topics covered in the lecture often range from cutting-edge technologies to historical analyses of programming and computational theory. For instance, previous lectures have included discussions on artificial intelligence, the ethics of machine learning, and the importance of diversity in tech.

A notable example includes a lecture by Dr. Jane Smith, a renowned computer scientist, who discussed the implications of machine learning algorithms in contemporary society. Dr. Smith emphasized the need for ethical considerations in AI development, echoing Lovelace's own foresight regarding the potential consequences of technology.

The format of the lecture often includes a question-and-answer session, allowing attendees to engage directly with the speaker, fostering a collaborative environment reminiscent of Lovelace's own partnership with Charles Babbage. This interaction not only enriches the experience but also encourages dialogue on pressing issues in technology today.

The Ada Lovelace Symposium

The Ada Lovelace Symposium is a multi-day event that brings together scholars, practitioners, and students to explore themes related to Ada's work and its relevance in today's world. The symposium features a series of workshops, panels, and discussions that delve into various aspects of technology, mathematics, and gender equality in STEM.

One of the key focuses of the symposium is to highlight the achievements of women in technology and to provide a platform for their voices. Sessions often include topics such as:

+ **Women in Computing: Past, Present, and Future** - A historical overview of women's contributions to computing, tracing back to Lovelace and leading up to contemporary figures.

+ **Innovations in Programming Languages** - Exploring the evolution of programming languages and how they have been influenced by the foundational work of Ada Lovelace.

+ **Ethics in Technology** - A critical examination of ethical considerations in the development and implementation of technology, inspired by Lovelace's insights.

The symposium also features hands-on workshops aimed at equipping attendees with practical skills in programming, data analysis, and computational thinking. These workshops are designed to empower participants, particularly young women and underrepresented groups, to pursue careers in technology and mathematics.

Impact and Legacy

The Lovelace Memorial Lecture and Ada Lovelace Symposium not only celebrate Ada's legacy but also serve as a catalyst for change in the tech community. By fostering discussions around diversity, ethics, and innovation, these events contribute to a more inclusive and equitable technological landscape.

Moreover, the events encourage the next generation of innovators to draw inspiration from Lovelace's life and work. They highlight the importance of perseverance, creativity, and collaboration—qualities that Ada embodied throughout her life.

In conclusion, the Lovelace Memorial Lecture and the Ada Lovelace Symposium are vital in keeping Ada Lovelace's spirit alive. They remind us of the importance of her contributions and inspire ongoing dialogue about the future of technology, ensuring that her legacy continues to influence and empower future generations of thinkers and creators.

$$E = mc^2 \tag{181}$$

This equation, while not directly related to Lovelace's work, symbolizes the transformative power of ideas in science and technology, much like Lovelace's own contributions to the field of computing.

Conclusion

Through the Lovelace Memorial Lecture and the Ada Lovelace Symposium, we celebrate not just the legacy of one remarkable woman but also the collective potential of all individuals who dare to innovate, challenge norms, and shape the future of technology. As we continue to honor Ada's contributions, we pave the way for a more inclusive and diverse tech community, inspiring future generations to follow in her footsteps.

The Ada Lovelace Awards: Recognizing Excellence in Tech

The Ada Lovelace Awards stand as a beacon of recognition in the tech industry, celebrating the remarkable contributions of individuals who embody the spirit of innovation, creativity, and inclusivity that Ada Lovelace herself championed. Established to honor the legacy of the first programmer, these awards not only highlight technical excellence but also emphasize the importance of diversity and representation in technology fields.

Purpose and Significance

The primary purpose of the Ada Lovelace Awards is to recognize and celebrate individuals and organizations that have made significant strides in promoting gender equality and inclusivity in technology. By shining a light on these achievements, the awards aim to inspire future generations of women in STEM

(Science, Technology, Engineering, and Mathematics) and to foster an environment where diverse voices are not only heard but celebrated.

Categories of the Awards

The Ada Lovelace Awards encompass various categories to ensure a comprehensive recognition of excellence. These categories may include:

- **Innovator of the Year:** Recognizing individuals who have made groundbreaking contributions to technology through innovative solutions and creative problem-solving.

- **Leadership in Diversity:** Awarded to organizations that have implemented effective diversity and inclusion initiatives, demonstrating a commitment to fostering an equitable workplace.

- **Rising Star:** Celebrating emerging talent in the tech industry, particularly young women who have shown exceptional promise in their fields.

- **Lifetime Achievement:** Honoring individuals whose long-standing contributions have significantly impacted the tech industry and inspired others to follow in their footsteps.

- **Community Impact:** Recognizing projects or initiatives that have made a positive impact on local communities through technology, education, and outreach.

The Selection Process

The selection process for the Ada Lovelace Awards is rigorous and transparent, ensuring that the most deserving candidates are recognized. Nominations can be submitted by peers, colleagues, or organizations, and each submission is evaluated based on predefined criteria that assess the impact, innovation, and relevance of the nominee's contributions.

The evaluation committee, composed of industry leaders and previous award recipients, reviews the nominations and selects finalists in each category. The winners are then announced during a prestigious ceremony that serves not only as a celebration but also as a platform for dialogue about the future of women in technology.

Impact of the Awards

The impact of the Ada Lovelace Awards extends beyond recognition; they serve as a catalyst for change within the tech industry. By highlighting the achievements of women and underrepresented groups, the awards challenge the status quo and encourage organizations to prioritize diversity and inclusion.

Moreover, the awards create role models for young girls and aspiring technologists. Seeing women celebrated for their contributions helps dismantle stereotypes and fosters a culture where everyone feels empowered to pursue careers in technology. The awards also generate media attention, bringing broader awareness to the issues of gender disparity and the importance of representation in tech.

Examples of Past Recipients

The Ada Lovelace Awards have celebrated numerous trailblazers since their inception. For instance, consider the case of Dr. Jane Smith, a computer scientist who developed an innovative algorithm for data encryption, significantly enhancing cybersecurity protocols. Her work not only advanced technology but also inspired a generation of young women to pursue careers in computer science.

Another notable recipient is the organization Tech for Good, which has implemented community outreach programs aimed at teaching coding skills to underprivileged youth. Their initiatives have not only empowered individuals but have also contributed to a more diverse tech workforce.

Conclusion

In conclusion, the Ada Lovelace Awards play a pivotal role in recognizing and promoting excellence in technology while advocating for gender equality and diversity. By honoring the contributions of individuals and organizations that align with Ada Lovelace's vision, these awards continue to inspire innovation and pave the way for a more inclusive future in the tech industry. As we celebrate these achievements, we also reaffirm our commitment to carrying forward Ada's legacy, ensuring that her spirit of creativity and resilience endures for generations to come.

$$\text{Impact} = \text{Innovation} + \text{Diversity} + \text{Community Engagement} \qquad (182)$$

The Ada Lovelace Awards exemplify how recognizing excellence can drive positive change, creating a tech landscape that reflects the richness of human experience and potential.

Local and Community-Led Ada Lovelace Events

In the spirit of Ada Lovelace, local and community-led events play a crucial role in celebrating her legacy and promoting the importance of women in technology. These grassroots initiatives not only honor Ada's contributions but also encourage community engagement, inspire future generations, and foster a supportive environment for aspiring female programmers.

Types of Local Events

Local events can take many forms, including workshops, coding boot camps, lectures, and hackathons. Each type of event serves a unique purpose, yet all share the common goal of empowering individuals through education and collaboration.

+ **Workshops:** Hands-on workshops provide participants with practical skills in programming and technology. These workshops often focus on specific languages or tools, such as Python, JavaScript, or data visualization. For instance, a workshop titled *"Code Like Ada: Introduction to Programming"* could guide participants through the basics of coding while highlighting Ada's pioneering work in the field.

+ **Hackathons:** Hackathons are intense, time-limited events where participants collaborate to create software projects. These events foster teamwork and innovation, often culminating in presentations that showcase the projects developed over the course of the hackathon. A local hackathon could be themed around *"Innovating for Change,"* encouraging teams to develop solutions that address social issues, much like how Ada envisioned the potential of the Analytical Engine.

+ **Lectures and Panels:** Inviting speakers from diverse backgrounds to discuss their experiences in tech can inspire attendees. A panel discussion titled *"Women in Tech: Past, Present, and Future"* could feature successful women in various tech roles, sharing their journeys and insights, thereby reinforcing the importance of representation.

+ **Community Meetups:** Regular meetups provide a space for individuals to network, share ideas, and collaborate on projects. These informal gatherings can facilitate mentorship opportunities and create a sense of belonging among participants.

Impact on the Community

Community-led events have a profound impact on both individual participants and the broader community. They help to:

1. **Build Confidence:** By providing a safe space for learning and experimentation, these events encourage participants to step out of their comfort zones. The supportive atmosphere can significantly boost confidence, particularly for women who may feel intimidated in male-dominated environments.

2. **Foster Collaboration:** Local events promote collaboration among participants, allowing them to share knowledge, resources, and experiences. This collaborative spirit mirrors Ada's own partnerships with contemporaries like Charles Babbage, emphasizing the importance of teamwork in innovation.

3. **Enhance Skills:** Workshops and hands-on activities equip participants with valuable skills that can be applied in their academic and professional pursuits. For example, a local coding boot camp could teach participants how to build their own websites, thereby enhancing their employability in the tech industry.

4. **Create Role Models:** By showcasing successful women in technology, these events help to create role models for younger generations. Seeing women in leadership positions can inspire girls to pursue careers in STEM fields, continuing Ada's legacy of breaking barriers.

Examples of Successful Local Events

Numerous communities around the world have successfully hosted local events that celebrate Ada Lovelace and promote women in technology. Some notable examples include:

- **Ada Lovelace Day Celebrations:** Many cities host annual Ada Lovelace Day celebrations, featuring talks, workshops, and networking opportunities. For instance, a city-wide celebration might include a series of events at local libraries, universities, and tech hubs, all centered around Ada's contributions and the importance of diversity in tech.

+ **Coding for Girls:** Some communities have established programs specifically aimed at young girls, such as *"Coding for Girls,"* where participants learn to code through fun and engaging projects. These programs often culminate in a showcase event where participants present their work to family and friends, fostering a sense of pride and accomplishment.

+ **Women Who Code Meetups:** Organizations like Women Who Code host local meetups that provide opportunities for women to connect, learn, and grow in their careers. These meetups often feature guest speakers, workshops, and collaborative projects, all aimed at supporting women in the tech community.

Challenges and Solutions

While local and community-led events have numerous benefits, they also face challenges. Common issues include:

+ **Funding and Resources:** Securing funding for events can be a significant hurdle. Communities can address this by seeking sponsorship from local businesses, applying for grants, or partnering with educational institutions that may have resources to share.

+ **Awareness and Participation:** Ensuring that the community is aware of these events and encouraging participation can be challenging. Utilizing social media, local news outlets, and community bulletin boards can help raise awareness. Additionally, creating engaging promotional materials that highlight the benefits of attending can attract more participants.

+ **Inclusivity:** It is essential to create an inclusive environment that welcomes individuals from diverse backgrounds. Event organizers can promote inclusivity by ensuring that events are accessible and by actively reaching out to underrepresented groups in tech.

Conclusion

Local and community-led Ada Lovelace events serve as vital platforms for celebrating Ada's legacy and empowering future generations of women in technology. By fostering collaboration, enhancing skills, and creating role models, these initiatives not only honor Ada Lovelace's contributions but also pave the way for a more inclusive and diverse tech landscape. As communities continue to embrace and celebrate Ada's spirit, they contribute to the ongoing fight for gender equality in technology, ensuring that her vision of a world where women thrive in STEM fields becomes a reality.

Amplifying Ada's Message: Social Media Campaigns and Online Movements

In the digital age, social media platforms have emerged as powerful tools for advocacy and awareness, allowing voices to be amplified and messages to reach global audiences. For Ada Lovelace, a pioneer in programming and a symbol of women in technology, social media campaigns have played a crucial role in celebrating her legacy and promoting gender equality in STEM fields. This section explores the strategies used to amplify Ada's message through social media and online movements, the theoretical frameworks underpinning these efforts, and the challenges faced in this digital advocacy landscape.

Theoretical Frameworks for Social Media Advocacy

Social media advocacy is rooted in several theoretical frameworks that guide how messages are crafted and disseminated. One prominent theory is the **Diffusion of Innovations** theory, proposed by Rogers (1962), which explains how new ideas and technologies spread within societies. According to this theory, the adoption of innovative practices occurs through a series of stages: knowledge, persuasion, decision, implementation, and confirmation. In the context of Ada Lovelace's legacy, social media campaigns aim to create awareness about her contributions, persuade individuals of her significance, and encourage them to engage with her story and the broader movement for women in technology.

Additionally, the **Social Identity Theory** (Tajfel & Turner, 1979) emphasizes the importance of group identity in shaping individual behavior. Campaigns that highlight Ada Lovelace's achievements resonate with individuals who identify as women in STEM or those advocating for gender equality. By fostering a sense of belonging and shared purpose, these campaigns motivate participants to engage actively and share content within their networks.

Key Campaigns and Movements

Numerous social media campaigns have emerged to honor Ada Lovelace and advocate for women in technology. One of the most notable is **Ada Lovelace Day**, celebrated annually on the second Tuesday of October. This global event encourages people to share stories of women in STEM, highlighting their contributions and achievements. The campaign leverages hashtags such as

#AdaLovelaceDay and #WomenInSTEM to create a sense of community and facilitate the sharing of resources, articles, and personal narratives.

Another impactful movement is the #ILookLikeAnEngineer campaign, which challenges stereotypes about engineers and promotes diversity in the field. Although not exclusively focused on Ada Lovelace, this campaign aligns with her legacy by showcasing the faces and stories of women in engineering and technology.   By using social media platforms like Twitter, Instagram, and Facebook, participants share their experiences and counteract the prevalent notion that engineering is a male-dominated profession.

Challenges in Amplifying Ada's Message

While social media campaigns have the potential to reach vast audiences, they are not without challenges. One significant issue is the **digital divide**, which refers to the gap between those who have access to digital technologies and those who do not. This divide disproportionately affects marginalized communities, limiting their participation in online movements. As a result, campaigns that rely solely on social media may inadvertently exclude voices that are crucial for a comprehensive understanding of gender equality in technology.

Moreover, social media platforms often grapple with issues of **misinformation** and **trolling**, which can undermine the effectiveness of campaigns. For instance, discussions around Ada Lovelace's contributions may be met with skepticism or derogatory comments that perpetuate gender stereotypes. Campaign organizers must navigate these challenges by fostering respectful dialogue and promoting evidence-based narratives about Ada's impact on computing.

Successful Examples of Social Media Engagement

Several successful examples illustrate how social media can effectively amplify Ada's message. The **Ada Lovelace Challenge**, initiated by various organizations, encourages participants to create and share content that highlights women in tech. Participants are invited to post videos, infographics, and blog posts that celebrate women in the field, using the hashtag #AdaChallenge. This campaign not only honors Ada's legacy but also empowers individuals to share their stories and inspire others.

Furthermore, organizations like **Girls Who Code** and **Women Who Code** regularly use social media to promote events, workshops, and initiatives aimed at increasing female representation in tech. By sharing success stories and resources, these organizations create a supportive online community that echoes Ada Lovelace's spirit of innovation and collaboration.

Conclusion

In conclusion, social media campaigns and online movements play a pivotal role in amplifying Ada Lovelace's message and promoting gender equality in technology. By leveraging theoretical frameworks such as the Diffusion of Innovations and Social Identity Theory, advocates can craft compelling narratives that resonate with diverse audiences. Despite challenges such as the digital divide and misinformation, successful campaigns like Ada Lovelace Day and the #ILookLikeAnEngineer movement demonstrate the power of social media in shaping public discourse and inspiring future generations of women in STEM. As we continue to celebrate Ada's legacy, it is essential to harness the potential of digital platforms to foster inclusivity, challenge stereotypes, and advocate for a more equitable tech landscape.

The Global Impact of Ada's Legacy Celebrations

Ada Lovelace Day, celebrated annually on the second Tuesday of October, serves as a global reminder of the contributions of women in science, technology, engineering, and mathematics (STEM). This celebration not only honors Ada's groundbreaking work as the first programmer but also aims to inspire the next generation of female innovators. The impact of these celebrations can be seen across various dimensions, from educational initiatives to cultural shifts in the perception of women in tech.

Educational Outreach and Initiatives

One of the most significant impacts of Ada's legacy celebrations is the emphasis on educational outreach. Events such as coding workshops, STEM fairs, and public lectures are organized worldwide to engage young minds. For instance, many schools incorporate Ada Lovelace's story into their curriculum, showcasing her as a role model for girls interested in technology.

These initiatives often include:

- **Coding Bootcamps:** Programs designed to teach girls and young women the basics of programming and computer science, often culminating in a project that they can showcase.

- **Mentorship Programs:** Pairing young women with female professionals in tech to provide guidance, support, and networking opportunities.

+ **Scholarships and Grants:** Financial assistance aimed at encouraging women to pursue degrees in STEM fields, inspired by Ada's legacy.

Cultural Shifts in Perception

The celebrations of Ada Lovelace's legacy contribute to a cultural shift in the perception of women in technology. By highlighting the achievements of Ada and other female pioneers, these events challenge the stereotypes that have long plagued the tech industry.

For example, media coverage of Ada Lovelace Day often includes stories of contemporary women in tech who are making significant contributions to the field. This visibility not only empowers young women but also encourages companies to adopt more inclusive hiring practices.

Global Participation and Collaboration

Ada Lovelace Day has transcended borders, with celebrations occurring in various countries around the globe. From hackathons in the United States to workshops in India, the global participation showcases a unified front in advocating for gender equality in STEM.

This international collaboration fosters a sense of community among women in technology, allowing them to share experiences, resources, and strategies for overcoming obstacles. The use of social media platforms has amplified these efforts, enabling participants to connect, share their stories, and inspire others.

Case Studies of Successful Celebrations

Several case studies exemplify the global impact of Ada's legacy celebrations:

+ **Ada Lovelace Day UK:** This event features a series of talks and workshops that highlight the achievements of women in STEM. It has successfully increased participation in STEM fields among young women in the UK.

+ **Ada Lovelace Day in Australia:** Celebrations include a national conference that brings together female tech leaders to discuss their journeys and the importance of diversity in technology.

+ **Global Online Events:** Virtual events allow participants from different countries to engage in discussions about women in tech, share resources, and collaborate on projects. These events have been particularly impactful during times of social distancing, maintaining community connections.

Challenges and Future Directions

Despite the positive impact of Ada's legacy celebrations, challenges remain. Gender bias and stereotypes persist in the tech industry, and while celebrations raise awareness, they must be coupled with tangible actions from organizations and governments to create lasting change.

Future directions for these celebrations could include:

+ **Increased Corporate Sponsorship:** Encouraging tech companies to sponsor events and initiatives that promote women in STEM.

+ **Policy Advocacy:** Using the platform of Ada Lovelace Day to advocate for policies that support women in the workplace, such as parental leave and equal pay.

+ **Sustainability Initiatives:** Focusing on the environmental impact of tech and how women can lead in creating sustainable solutions.

In conclusion, the global impact of Ada's legacy celebrations extends beyond mere recognition; they serve as a catalyst for change, inspiring future generations, challenging cultural norms, and fostering a community dedicated to promoting gender equality in technology. As we continue to celebrate Ada Lovelace's contributions, we must also commit to ensuring that her legacy lives on through actionable initiatives that empower women in STEM for years to come.

Ada Lovelace's Birthday: A Day to Reflect on Her Indelible Contributions

Every year, on December 10th, the world pauses to celebrate the birthday of Ada Lovelace, a woman whose contributions to mathematics and computing resonate through the ages. This day serves as a powerful reminder of her groundbreaking work and the impact it has had on modern technology. Ada Lovelace was not just a pioneer of programming; she was a visionary who foresaw the potential of machines to transcend mere calculation and enter the realm of creativity and innovation.

A Celebration of Legacy

Ada's birthday is not merely a date on the calendar; it is a global celebration of women in STEM (Science, Technology, Engineering, and Mathematics). Schools, universities, and tech companies around the world engage in activities that honor her legacy, including workshops, lectures, and coding events aimed at inspiring the next generation of female technologists.

For example, many organizations host coding competitions in Ada's name, encouraging young women to explore programming and computational thinking. These events often culminate in awards that recognize outstanding achievements in technology, ensuring that Ada's spirit of innovation lives on.

Reflecting on Contributions

On this day, we reflect on Ada's indelible contributions to the field of computing. One of her most significant achievements is the creation of what is now recognized as the first algorithm intended for implementation on a machine, specifically Charles Babbage's Analytical Engine. In her notes, she articulated how the machine could be programmed to perform complex calculations beyond simple arithmetic.

Her famous equation, often referred to as the Lovelace Note, can be expressed as:

$$\text{Algorithm} = \sum_{i=1}^{n} f(i)$$

Where $f(i)$ represents the function that the Analytical Engine would execute for each value of i. This foundational concept laid the groundwork for modern programming languages, where algorithms are a central component.

The Importance of Recognition

Recognizing Ada Lovelace's contributions is crucial in addressing the gender disparities that persist in the tech industry. By celebrating her birthday, we not only honor her legacy but also highlight the ongoing challenges faced by women in technology. Events held on this day often include discussions about gender equality, representation, and the importance of diversity in tech fields.

For instance, many speakers at Ada Lovelace Day events share personal stories about their journeys in STEM, emphasizing the need for mentorship and support for young women. This reflection fosters a sense of community and encourages collaboration among aspiring female programmers.

Inspiring Future Generations

Ada's birthday serves as a call to action for educators and industry leaders alike. By integrating her story into educational curricula, we can inspire young minds to explore the world of technology. Schools may host workshops that teach students about programming languages and computational thinking, using Ada's work as a springboard for discussion.

Moreover, organizations can establish scholarships and mentorship programs in Ada's name, empowering young women to pursue careers in technology. For example, the Ada Lovelace Young Technologist Scholarship provides financial support to female students pursuing degrees in computer science and engineering, ensuring that Ada's legacy continues to inspire future generations.

Conclusion

In conclusion, Ada Lovelace's birthday is a significant occasion that transcends mere celebration. It is a day for reflection, recognition, and inspiration. By honoring her contributions, we not only pay tribute to a remarkable woman but also commit ourselves to fostering an inclusive and equitable tech industry. As we celebrate her life and work, let us remember that the spirit of innovation and creativity she embodied continues to thrive, urging us all to dream big and break barriers.

As we gather to celebrate Ada Lovelace on December 10th, let us carry forward her legacy by empowering the next generation of innovators, ensuring that her contributions are never forgotten and that her vision for a future of technology is realized. After all, as Ada herself once said, "That brain of mine is something more than merely mortal; as time will show." And indeed, time has shown just how profound her impact has been.

Educating and Inspiring Future Generations

Ada's Role as an Icon and Role Model for Young Programmers

Ada Lovelace, often celebrated as the first computer programmer, serves as a beacon of inspiration for young programmers, particularly young women aspiring to enter the technology field. Her legacy transcends the mere historical acknowledgment of her contributions to computing; it embodies the spirit of innovation, resilience, and the relentless pursuit of knowledge.

The Symbol of Female Empowerment in Technology

In a male-dominated field, Ada Lovelace stands out not just as a pioneer but as a symbol of female empowerment. Her life story highlights the challenges women have historically faced in STEM (Science, Technology, Engineering, and Mathematics) fields. Young programmers can draw strength from Ada's determination to break barriers, making her an essential role model.

Educational Impact

Educational initiatives that incorporate Ada Lovelace's story into curricula have proven effective in inspiring students. For instance, the integration of her biography into computer science classes can spark interest in programming among students who may not have considered it otherwise. By presenting Ada as a relatable figure, educators can motivate young learners to explore the realms of mathematics and coding.

Mentorship and Representation

Ada's legacy emphasizes the importance of mentorship and representation in technology. Young programmers, especially girls, benefit from seeing women in prominent roles within the tech industry. Organizations that promote female role models and mentorship programs can create environments where young women feel empowered to pursue careers in programming. For example, programs like "Girls Who Code" and "Black Girls Code" draw inspiration from Ada's legacy, encouraging young girls to develop their programming skills and fostering a sense of community.

Theoretical Foundations of Programming

Understanding the theoretical foundations of programming can be daunting for beginners. However, Ada's work on the Analytical Engine laid the groundwork for modern programming languages. By introducing concepts such as loops and conditional statements, she made it possible for future generations to build upon her ideas. The equation for a simple loop in programming can be illustrated as follows:

$$\text{for } i = 1 \text{ to } n \text{ do } \{\text{execute code}\} \tag{183}$$

This structure, while simple, is at the core of many programming languages today, showcasing the relevance of Ada's contributions in a tangible way for young learners.

Problem-Solving and Creativity

Ada's approach to problem-solving was characterized by creativity and analytical thinking. Encouraging young programmers to think outside the box is essential in fostering innovation. For instance, when teaching programming concepts, educators can use real-world problems that require creative solutions. An example might be:

> **Problem:** Create a program that analyzes a dataset of temperatures and determines the average temperature for each month.

This problem not only requires programming skills but also encourages students to think critically about data analysis, a skill that Ada exemplified through her work.

Building a Community of Innovators

Ada Lovelace's legacy is not just about her individual achievements; it's about the community she inspires. By fostering a culture of collaboration and support among young programmers, we can encourage innovation and creativity. Hackathons, coding clubs, and collaborative projects can provide platforms for young programmers to share ideas and learn from one another.

For example, consider a coding club that focuses on developing applications for social good. A project could involve creating an app that helps users track their carbon footprint. This not only teaches programming skills but also instills a sense of responsibility toward societal issues, mirroring Ada's vision of using technology for the betterment of humanity.

The Legacy of Lifelong Learning

Finally, Ada Lovelace's life is a testament to the importance of lifelong learning. Her insatiable curiosity drove her to explore various disciplines, from mathematics to philosophy. Young programmers should be encouraged to adopt a similar mindset, embracing continuous learning and exploration.

In the rapidly evolving tech landscape, the ability to adapt and learn new skills is crucial. Encouraging young programmers to pursue knowledge beyond their immediate interests can lead to innovative thinking and problem-solving capabilities.

In conclusion, Ada Lovelace's role as an icon and role model for young programmers is multifaceted. Her legacy inspires empowerment, creativity, and a commitment to lifelong learning. By celebrating her contributions and integrating her story into educational frameworks, we can cultivate a new generation of innovators ready to take on the challenges of tomorrow.

Incorporating Ada's Story into STEM Education Curricula

Incorporating Ada Lovelace's story into STEM education curricula serves not only to honor her legacy but also to inspire and empower the next generation of innovators. By weaving her narrative into various aspects of STEM education, educators can create a more inclusive and engaging learning environment that highlights the contributions of women in technology and mathematics.

Theoretical Framework

The integration of historical figures like Ada Lovelace into STEM curricula can be grounded in several educational theories, including constructivism and culturally relevant pedagogy. Constructivism posits that students learn best when they can connect new knowledge to their existing understanding. By introducing Ada's story, educators can help students see the relevance of mathematics and programming in a real-world context.

Culturally relevant pedagogy emphasizes the importance of including diverse perspectives in education. Ada's unique background as a woman in a male-dominated field provides a powerful example for students, particularly girls and underrepresented minorities, illustrating that they too can pursue careers in STEM.

Curricular Integration Strategies

To effectively incorporate Ada's story into STEM education, educators can employ several strategies:

- **Biographical Studies:** Introduce students to Ada's life through biographical readings and discussions. This can include her challenges, achievements, and the historical context of her work. For example, students can read excerpts from her correspondence with Charles Babbage, analyzing her insights and contributions to the development of the Analytical Engine.

- **Project-Based Learning:** Encourage students to engage in project-based learning activities that relate to Ada's work. For instance, students can create their own algorithms inspired by Ada's early programming concepts, allowing them to apply mathematical principles in a hands-on manner. An example project could involve programming a simple computational task that mimics the functions of the Analytical Engine, thereby making abstract concepts tangible.

+ **Interdisciplinary Approaches:** Integrate Ada's story across various subjects, including history, literature, and art. Students can explore the societal implications of Ada's work, her relationship with her father, Lord Byron, and her impact on the feminist movement in STEM. Art projects could involve creating visual representations of Ada's contributions, such as infographics that summarize her life and achievements.

+ **STEM Role Models:** Highlight Ada as a role model by discussing her perseverance and innovative thinking. Invite guest speakers from various STEM fields, particularly women, to share their experiences and relate them to Ada's legacy. This connection can help students see the ongoing relevance of Ada's contributions in contemporary technology and inspire them to follow in her footsteps.

Real-World Applications

To further ground Ada's story in real-world applications, educators can present case studies of modern technologies influenced by her ideas. For instance, discussions about programming languages and their evolution can include references to the Ada programming language, named in her honor. Educators can analyze the syntax and structure of this language, drawing parallels to Ada's original concepts.

$$\text{Algorithm: } A = B + C \tag{184}$$

This simple algorithm can be a starting point for students to create more complex programs, illustrating the foundational nature of Ada's contributions to computer science.

Assessment and Reflection

Assessment strategies should include reflective components where students can articulate what they have learned about Ada Lovelace and her impact on STEM. This can take the form of written reflections, presentations, or creative projects that demonstrate their understanding of her contributions and the challenges she faced.

For example, students could be tasked with answering the following prompt:

"How does Ada Lovelace's story inspire you to pursue your interests in STEM? Provide specific examples of how her work relates to modern technology."

Challenges and Considerations

While incorporating Ada's story into STEM curricula is beneficial, educators may face challenges such as time constraints and the need for professional development to effectively teach these concepts. Additionally, educators should be mindful of the diverse backgrounds of their students and strive to create an inclusive environment that resonates with all learners.

Conclusion

In conclusion, incorporating Ada Lovelace's story into STEM education curricula not only honors her legacy but also enriches the learning experience for students. By employing diverse teaching strategies and fostering an inclusive environment, educators can inspire future generations to pursue careers in STEM, breaking down barriers and fostering a culture of innovation. Ada Lovelace's contributions serve as a reminder that the world of technology is not only for a select few but is open to all who dare to dream and innovate.

The Importance of Female Representation in Tech Role Models

In the ever-evolving landscape of technology, the representation of women in tech roles is not just a matter of equity; it is a crucial factor in fostering innovation and creativity. The underrepresentation of women in the technology sector has been a persistent issue, leading to a significant gap in perspectives and ideas that are vital for the development of inclusive technology solutions. Female role models in tech serve as beacons of inspiration, encouraging young women to pursue careers in science, technology, engineering, and mathematics (STEM).

The Current Landscape of Female Representation

Statistics reveal a stark reality: women hold only 26% of computing jobs in the United States, a figure that has remained relatively stagnant over the past few decades [1]. This lack of representation extends to leadership roles, where women occupy only 11% of executive positions in Silicon Valley [2]. This disparity not only affects the workforce but also impacts the design and functionality of technology products, as diverse teams are known to produce more innovative solutions.

Theoretical Framework: Social Learning Theory

To understand the importance of female representation in tech role models, we can apply *Social Learning Theory*, which posits that individuals learn behaviors, values, and attitudes through observation and imitation of role models [4]. This theory emphasizes the significance of seeing women in tech roles, as it can inspire young girls to envision themselves in similar positions. When girls see women succeeding in technology, it can enhance their self-efficacy and motivation to pursue STEM fields.

$$\text{Self-Efficacy} = \frac{\text{Successful Experiences} + \text{Vicarious Experiences}}{\text{Total Experiences}} \tag{185}$$

This equation illustrates that self-efficacy is influenced not only by personal achievements but also by the successes of others. Hence, the visibility of female role models can significantly bolster the confidence of aspiring young female technologists.

Challenges Faced by Women in Tech

Despite the progress made, women in tech still face numerous challenges, including gender bias, workplace discrimination, and a lack of mentorship opportunities. A study conducted by *McKinsey & Company* found that women in tech are **1.5 times** more likely than men to be promoted to manager positions, yet they are still underrepresented in senior leadership roles [3]. This phenomenon is often referred to as the *"leaky pipeline,"* where women drop out of the tech field at various stages due to systemic barriers.

The Impact of Role Models on Career Aspirations

Research indicates that having a female role model in tech can significantly influence a young girl's decision to pursue a career in STEM. For instance, a study by *Harvard Business Review* found that girls who have female role models in their communities are more likely to express interest in STEM fields and pursue related educational paths [5].

Moreover, initiatives like *Girls Who Code* and *Black Girls Code* have successfully highlighted female role models in tech, providing mentorship and resources that empower young women to enter the technology sector. These organizations not only cultivate interest in coding and technology but also create a supportive community that fosters resilience and confidence.

Examples of Inspiring Female Role Models

Several prominent women in technology exemplify the impact of strong role models. Ada Lovelace, often regarded as the first computer programmer, serves as a historical figure whose legacy continues to inspire generations. Modern figures such as *Reshma Saujani*, the founder of Girls Who Code, and *Sheryl Sandberg*, COO of Facebook, have made significant strides in advocating for women's representation in tech.

- **Reshma Saujani** has been instrumental in creating coding programs for girls, emphasizing the importance of female representation in the tech workforce.

- **Sheryl Sandberg** has not only broken glass ceilings in Silicon Valley but has also authored books like *Lean In*, encouraging women to pursue leadership roles.

These role models not only demonstrate what is possible but also actively work to dismantle the barriers that hinder women's progress in technology.

Conclusion: The Path Forward

To cultivate a more inclusive tech industry, it is imperative to increase the visibility of female role models and create environments where young women feel empowered to pursue careers in STEM. Educational institutions, organizations, and companies must prioritize initiatives that promote female representation and mentorship in tech. By fostering diverse role models, we can inspire the next generation of innovators and ensure that the technology of the future is reflective of the diverse world we live in.

In conclusion, the importance of female representation in tech role models cannot be overstated. As we continue to advocate for gender equality in the technology sector, let us celebrate and amplify the voices of women who are making waves in this dynamic field. By doing so, we not only honor their contributions but also pave the way for future generations of women to thrive in technology.

Bibliography

[1] National Center for Women & Information Technology. (2021). *Women in Tech: The Facts.*

[2] Pew Research Center. (2020). *Women and Men in STEM: A Gender Gap in the Tech Workforce.*

[3] McKinsey & Company. (2020). *Women in the Workplace 2020.*

[4] Bandura, A. (1977). *Social Learning Theory.* Englewood Cliffs, NJ: Prentice Hall.

[5] Harvard Business Review. (2019). *The Impact of Female Role Models on Girls' Aspirations.*

The Need for Inclusive Education and Mentorship Programs

In the rapidly evolving landscape of technology, the importance of inclusive education and mentorship programs cannot be overstated. These programs serve as critical frameworks that help dismantle barriers, promote diversity, and foster a culture of innovation. As we reflect on the legacy of Ada Lovelace, it becomes evident that her pioneering spirit must be matched with contemporary efforts to ensure that future generations of innovators, particularly women and underrepresented minorities, have equitable access to opportunities in STEM fields.

Theoretical Framework

The need for inclusive education is grounded in several educational theories, including Social Constructivism and Critical Pedagogy. Social Constructivism posits that knowledge is constructed through social interactions and experiences, emphasizing the importance of collaborative learning environments. In this context, mentorship programs can provide the necessary scaffolding for students, allowing them to navigate complex concepts in mathematics and technology through guided experiences.

Critical Pedagogy, on the other hand, advocates for an educational approach that challenges social injustices and empowers marginalized groups. This theory underscores the necessity of creating curricula that reflect diverse perspectives and experiences, thereby making learning more relevant and engaging for all students. By integrating these theoretical frameworks into educational practices, we can cultivate an inclusive atmosphere that values every learner's contributions.

Current Challenges

Despite the theoretical underpinnings supporting inclusive education, significant challenges remain. One of the primary issues is the persistence of gender bias and stereotypes within educational institutions. Research has shown that girls often receive less encouragement in STEM subjects compared to their male counterparts. According to a study by the American Association of University Women (AAUW), girls are less likely to pursue advanced mathematics and science courses due to a lack of confidence and the perception that these fields are male-dominated.

Furthermore, the absence of role models and mentors in STEM can exacerbate feelings of isolation among female students. A report by the National Science Foundation (NSF) indicates that mentorship is a critical factor in retaining women in STEM careers. Without access to mentors who can provide guidance, support, and networking opportunities, many talented individuals may abandon their aspirations in these fields.

Successful Examples of Inclusive Programs

Several successful programs have emerged as models for fostering inclusivity in STEM education. One such initiative is the **Girls Who Code** program, which aims to close the gender gap in technology by providing young girls with coding education and mentorship. Through after-school clubs and summer immersion programs, participants gain hands-on experience in programming while building a supportive community of peers and mentors.

Another noteworthy example is the **Black Girls Code** initiative, which focuses on empowering girls of color by teaching them computer programming skills and encouraging them to pursue careers in tech. This program not only provides technical training but also emphasizes the importance of cultural identity and representation in technology.

Furthermore, universities such as **MIT** and **Stanford** have developed mentorship programs that connect students from underrepresented backgrounds with industry professionals. These initiatives are designed to provide guidance, networking opportunities, and career development resources, thereby enhancing the educational experience and fostering a sense of belonging.

Recommendations for Implementation

To effectively address the need for inclusive education and mentorship programs, several recommendations can be made:

1. **Curriculum Development:** Educational institutions should prioritize the integration of diverse perspectives into STEM curricula. This can be achieved by incorporating case studies, examples, and contributions from women and underrepresented groups in technology.

2. **Mentorship Training:** Training programs should be established for mentors to equip them with the skills necessary to support and inspire their mentees. This training should focus on understanding the unique challenges faced by underrepresented students and developing strategies to foster an inclusive environment.

3. **Partnerships with Industry:** Schools and universities should collaborate with tech companies to create internship and mentorship opportunities for students. These partnerships can facilitate real-world experiences and connections that are crucial for career advancement.

4. **Awareness Campaigns:** Initiatives aimed at raising awareness about the importance of diversity in STEM should be implemented. Campaigns can highlight successful female role models in technology, thereby inspiring young girls to pursue careers in these fields.

Conclusion

In conclusion, the need for inclusive education and mentorship programs is paramount in shaping the future of technology. By embracing diverse perspectives, providing mentorship opportunities, and fostering supportive learning environments, we can honor Ada Lovelace's legacy and empower the next generation of innovators. As we continue to break down barriers and challenge stereotypes, we must remain committed to creating a more equitable and inclusive landscape in STEM education. This is not just a moral imperative; it is essential for the advancement of technology and society as a whole.

Ada Lovelace Young Technologist Scholarship: Empowering Young Innovators

The Ada Lovelace Young Technologist Scholarship is a pioneering initiative aimed at fostering the next generation of innovators in science, technology, engineering, and mathematics (STEM). Named after the first programmer, Ada Lovelace, this scholarship embodies the spirit of creativity, resilience, and visionary thinking that Ada herself exemplified. The scholarship is designed to empower young minds, particularly those from underrepresented backgrounds, by providing them with the resources, mentorship, and opportunities needed to thrive in the tech industry.

Objectives of the Scholarship

The primary objectives of the Ada Lovelace Young Technologist Scholarship include:

- **Financial Support:** To alleviate the financial burden on students pursuing STEM education, the scholarship provides monetary awards that can be used for tuition, books, and other educational expenses.

- **Mentorship Programs:** Recipients are paired with industry professionals who provide guidance, support, and insights into navigating the challenges of a tech career.

- **Networking Opportunities:** The scholarship facilitates connections with peers and established professionals through workshops, conferences, and tech events, fostering a sense of community and collaboration.

- **Skill Development:** Workshops and training sessions are organized to enhance technical skills, including programming, data analysis, and project management, equipping students with the tools they need for success.

Eligibility Criteria

To ensure that the scholarship reaches those who can benefit the most, the following eligibility criteria are established:

+ Applicants must be high school seniors or current undergraduate students pursuing a degree in a STEM field.

+ A demonstrated commitment to community service or involvement in initiatives that promote diversity in tech is required.

+ Applicants must submit an essay outlining their passion for technology, their vision for the future, and how they plan to contribute to the field.

+ Letters of recommendation from teachers, mentors, or community leaders are required to support the application.

Application Process

The application process for the Ada Lovelace Young Technologist Scholarship is designed to be straightforward and accessible. It includes the following steps:

1. **Online Application:** Interested candidates must complete an online application form, providing personal information, academic achievements, and extracurricular activities.

2. **Essay Submission:** Applicants must submit a 1,000-word essay reflecting their passion for technology and their aspirations in the field.

3. **Recommendation Letters:** Two letters of recommendation must be submitted, highlighting the applicant's strengths and potential in STEM.

4. **Interview:** Shortlisted candidates may be invited for an interview with the scholarship committee to discuss their application in more detail.

Impact and Success Stories

The impact of the Ada Lovelace Young Technologist Scholarship is profound. By providing financial support and mentorship, the scholarship has enabled numerous young innovators to pursue their dreams in technology.

> **Example**
>
> Consider the case of Sarah, a scholarship recipient from a low-income background. With the financial assistance from the scholarship, she was able to attend a prestigious university where she majored in computer science. Sarah's experience with her mentor, a successful software engineer, helped her navigate the challenges of her coursework and secure internships that would have otherwise been inaccessible. Today, Sarah is a lead developer at a tech startup, advocating for diversity in the industry and mentoring other young women in tech.

Challenges and Future Directions

While the Ada Lovelace Young Technologist Scholarship has made significant strides in empowering young innovators, challenges remain.

+ **Awareness and Outreach:** Increasing awareness about the scholarship in underserved communities is crucial to ensure that eligible candidates apply.

+ **Sustaining Funding:** Securing ongoing financial support from donors and corporate sponsors is essential for the scholarship's longevity.

+ **Measuring Impact:** Developing metrics to assess the long-term impact of the scholarship on recipients' careers and contributions to the tech industry is necessary for continuous improvement.

Future directions for the scholarship include expanding the program to include more recipients each year, offering additional workshops focused on emerging technologies, and creating an alumni network to support past recipients in their professional journeys.

Conclusion

The Ada Lovelace Young Technologist Scholarship stands as a beacon of hope and opportunity for young innovators. By honoring Ada Lovelace's legacy, the scholarship not only empowers individuals to pursue their passions in technology but also contributes to a more diverse and inclusive tech industry. As we continue to celebrate Ada's contributions, we must also commit to nurturing the talents of the next generation, ensuring that the spirit of innovation lives on for years to come.

Ada Lovelace Classroom Grants: Supporting Teacher Excellence

The Ada Lovelace Classroom Grants are designed to empower educators by providing financial support to enhance STEM education in classrooms across the globe. These grants aim to recognize and reward teachers who are committed to fostering a love for mathematics, science, and technology among their students, particularly girls and underrepresented minorities in the field.

The Importance of Teacher Excellence

Educators play a crucial role in shaping the minds of future innovators. Research has shown that effective teaching practices significantly impact student engagement and achievement, particularly in STEM subjects. According to [1], the influence of a teacher on student learning can be quantified, with effect sizes demonstrating that quality instruction is one of the most significant factors contributing to student success.

$$\text{Effect Size} = \frac{\text{Mean of Treatment Group} - \text{Mean of Control Group}}{\text{Standard Deviation of Control Group}} \tag{186}$$

This equation illustrates how we can measure the impact of different teaching methods, emphasizing the need for ongoing professional development and support for teachers. The Ada Lovelace Classroom Grants are a step towards ensuring that educators have the resources they need to implement innovative teaching strategies.

Grant Objectives

The objectives of the Ada Lovelace Classroom Grants include:

- **Fostering Innovation:** Encouraging teachers to develop and implement creative lesson plans that integrate technology and hands-on learning experiences.

- **Enhancing Resources:** Providing funding for classroom materials, technology, and tools that facilitate effective STEM instruction.

- **Supporting Professional Development:** Enabling teachers to attend workshops, conferences, and training sessions that enhance their skills and knowledge in STEM education.

+ **Encouraging Collaboration:** Promoting partnerships between schools, local businesses, and community organizations to create a supportive network for educators and students.

Application Process

The application process for the Ada Lovelace Classroom Grants is designed to be accessible and straightforward. Teachers are invited to submit proposals that outline their project ideas, including:

+ **Project Description:** A detailed overview of the proposed project, including objectives, methodologies, and expected outcomes.

+ **Budget:** An itemized budget outlining how the grant funds will be allocated to support the project.

+ **Impact Assessment:** A plan for evaluating the effectiveness of the project and its impact on student learning and engagement.

Selected projects will receive funding ranging from $500 to $5,000, depending on the scope and scale of the initiative.

Examples of Funded Projects

Several innovative projects have been funded through the Ada Lovelace Classroom Grants, showcasing the diverse ways in which educators are enhancing STEM education:

+ **Coding for Kids:** A project that introduced coding and programming concepts to elementary school students through interactive games and robotics. The project aimed to demystify technology and encourage girls to explore careers in computer science.

+ **STEM in Nature:** A program that integrated environmental science with technology by utilizing outdoor classrooms and field studies. Students engaged in hands-on experiments to understand ecological systems and the impact of technology on the environment.

+ **Math and Art Fusion:** An interdisciplinary project that combined mathematics and art to teach geometric concepts through creative expression. Students created art pieces that incorporated mathematical principles, fostering a deeper understanding of both subjects.

These examples illustrate the potential of the Ada Lovelace Classroom Grants to inspire educators and transform the learning experiences of students.

Conclusion

The Ada Lovelace Classroom Grants represent a commitment to supporting teacher excellence and innovation in STEM education. By providing financial resources and encouraging creative teaching practices, these grants aim to cultivate the next generation of thinkers, creators, and leaders in technology. As we celebrate Ada Lovelace's legacy, we also recognize the vital role that educators play in shaping the future of our society. Through initiatives like the Ada Lovelace Classroom Grants, we can ensure that every student has the opportunity to explore their passions and reach their full potential in the world of STEM.

Bibliography

[1] Hattie, J. (2009). *Visible Learning: A Synthesis of Over 800 Meta-Analyses Relating to Achievement.* Routledge.

Ada Lovelace Coding Clubs: Fostering a Love for Programming

In an age where technology is woven into the very fabric of our lives, fostering a love for programming among young minds is not just beneficial; it is essential. The Ada Lovelace Coding Clubs serve as a beacon of inspiration, offering a nurturing environment where children, especially girls, can explore the world of coding and technology. These clubs are designed to empower the next generation of innovators by providing them with the tools, resources, and community support they need to thrive in the tech landscape.

The Mission of Ada Lovelace Coding Clubs

The primary mission of the Ada Lovelace Coding Clubs is to create an inclusive space where participants can learn programming skills through hands-on projects and collaborative learning. By focusing on real-world applications and problem-solving, these clubs aim to demystify coding and make it accessible to everyone, regardless of their background or prior experience.

The clubs emphasize the importance of creativity in programming, encouraging members to see themselves as not just coders, but as creators and innovators. Through engaging activities, members can witness firsthand how programming can be a powerful tool for expression and change.

Curriculum Overview

The curriculum of the Ada Lovelace Coding Clubs is carefully crafted to cater to various skill levels, ensuring that every participant can find their footing in the world of coding. Key components of the curriculum include:

+ **Introduction to Programming Concepts:** Members are introduced to fundamental programming concepts such as variables, loops, and conditionals using block-based programming languages like Scratch. This visual approach helps to solidify their understanding before moving on to text-based languages.

+ **Project-Based Learning:** Participants engage in hands-on projects that allow them to apply their newly acquired skills. Projects range from creating simple games to developing interactive stories, providing a tangible sense of accomplishment.

+ **Collaboration and Teamwork:** The clubs encourage collaboration through group projects, fostering a sense of community and teamwork. Members learn to communicate their ideas effectively and work together to solve problems, mirroring real-world tech environments.

+ **Guest Speakers and Workshops:** Regular workshops and talks by industry professionals provide insights into various tech careers and the importance of diversity in the field. These sessions inspire participants to envision themselves in roles they may not have previously considered.

+ **Mentorship Opportunities:** Each club pairs participants with mentors who guide them through their learning journey, providing support, encouragement, and personalized feedback.

Theoretical Foundations of Coding Education

The pedagogical approach of the Ada Lovelace Coding Clubs is grounded in several educational theories that emphasize experiential learning, constructivism, and social learning.

Experiential Learning: Drawing from Kolb's Experiential Learning Theory, the clubs prioritize learning through experience. Participants engage in coding activities that allow them to reflect on their experiences, conceptualize their learning, and apply it to new situations.

Constructivism: The clubs align with constructivist principles, where learners build their understanding through active engagement. By encouraging participants to create their projects, they construct knowledge that is meaningful and relevant to them.

Social Learning: Bandura's Social Learning Theory underscores the importance of observation and imitation in learning. In the clubs, members learn from one another, sharing insights and strategies, thus reinforcing their understanding of programming concepts.

Addressing Common Challenges in Coding Education

While fostering a love for programming, the Ada Lovelace Coding Clubs also address common challenges that learners face:

- **Imposter Syndrome:** Many young coders, particularly girls, may feel inadequate in their abilities. The clubs combat this by celebrating small wins and creating a culture of support and encouragement.

- **Access to Resources:** Not all participants may have access to computers or the internet at home. The clubs provide necessary resources, ensuring that every member has the tools they need to succeed.

- **Retention of Interest:** Keeping young learners engaged can be challenging. The clubs regularly update their projects and incorporate current trends in technology to maintain excitement and relevance.

Examples of Successful Projects

To illustrate the impact of the Ada Lovelace Coding Clubs, here are a few examples of successful projects completed by participants:

1. Interactive Storytelling: Members created an interactive story using Scratch, where users could choose different paths for the characters. This project not only taught them programming fundamentals but also allowed them to express their creativity through storytelling.

2. Game Development: Participants collaborated to design and develop a simple video game. They learned about game mechanics, user interface design, and debugging, culminating in a showcase where they presented their games to family and friends.

3. Community Service Projects: Some clubs initiated projects aimed at solving community issues, such as creating a website for a local charity. This not only enhanced their coding skills but also instilled a sense of social responsibility.

The Future of Ada Lovelace Coding Clubs

As the tech landscape continues to evolve, the Ada Lovelace Coding Clubs remain committed to adapting their programs to meet the needs of future generations. By integrating emerging technologies such as artificial intelligence and robotics into their curriculum, they ensure that participants are not only consumers of technology but also creators of it.

In conclusion, the Ada Lovelace Coding Clubs play a pivotal role in fostering a love for programming among young learners. By providing a supportive and engaging environment, these clubs empower the next generation to embrace technology, challenge stereotypes, and become the innovators of tomorrow. As we celebrate Ada Lovelace's legacy, we also look forward to the bright future of young programmers who will carry her spirit of innovation and creativity into the digital age.

The Impact of Ada's Story on Girls' Interest in Technology

Ada Lovelace, often celebrated as the first programmer, serves as an enduring symbol of women's contributions to technology and mathematics. Her story resonates with girls and young women, inspiring them to explore careers in STEM (Science, Technology, Engineering, and Mathematics). This section delves into the various ways Ada's legacy has influenced girls' interest in technology, supported by relevant theories and examples.

The Power of Role Models

Research shows that role models significantly impact young people's career aspirations. According to social cognitive theory, individuals are more likely to pursue careers in fields where they see successful figures who share similar backgrounds or characteristics. Ada Lovelace's narrative provides girls with a historical figure they can relate to—a woman who defied societal norms to pursue her passion for mathematics and computing.

For instance, initiatives like Ada Lovelace Day, which celebrates women in STEM, highlight her achievements and encourage girls to envision themselves in similar roles. Events surrounding this day often feature speakers who share their journeys in technology, creating a sense of community and belonging for young girls.

Educational Programs and Curriculum Integration

Incorporating Ada's story into educational curricula has proven effective in fostering interest in technology among girls. Programs that introduce students to Ada's contributions not only educate them about her work but also contextualize the importance of diversity in tech. For example, the incorporation of Ada Lovelace's biography into mathematics and computer science classes can spark discussions about gender equality and the historical barriers women faced in these fields.

Organizations like Girls Who Code have embraced this approach, utilizing Ada's story as a motivational tool. By presenting Ada as a pioneer, they encourage girls to pursue coding and programming, thereby addressing the gender gap in technology.

Inspiring Innovation and Creativity

Ada Lovelace's work on the Analytical Engine exemplifies creativity in technology. She envisioned a machine that could perform complex calculations and even generate music. By showcasing her innovative spirit, educators can inspire girls to think outside the box and embrace their creativity in tech.

For example, coding camps and workshops that incorporate artistic elements—such as creating visual art through programming—allow girls to explore technology in a fun and engaging way. These programs often reference Ada's contributions to emphasize that technology is not just about numbers and logic; it can also be a medium for artistic expression.

Community and Support Networks

Ada's story has also led to the formation of various community networks aimed at supporting girls in technology. Online platforms and local organizations provide safe spaces for girls to share their experiences, seek mentorship, and collaborate on projects. These networks emphasize the importance of community in overcoming challenges and fostering a sense of belonging.

For instance, the Ada Lovelace Foundation actively promotes initiatives that empower girls and women in tech. By providing resources, mentorship programs, and scholarships, they honor Ada's legacy while addressing the ongoing challenges women face in the industry.

Quantifying the Impact

The impact of Ada's story on girls' interest in technology can be quantified through various metrics. Surveys conducted by organizations like Code.org indicate that girls exposed to female role models in tech are more likely to express interest in pursuing computer science. For instance, a study found that girls who learned about Ada's contributions were 30% more likely to consider a career in technology compared to those who did not.

Furthermore, programs that celebrate Ada's legacy report increased participation rates among girls in coding and robotics clubs. This increase demonstrates a tangible shift in interest, showcasing the effectiveness of leveraging Ada's story to inspire future generations.

Conclusion

In conclusion, Ada Lovelace's story serves as a powerful catalyst for increasing girls' interest in technology. By providing relatable role models, integrating her narrative into educational programs, fostering creativity, and building supportive communities, we can continue to inspire young women to pursue careers in STEM. Ada's legacy not only honors her contributions but also paves the way for future innovators, ensuring that the tech industry remains diverse and inclusive. As we celebrate Ada Lovelace, we also celebrate the countless girls who will follow in her footsteps, breaking barriers and reshaping the future of technology.

Empowering the Next Generation: Ada Lovelace's Gift to Young Minds

Ada Lovelace, often heralded as the first programmer, left behind a legacy that transcends time, inspiring countless generations of young minds. Her contributions to mathematics and computing not only laid the groundwork for modern programming but also serve as a beacon of encouragement for aspiring innovators, particularly young women in STEM. In this section, we will explore how Ada's story empowers the next generation, focusing on educational initiatives, mentorship programs, and the importance of representation in technology.

The Importance of Role Models in STEM

Role models play a crucial role in shaping the aspirations of young individuals. Ada Lovelace's journey from a noblewoman to a pioneering mathematician demonstrates that passion and intellect can defy societal norms. By showcasing Ada's life, we can instill a sense of possibility in young girls who might otherwise feel discouraged from pursuing careers in technology and engineering.

Research indicates that students, particularly girls, are more likely to pursue STEM fields when they see successful women in those roles. According to a study by the American Association of University Women (AAUW), girls who have female role models in STEM are more likely to express interest in these fields and pursue related educational paths. Ada Lovelace serves as a historical figure who embodies the potential of women in technology, inspiring young minds to envision themselves as future innovators.

Incorporating Ada's Story into STEM Education Curricula

Integrating Ada Lovelace's narrative into educational curricula can enhance students' understanding of the historical context of technology and mathematics. By including her story, educators can highlight the intersection of creativity and logic, demonstrating that programming is not just about coding but also about problem-solving and innovative thinking.

For example, educators can develop lesson plans that explore Ada's work on the Analytical Engine, emphasizing her visionary insights into programming. Students can engage in hands-on activities that mimic the principles of early computing, such as creating algorithms or programming simple tasks using modern programming languages. This practical application of Ada's theories can foster a deeper appreciation for the evolution of technology.

The Role of Mentorship Programs

Mentorship programs are vital in supporting young women in their pursuit of STEM careers. By connecting students with mentors who can provide guidance, encouragement, and real-world experience, these programs can help young minds navigate the challenges of entering male-dominated fields.

Organizations such as Girls Who Code and the Ada Lovelace Foundation are dedicated to providing mentorship opportunities for girls interested in technology. These initiatives not only empower young women to develop their skills but also create a supportive community where they can share their experiences and challenges.

A study by the National Mentoring Partnership found that mentees who have strong relationships with their mentors are more likely to pursue higher education and careers in their fields of interest. By fostering these connections, we can ensure that Ada's legacy continues to inspire and empower future generations.

Fostering a Love for Programming

To truly empower the next generation, we must cultivate a love for programming and problem-solving from an early age. Coding clubs, workshops, and summer camps can provide fun and engaging environments for young learners to explore technology. These initiatives can introduce students to programming languages such as Python, Scratch, or JavaScript, allowing them to create their own projects and express their creativity through code.

For instance, a coding club inspired by Ada Lovelace could focus on developing projects that align with her interests, such as creating simple algorithms or designing games that incorporate mathematical concepts. By linking programming to creativity and personal expression, we can make technology accessible and appealing to young minds.

The Impact of Ada's Story on Girls' Interest in Technology

Ada Lovelace's story has the potential to significantly impact girls' interest in technology. By sharing her achievements and struggles, we can show young women that they are not alone in their journey.

For example, the celebration of Ada Lovelace Day serves as an annual reminder of the contributions women have made to technology. Events and activities organized around this day can inspire young girls to learn about Ada's life and the importance of women in STEM. By participating in discussions, workshops, and competitions, girls can see themselves as part of a larger narrative of innovation and creativity.

Empowering Through Technology and Innovation

Finally, empowering the next generation also means encouraging them to innovate and create their own technologies. By fostering a mindset of curiosity and experimentation, we can inspire young minds to think critically about the world around them and seek solutions to real-world problems.

For instance, students can be challenged to develop projects that address social issues, such as creating apps that promote sustainability or coding games that educate users about health and wellness. By linking technology to meaningful causes, we can motivate young innovators to use their skills for positive change.

Conclusion

In conclusion, Ada Lovelace's legacy is a powerful tool for empowering the next generation of innovators. By incorporating her story into educational curricula, providing mentorship opportunities, fostering a love for programming, and encouraging innovation, we can inspire young minds to pursue careers in technology. As we celebrate Ada's contributions, let us continue to champion the importance of diversity and representation in STEM, ensuring that her gift to young minds endures for generations to come.

By nurturing the potential of every young person, we honor Ada Lovelace's legacy and pave the way for a future filled with creativity, innovation, and equality in technology.

Continuing the Fight for Gender Equality in Tech

The Persistence of Gender Bias and Discrimination in the Tech Industry

The tech industry, often heralded as a bastion of innovation and progress, continues to grapple with the insidious persistence of gender bias and discrimination. Despite decades of advocacy for equality, women remain underrepresented in technology roles and leadership positions. This systemic issue is deeply rooted in societal norms, historical precedents, and institutional practices that perpetuate inequality.

Historical Context

To understand the current landscape, we must first acknowledge the historical context. The tech industry, which burgeoned in the late 20th century, was predominantly male-dominated. This male-centric culture not only shaped the industry's development but also established norms that marginalized women's contributions. Figures like Ada Lovelace, who was pivotal in the early days of computing, have often been relegated to the sidelines of history, overshadowed by their male counterparts.

Statistical Evidence of Gender Disparities

Statistical data reveals the stark reality of gender disparities in tech. According to a 2021 report by the National Center for Women & Information Technology (NCWIT), women hold only 26% of computing jobs in the United States. Furthermore, women of color face even greater challenges, with Black and Hispanic women representing only 3% and 1% of the computing workforce, respectively. This underrepresentation is not merely a numbers game; it translates into a lack of diverse perspectives in product development, leadership, and innovation.

Theoretical Frameworks

Several theoretical frameworks help elucidate the persistence of gender bias in tech.

Social Role Theory   posits that societal expectations about gender roles influence individuals' behavior and career choices. Women are often socialized to prioritize communal roles over agentic ones, which can lead to a reluctance to pursue careers in competitive fields like technology.

Implicit Bias Theory   further explains how unconscious biases affect hiring and promotion practices. Studies have shown that identical resumes are evaluated differently based on the perceived gender of the candidate, with male candidates often receiving preferential treatment. For instance, a study published in the journal *Proceedings of the National Academy of Sciences* found that both male and female evaluators rated male applicants as more competent and hireable than equally qualified female applicants.

Examples of Gender Bias in Tech

Real-world examples illustrate the pervasiveness of gender bias in the tech industry. High-profile incidents, such as the fallout from the "Google Memo" in 2017, highlighted the toxic environment for women in tech. The memo, which argued that biological differences explain the gender gap in tech, sparked outrage and ignited discussions about the culture of misogyny that persists in many tech companies.

Moreover, the case of Ellen Pao, who sued venture capital firm Kleiner Perkins for gender discrimination, brought attention to the challenges women face in securing equal opportunities in male-dominated environments. Although Pao lost the case, her story resonated widely, inspiring many women to speak out against discrimination and advocate for change.

Barriers to Advancement

Women in tech encounter numerous barriers to advancement, including:

- **Lack of Mentorship and Sponsorship:** Women often lack access to mentors and sponsors who can advocate for their career advancement. This absence is detrimental, as mentorship plays a critical role in professional development.

- **Workplace Culture:** Many tech companies maintain cultures that are unwelcoming to women. This can manifest through microaggressions, exclusion from informal networks, and a lack of support for work-life balance.

- **Pay Inequity:** Gender pay gaps persist in the tech industry, with women earning approximately 83 cents for every dollar earned by their male counterparts in similar roles. This inequity not only affects women's financial stability but also perpetuates the perception that their work is less valuable.

The Role of Policy and Advocacy

Addressing gender bias and discrimination in tech requires systemic change. Policies aimed at promoting diversity and inclusion are essential. Initiatives such as the *Equal Pay Act* and affirmative action programs are critical in creating equitable workplaces. Furthermore, advocacy organizations like *Girls Who Code* and *Women Who Code* play a vital role in empowering women through education, networking, and mentorship opportunities.

Conclusion

The persistence of gender bias and discrimination in the tech industry is a multifaceted issue that demands attention and action. As we look to the future, it is imperative to honor the legacy of pioneers like Ada Lovelace by continuing to challenge the status quo and advocate for a more inclusive and equitable tech landscape. By recognizing and addressing the systemic barriers that women face, we can foster an environment where innovation thrives, driven by diverse perspectives and inclusive practices.

Ada's Advocacy for Equal Opportunities and Representation

Ada Lovelace, often celebrated as the first programmer, was not only a pioneer in the realm of computing but also an early advocate for equal opportunities and representation, particularly for women in the male-dominated fields of mathematics and technology. Her life and work serve as a testament to the importance of diversity in innovation and the necessity of creating spaces where all individuals can thrive, regardless of gender.

Historical Context

In the 19th century, the landscape of education and professional opportunities was starkly divided along gender lines. Women were largely excluded from formal education in mathematics and science, with societal norms dictating that these fields were unsuitable for their delicate sensibilities. Ada, however, was fortunate to have a mother, Lady Anne Isabella Byron, who recognized her daughter's potential and encouraged her intellectual pursuits. This familial support was critical in shaping Ada's path, allowing her to defy the conventions of her time.

Theoretical Framework

The advocacy for equal opportunities can be understood through various theoretical lenses, including Feminist Theory and Social Justice Theory. Feminist Theory critiques the historical and systemic inequalities that have marginalized women's contributions to various fields. It emphasizes the need for representation and equal access to resources, which can be summarized by the following equation:

$$\text{Equity} = \frac{\text{Access to Opportunities}}{\text{Barriers to Participation}}$$

In this equation, equity is achieved when access to opportunities is maximized while barriers to participation are minimized. Ada's life exemplifies this pursuit of equity, as she not only sought opportunities for herself but also envisioned a future where women could equally participate in scientific discourse.

Problems Faced by Women in STEM

Despite Ada's groundbreaking contributions, the issues of gender bias and discrimination in STEM fields persist today. Studies have shown that women in technology often face numerous barriers, including:

- **Stereotyping:** Women are frequently stereotyped as being less capable in technical roles, which can lead to self-doubt and decreased participation.

- **Lack of Representation:** Women remain underrepresented in STEM, with only 28% of the workforce in science and engineering being female as of 2020.

+ **Pay Gap:** Women in technology earn, on average, 82 cents for every dollar earned by their male counterparts, highlighting the economic disparities that continue to exist.

+ **Workplace Culture:** A culture that often prioritizes masculine traits can alienate women, leading to higher turnover rates and decreased job satisfaction.

These barriers not only hinder individual careers but also stifle innovation by limiting the diversity of thought and experience in technological development.

Ada's Vision for Representation

Ada envisioned a world where women's contributions to science and technology were recognized and valued. She understood that representation was crucial for progress. In her correspondence with Charles Babbage, she articulated her belief that the Analytical Engine could be used for more than just calculations; it could be a tool for creativity and innovation. This perspective resonates with contemporary discussions about the importance of diverse teams in driving innovation.

Modern Examples of Advocacy

In the spirit of Ada's advocacy, numerous organizations and initiatives have emerged to promote equal opportunities and representation in STEM fields:

+ **Girls Who Code:** This organization aims to close the gender gap in technology by equipping young girls with the skills and resources needed to succeed in computer science.

+ **Women in Technology International (WITI):** WITI focuses on empowering women in technology through networking, education, and professional development.

+ **Ada Lovelace Day:** An annual event that celebrates the achievements of women in STEM, encouraging girls to pursue careers in these fields.

These initiatives echo Ada's vision and work towards dismantling the barriers that have historically restricted women's participation in technology.

Conclusion

Ada Lovelace's advocacy for equal opportunities and representation was revolutionary for her time and remains critically relevant today. Her legacy inspires ongoing efforts to create inclusive environments in STEM, where diversity is not only welcomed but celebrated. As we continue to navigate the complexities of gender inequality in technology, we must remember Ada's pioneering spirit and her belief in the transformative power of representation. By honoring her contributions, we can pave the way for future generations of innovators, ensuring that the doors Ada opened remain wide for all who wish to enter.

Promoting Diversity and Inclusion in Hiring and Leadership

In the ever-evolving landscape of technology, promoting diversity and inclusion in hiring and leadership is not merely a trend but a necessity. The tech industry, historically dominated by a homogeneous group, has begun to recognize the myriad benefits that diverse teams bring to innovation, creativity, and problem-solving. This section delves into the theories underpinning diversity, the challenges faced, and actionable strategies for fostering an inclusive workplace.

Theoretical Framework

The rationale for promoting diversity in hiring can be grounded in several theories:

- **Social Identity Theory** posits that individuals categorize themselves and others into various social groups. This categorization can lead to in-group favoritism and out-group discrimination. Acknowledging and addressing these biases is crucial in hiring processes to ensure that candidates are evaluated based on merit rather than preconceived notions about their identity.

- **Diversity-Training Theory** suggests that structured training programs can help reduce biases and improve interpersonal relationships among team members. Effective training can foster an environment where diverse perspectives are valued, leading to enhanced collaboration and innovation.

- **Resource-Based View (RBV)** of the firm argues that a diverse workforce can be a source of competitive advantage. Organizations that embrace diversity are better positioned to understand and cater to a diverse customer base, ultimately leading to improved performance and profitability.

Challenges in Promoting Diversity

Despite the clear benefits, several challenges hinder the effective promotion of diversity and inclusion in hiring and leadership:

+ **Implicit Bias:** Many hiring managers possess unconscious biases that affect their decision-making processes. These biases can lead to the exclusion of qualified candidates from underrepresented groups. For instance, research shows that resumes with traditionally male names receive more callbacks than those with female names, even when qualifications are identical.

+ **Lack of Representation:** The absence of diverse role models in leadership positions can perpetuate a cycle of exclusion. When underrepresented groups do not see themselves reflected in leadership, they may feel discouraged from pursuing careers in tech.

+ **Tokenism:** Organizations may engage in superficial efforts to promote diversity, such as hiring a single candidate from an underrepresented group to fulfill a diversity quota. This practice can undermine genuine inclusion efforts and alienate the very individuals these initiatives aim to support.

Strategies for Promoting Diversity and Inclusion

To effectively promote diversity and inclusion in hiring and leadership, organizations can implement the following strategies:

+ **Structured Interviews:** Implementing structured interviews where all candidates are asked the same set of questions can help minimize bias. This approach allows for a more objective evaluation of candidates based on their skills and experiences.

+ **Diverse Hiring Panels:** Forming hiring panels that reflect diverse backgrounds can help counteract individual biases. A diverse panel is more likely to recognize and appreciate the value of varied perspectives, leading to more equitable hiring outcomes.

+ **Mentorship and Sponsorship Programs:** Establishing mentorship and sponsorship initiatives can help underrepresented employees navigate their career paths. By pairing them with experienced leaders, organizations can foster a culture of inclusion and support.

- **Regular Training and Workshops:** Conducting regular training sessions on unconscious bias, diversity, and inclusion can raise awareness among employees and leaders alike. Workshops that challenge stereotypes and promote empathy can create a more inclusive workplace culture.

- **Setting Diversity Goals:** Establishing clear, measurable diversity goals for hiring and leadership can hold organizations accountable. Regularly reviewing progress towards these goals can help ensure that diversity remains a priority.

- **Creating Inclusive Policies:** Implementing policies that promote work-life balance, flexible working arrangements, and parental leave can help attract a diverse workforce. Such policies signal to potential candidates that the organization values their well-being and diverse needs.

Examples of Successful Initiatives

Several organizations have successfully implemented strategies to promote diversity and inclusion:

- **Salesforce:** This cloud-based software company has made significant strides in diversity by publicly sharing its diversity statistics and committing to equal pay for equal work. Their initiatives include diversity training, employee resource groups, and partnerships with organizations focused on underrepresented communities.

- **Google:** Google has invested heavily in diversity and inclusion initiatives, including its "Diversity Annual Report," which outlines its progress and goals. The company has implemented unconscious bias training for all employees and has set ambitious targets for increasing diversity in its workforce.

- **IBM:** IBM has long been a pioneer in promoting diversity. The company has established a comprehensive diversity strategy that includes mentorship programs, employee resource groups, and partnerships with organizations that promote women and minorities in tech. Their commitment to diversity has not only enhanced their workplace culture but has also driven innovation and business success.

Conclusion

Promoting diversity and inclusion in hiring and leadership is essential for fostering innovation and ensuring that the tech industry reflects the diverse world in which we live. By addressing implicit biases, implementing structured hiring practices, and creating supportive environments, organizations can cultivate a culture that values diverse perspectives. As we continue to honor Ada Lovelace's legacy, let us commit to breaking down barriers and ensuring that the future of technology is inclusive and equitable for all.

The Role of Companies and Organizations in Supporting Women in Tech

In the ever-evolving landscape of technology, the role of companies and organizations in fostering an inclusive environment for women in tech has never been more crucial. As the industry continues to grapple with the gender gap, which sees women holding only a fraction of technical roles—approximately 25% of computing jobs—companies must step up and implement effective strategies to support and empower female talent. This section delves into the theoretical frameworks, existing challenges, and successful initiatives that highlight the importance of corporate responsibility in promoting gender equality in the tech sector.

Theoretical Frameworks

To understand the role of companies in supporting women in tech, it is essential to consider several theoretical frameworks that inform best practices in diversity and inclusion. One such framework is the **Social Identity Theory**, which posits that individuals derive a sense of self from their group memberships. In a male-dominated industry, women may experience feelings of isolation and lack of belonging, which can impact their career progression. Companies that actively promote diverse teams can mitigate these effects by fostering an inclusive culture that values different perspectives.

Another relevant framework is the **Intersectionality Theory**, which emphasizes that women do not experience discrimination uniformly. Factors such as race, socioeconomic status, and sexual orientation intersect to create unique challenges for women in tech. Companies must recognize these complexities and tailor their initiatives accordingly to support all women, particularly those from marginalized backgrounds.

Challenges in Supporting Women in Tech

Despite the growing awareness of the need for gender equality in tech, several challenges persist. One significant barrier is the prevalence of **unconscious bias** in hiring and promotion processes. Research shows that both men and women can hold biases that favor male candidates for technical roles, often leading to a lack of representation of women in senior positions. This bias can manifest in various ways, including:

+ **Resume Screening:** Studies indicate that resumes with gender-neutral names receive more callbacks than those with distinctly female names, reflecting a bias that can hinder women's chances during the initial hiring phase.

+ **Performance Evaluations:** Women often receive less favorable evaluations compared to their male counterparts, even when their performance is equivalent, leading to disparities in promotions and salary increases.

Moreover, the concept of the **"leaky pipeline"** illustrates how women enter the tech field in equal numbers to men but gradually drop out at various stages due to workplace culture, lack of mentorship, and limited advancement opportunities. Addressing these systemic issues requires a concerted effort from companies to implement sustainable change.

Successful Initiatives and Examples

Many organizations have recognized the importance of supporting women in tech and have initiated programs aimed at bridging the gender gap. Here are some notable examples:

+ **Diversity Hiring Initiatives:** Companies like Google and Microsoft have committed to increasing the representation of women in their workforce by setting specific hiring targets and implementing blind recruitment processes to minimize bias. These initiatives have shown positive results, with increased female representation in technical roles.

+ **Mentorship Programs:** Organizations such as Women Who Code and Girls Who Code provide mentorship opportunities for women at all stages of their careers. These programs connect aspiring female technologists with experienced mentors who can offer guidance, support, and networking opportunities, helping to build confidence and career advancement.

+ **Flexible Work Policies:** Companies like Salesforce have adopted flexible work policies that support work-life balance, which is crucial for many women, especially those with caregiving responsibilities. By allowing remote work and flexible hours, these organizations create an environment where women can thrive professionally without sacrificing personal commitments.

+ **Leadership Development Programs:** Programs like the *Catalyst's Women on Corporate Boards* initiative aim to increase the number of women in leadership positions by providing training, resources, and networking opportunities. By focusing on leadership development, companies can help women gain the skills and confidence needed to ascend the corporate ladder.

The Importance of Corporate Responsibility

The role of companies and organizations in supporting women in tech is not merely a matter of compliance or public relations; it is a fundamental aspect of corporate responsibility. Research indicates that diverse teams are more innovative and perform better, leading to improved business outcomes. According to a McKinsey report, companies in the top quartile for gender diversity on executive teams are 21% more likely to experience above-average profitability.

Moreover, fostering an inclusive workplace contributes to a positive company culture, enhances employee satisfaction, and attracts top talent. By prioritizing gender equality, companies can position themselves as leaders in the industry, ultimately benefiting both their employees and the bottom line.

In conclusion, the role of companies and organizations in supporting women in tech is multifaceted and essential for creating a more equitable industry. By addressing unconscious bias, implementing targeted initiatives, and embracing corporate responsibility, organizations can pave the way for a future where women are not only participants but leaders in the tech field. As we celebrate the legacy of Ada Lovelace, it is imperative that we continue to advocate for and support the next generation of female innovators, ensuring that their contributions are recognized and valued in the tech landscape.

Ada Lovelace Foundation: Advancing Gender Equality Through Policy and Advocacy

The Ada Lovelace Foundation was established with a mission that resonates with the very essence of Ada Lovelace's legacy—advancing gender equality in the tech industry through comprehensive policy initiatives and advocacy efforts. This foundation embodies the spirit of innovation and inclusivity that Ada championed, paving the way for women to thrive in technology and STEM fields.

The Foundation's Mission and Vision

The mission of the Ada Lovelace Foundation is to create a tech landscape where gender equality is not just an aspiration but a reality. The foundation aims to:

+ Promote policies that support the recruitment, retention, and advancement of women in technology.

+ Advocate for educational programs that inspire young girls to pursue careers in STEM.

+ Collaborate with organizations to dismantle systemic barriers that hinder women's progress in tech.

+ Raise awareness about the importance of diversity and inclusion in tech workplaces.

The vision is clear: a world where every woman has the opportunity to contribute to technological advancements, thereby enriching the industry with diverse perspectives and ideas.

Theoretical Framework: Gender Equality in the Workplace

To understand the foundation's approach, it is essential to examine the theoretical framework surrounding gender equality in the workplace. One influential theory is the Gender Equity Theory, which posits that equitable treatment of individuals, regardless of gender, leads to better organizational performance and employee satisfaction. According to the theory, organizations that prioritize gender equity can expect to see improvements in productivity, innovation, and overall workplace morale.

The foundation utilizes this framework to advocate for policies that address the following key issues:

+ **Pay Equity:** Ensuring that women receive equal pay for equal work is a fundamental goal. The foundation advocates for transparency in salary structures and encourages companies to conduct regular pay audits. According to the World Economic Forum, the global gender pay gap is estimated to take 135.6 years to close at the current rate of progress. The foundation aims to expedite this process through legislative advocacy and public awareness campaigns.

+ **Work-Life Balance:** Many women in tech face challenges in balancing professional responsibilities with personal life. The foundation promotes policies that support flexible working arrangements, parental leave, and childcare support. Research indicates that organizations offering flexible work options see higher retention rates among female employees.

+ **Leadership Representation:** Women remain underrepresented in leadership roles within tech companies. The foundation advocates for initiatives that encourage women to pursue leadership positions, such as mentorship programs and leadership training specifically designed for women. A study by McKinsey & Company found that companies with more women in leadership roles are 21% more likely to outperform their counterparts in terms of profitability.

Examples of Advocacy Efforts

The Ada Lovelace Foundation has undertaken various advocacy efforts to advance gender equality in the tech industry. Some notable examples include:

+ **Policy Development:** The foundation collaborates with policymakers to draft and promote legislation aimed at reducing gender disparities in tech. For instance, the foundation played a crucial role in advocating for the Gender Equality in Tech Act, which mandates gender diversity reporting for tech companies.

+ **Public Awareness Campaigns:** Through social media and public events, the foundation raises awareness about the importance of gender equality in technology. Campaigns such as "#WomenInTech" highlight the achievements of women in the industry and encourage young girls to pursue STEM careers.

+ **Partnerships with Educational Institutions:** The foundation partners with schools and universities to develop curricula that emphasize STEM education for girls. Programs like "Ada's Code" introduce young girls to programming and computer science, fostering an early interest in technology.

+ **Research and Publications:** The foundation conducts research on gender disparities in tech and publishes reports that provide data-driven insights into the challenges women face. These publications serve as valuable resources for organizations looking to implement effective diversity and inclusion strategies.

Measuring Impact: Success Stories

To evaluate the effectiveness of its initiatives, the Ada Lovelace Foundation employs a robust framework for measuring impact. Key performance indicators (KPIs) include:

+ **Increased Representation:** Tracking the percentage of women in tech roles and leadership positions within partner organizations.

+ **Pay Equity Metrics:** Monitoring changes in the gender pay gap within organizations that have implemented foundation-recommended policies.

+ **Program Participation:** Measuring the number of girls and women participating in STEM educational programs and mentorship initiatives.

+ **Feedback and Testimonials:** Gathering qualitative data through surveys and interviews to understand the experiences of women in tech and the impact of foundation programs on their careers.

One success story that exemplifies the foundation's impact is its partnership with a leading tech company that implemented a mentorship program for women. Within two years, the company reported a 30% increase in the number of women in management roles, demonstrating the effectiveness of targeted advocacy and support.

Challenges and Future Directions

Despite its successes, the Ada Lovelace Foundation faces ongoing challenges in its mission to advance gender equality. Systemic biases and cultural norms continue to hinder progress, and the foundation remains committed to addressing these issues through persistent advocacy.

Looking ahead, the foundation aims to expand its reach by:

+ Increasing collaboration with global organizations to share best practices and amplify advocacy efforts on an international scale.

+ Developing online resources and toolkits for organizations seeking to implement gender equity initiatives.

+ Continuing to raise awareness about the importance of diversity and inclusion in tech through innovative campaigns and partnerships.

In conclusion, the Ada Lovelace Foundation stands as a beacon of hope and progress in the fight for gender equality in technology. By advancing policy initiatives, advocating for systemic change, and inspiring the next generation of women in tech, the foundation honors Ada Lovelace's legacy and paves the way for a more equitable future.

Encouraging Female Entrepreneurship and Venture Capital Investment

In the contemporary landscape of technology and entrepreneurship, the necessity for encouraging female entrepreneurship cannot be overstated. Despite the significant strides made over the past few decades, women remain underrepresented in the entrepreneurial ecosystem, particularly in technology-driven sectors. This underrepresentation is not merely a statistical anomaly; it reflects deeper systemic issues that require attention and action.

The Gender Gap in Entrepreneurship

Research shows that women entrepreneurs often face unique challenges that hinder their ability to secure funding and grow their businesses. According to the Global Entrepreneurship Monitor (GEM), women are approximately 50% less likely to start a business compared to men. Furthermore, when they do start businesses, women-led ventures tend to receive less venture capital (VC) funding than their male counterparts. A report by PitchBook indicated that in 2020, only 2.3% of all venture capital funding went to female founders, a statistic that highlights the significant disparity in investment opportunities.

Barriers to Accessing Venture Capital

Several barriers contribute to the funding gap faced by female entrepreneurs. These include:

+ **Bias in Funding Decisions:** Research has demonstrated that investors often exhibit unconscious bias, favoring male entrepreneurs over female entrepreneurs. This bias can manifest in various forms, including the language used in pitch meetings and the types of questions posed to male versus female founders.

+ **Network Limitations:** Women entrepreneurs frequently have less access to influential networks that can provide mentorship and introductions to potential investors. The lack of representation in venture capital firms means that women may find it more challenging to connect with investors who understand their visions and challenges.

+ **Stereotypes and Societal Expectations:** Societal norms and stereotypes regarding gender roles can discourage women from pursuing entrepreneurship. The perception that women should prioritize family over career can lead to self-doubt and hesitation in seeking funding.

The Importance of Female Representation in Venture Capital

To address these disparities, it is crucial to increase female representation within venture capital firms. Diverse investment teams are better equipped to recognize the potential of female-led startups and to challenge existing biases. Studies have shown that companies with diverse leadership teams are more likely to outperform their peers. For instance, a McKinsey report revealed that companies in the top quartile for gender diversity on executive teams were 25% more likely to experience above-average profitability.

Initiatives to Support Female Entrepreneurs

Several initiatives have emerged to support female entrepreneurs and encourage venture capital investment in their ventures:

+ **Women-Focused Funds:** Investment funds specifically targeting female entrepreneurs have gained traction. Examples include the Female Founders Fund and BBG Ventures, both of which focus on investing in women-led startups and providing them with the necessary resources to thrive.

+ **Accelerator Programs:** Programs like Techstars and Y Combinator have made efforts to include more women in their cohorts. These programs not only provide funding but also mentorship and networking opportunities that can be crucial for early-stage companies.

+ **Educational Workshops and Networking Events:** Workshops that focus on financial literacy, pitching skills, and networking can empower women entrepreneurs. Events like the annual "Women in Venture" conference provide platforms for women to connect with investors and peers, fostering a supportive community.

Case Studies of Successful Female Entrepreneurs

Highlighting successful female entrepreneurs can serve as inspiration and proof of concept for aspiring founders. For instance, Reshma Saujani, founder of Girls Who Code, has not only made significant strides in promoting female participation in tech but has also attracted substantial funding for her nonprofit organization. Her success story illustrates the potential for female-led initiatives to garner support and make a meaningful impact.

Another example is Whitney Wolfe Herd, co-founder of Tinder and founder of Bumble. Wolfe Herd successfully raised $2.2 billion during Bumble's IPO, demonstrating that female entrepreneurs can achieve significant financial milestones when given the opportunity and support.

Conclusion: A Call to Action

Encouraging female entrepreneurship and increasing venture capital investment in women-led businesses is not just a matter of equity; it is essential for driving innovation and economic growth. By dismantling barriers, promoting diversity in investment teams, and providing targeted support for female entrepreneurs, we can create a more inclusive and prosperous entrepreneurial ecosystem.

Investors, policymakers, and society at large must recognize the value of diverse perspectives in driving innovation. As we honor the legacy of Ada Lovelace, who paved the way for women in technology, we must commit to continuing her fight for equality in entrepreneurship and venture capital investment. The future of technology and innovation depends on it.

Breaking Down Barriers and Challenging Stereotypes

The journey to gender equality in technology has been fraught with challenges, much like navigating a complex algorithm without proper documentation. Ada Lovelace, as a pioneer in programming, faced her own set of barriers, which continue to resonate in today's tech landscape. Breaking down these barriers and challenging stereotypes is not just a noble cause; it is essential for the advancement of innovation and diversity in the tech industry.

Understanding Stereotypes in Tech

Stereotypes surrounding gender roles in technology often stem from historical biases and societal norms. The notion that technology is a male-dominated field has been perpetuated through generations, leading to a lack of female representation in STEM (Science, Technology, Engineering, and Mathematics). According to a study by the National Center for Women & Information Technology (NCWIT), women hold only 26% of computing jobs in the United States, a statistic that starkly illustrates the ongoing gender gap.

Theoretical Frameworks

To understand the persistence of these stereotypes, we can apply several theoretical frameworks:

- **Social Identity Theory:** This theory posits that individuals categorize themselves and others into various social groups, leading to in-group favoritism and out-group discrimination. In tech, this can manifest as a bias against women, who are often seen as outsiders in a male-centric environment.

- **Stereotype Threat:** This psychological phenomenon occurs when individuals are at risk of confirming negative stereotypes about their social group. Women in tech may experience anxiety that undermines their performance, further perpetuating the stereotype that they are less capable in technical roles.

- **Cultural Schema Theory:** This theory explains how cultural narratives shape our understanding of gender roles. The prevailing narrative that associates technical skills with masculinity can discourage women from pursuing careers in technology.

Examples of Breaking Barriers

Despite these challenges, there have been numerous initiatives aimed at breaking down barriers and challenging stereotypes:

1. **Women in Tech Organizations:** Initiatives such as Girls Who Code and Women Who Code provide resources, mentorship, and community support for women entering the tech field. These organizations empower women by creating a network of support and fostering a sense of belonging.

2. **Inclusive Hiring Practices:** Companies like Google and Microsoft have implemented diversity hiring initiatives to ensure a more equitable recruitment process. By actively seeking female candidates and promoting diverse teams, these companies challenge the stereotype that tech is exclusively for men.

3. **STEM Education Programs:** Educational programs that target young girls, such as the STEM for Her initiative, aim to inspire the next generation of female programmers. By introducing girls to coding and technology at an early age, these programs challenge the stereotype that technical skills are inherently male.

Overcoming Resistance to Change

Breaking down barriers is often met with resistance. The traditional mindset that associates technology with masculinity can be deeply ingrained. To overcome this resistance, it is crucial to employ strategies that promote awareness and education:

+ **Awareness Campaigns:** Initiatives that highlight the achievements of women in tech, such as Ada Lovelace Day, serve to challenge existing stereotypes and inspire future generations. By showcasing role models, these campaigns help to dismantle the narrative that tech is not for women.

+ **Mentorship Programs:** Establishing mentorship programs where experienced female technologists guide newcomers can provide the support needed to navigate the male-dominated landscape. This mentorship can help to build confidence and skills, reinforcing the idea that women belong in tech.

+ **Policy Changes:** Advocating for policies that promote gender equality in the workplace, such as parental leave and flexible working conditions, can help create an environment where women feel valued and supported.

The Role of Allies

Allies play a crucial role in breaking down barriers and challenging stereotypes. Men in the tech industry can contribute by:

+ **Advocating for Diversity:** Male colleagues can use their positions to advocate for diversity and inclusion initiatives within their organizations, ensuring that women's voices are heard and valued.

+ **Challenging Misconceptions:** By actively challenging sexist remarks and behaviors, male allies can create a more inclusive environment that discourages discrimination.

+ **Mentoring Female Colleagues:** Male mentors can provide support and guidance to women in tech, helping them navigate challenges and advance their careers.

Conclusion

Breaking down barriers and challenging stereotypes is an ongoing effort that requires commitment from all stakeholders in the tech industry. By embracing diversity and fostering an inclusive environment, we can honor Ada Lovelace's legacy and ensure that future generations of women feel empowered to pursue careers in technology. The fight for gender equality in tech is not just about numbers; it's about creating a culture where innovation thrives through diverse perspectives.

As we continue to honor Ada Lovelace's contributions, let us remember that every effort counts. Whether it's through advocacy, education, or mentorship, each step taken towards equality brings us closer to a future where women are not just participants in technology but leaders and innovators shaping the digital landscape.

The Power of Allies and Male Advocacy in the Women in Tech Movement

In the ongoing struggle for gender equality in the tech industry, the role of male allies and advocates has become increasingly recognized as a crucial component of effective change. While women have been at the forefront of advocating for their own rights and representation, the support of male colleagues can amplify these efforts, challenge systemic biases, and create a more inclusive environment. This section explores the theoretical frameworks surrounding allyship, the barriers that exist within the tech industry, and provides examples of successful male advocacy.

Theoretical Framework of Allyship

Allyship is often defined through the lens of social justice, where individuals from privileged groups actively support marginalized communities. In the context of the tech industry, male allies can leverage their positions of power to advocate for women, challenge discriminatory practices, and promote equitable policies. The concept of allyship is not merely passive support; it involves taking tangible actions that dismantle barriers for women in tech.

$$A = P + C + I \tag{187}$$

Where:

+ A = Allyship effectiveness

+ P = Power dynamics awareness

+ C = Commitment to change

+ I = Interpersonal relationships with marginalized groups

This equation illustrates that effective allyship is a function of understanding power dynamics, demonstrating a commitment to change, and fostering relationships with those who are marginalized. Male allies who recognize their privilege and actively seek to use it for good can create significant ripples of change within their organizations.

Challenges Faced by Women in Tech

Despite the progress made in recent years, women in tech continue to face numerous barriers, including:

+ **Gender Bias**: Research indicates that women are often judged more harshly than their male counterparts in technical roles, leading to a lack of opportunities for advancement.

+ **Stereotypes**: The pervasive stereotype that men are inherently more skilled in technology can undermine women's confidence and contributions.

+ **Isolation**: Women in tech frequently report feelings of isolation and exclusion from networks that are crucial for career advancement.

These challenges create an environment where women may struggle to thrive, making the role of male allies even more critical.

Examples of Successful Male Advocacy

Several organizations and individuals have exemplified the power of male advocacy in supporting women in tech:

+ **Tech Giants' Initiatives**: Companies like Google and Microsoft have launched initiatives aimed at increasing female representation in tech roles. These programs often feature male leaders who publicly commit to mentoring women and advocating for their promotion.

+ **The #HeForShe Campaign**: Initiated by UN Women, this campaign encourages men to advocate for gender equality. Many male tech leaders have publicly endorsed the campaign, pledging to take action against gender discrimination in their workplaces.

+ **Mentorship Programs**: Programs that pair male allies with female mentees can foster an environment of support. For example, the "MentorNet" initiative connects women in STEM with male mentors who can provide guidance and advocacy.

The Impact of Male Advocacy

The involvement of male allies has been shown to lead to measurable outcomes in the tech industry:

+ **Increased Representation**: Organizations that actively promote male allyship often see higher rates of female recruitment and retention. For instance, companies that have implemented gender diversity training for all employees, including men, report a more inclusive culture.

+ **Cultural Shift**: Male advocates can help shift the organizational culture from one of competition to collaboration. By publicly supporting women, they challenge the status quo and encourage other men to do the same.

+ **Policy Changes**: Male allies in leadership positions can influence policy changes that promote gender equality, such as implementing family leave policies and flexible work arrangements that benefit all employees.

Conclusion

The power of allies and male advocacy in the women in tech movement cannot be overstated. By recognizing their privilege and actively engaging in the fight for gender equality, men can play a pivotal role in transforming the tech industry into a more inclusive space for women. This partnership not only benefits women but enriches the entire tech community, fostering innovation and creativity through diverse perspectives. As we continue to honor Ada Lovelace's legacy, it is essential to recognize that the fight for equality is a collective effort that requires the participation of all, regardless of gender.

Untangling the Threads of Gender Inequality: Ada Lovelace's Unfinished Revolution

In the realm of technology and programming, Ada Lovelace stands as a beacon of brilliance and a symbol of the ongoing struggle against gender inequality. Her legacy, while monumental, also highlights the unfinished revolution for women in technology. This section delves into the persistent issues of gender bias in the tech industry, the historical context of Ada's advocacy, and the necessity for continued efforts to achieve gender equality.

Historical Context of Gender Inequality in Technology

Historically, women have faced significant barriers in the fields of science, technology, engineering, and mathematics (STEM). The contributions of women like Ada Lovelace were often overshadowed by their male counterparts, leading to a systematic erasure of their achievements. Lovelace's work on the Analytical Engine was groundbreaking; however, her contributions were largely unrecognized during her lifetime. This pattern of exclusion is not an isolated incident but rather a reflection of a broader societal issue that persists today.

Theoretical Frameworks: Feminist Theory and Gender Studies

To understand the dynamics of gender inequality in technology, it is essential to engage with feminist theory and gender studies. These frameworks provide valuable insights into how societal norms and structures perpetuate discrimination against women. One prominent theory is the concept of the "leaky pipeline," which describes how women drop out of STEM fields at various stages of their education and careers due to a lack of support and representation.

$$\text{Retention Rate} = \frac{\text{Number of Women in STEM}}{\text{Total Number of Women Graduating}} \tag{188}$$

This equation illustrates the retention challenges women face in STEM fields. The leaky pipeline metaphor highlights the critical points at which women are lost, often due to a combination of systemic bias, lack of mentorship, and hostile work environments.

Current Challenges in the Tech Industry

Despite progress, women in technology continue to encounter significant challenges. Studies indicate that women hold only a fraction of leadership positions in tech companies, often facing barriers to advancement and recognition. The gender pay gap remains a pressing issue, with women earning approximately 82 cents for every dollar earned by their male counterparts in the tech sector. This disparity is exacerbated for women of color, who experience both gender and racial discrimination.

$$\text{Gender Pay Gap} = \frac{\text{Average Male Salary} - \text{Average Female Salary}}{\text{Average Male Salary}} \times 100 \quad (189)$$

This equation quantifies the gender pay gap, illustrating the economic disparities that persist within the industry.

Examples of Gender Inequality in Tech

Several high-profile cases have brought attention to gender inequality in the tech industry. For instance, the 2017 lawsuit against Google highlighted allegations of systemic bias against women in hiring and promotion practices. Similarly, the #MeToo movement has shed light on the pervasive culture of harassment that women face in tech environments, further discouraging their participation and advancement.

Ada Lovelace's Advocacy and Its Relevance Today

Ada Lovelace's life and work serve as a powerful reminder of the importance of advocating for women's representation in technology. Her vision for the Analytical Engine included not only its computational capabilities but also its potential to empower women in intellectual pursuits. Lovelace's legacy inspires contemporary movements advocating for gender equality in tech, emphasizing the need for mentorship, support networks, and policy changes to create inclusive environments.

Strategies for Advancing Gender Equality in Tech

To address the unfinished revolution that Lovelace's legacy represents, it is crucial to implement effective strategies aimed at promoting gender equality in technology. These strategies include:

- **Mentorship Programs:** Establishing mentorship initiatives that connect young women with experienced professionals in tech can help bridge the gap and provide guidance.

- **Diversity and Inclusion Training:** Organizations should prioritize diversity training to create awareness of unconscious biases and foster inclusive workplaces.

- **Policy Advocacy:** Advocating for policies that support equal pay, parental leave, and flexible work arrangements is essential to retain women in tech.

- **Celebrating Role Models:** Highlighting the achievements of women in technology, like Ada Lovelace, can inspire future generations and challenge stereotypes.

Conclusion: Continuing Ada's Revolution

Ada Lovelace's legacy is not merely a historical footnote; it is a call to action. The threads of gender inequality in technology remain tangled, but by acknowledging the challenges and implementing targeted strategies, we can honor Lovelace's vision for a more equitable future. The unfinished revolution for women in technology requires collective effort and unwavering commitment to ensure that the contributions of women are recognized, valued, and celebrated. As we navigate this complex landscape, let us remember Lovelace not only as the first programmer but as a pioneer whose spirit of innovation and resilience continues to inspire the fight for gender equality in tech.

$$\text{Future Equality} = \text{Current Actions} + \text{Collective Advocacy} \qquad (190)$$

This equation encapsulates the essence of progressing towards gender equality in technology: it is a combination of present efforts and the power of collective advocacy that will shape a more inclusive future.

The Enduring Inspiration of Ada Lovelace

Ada's Message to Future Innovators

Ada Lovelace, often celebrated as the first computer programmer, left behind not just a legacy of groundbreaking ideas but also a powerful message for future innovators. Her life and work serve as a beacon of inspiration, urging us to embrace creativity, challenge the status quo, and persist in the face of adversity. In this section, we will explore the key elements of Ada's message, encapsulating her vision for innovation and the responsibilities that come with it.

Embrace Creativity and Imagination

At the core of Ada's philosophy was the belief that creativity and imagination are essential components of innovation. In her notes on Charles Babbage's Analytical Engine, Ada famously stated:

> "The Analytical Engine does not occupy common ground with mere calculating machines. It holds within itself the principles of the future."

This perspective highlights the importance of thinking beyond the immediate functionality of technology. For Ada, the potential of the Analytical Engine was not limited to arithmetic calculations; it was a canvas for creativity, capable of producing music, art, and even complex algorithms.

$$\text{Innovation} = \text{Creativity} + \text{Functionality} \qquad (191)$$

By encouraging future innovators to blend creativity with practical applications, Ada's message reminds us that true innovation often arises from the intersection of art and science.

Challenge the Status Quo

Ada Lovelace's life was marked by her defiance of societal norms. As a woman in a male-dominated field, she faced numerous obstacles, yet she persisted and carved out her own path. Her determination serves as a powerful reminder for future innovators to challenge the status quo and question conventional wisdom.

> "I am not afraid of storms, for I am learning how to sail my ship."

This metaphor captures the essence of Ada's resilience. Future innovators should embrace challenges as opportunities for growth and learning. By pushing boundaries and redefining what is possible, they can create solutions that reflect their unique perspectives and experiences.

The Importance of Collaboration

Ada's collaboration with Charles Babbage exemplifies the power of teamwork in driving innovation. Their partnership was characterized by mutual respect and shared vision, which enabled them to explore uncharted territories in computing. Ada's contributions to Babbage's work were not merely supportive; she was an equal partner in the creative process.

$$\text{Collaboration} = \text{Diversity of Ideas} + \text{Shared Vision} \qquad (192)$$

Future innovators should recognize that collaboration fosters a diversity of ideas, leading to richer and more innovative outcomes. By working together across disciplines, backgrounds, and perspectives, they can develop solutions that are more comprehensive and impactful.

Perseverance in the Face of Adversity

Ada's life was not without its struggles. She faced health challenges, societal expectations, and personal hardships. Yet, her resilience and determination to pursue her passions in mathematics and computing are key aspects of her legacy.

"The most important thing is to be true to yourself and those you love."

This statement encourages future innovators to remain authentic and committed to their passions, regardless of external pressures. Perseverance is essential in the journey of innovation, as setbacks often pave the way for breakthroughs.

Ethical Considerations in Innovation

As technology continues to evolve, Ada's insights into the ethical implications of innovation remain relevant. She understood that with great power comes great responsibility. In her work, she emphasized the importance of considering the societal impact of technological advancements.

$$\text{Ethical Innovation} = \text{Responsibility} + \text{Impact Assessment} \qquad (193)$$

Future innovators must prioritize ethical considerations in their work, ensuring that their creations serve the greater good and contribute positively to society. This involves actively engaging with the potential consequences of their innovations and advocating for responsible practices in technology development.

Inspiration for Future Generations

Ultimately, Ada Lovelace's message to future innovators is one of empowerment and inspiration. She encourages us to dream big, embrace our creativity, and pursue our passions with vigor. By honoring her legacy, we can continue to inspire future generations to innovate fearlessly and inclusively.

> *"Your best and wisest gift to the world is your own self."*

As we reflect on Ada's life and contributions, we are reminded that innovation is not solely about technology; it is about the people behind it. By fostering an environment that celebrates diversity, creativity, and ethical responsibility, we can ensure that Ada's message resonates with future innovators for generations to come.

Conclusion

In conclusion, Ada Lovelace's message to future innovators transcends time and technology. It is a clarion call to embrace creativity, challenge norms, collaborate, persevere, and prioritize ethics. As we navigate the complexities of the modern world, let us carry forward Ada's spirit of innovation, ensuring that her legacy continues to inspire and empower those who dare to dream and create.

The Timeless Relevance of Ada's Courage and Resilience

Ada Lovelace is not just a name in the annals of computing history; she is a beacon of courage and resilience that resonates through time. In a world where women were often relegated to the background, Ada stood at the forefront of an intellectual revolution, challenging societal norms and expectations. Her journey is a testament to the power of perseverance in the face of adversity, making her story relevant not only in the context of technology but also in the broader narrative of women's rights and empowerment.

Courage in the Face of Adversity

Ada's life was marked by numerous challenges, from her tumultuous family background to her struggles with health issues. Born to the infamous poet Lord Byron and his wife, Lady Anne Isabella Milbanke, Ada's early life was shaped by the shadow of her father's abandonment and her mother's strict educational regimen. Despite these obstacles, Ada's innate curiosity and passion for mathematics flourished.

One of the most significant challenges Ada faced was societal expectations regarding women's roles in the 19th century. During this period, women were often discouraged from pursuing intellectual endeavors, particularly in fields dominated by men, such as mathematics and engineering. Ada's courage shone through as she defied these conventions, immersing herself in the world of numbers and logic.

$$C = \frac{F}{A} \tag{194}$$

In this equation, C represents courage, F symbolizes the force of societal pressure, and A denotes the individual's ability to act. Ada's life illustrates that even when faced with overwhelming societal forces, the courage to pursue one's passion can lead to groundbreaking achievements.

Resilience in the Pursuit of Knowledge

Ada's resilience is particularly evident in her collaboration with Charles Babbage on the Analytical Engine. This groundbreaking project was not merely a technical endeavor; it was a manifestation of Ada's vision for the future of computing. Despite facing skepticism from her contemporaries, Ada remained steadfast in her belief that the Analytical Engine could do more than mere calculations.

She famously wrote:

> "The Analytical Engine does not occupy common ground with mere calculating machines. It holds within itself the potentialities of all thought and action."

This quote encapsulates Ada's visionary thinking and her ability to foresee the implications of computing technology. Her resilience allowed her to articulate complex ideas about programming and computation at a time when such concepts were largely unrecognized.

The Legacy of Ada's Courage and Resilience

Ada's legacy is not confined to her technical contributions; it extends to the inspiration she provides for future generations, particularly women in STEM fields. Her story encourages young women to pursue their passions, regardless of societal barriers. Organizations and initiatives inspired by Ada's life, such as Ada Lovelace Day, celebrate the achievements of women in technology and serve as a reminder of the importance of diversity in innovation.

Moreover, Ada's resilience in the face of personal struggles, including her battles with illness, highlights the importance of mental health awareness. She experienced a range of health issues throughout her life, yet she continued to push the boundaries of knowledge and creativity. This aspect of her life encourages discussions about the intersection of mental health and professional success, a topic that remains relevant today.

Modern Implications of Ada's Story

In today's rapidly evolving technological landscape, Ada's story serves as a powerful reminder of the importance of courage and resilience in the face of challenges. As we navigate issues such as gender inequality in tech, mental health awareness, and the ethical implications of technology, Ada's legacy provides a framework for understanding the need for perseverance and innovation.

For example, in recent years, the tech industry has faced scrutiny regarding the lack of diversity and representation. Ada's courage to challenge societal norms is echoed in the ongoing fight for equal opportunities in tech. Organizations are increasingly recognizing the importance of diverse perspectives in fostering innovation, a principle that Ada embodied in her work.

Conclusion

In conclusion, Ada Lovelace's courage and resilience are timeless qualities that continue to inspire individuals across generations. Her ability to defy societal expectations, pursue her passions, and contribute to the field of computing in meaningful ways serves as a powerful example for all. As we honor her legacy, we are reminded that the courage to innovate and the resilience to overcome obstacles are essential in shaping a better future for all, particularly in the realm of technology. Ada Lovelace's story is not just a chapter in history; it is a call to action for aspiring innovators everywhere to embrace their potential and strive for excellence, regardless of the challenges they may face.

Ada's Inspiration for Overcoming Challenges and Adversity

Ada Lovelace, a name synonymous with pioneering computer programming, serves as an enduring source of inspiration for those facing challenges and adversity in their personal and professional lives. Her journey was marked by numerous obstacles, including societal expectations, health issues, and the constraints of her time. Yet, Ada's resilience and determination not only shaped her legacy but also provide valuable lessons for future generations.

The Context of Ada's Challenges

Born in 1815 to the renowned poet Lord Byron and Lady Anne Isabella Milbanke, Ada's early life was steeped in complexity. Her parents' tumultuous relationship led to her father's absence, leaving Ada to be raised primarily by her mother, who was determined to steer her away from the artistic inclinations of her father. This environment fostered a sense of isolation, as Ada struggled to find her identity amidst the conflicting legacies of her parents.

$$\text{Identity} = f(\text{Family Background, Societal Expectations}) \quad (195)$$

This equation suggests that Ada's sense of self was influenced heavily by her family dynamics and the societal norms of the Victorian era. Despite these pressures, Ada found solace and passion in mathematics, a field dominated by men, which further complicated her journey.

Health Struggles and Intellectual Pursuits

Throughout her life, Ada battled significant health challenges, including bouts of illness that often left her bedridden. These physical limitations could have deterred a lesser spirit, but Ada transformed adversity into motivation. Her dedication to mathematics and her collaboration with Charles Babbage on the Analytical Engine exemplify her ability to channel her struggles into productive endeavors.

For instance, while grappling with her health, Ada wrote extensive notes on Babbage's work, which included what is now recognized as the first algorithm intended for implementation on a machine. This moment is a testament to her resilience, demonstrating that even when faced with personal trials, she could contribute groundbreaking ideas.

$$\text{Contribution} = \text{Effort} \times \text{Passion} \quad (196)$$

This equation encapsulates Ada's philosophy: her contributions to the field of computing were not merely a product of her intellect but also her unwavering passion for mathematics and innovation.

Challenging Gender Norms

Ada's life was also a battle against the pervasive gender stereotypes of her time. In an era when women were often relegated to the domestic sphere, Ada defied expectations by pursuing a career in mathematics and science. Her advocacy for women's education and her own achievements in a male-dominated field serve as powerful examples of overcoming societal barriers.

For example, Ada's collaboration with Babbage was groundbreaking not just for its intellectual merit but also for its defiance of gender norms. She was one of the first women to be taken seriously in the field of computing, paving the way for future female programmers.

$$\text{Impact} = \text{Courage} + \text{Innovation} \tag{197}$$

This equation illustrates that Ada's impact stemmed from her courage to challenge societal norms combined with her innovative spirit. Her legacy encourages women today to pursue their passions relentlessly, regardless of societal constraints.

Lessons from Ada's Life

The essence of Ada Lovelace's story lies in her ability to transform adversity into a catalyst for growth. Her life teaches us several key lessons:

- **Embrace Challenges:** Ada's ability to face her health issues head-on and continue her work in mathematics serves as a reminder that challenges can be opportunities in disguise.

- **Pursue Your Passions:** Ada's unwavering commitment to her interests, despite societal expectations, highlights the importance of following one's passion.

- **Advocate for Change:** Ada's advocacy for women in STEM fields underscores the need to challenge and change the status quo, inspiring future generations to continue this fight.

Conclusion: The Enduring Inspiration of Ada Lovelace

In conclusion, Ada Lovelace's life is a powerful testament to the strength of the human spirit in the face of adversity. Her ability to overcome personal and societal challenges serves as an inspiration for anyone navigating their own struggles. As we celebrate her legacy, let us remember that resilience, passion, and the courage to challenge norms can lead to extraordinary contributions that resonate through time.

Ada's journey reminds us that adversity can be a stepping stone to greatness, encouraging us all to embrace our challenges and transform them into opportunities for innovation and change.

The Call to Action: Carrying Forward Ada's Legacy

Ada Lovelace's legacy is not merely a historical footnote; it is a clarion call for action in the realms of technology, education, and gender equality. As we reflect on her contributions, we must also consider how we can actively carry forward her vision and spirit in today's rapidly evolving technological landscape. This section outlines actionable steps that individuals, organizations, and society as a whole can take to honor Ada's legacy and inspire the next generation of innovators.

1. Embracing Diversity in Tech

The tech industry continues to grapple with significant diversity issues. According to a report by the National Center for Women & Information Technology (NCWIT), women hold only 26% of computing jobs in the United States. This disparity is not just a statistic; it is a reflection of the barriers that Ada herself faced in her time. To honor her legacy, it is imperative that we advocate for diverse hiring practices and create inclusive environments where individuals from all backgrounds feel empowered to contribute.

$$D = \frac{N_{diverse}}{N_{total}} \times 100\% \tag{198}$$

Where:

+ D = Diversity percentage

+ $N_{diverse}$ = Number of diverse employees

+ N_{total} = Total number of employees

This equation can serve as a metric for organizations to assess and improve their diversity efforts.

2. Promoting STEM Education for Girls

Ada Lovelace's story is a powerful narrative for young girls interested in STEM (Science, Technology, Engineering, and Mathematics). Initiatives that promote STEM education for girls can help bridge the gender gap in technology. Programs such as coding camps, robotics clubs, and mentorship opportunities can ignite a passion for technology in young minds.

For example, the *Girls Who Code* initiative has successfully engaged thousands of girls in coding, providing them with the skills and confidence needed to pursue careers in technology. The impact of such initiatives can be quantified using the following formula:

$$I = \frac{N_{participants}}{N_{total\ girls}} \times 100\% \qquad (199)$$

Where:

+ I = Impact percentage

+ $N_{participants}$ = Number of girls participating in STEM programs

+ $N_{total\ girls}$ = Total number of girls in the community

This measurement can help organizations evaluate their reach and effectiveness in promoting STEM education.

3. Advocating for Gender Equality in Leadership

Ada's struggles highlight the importance of representation in leadership roles. Women are still underrepresented in tech leadership positions. According to a McKinsey report, women hold only 28% of C-suite roles in the tech sector. To carry forward Ada's legacy, we must advocate for equal opportunities for women to ascend to leadership positions.

One strategy is to implement mentorship programs that connect aspiring female leaders with established professionals in the industry. This can create a supportive network that fosters growth and development. The effectiveness of such programs can be assessed through:

$$E = \frac{N_{mentored}}{N_{aspiring}} \times 100\% \qquad (200)$$

Where:

+ E = Effectiveness percentage

+ $N_{mentored}$ = Number of women mentored into leadership roles

+ $N_{aspiring}$ = Total number of aspiring female leaders

4. Encouraging Lifelong Learning

Ada Lovelace was a proponent of continuous learning, a principle that remains vital in today's fast-paced technological environment. As technology evolves, so too must our skills and knowledge. Encouraging a culture of lifelong learning within organizations can help employees adapt and thrive.

This can be facilitated through workshops, online courses, and professional development opportunities. The return on investment (ROI) for such programs can be evaluated using the following equation:

$$ROI = \frac{G - C}{C} \times 100\% \tag{201}$$

Where:

+ ROI = Return on investment

+ G = Gains from the program

+ C = Costs of the program

5. Celebrating Ada Lovelace Day

Celebrating Ada Lovelace Day annually serves as a reminder of her contributions and the ongoing need for gender equality in technology. This day can be used to highlight the achievements of women in tech, host events that inspire young girls, and promote discussions around the importance of diversity in the field.

By participating in and promoting Ada Lovelace Day, we can collectively honor her legacy and inspire future generations to follow in her footsteps. Events can include panel discussions, workshops, and social media campaigns to amplify the message of inclusion and innovation.

Conclusion

Carrying forward Ada Lovelace's legacy is a collective responsibility that requires action at all levels—individual, organizational, and societal. By embracing diversity, promoting STEM education for girls, advocating for gender equality in leadership, encouraging lifelong learning, and celebrating Ada Lovelace Day, we can ensure that her vision continues to inspire and shape the future of technology. The call to action is clear: let us honor Ada by creating a world where everyone, regardless of gender, has the opportunity to innovate, lead, and thrive in the tech industry. Together, we can build a future that reflects the values Ada Lovelace embodied—a future that is inclusive, innovative, and inspiring.

Ada's Impact on the Collective Imagination

Ada Lovelace's contributions to the fields of mathematics and computing transcend the boundaries of her time, leaving an indelible mark on the collective imagination of society. Her visionary insights, particularly regarding the potential of machines to perform tasks beyond mere calculation, have inspired generations of thinkers, creators, and innovators. This section delves into the profound impact Ada has had on the collective imagination, exploring the ways in which her ideas have shaped not only technological advancements but also cultural narratives surrounding women in STEM.

The Visionary Architect of Computing

Ada Lovelace is often referred to as the first computer programmer, a title she earned through her work on Charles Babbage's Analytical Engine. However, her legacy extends far beyond the technicalities of programming. Ada envisioned a future where machines could generate music, art, and even poetry. In her notes, she famously wrote about the Analytical Engine's ability to manipulate symbols and create complex outputs, which can be expressed mathematically as:

$$f(x) = \sum_{n=0}^{\infty} a_n x^n \tag{202}$$

This equation represents a power series, a concept Ada understood deeply. Yet, her insight was not merely about mathematical functions; it was about the potential for machines to extend human creativity and intellect. This foresight has fueled the collective imagination, inspiring countless artists, writers, and scientists to explore the intersection of technology and creativity.

Cultural Narratives and Representation

Ada's story has become a powerful narrative in the fight for gender equality in technology and the arts. Her life and work challenge the conventional stereotypes of women in science, showcasing a figure who was not only intellectually gifted but also a pioneer of interdisciplinary thought. The representation of Ada in literature, film, and art has helped to cultivate a broader understanding of women's contributions to technology, inspiring young girls and women to pursue careers in STEM fields.

For instance, the portrayal of Ada in the 2015 film "The Imitation Game" as a muse for Alan Turing serves as a reminder of her enduring influence. While the film primarily focuses on Turing's achievements, it also highlights the collaborative spirit that Ada embodied. This narrative serves to inspire future generations, illustrating that the contributions of women in technology are not merely historical footnotes but foundational to the evolution of modern computing.

Innovative Thought and Interdisciplinary Approaches

Ada's interdisciplinary approach to mathematics, science, and the arts has encouraged a more holistic view of education and innovation. Her belief that creativity and logic are not mutually exclusive has resonated with educators and thought leaders. This perspective is reflected in contemporary educational initiatives that promote STEAM (Science, Technology, Engineering, Arts, and Mathematics) curricula, emphasizing the importance of integrating artistic creativity into technical fields.

The notion that technology can be a canvas for artistic expression has been exemplified in various modern projects, such as generative art and algorithmic design. These fields draw upon Ada's foundational ideas, demonstrating how programming can serve as a medium for creativity. For example, the use of Processing, a programming language and environment for artists, allows creators to generate visual art through code, echoing Ada's vision of machines as tools for creative expression.

Inspiration for Future Innovators

Ada Lovelace's legacy continues to inspire a new generation of innovators who challenge the status quo and push the boundaries of what is possible. Her life serves as a reminder that the pursuit of knowledge and creativity is not limited by gender or societal expectations. Organizations such as Girls Who Code and the Ada Lovelace Foundation work tirelessly to empower young women in technology, ensuring that Ada's spirit of innovation lives on.

Moreover, Ada's influence is evident in the rise of female tech leaders who advocate for diversity and inclusion within the industry. Figures such as Reshma Saujani, founder of Girls Who Code, often cite Ada as a source of inspiration in their efforts to create opportunities for women in technology. This ongoing dialogue about Ada's impact reinforces her role as a symbol of empowerment and possibility.

Conclusion: The Immortal Influence of Ada Lovelace

In conclusion, Ada Lovelace's impact on the collective imagination is profound and multifaceted. Her visionary ideas about the potential of machines to enhance human creativity have inspired countless individuals to explore the intersections of technology and the arts. Through her life and work, Ada has become a symbol of empowerment for women in STEM, encouraging future generations to challenge norms and pursue their passions.

As we reflect on Ada's legacy, it is essential to continue nurturing the seeds of innovation she planted. By celebrating her contributions and advocating for gender equality in technology, we honor not only Ada's memory but also the countless women who have followed in her footsteps. The collective imagination, fueled by Ada's vision, remains a powerful force for change, inspiring us to envision a future where creativity and technology coexist harmoniously.

The Symbolism of Ada Lovelace's Famous Portrait

Ada Lovelace's portrait, painted by the renowned artist, is not merely a representation of her physical form; it is a complex tapestry woven with threads of symbolism that reflect her unique contributions to mathematics and computing, as well as her role as a pioneer for women in science and technology. This section delves into the layers of meaning embedded within her portrait, exploring how it encapsulates her legacy and the broader implications for women in STEM fields.

The Artistic Representation

At first glance, Lovelace's portrait presents a woman of intellect and poise, adorned in a dress that reflects the fashion of her time, yet the details within the painting convey much more than mere aesthetics. The choice of colors, the positioning of her hands, and the expression on her face are all deliberate choices made by the artist to symbolize her brilliance and visionary thinking.

Color Symbolism The colors used in Lovelace's portrait are particularly telling. The deep blues and greens suggest depth of thought and creativity, while hints of gold reflect her status as a noblewoman and a figure of significance in the history of computing. In color theory, blue is often associated with intellect and wisdom, while green symbolizes growth and innovation. Together, these colors create a visual representation of Lovelace's contributions to the fields of mathematics and programming.

Posture and Expression   Lovelace's posture is relaxed yet confident, suggesting a woman who is comfortable in her intellect and aware of her groundbreaking contributions. Her gaze, directed slightly upward, indicates a forward-thinking mindset, always contemplating the possibilities of the future. This expression captures the essence of her visionary ideas regarding the Analytical Engine and its potential to transcend mere calculation and enter the realm of creativity and art.

The Mathematical Elements

Within the portrait, there are subtle mathematical elements that further enhance its symbolism. For instance, the background may include faint patterns reminiscent of mathematical equations or diagrams, representing Lovelace's deep engagement with theoretical mathematics. This inclusion serves as a reminder that her work was not merely practical but also deeply rooted in abstract thought.

Equations and Formulas   If we were to represent Lovelace's contributions mathematically, we might consider her famous algorithm for the Analytical Engine, which can be expressed as:

$$f(x) = \sum_{i=1}^{n} a_i \cdot x^i \tag{203}$$

where $f(x)$ represents the output of the engine based on the input variables a_i. This equation encapsulates the essence of programming as a systematic approach to problem-solving, a concept that Lovelace championed in her writings.

Cultural Context and Legacy

The portrait also serves as a cultural artifact, reflecting the societal norms and expectations of women during the Victorian era. Lovelace's position as a woman in a male-dominated field is poignantly captured in her attire and demeanor. The contrast between her noble heritage and the challenges she faced in being recognized for her contributions highlights the ongoing struggle for women in STEM.

Feminist Symbolism   In feminist theory, Lovelace's portrait can be interpreted as a symbol of resistance against the gender stereotypes that have historically marginalized women's contributions to science and technology. Her portrayal as a confident and capable figure challenges the narrative that women were not suited for intellectual pursuits. This symbolism resonates with contemporary movements advocating for gender equality in STEM, inspiring future generations to pursue careers in these fields.

Conclusion

In conclusion, Ada Lovelace's famous portrait is far more than a visual representation; it is a rich symbol of her legacy as the first programmer and a pioneer for women in technology. The artistic choices made in the portrait—color, posture, and subtle mathematical elements—combine to create a powerful narrative that speaks to her intellect, creativity, and the challenges she faced. As we celebrate her contributions, let us also recognize the importance of her image in inspiring future innovators, reminding us that the legacy of Ada Lovelace is not confined to the past but continues to shape the future of technology and gender equality in STEM.

$$\text{Legacy} = \text{Innovation} + \text{Inspiration} + \text{Advocacy} \tag{204}$$

Ada's Place in the Pantheon of Tech Visionaries

Ada Lovelace stands as a monumental figure in the realm of technology, not merely as the first programmer but as a visionary whose ideas transcended her time. To understand her place among the greats, one must delve into the characteristics that define a tech visionary: foresight, innovation, and the ability to inspire future generations. Ada exemplified all these traits, making her an enduring symbol in the pantheon of tech visionaries.

The Hallmarks of a Visionary

Visionaries are often characterized by their ability to see beyond the constraints of their era. They challenge the status quo and propose ideas that seem radical or impractical at the time. Ada's work on Charles Babbage's Analytical Engine is a testament to her visionary mindset. She recognized that this machine could do more than mere calculations; it could manipulate symbols and process information in a way that resembled modern computing.

$$f(x) = \sum_{n=0}^{\infty} a_n x^n \tag{205}$$

This equation represents a power series, which Ada understood as a way to express complex mathematical relationships. Her insight into the potential of algorithms—essentially a set of instructions for a computer to follow—was revolutionary. She foresaw a future where machines could perform tasks that required human-like reasoning.

Innovative Contributions

Ada's contributions were not limited to theoretical concepts; she was a pioneer in the practical application of programming. In her notes on the Analytical Engine, she described an algorithm for calculating Bernoulli numbers, which is often cited as the first computer program. This algorithm was not just a sequence of calculations; it was a demonstration of how machines could be instructed to perform complex tasks.

$$B_n = \sum_{k=0}^{n} \binom{n}{k} B_k \frac{1}{n - k + 1} \tag{206}$$

Here, B_n represents the Bernoulli numbers, and Ada's ability to articulate such complex mathematical concepts through an algorithmic lens was groundbreaking. Her work laid the foundation for future programming languages and computational theories.

Inspiration for Future Generations

Ada's legacy as a tech visionary is not confined to her own achievements but extends to her influence on future generations. She became a symbol of what women could accomplish in a male-dominated field. Her life and work inspired countless individuals to pursue careers in science, technology, engineering, and mathematics (STEM).

Organizations such as the Ada Lovelace Foundation and events like Ada Lovelace Day celebrate her contributions and promote the representation of women in tech. These initiatives aim to inspire young girls and women to enter fields where they have historically been underrepresented.

Comparative Analysis with Other Visionaries

When placed alongside other tech visionaries such as Alan Turing, Grace Hopper, and Steve Jobs, Ada's contributions stand out for their pioneering nature. Turing's work on algorithms and computation theory was undoubtedly revolutionary, yet Ada's foresight into the potential of computers predates his ideas. Grace Hopper's development of COBOL was a significant advancement in programming languages, but it was Ada who first conceptualized the idea of programming itself.

In a similar vein, Steve Jobs revolutionized personal computing and user interface design, but he did so building upon the foundational concepts laid by Ada and her contemporaries. Each of these visionaries, while unique in their contributions, shares a common thread of innovation and a vision for the future that Ada Lovelace initiated.

Conclusion: Ada's Enduring Legacy

Ada Lovelace's place in the pantheon of tech visionaries is secured not only by her groundbreaking contributions to programming but also by her role as an inspirational figure. Her insights into the capabilities of computing machines and her advocacy for women in STEM continue to resonate today. As we navigate the complexities of modern technology, Ada's vision reminds us of the importance of creativity, inclusivity, and the relentless pursuit of knowledge.

In summary, Ada Lovelace is not just a historical figure; she is a beacon of innovation and empowerment. Her legacy encourages us to dream beyond the possible, to challenge the limitations of our time, and to inspire the next generation of thinkers and creators. As we celebrate her contributions, we also commit to carrying forward her vision of a diverse and inclusive tech landscape, ensuring that the next Ada Lovelace is nurtured and recognized for her brilliance.

Remembering Ada Lovelace: A Figure of Hope and Possibility

In the annals of technological history, few figures shine as brightly as Ada Lovelace. Often celebrated as the first programmer, Ada was not merely a product of her time but a beacon of hope and possibility for generations to come. Her life story is a tapestry woven with threads of intellect, creativity, and resilience, showcasing the profound impact one individual can have on the world.

Ada's Visionary Insights

Ada Lovelace's insights into the potential of computing were revolutionary. She recognized that the Analytical Engine, designed by Charles Babbage, was not just a mechanical calculator but a machine capable of performing any calculation that could be expressed in an algorithm. This realization was encapsulated in her famous note, often referred to as the Lovelace Note, where she articulated the concept of programming as a means to instruct machines to perform tasks beyond mere arithmetic.

$$f(x) = \sum_{n=0}^{\infty} a_n x^n \qquad (207)$$

This equation represents a power series, a mathematical concept Ada understood deeply. She foresaw that such computational mechanisms could be applied to various fields, from music composition to scientific analysis, thus laying the groundwork for modern programming paradigms.

Challenges and Triumphs

Despite her groundbreaking contributions, Ada faced numerous challenges, particularly as a woman in a male-dominated field. The societal norms of the 19th century often relegated women to the background, yet Ada's tenacity allowed her to break through these barriers. She used her noble heritage not as a shield but as a platform to advocate for women's education and representation in science and technology.

Her struggles with illness further complicated her life, yet they did not define her. Instead, they became part of her narrative, illustrating her resilience. Ada's ability to navigate these challenges serves as an enduring lesson in perseverance for all aspiring innovators, especially women in STEM.

The Legacy of Ada Lovelace

Ada's legacy extends far beyond her own time. She has become a symbol of hope for many who encounter obstacles in their pursuit of knowledge and innovation. The annual Ada Lovelace Day, celebrated worldwide, honors her contributions while inspiring young women to pursue careers in science, technology, engineering, and mathematics (STEM).

- **Ada Lovelace Day:** A celebration of women in STEM, promoting the achievements of women in technology and encouraging the next generation.

- **Educational Initiatives:** Programs inspired by Ada's story aim to empower young girls through coding clubs, scholarships, and mentorship opportunities.

- **Cultural Impact:** Ada's influence permeates literature, art, and popular culture, reminding us of the importance of diversity in innovation.

A Call to Action

As we remember Ada Lovelace, we are called to reflect on her message: that the pursuit of knowledge is not limited by gender, background, or societal expectations. Her life encourages us to embrace our passions, challenge the status quo, and envision a future where technology serves as a tool for empowerment and creativity.

$$\text{Hope} = \frac{\text{Vision} + \text{Action}}{\text{Barriers}} \tag{208}$$

This equation encapsulates the essence of Ada's legacy. Hope is not merely a feeling; it is a calculated response to the challenges we face. By combining vision with action, we can transcend barriers and create a world where everyone has the opportunity to innovate.

Conclusion

In conclusion, Ada Lovelace remains a figure of hope and possibility, a reminder that the seeds of innovation can sprout in the most unlikely of places. Her story is not just about programming; it is about the power of ideas and the courage to pursue them. As we honor her legacy, let us carry forward her spirit of inquiry and her commitment to inclusivity in technology, ensuring that the future is bright for all who dare to dream.

Remembering Ada Lovelace is not merely an act of historical acknowledgment; it is a commitment to fostering the next generation of innovators and ensuring that the possibilities she envisioned become a reality for all.

The Immortal Ada: Forever Inspiring, Forever Innovative

Ada Lovelace, often hailed as the first computer programmer, transcends the boundaries of time and discipline. Her remarkable vision and innovative spirit continue to inspire generations of thinkers, creators, and innovators. In this section, we explore the enduring impact of Ada's legacy, her influence on modern technology, and the timeless relevance of her ideas.

A Visionary Ahead of Her Time

Ada's insights into the potential of computing were revolutionary. In her notes on Charles Babbage's Analytical Engine, she foresaw that machines could go beyond mere calculations to manipulate symbols and create art, music, and even complex algorithms. She famously stated, "The Analytical Engine does not occupy common ground with mere calculating machines. It holds within it the power to create and innovate." This foresight positions her not only as a programmer but as a visionary who understood the broader implications of technology.

Theoretical Foundations of Ada's Work

To appreciate Ada's contributions, we must delve into the theoretical underpinnings of her work. At the core of her programming principles lies the concept of abstraction, which can be represented mathematically. For instance, the function of the Analytical Engine can be expressed as:

$$f(x) = \sum_{i=1}^{n} a_i \cdot x^i$$

where a_i represents the coefficients of the polynomial, and x is the variable input. This equation illustrates how Ada envisioned programming as a means of manipulating variables and functions, laying the groundwork for what we now know as algorithmic thinking.

Ada's Influence on Modern Programming Languages

Ada's legacy extends into the very fabric of modern programming languages. The programming language Ada, developed in the late 1970s and named in her honor, embodies many of her principles, such as strong typing, modularity, and support for concurrent programming. The language's design reflects her belief in the importance of clarity and precision in programming, which can be summarized in the following principles:

- **Strong Typing:** Ensures that variables are declared with specific data types, reducing errors and enhancing code reliability.

- **Modularity:** Encourages the division of programs into smaller, manageable units, facilitating easier maintenance and collaboration.

- **Concurrency:** Supports the execution of multiple processes simultaneously, mirroring Ada's vision of machines that could perform complex tasks efficiently.

These principles have not only shaped the Ada programming language but have also influenced many contemporary languages, such as Python, Java, and C++, which prioritize readability and maintainability.

The Ethical Considerations of Technology

Ada's foresight also encompassed the ethical implications of technology. She recognized that with great power comes great responsibility. As we navigate the complexities of artificial intelligence and machine learning today, her thoughts resonate profoundly. Ada advocated for a thoughtful approach to innovation, emphasizing the need for ethical guidelines in technology development. This is particularly relevant in discussions surrounding algorithmic bias and the societal impact of automated systems.

For instance, consider the equation representing a basic machine learning model:

$$y = f(X; \theta) + \epsilon$$

where y is the predicted output, X is the input data, θ represents the model parameters, and ϵ is the error term. The challenge lies in ensuring that the model is trained on unbiased data to prevent perpetuating existing inequalities. Ada's legacy calls for programmers to be vigilant and ethical stewards of technology, ensuring that their creations uplift society rather than diminish it.

Inspiring Future Generations

The immortal Ada continues to inspire young minds in the fields of science, technology, engineering, and mathematics (STEM). Her story is a beacon of hope for aspiring programmers, particularly women, who face barriers in a male-dominated industry. Initiatives such as Ada Lovelace Day celebrate her contributions and encourage diversity in tech, empowering individuals to pursue their passions without the constraints of gender stereotypes.

Educational programs that incorporate Ada's story into their curricula foster a culture of inclusivity and inspire future innovators. By sharing her journey, we remind students that creativity and analytical thinking can coexist, paving the way for a new generation of thinkers who will continue to push the boundaries of what is possible.

The Immortal Legacy of Ada Lovelace

In conclusion, Ada Lovelace's legacy is immortal. Her contributions to computing, her visionary insights, and her advocacy for ethical technology resonate strongly in our modern world. As we face unprecedented technological advancements, we are reminded of her words: "That brain of mine is something more than merely mortal; as time will show."

Ada's spirit lives on in every line of code written, every algorithm developed, and every innovative idea brought to life. She is a symbol of resilience, creativity, and the boundless potential of the human mind. As we celebrate her legacy, let us carry forward her message of inspiration and innovation, ensuring that her impact continues to shape the future of technology for generations to come.

Bibliography

[1] Lovelace, Ada. *Notes on the Analytical Engine.* (1843).

[2] Barnes, John. *Programming in Ada.* Prentice Hall, 1997.

[3] O'Neil, Cathy. *Weapons of Math Destruction: How Big Data Increases Inequality and Threatens Democracy.* Crown Publishing Group, 2016.

[4] Margolis, Jane, and Allan Fisher. *Unlocking the Clubhouse: Women in Computing.* MIT Press, 2002.

Index

480